On Global Citizenship

CRITICAL POWERS

Series Editors:

Bert van den Brink (University of Utrecht),
Antony Simon Laden (University of Illinois, Chicago),
Peter Niesen (University of Hamburg) and
David Owen (University of Southampton).

Critical Powers is dedicated to constructing dialogues around innovative and original work in social and political theory. The ambition of the series is to be pluralist in welcoming work from different philosophical traditions and theoretical orientations, ranging from abstract conceptual argument to concrete policy-relevant engagements, and encouraging dialogue across the diverse approaches that populate the field of social and political theory. All the volumes in the series are structured as dialogues in which a lead essay is greeted with a series of responses before a reply by the lead essayist. Such dialogues spark debate, foster understanding, encourage innovation and perform the drama of thought in a way that engages a wide audience of scholars and students.

Forthcoming titles include:

Justice, Democracy and the Right to Justification, Rainer Forst
Autonomy Gaps, Joel Anderson
Rogue Theodicy – Politics and Power in the Shadow of Justice,
Glen Newey

On Global Citizenship

James Tully in Dialogue

James Tully

Bloomsbury Academic
An imprint of Bloomsbury Publishing Plc

B L O O M S B U R Y
LONDON • NEW DELHI • NEW YORK • SYDNEY

Bloomsbury Academic

An imprint of Bloomsbury Publishing Plc

50 Bedford Square	1385 Broadway
London	New York
WC1B 3DP	NY 10018
UK	USA

www.bloomsbury.com

BLOOMSBURY and the Diana logo are trademarks of Bloomsbury Publishing Plc

First published 2014
Reprinted 2014

© James Tully and contributors, 2014

James Tully has asserted his right under the Copyright, Designs and
Patents Act, 1988, to be identified as Author of this work.

British Library Cataloguing-in-Publication Data
A catalogue record for this book is available from the British Library.

ISBN: HB:	978-1-8496-6492-9
PB:	978-1-8496-6493-6
ePDF:	978-1-8496-6516-2
ePub:	978-1-8496-6501-8

Library of Congress Cataloging-in-Publication Data
Tully, James, 1946-
On global citizenship : James Tully in dialogue / James Tully.
pages cm
ISBN 978-1-84966-492-9 (hardback) – ISBN 978-1-84966-493-6 (paperback) –
ISBN 978-1-84966-501-8 (epub) 1. World citizenship–Philosophy. 2. Tully, James,
1946—Political and social views. I. Title.
JZ1320.4.T85 2014
323.6–dc23
2014002707

Series: Critical Powers

Typeset by Newgen Knowledge Works (P) Ltd., Chennai, India
Printed and bound in Great Britain

Contents

List of Contributors

Duncan Bell is a senior lecturer in the Department of Politics and International Studies at the University of Cambridge, and a Fellow of Christ's College. He is the author of *The Idea of Greater Britain: Empire and the Future of World Order, 1860–1900* (Princeton University Press, 2007), and several edited collections, the most recent of which is (with Joel Isaac) *Uncertain Empire: American History and the Idea of the Cold War* (Oxford University Press, 2012).

Robin Celikates is associate professor of political and social philosophy at the Department of Philosophy at the University of Amsterdam and an associated member of the Institut für Sozialforschung (Institute for Social Research) in Frankfurt am Main. His most recent book is *Kritik als soziale Praxis. Gesellschaftliche Selbstverständigung und kritische Theorie* (Criticism as Social Practice. Social Self-Understanding and Critical Theory), with a preface by Axel Honneth (Campus, 2009).

Adam Dunn is a visiting fellow at the Centre for Citizenship, Globalization and Governance at the University of Southampton. He is currently completing a book manuscript on Hannah Arendt: Judgment, Action and Institutions.

Bonnie Honig is Nancy Duke Lewis Professor in the Departments of Modern Culture and Media (MCM) and Political Science at Brown University. Her most recent book is *Antigone, Interrupted* (Cambridge University Press, 2013).

Anthony Laden is professor of philosophy, and Chair, of the Department of Philosophy at the University of Illinois Chicago. His most recent book is *Reasoning: A Social Picture* (Oxford University Press, 2012).

Andrew Mason is professor of political theory in the Department of Politics and International Studies at the University of Warwick. His most recent book is *Living Together as Equals: The Demands of Citizenship* (Oxford University Press, 2012).

David Owen is professor of social and political philosophy in the Department of Politics and International Relations at the University of Southampton. His most recent book is *Nietzsche's Genealogy of Morality* (Acumen Press, 2007).

Marc Stears is professor of political theory, university lecturer, and fellow, University College (currently on leave as chief speechwriter to the leader of the opposition, Rt Hon Ed Miliband, MP). His most recent book is *Demanding Democracy: American Radicals in Search of a New Politics* (Princeton University Press, 2010).

James Tully is distinguished professor of political science, law, indigenous governance and philosophy at the University of Victoria. He is fellow of the Royal Society of Canada and emeritus fellow of the Trudeau Foundation. In 2010 he was awarded the Killam Prize in the Humanities for his outstanding contribution to scholarship and Canadian public life. His two-volume work, *Public Philosophy in a New Key* (Cambridge University Press, 2008), was awarded the C. B. Macpherson Prize by the Canadian Political Science Association for the best book in political theory written in English or French in Canada 2008–10. He is consulting editor of the journals *Political Theory* and *Global Constitutionalism*, co-editor of the *Clarendon Works of John Locke* and former co-editor of the *Cambridge Ideas in Context Series*.

Series Editor's Foreword

On Global Citizenship and Public Philosophy

James Tully's lead essay for this volume offers a substantive reflection on citizenship as the main upshot of his investigations of contemporary global politics. In this essay, Tully distinguishes two modes of citizenship – modern/civil and diverse/civic – that align with 'restricted' and 'open' practices of democracy. The 'modern citizen' stands towards citizenship as a status-securing liberty within an institutional framework of rules that compose democratic rule, whereas the 'diverse citizen' is oriented towards citizenship as the freedom of participation – as actors in contexts of governance engaged in democratic praxis, not the citizen of an institution (e.g. a state) but the free citizen of the 'free city': that is, any kind of civic world or democratic 'sphere' that comes into being among them. Tully's aim is to show us that when we adopt this civic stance it becomes clear that another world is not simply possible but actual, that civic citizens engaged in contesting norms of governance from local to global contexts and in cooperatively organizing themselves are a widespread feature of our common world.

This essay is also, however, an exemplification of an approach to political philosophy that Tully terms 'public philosophy' – and in order to contextualize Tully's essay as well as the responses to it, it may be helpful to offer a sketch of this approach.

For Tully, political theory is to be understood as the methodical extension of the self-reflective character of historically situated practices of practical reasoning and not as a distinct higher-order activity of theoretical reflection on these situated practices of practical reasoning. As such political theory is not oriented to legislating the nature and limits of practical reason (e.g. by trying to provide a general theory of justice) but to the reflective elucidation and negotiation of the contents and bounds of practical reason. The authority of the reasons offered by political theory are not to be seen as modelled on the commands of a rational legislator specifying, for example, the form of the just society but rather as more akin to invitations to consider looking at our political relationship in a different way. We can distinguish three steps in Tully's 'public philosophy' that comprise its critical activity.

The first is that, following Wittgenstein, Skinner and Foucault, it grants a primacy to practice, that is, it focuses on the practices of governance and the exercise of freedom within and over the norms of these practices that shapes the forms of thought, conduct and subjectivity characteristic of the present. From Wittgenstein, Tully draws out the point that Arendt's understanding of the practice of freedom – of speaking and acting differently in the course of a language game and so modifying or transforming the game – is not a special feature of politics or a form of freedom restricted to certain modes of human interaction but, rather, is a general feature of human practices and relationships. Tully takes Skinner and Foucault to be the primary inheritors of this outlook. In the case of Skinner, this involves tracing the intersubjective conventions that govern political reflection in a given context in order to show how political actors in that context have exercised their freedom in modifying those conventions. In the case of Foucault, it involves providing a genealogy of the problematizations in terms of which we understand ourselves as bound by certain limits; a genealogy which is, at the same time, a redescription of those limits. Foucault's approach shares both Arendt's understanding of the activity of freedom as modification or transformation of games of governance and the view of Wittgenstein and Skinner that such freedom is a feature of any and all human practices, but Foucault also develops Nietzsche's point that this activity of freedom is an *agonistic* relationship and, thereby, links the following elements together: the practice of freedom, the modification of the rules governing the relationships among players in the course of a game and agonistic activity. Public philosophy in Tully's sense begins with the calling into question, and concern to modify, a game of government on the part of those subject to it. In this respect, it is best construed as an expression and an enabling of the agonistic activity of freedom.

The second step is that Tully does not attempt to develop a normative theory as a way of adjudicating or evaluating the calling into question of the game of government. Rather public philosophy engages in what might be termed 'redescription with critical intent'. First, public philosophy focuses on disclosing the historically contingent conditions of possibility for the practices of governance in question and the form of problematization that it exhibits before, second, offering a redescription that alters the self-understanding of those subject to it, and struggling within it, in ways that enable them to perceive the arbitrary constraints in what is given as universal, necessary and obligatory. Public philosophy achieves this objective through two elements. The first, adopting Wittgenstein's practice of perspicuous representation, is designed to bring to light the unexamined conventions of the language games within which the problem and proposed solutions to it arise. The second, combining Foucault with the Cambridge School, is a genealogical account of these language games designed to free us from the hold of these unexamined conventions.

The third and final step in Tully's critical activity is that this historical and critical relation to the present does not stop at calling a limit into question and engaging in a dialogue over its possible transformation, but also attempts to establish an ongoing mutual relation with the concrete struggles, negotiations and implementations of citizens who experiment with modifying the practices on the ground. Public philosophy does not aim to speak for those subject to government, but rather aims to provide them with resources for speaking for themselves.

This practice of political theory was given initial, and incomplete, expression in *Strange Multiplicity* where Tully addresses the question of the constitutional accommodation of cultural diversity. A critical survey identifies a range of conventions that inform contemporary constitutionalism and serve to exclude or assimilate cultural diversity. A genealogical investigation of contemporary constitutionalism identifies two distinct modes of constitutionalism – modern and common – which exhibit radically different practical attitudes to the issue of accommodating cultural diversity. The former, which is dominant, adopts a monological perspective and unilaterally gives expression to a claim to establish just constitutional rules (where this claim is predicated on the stages view of history that identifies the modern European state with a republican constitution as the rational form of polity). Tully shows how this practical attitude was forged in and through the imperialist context of Europe's encounter with the New World as a way of justifying the appropriation of land without native consent (e.g. Locke), the denial of international standing to aboriginal peoples (e.g. Kant and Vattel) and the destruction of aboriginal culture and customs in the name of enlightened progress (e.g. Pufendorf, Sieyes and Paine). By contrast, common constitutionalism adopts a dialogical perspective which expresses the anti-theoretical claim that constitution-making is a practical skill guided by the conventions of mutual recognition, consent and cultural continuity. Tully provides a series of examples of how this practical attitude led to the acknowledgement of aboriginal peoples and a conceptualization of a constitution as a form of accommodation of cultural diversity. In the light of this genealogical account, the struggles of aboriginal peoples can now be seen as anti-imperial struggles for self-rule generated by the imposition of modern constitutionalism and resolvable through the practice of common constitutionalism.

Following *Strange Multiplicity*, Tully worked further on freedom and power, coming to see that these struggles are best conceived agonistically, not as struggles *for* recognition but as struggles *over* recognition. It is not a matter of aiming at dialogical consensus on a just final settlement since there can always be reasonable dissensus concerning any such settlement. Rather it is a matter of following practices of civic freedom such that those subject to a practice of governance can contest and transform it. It is this step that completes Tully's understanding of the approach that he comes to call 'public philosophy' and which leads him to elaborate the implications of his revised view of freedom for multinational democracy and extend his analysis to encompass the history of Western imperialism before and after decolonization as well as contemporary global politics and international law. These elements are drawn together in his most major work to date: the two-volume *Public Philosophy in a New Key* – and further extended in the essay on citizenship offered in this volume. As this essay makes clear, Tully's public philosophy is an invitation to take up the civic stance and to practise freedom.

David Owen

Part One

Lead Essay

1

On Global Citizenship

James Tully

1. Introduction: Global citizenship as negotiated practices

'Global citizenship' has emerged as the locus of struggles on the ground and of reflection and contestation in theory.[1] This is scarcely surprising. Many of the central and most enduring struggles in the history of politics have taken place *in* and *over* the language of citizenship and the activities and institutions into which it is woven. One could say that the hopes and dreams and fears and xenophobia of centuries of individual and collective political actors are expressed in the overlapping and conflicting histories of the uses of the language of citizenship, the forms of life in which they have been employed and the locales in which they take place. This motley ensemble of contested languages, activities and institutions constitutes the inherited *field* of citizenship today.[2]

---

[1] For an introduction to this broad field see H. Anheier, M. Glasius, M. Kaldor and F. Holland, eds, *Global Civil Society 2004–2005*, London: Sage, 2004; L. Amoore, eds, *The Global Resistance Reader*, London: Routledge, 2005; J. Brodie, 'Introduction: Globalization and Citizenship beyond the Nation State', *Citizenship Studies* 8 (4): 323–32, 2004; N. Dower, *An Introduction to Global Citizenship*, Edinburgh: Edinburgh University Press, 2003; N. Dower and J. Williams, eds, *Global Citizenship: A Critical Introduction*, New York: Routledge, 2002; D. Held and A. McGrew, eds, *The Global Transformations Reader: An Introduction to the Globalization Debate*, 2nd edn, Cambridge: Polity, 2003; C. McKinnon and I. Hampsher-Monk, eds, *The Demands of Citizenship*, London: Continuum, 2000.

[2] I mean by 'field' the field of human action, the field of academic research and the ecological field in which these are carried on. Similarly, 'language of citizenship' refers to the broad range of vocabularies or discourses of citizenship practices, policies and theories.

The language of 'global' and 'globalization' and the activities, institutions and processes to which it refers and in which it is increasingly used, while more recent than citizenship, comprise a similarly central and contested domain. Globalization has become a shared yet disputed vocabulary in terms of which rival interpretations of the ways humans and their habitats are governed globally are presented and disputed in both practice and theory. It thus constitutes a similarly contested *field* of globalization.

When 'globalization' and 'citizenship' are combined they not only bring their contested histories of meanings with them, their conjunction brings into being a complex new field that raises new questions and elicits new answers concerning the meaning of, and relationship between, global governance and global citizenship. When we enquire into global citizenship, therefore, we are already thrown into this remarkably complex inherited field of contested languages, activities, institutions, processes and the environs in which they take place. This conjoint field is the problematization of global citizenship: The way that formerly disparate activities, institutions, processes and languages have been gathered together under the rubric of 'global citizenship', becomes the site of contestation in practice, and formulated as a problem in research, policy and theory, to which diverse solutions are presented and debated.[3]

The reason why the uses of 'citizenship', 'globalization' and 'global citizenship' are contestable, rather than fixed and determinant, is, as Wittgenstein classically argued, because there is neither an essential set of necessary and sufficient criteria for the correct use of such concepts nor a calculus for their application in particular cases. The art of understanding a concept like 'global citizenship' is *not* the application of a universal rule to particular cases. Rather, the uses of such complex concepts in different cases and contexts do not have one set of properties in common, but – from case to case – an indeterminate

---

[3] For this approach see J. Tully, *Public Philosophy in a New Key*, 2 vols, Cambridge: Cambridge University Press, 2008, volume I, chapters 1 and 3.

family of overlapping and crisscrossing 'similarities, relationships, and a whole series of them at that'. What 'we see', therefore, is not a single rule (definition or theory) being applied in every case, but, rather, 'a complicated network of similarities overlapping and criss-crossing: sometimes overall similarities, sometimes similarities of detail'.[4] A language user learns how to use a concept by apprenticeship in the practice of use and discrimination in everyday life, by invoking (defeasible) similarities and dissimilarities with other cases and responding to counterarguments when challenged, and thereby gradually acquiring the abilities to use language in normative and critical ways in new contexts.[5]

Since the use of concepts with complex histories 'is not everywhere circumscribed by rules', Wittgenstein continues, 'the extension of the concept is *not* closed by a frontier'.[6] It is almost always possible, to some indeterminate extent, to question a given normal use, invoke slightly different similarities with other historical uses or interpret a shared criterion differently, and argue that the term can be extended in an unexpected and unpredictable way, which is nevertheless 'related' to other, familiar uses, and to *act* on it (and sometimes the act *precedes* the argumentation for the novel use).[7] Use, and therefore meaning, is not the application of a transcendental or official theory of citizenship. It is an indeterminate spatio-temporal 'negotiated practice' among partners in relations of dialogical interlocution and practical interaction in which the possibility of going on differently is always present.[8] This pragmatic linguistic freedom of enunciation and initiation – of contestability and speaking otherwise – within the weighty constraints of the inherited relations of use and meaning is, as we shall see, internally related to

---

[4] L. Wittgenstein, *Philosophical Investigations*, Oxford: Blackwell, 1997; for an exploration of this account of learning and understanding language see Tully, *Public Philosophy* I, chapter 2.

[5] Wittgenstein, *Philosophical Investigations*, p. 75.

[6] Ibid., 68.

[7] Ibid.; note also p. 75.

[8] See J. Medina, *The Unity of Wittgenstein's Philosophy: Necessity, Intelligibility, and Normativity*, Albany: SUNY Press, 2002, pp. 141–94; J. Medina, *Language*, London: Continuum, 2005, pp. 139–67.

a practical (extralinguistic) freedom of enactment and improvization within the inherited relations of power in which the vocabulary is used.[9] It is the reason why the history of citizens and citizenship is not the unfolding of some transhistorical definition that the grand theories claim it to be. It is not the endless repetition of the same formula, stages of historical development towards a predictable end, an instrument controlled by the hegemonic class or the dialectical overcoming of antagonistic forces. Unfortunately for theorists and fortunately for human beings, it is precisely the unpredictable 'deeds and events we call historical'.[10]

The creation of the conjunction 'global citizenship' could be seen as a prime exemplar of the innovative freedom of citizens and non-citizens to contest and initiate something new in the practice of citizenship. The multiplicity of contests that extend citizenship into the field of globalization (conceived formerly as a realm of predictable historical processes impervious to civic action), could be construed as the initiatory act of global citizenship that opens a new field of possibilities of another, more democratic world. While partly true, the actual existing inherited field of global citizenship is much more complex, and the possibilities of initiating and carrying on civic action much more contextually situated within the field, than this abstract formulation could unintentionally lead one to believe. If we wish to become effective global citizens then there is no alternative to undergoing the apprenticeship of learning our way around this complicated field and coming to acquire the practical abilities of thinking and acting within it and the critical abilities of seeing the concrete possibilities of going beyond its limits. This exploration of the field is thus an apprenticeship manual in becoming who we can be – local *and* global citizens.

---

[9] This contextual freedom of enunciation and enactment (words and deeds) is an aspect of civic freedom (Subsection 5).

[10] H. Arendt, 'What is Freedom?', in *Between Past and Future: Eight Exercises in Political Thought*, Harmondsworth: Penguin, 1977, p. 169; see Tully, *Public Philosophy* I, chapter 4.

2. Two modes of citizenship: Preliminary sketch

Among the many contested meanings and corresponding practices of global citizenship I would like to focus on two and their traditions of interpretation. Many of the most important struggles around the globe today are *over* these two modes of global citizenship and the struggles themselves consist in *their* enactment. Here a 'mode of citizenship' refers to the ensemble comprised of a distinctive language of citizenship and its traditions of interpretation on the one hand and the corresponding practices and institutions to which it refers and in which it is used on the other.[11] The two I wish to examine have been interpreted in different ways and related to different traditions of citizenship under different names in a wide variety of academic and activist literature: for example, global citizenship from above *versus* global citizenship from below, low intensity *versus* high intensity global citizenship, representative *versus* direct, hegemonic *versus* counter-hegemonic, cosmopolitan *versus* place-based, universal *versus* multiversal. I call these two families 'modern' and 'diverse' citizenship. I call modern citizenship in a modern state 'civil' citizenship and in a global context 'cosmopolitan' citizenship. The corresponding names of diverse citizenship are 'civic' and 'glocal'. 'Glocal' and 'glocalization' in the diverse citizenship tradition refer to the global networking of local practices of civic citizenship in contrast to the use of 'global' and 'globalization' in modern/cosmopolitan citizenship.[12] The comparative explication of these two historical and contemporary vocabularies and the practices in which they are used aims to bring to light the shared field of citizenship from their different orientations. I begin with a

---

[11] This account of modes of citizenship is adapted from Wittgenstein's concept of language-games and Foucault's concept of practical systems. See Tully, *Public Philosophy* I, chapters 1–3. In these chapters I have used the general category of practices rather than modes. However, in this case, citizenship is taken as a practice in one tradition and an institution in the other, so the use of practice as the generic term would elide this crucial difference.

[12] I am indebted to Warren Magnusson for introducing me to the concept of and literature on glocal citizenship.

preliminary sketch of two general aspects of citizenship as a way of introducing them.[13]

The first and most familiar aspect is that modern citizenship is the modular form of citizenship associated with the historical processes of modernization and colonization: that is, (1) the modernization of the West into modern nation states with representative governments, a system of international law, the decolonization of European empires, supranational regime formations and the development of global civil society; and, in tandem, (2) the dependent modernization and citizenization of the non-West through colonization, the Mandate System, post-decolonization nation-building and global governance of the former colonies. The language of modern citizenship, in its civil and cosmopolitan forms, presents successive idealizations of modern Euroamerican citizenship as the uniquely universal module for all human societies. This allegedly universal mode of citizenship is also presented as the product of universal historical processes or stages of development under successive discourses of progress – civilization, modernization, constitutionalization, democratization and now globalization – that began in Europe and have been spread around the world by Euroamerican expansion and continuing hegemony. These two features of modern citizenship – a universal *institutional* form of citizenship conjoined with a universal set of historical processes that bring it to the non-West under Western tutelage – are articulated and debated in, respectively, modern normative theories of citizenship and social scientific theories of modernization from the eighteenth century to today.

In contrast, diverse citizenship is associated with a diversity or multiplicity of different *practices* of citizenship in the West and non-West. The language of diverse citizenship, both civic and glocal, presents citizenship as a situated or 'local' practice that takes countless forms in different locales. It is not described in terms of universal institutions and historical processes, but in terms of grass roots democratic or civic

---

[13] This preliminary sketch is developed in more detail in the following sections and it draws on the chapters in Tully, *Public Philosophy*.

activities of the 'governed' (the people) in the specific relationships of governance in specific locales and the glocal activities of networking with other local practices. Whereas modern citizenship focuses on citizenship as a universalizable legal status underpinned by institutions and processes of rationalization that enable and circumscribe the possibility of civil activity (an institutional/universal orientation), diverse citizenship focuses on the singular civic activities and improvizations of the governed in any practice of government and the diverse ways these are more or less institutionalized or blocked in different contexts (a civic activity/ contextual orientation). Citizenship is not a status given by the institutions of the modern constitutional state and international law, but negotiated practices in which one becomes a citizen through participation.

Second, the language of modern citizenship, especially the theories, histories and comparative taxonomies, not only elaborate a theory of modern citizenship with its membership codes, rights and duties and corresponding institutional preconditions, it also characterizes all other practices of citizenship in relation to its unique form as the universal standard. Other modes of citizenship are classified as either not really citizenship at all (not meeting any of the modern criteria) or, if some modern criteria are present, as primitive, pre-modern, traditional or customary stages of proto-citizenship on the historical path (cultural, economic, cognitive, political) to full modern citizenship as the telos, and as requiring some form of direct or indirect guidance from the self-described more advanced, civilized or developed races, nations or peoples. That is, the kind of *critical theory* that has accompanied modern citizenship since the eighteenth century critically organizes all other forms of citizenship in the world as 'lower' or 'inferior' in relationship to its form as the regulative ideal. This feature of the language of modern citizenship is called the 'subalternization' or colonization of other forms of citizenship: bringing them to language under a description of their subalternity or coloniality relative to modern citizenship.[14]

[14] W. D. Mignolo, *Local Histories/Global Designs: Coloniality, Subaltern Knowledges and Border Thinking*, Princeton: Princeton University Press, 2000.

The language of diverse citizenship, in contrast, characterizes other forms of citizenship as singular and historically contingent and critically compares them in terms of various similar and dissimilar aspects and from the perspectives and normative criteria of each.[15] From these perspectival and critical comparisons, modern citizenship (like all forms of citizenship) is seen as one singular, historical form of citizenship among others, with its strengths and weaknesses relative to others, yet presenting itself in false (circular) claims to universality (formulated in different ways over the last 200 years) that legitimate its global imposition. That is, the kind of *critical attitude* that accompanies practices of diverse citizenship and contextualizes or 'provincializes' modern citizenship and its universalizing language, usually but not necessarily by a historical or genealogical contextualization.[16] The aim of this critical attitude is to free us from the hold of the globally dominant language of modern citizenship as the pre-emptive language of disclosure of all forms of citizenship and enable us to see it as one language among others. In so doing, it de-universalizes modern citizenship (for, as we have seen, its claim to universality is internal to the globally dominant language of modern citizenship) and de-subalternizes other modes of citizenship (discloses them in their local languages and histories). Modern citizenship can thus be put in its place as one singular (and imperious) mode in a global field of diverse alternatives and the critical work of comparisons and contrasts from different perspectives and norms of assessment can begin. This difficult practice of situated critical freedom is not a change in theory but in attitude or ethos – in the way one sees and acts in the world of citizenship and its possibilities.[17]

---

[15] That is, the diverse tradition studies citizenship in the comparative and analogical way Wittgenstein outlines in the Introduction. For these two contrasting genres of reasoning, the modern and the diverse, see Tully, *Public Philosophy* I, chapter 1.

[16] See D. Chakrabarty, *Provincializing Europe: Postcolonial Thought and Historical Difference*, Princeton: Princeton University Press, 2000; and D. Chakrabarty, *Habitations of Modernity: Essays in the Wake of Subaltern Studies*, Chicago: University of Chicago Press, 2002.

[17] For the contrast between a 'critical theory' and a 'critical attitude' see Tully, *Public Philosophy* I, chapter 3.

Section One: Modern Citizenship

3. Modern civil citizenship

The tradition of modern citizenship takes as its empirical and normative exemplar the form of citizenship characteristic of the modern nation state.[18] Citizenship (both civil and cosmopolitan) is defined in relation to two clusters of institutional features of modern nation states: the constitutional rule of law (*nomos*) and representative government (*demos*). The constitutional rule of law is the first condition of citizenship. The 'civil' law (a formal legal order) and its enforcement by a coercive authority establishes (literally 'constitutes') the conditions of civilization, the city (*civitas*), citizenship, civil society, civil liberty and civility (hence 'civil' citizenship). By definition the 'outside' is the realm of the uncivilized: barbarism, savagery, the state of nature or war or the uncertainty of informal, customary law and unenforceable natural law. A person has the status of citizenship in virtue of being subject to civil law in two senses: to an established and enforced system of law and to the 'civilizing', pacifying or socializing force of the rule of law on the subjectivity (self-awareness and self-formation) of those who are constrained to obey over time. This is why cosmopolitan citizenship and global civil society depend on some form of legalization or constitutionalization of the global order analogous (in various ways) to the modern nation state.

Relative to the constitutional rule of law, modern citizenship is defined as a status (state or condition). This civil status is usually

---

[18] For the background to Section Two see J. Tully, *Strange Multiplicity: Constitutionalism in an Age of Diversity*, Cambridge: Cambridge University Press, 1995 as well as Tully, *Public Philosophy* I, chapter 6, and Tully, *Public Philosophy* II, chapters 1, 2, 4 and 7; C. Tilly, *Democracy*, Cambridge: Cambridge University Press, 2007; D. Held, *Models of Democracy*, Cambridge: Polity, 1996; J. Dunn, *Democracy: A History*, Toronto: Penguin Canada, 2005; M. R. Ishay, *The History of Human Rights: From Ancient Times to the Globalization Era*, Berkeley: University of California Press, 2004; S. Halperin, *War and Social Change in Modern Europe: The Great Transformation Revisited*, Cambridge: Cambridge University Press, 2004; Q. Skinner and B. Stråth, eds, *States and Citizens: History, Theory, Prospects*, Cambridge: Cambridge University Press, 2003; E. Wood, *Democracy against Capitalism: Renewing Historical Materialism*, Cambridge: Cambridge University Press, 1995; and the references in note 1.

explicated and defined in terms of the historical development of four rights (liberties) and duties of formally equal individual subjects of an association of constitutional rule of law and representative government. The association can be either the modern nation state, including its subordinate provinces and cities, or its analogous associations for cosmopolitan citizenship (international law, the United Nations (UN), global governance institutions). I will start with the four tiers of citizenship rights and duties within modern nation states as they are the basis of modern/cosmopolitan global citizenship.

The first and indispensable tier of rights is the set of 'civil liberties' (the liberties of the moderns or private autonomy) of the modern liberal tradition. This set includes the liberty of the person and of speech, thought and faith, the right to own private property and enter into contracts and the right to formal equality before the law. In virtue of these civil liberties citizens are 'at liberty' to engage in these activities if they choose (an opportunity status) and are protected by the law from 'interference' in the spheres where these rights can be exercised: of free speech and voluntary association, the market and the law. They are classic 'negative' liberties, protecting citizens from interference in these spheres.

Civil liberties and the rights of the person thus presuppose and are predicated of a human being with a distinctively modern or 'juridical' form of subjectivity situated in a set of modern institutional and educational preconditions. A modern person must be able to see oneself and others from the 'universal' standpoint of abstraction and freedom from relationships with others and, as such, independent rather than dependent (in relationships with others) or autonomous rather than heteronymous (determined by something other than one's self-legislating will). This modern subjectivity of civil personhood developed historically from the Roman legal dichotomy between the master, who possesses liberty because he is subject to his own will, and the slave, who lacks liberty because he is subject to the will of another. From the standpoint of formal and abstract independence and equality, civil persons are then at liberty to enter into relationships with each other on the basis of consent and contracts (irrespective of substantive inequalities). These relationships are 'free' relationships because the contracting parties give their consent. The collective analogue is the civil understanding of the right of self-determination of peoples. A people is said to be able to stand back and abstract itself from inherited relationships both among its individual members and between it and other peoples and – in a mythologized, historical constitutional convention or a hypothetical thought experiment – reach agreement on the basic laws they will subject themselves to and the international laws they will enter into with other peoples. In obeying the law, they obey their own will and remain at liberty.

At the centre of these civil liberties is the modern liberty to participate in the private economic sphere and not to be interfered within it; the right to own property and enter into contracts. This is the modern liberty to engage in the capitalist economy (market freedoms and free trade): to sell one's labouring abilities on the market for a wage to a corporation or, for those with the capital, to establish a corporation, hire the labour of and sell products competitively on the free market to consumers. Private corporations in the late nineteenth century gained recognition as 'persons' with the corresponding civil liberty of private autonomy (negative liberty). Thus, paradoxically from a civic perspective, the first right of modern citizenship is to participate in the private realm and to be protected from interference by the citizenry and its representatives. This form of participation in the economic sphere ('commercial society') is primary – *the* liberty of the moderns.

The modern civil liberty of private property and contracts accordingly presupposes the historical dispossession of people from access to land and resources through their local laws and non-capitalist economic organizations; the Enclosure of the commons; the accumulation of dispossessed workers into a 'free' market of wage labourers and consumers; the concentration of the means of production in private corporations and the imposition of modern legal systems of property law, contract law, labour law and trade law that constitute and protect the system of free markets and free trade. Thus, modern citizenship, in its basic commitment to the civil liberty of private property and contracts, is grounded in and dependent on the spread of these institutions of capitalism.[19] It is also the major justification for the spread of these institutions – as the basis of modern liberty. Accordingly, it is not only the coercive imposition of civil law acting alone that is said to civilize the uncivilized natives. Capitalist 'commerce', which, by rendering every person and society economically interdependent and competitive within an imposed structure of law and contractual relationships, pacifies, refines, polishes, makes predictable and – in concert with the law and representative governments – leads a crooked humanity, behind its back and despite its natural asociality, towards perpetual peace.

The second tier of liberties of modern citizenship is defined in relation to the second cluster of modern institutions: representative government. It consists in the rights to participate in these institutions if one chooses. In the language of modern citizenship 'democracy' and 'democratic' are equated with and restricted to 'representative government' and 'democratization' with the historical processes that bring these representative institutions and participatory rights into being. Other forms of democracy, if they are discussed *as* democracies, are described and subalternized in relation to representative government as the universal and regulative ideal of democracy. These rights of the modern democratic tradition are called public autonomy or the liberties of the ancients. They comprise the ways the *demos* – the citizenry of a nation state as a whole – legally exercise their popular sovereignty. The exercise of these 'democratic' rights enables the people to have a democratic say with respect to the laws and constitutions to which they are subject (and from which their citizenship derives) and thereby to balance the constitutional rule of law with the demands of democracy (the rule of the people) in a modern (representative) form. This representative form of democratic participation is contrasted with direct democracy, which is characterized as an 'earlier' form, incompatible with the size, complexity

[19] This summary draws on both Adam Smith and Karl Marx on what they called 'primitive accumulation'. See K. Marx, *Capital: A Critique of Political Economy*, Volume I, London: Penguin Classics, 1990, pp. 873–940. For the recent literature see note 18.

and individual liberties of modern polities. Modern democratic rights include: the right to vote for representatives in elections, join parties, interest groups, non-governmental organizations and social movements, stand for election, assemble, dissent and demonstrate in the civil or public sphere, freedom of the (private) press, engage in democratic deliberations, litigate in the Courts, exchange public reasons over ratifying constitutional amendments or participate in a constituent assembly and engage in civil disobedience and accept the punishment.

Like civil liberties and their institititional preconditions, these democratic liberties presuppose historically the dispossession of people from access to political power through pre-existing local forms of citizenship and the channelling of democratic citizenship into participation in the official public sphere of modern, Western representative governments and their global analogues. These historical 'processes' are described as freeing people from pre-modern forms of subjection and bringing democratic citizenship to them. Participation is equated with activities of public arguing (deliberating), bargaining (organizing, negotiating and protesting) and litigating over changing the laws, since political power, the object of democratic participation, is presumed to be exercised through the rule of law. The aim is to ensure that the law is not imposed unilaterally on those subject to it, but that they may, if they choose, have a representative say in making or amending the laws, and thus see themselves, abstractly and representatively, as co-articulators of the laws. This form of participation thus takes place (in both practice and theory) within and reproduces the ground plan of modern citizenship because the people participate *as* juridical citizens exercising democratic rights within modern institutions and under the priority of first tier civil liberties.[20]

---

[20] This juridical framework of individual democratic participation also enframes the modern collective right of self-determination in which a people have the right to form a modern state with the characteristic institutions and within the international state system (or, if they are a people within a modern state, then they must determine themselves within the constitutional constraints of that state – 'internal' self-determination). See Subsection 4 as well as Tully, *Public Philosophy* I, chapter 8, and *Public Philosophy* II, chapter 5.

The second tier democratic liberties are circumscribed by the first tier civil liberties in three main ways. Their exercise is optional. Members of a modern political association are citizens and the association is democratic whether or not they exercise their participatory rights. To make participation a requirement of citizenship is to violate the civil liberty not to be interfered with and thus is inconsistent with modern liberty. Second, the primary use and justification of these rights in the modern tradition is to fight for laws that protect the private autonomy of the moderns from too much governmental interference or domination – to protect the private liberty of the modern individual. Third, these rights cannot be extended and exercised in the private sphere (as in economic democracy in the workplace) for this would interfere with tier one liberties. When the leaders of the great powers today (the G8) speak of the spread of 'freedom' and 'democracy' in Afghanistan, Iraq and elsewhere in sound bites, they are referring to the module of tier one (freedom) and tier two (democracy) rights of citizenship and their underlying institutions of the rule of law, markets, eventual representative government and the military as the imposition and enforcement institution.

The third and weakest tier of modern rights of citizenship comprises the social and economic rights of the modern social democratic tradition. These are the citizenship rights won over the last two centuries by working-class movements struggling within the historically established priority and constraints of tiers one and two liberties in nation states and international law. They are a response to the horrendous, substantive inequalities in wealth, well-being, living conditions and forms of social power that go along with the unrestrained formal independence and equality of first tier civil liberties and the limited democratic rights of the second tier. The modern social democratic argument for them is that they are the minimum conditions of the worst off actually being able to exercise their civil and democratic liberties.[21] The argument

---

[21] The substantive inequalities across class, gender, race, ethnicity, regions and the North and Global South open up an enormous gap between the formal possession of a legal right and the actual wherewithal to exercise it effectively, yet the possession of the right is often equated with 'being able to' exercise it or being 'at liberty' to exercise it, thereby eliding this de facto disenfranchisement of millions of human beings.

against them is that they violate the economic liberties of the moderns by interfering in the private sphere and economic competition, and thus must be subordinated to tier one civil liberty and the limits of tier two. When the capitalist countries triumphed over the socialist countries at the end of the Cold War the bargaining power of Western socialist and social democratic movements was undermined and neoliberal governments were able to dismantle many hard-won social and economic rights nationally and internationally in the name of spreading market freedoms and democratic freedoms.

The fourth tier of citizenship rights consists of modern minority rights of multiculturalism, religious and ethnic groups, multiple nations within states and indigenous peoples. These rights appear to some modern theorists to violate one premise of modern citizenship, the primacy of the individual legal subject. However, minority rights can be defined as rights that, first, protect the individual members of minorities from interference or dominance by the majority (and by the powerful within the minority) and, second, empower members of minorities to exercise their civil and democratic liberties in more effective ways than through the institutions of the majority society. They thus can be designed to enhance, rather than to challenge, the spread of modern citizenship. This is the major way they have been implemented within modern nation states and international law. That is, they too presuppose the dispossession of 'minorities' of their diverse forms of legal, governmental and economic organization and their integration into replication forms of modern citizenship.

Within Europe, this modular form of modern citizenship became paramount during the centralization and consolidation of the modern constitutional representative nation state and the capitalist economy. Diverse local and regional forms of laws, governments and citizenship – of village commons, urban communes, counties, regional leagues – where they were not destroyed completely, were marginalized or transformed and subordinated as they were brought under the rationalization of the central institutions of the modern nation state. Modern citizenship was nationalized as local citizenship was subalternized. Generations of 'locals' were gradually socialized by education, urbanization, military duty, industrialization and techniques of citizenization to see themselves first and foremost as members of an abstract and disembedded imaginary community of nation, demos and nomos of formally equal citizens. In virtue of possessing the individual liberties of modern citizenship attached to the central legal and representative institutions, they were encouraged to see themselves as participating in a similarly abstract imaginary of the sovereignty of the people. The violent dispossessions and transformations, and the countless civic resistances to them, were described and justified in the social-scientific and normative theories and traditions of modern, state-centred citizenship as processes of modernization and making the modern identity. These 'uneven' processes are said to free individuals from dependency on unfree pre-modern ways and progressively make him and then her free and equal citizens with four tiers of rights and duties, correlative to the four aspects of a fully modern identity, and with the corresponding differentiation of institutionalized value spheres in which to exercise them.

Citizens and especially non-citizens – such as the poor, the propertyless, women, immigrants, excluded 'races' and others – struggled and continue to struggle within and against these 'civilizing processes' in Europe. When they were not struggling for local forms of self-government, they fought to be included in modern citizenship, to extend the use of political rights beyond the official public sphere, to gain social and economic rights that do more than prepare one for the market and for minority rights that protect alternative cultural, legal, political and economic organization. These struggles were and are against the powerful actors who strive to circumscribe citizenship to tier one civil liberties and a limited module of democratic rights.[22] Since these types of struggle are *for* new kinds of citizenship and by means of people who are not official citizens, or official citizens who often act beyond the official limits of citizenship of their generation, they cannot be called practices of citizenship in the modern tradition. They

---

[22] Ishay, *History of Human Rights*, pp. 63–244.

are classified as acts of civil disobedience or rebellion. If these illegal struggles are successful and the extensions institutionalized, then the extensions are redescribed retrospectively as stages in the development of modern citizenship and incorporated within its framework, as in the cases of working-class struggles giving rise to social and economic rights, women gaining recognition as citizens, civil rights movements and recognition of cultural minorities. Thus, what are seen as activities *of* citizenship by the civic tradition – struggles for new forms of recognition and extensions of citizenship – fall outside of modern citizenship with its institutional/status orientation.

4. The globalization of civil and cosmopolitan citizenship

I want now to examine how the modular form of modern citizenship has been spread around the globe as 'global citizenship'. It has been and continues to be globalized in two forms. First, the tripartite module of a modern nation state, the underlying institutions that modern citizenship presupposes, and, once these preconditions are in place, the specific institutions of modern *civil* citizenship has been and continues to be spread around the world, as various stages of development, as the universal form of political association recognized as the bearer of fully legitimate political authority (sovereignty) under international law. Second, a modular form of modern *cosmopolitan* citizenship has been and continues to be spread as the universal form of global citizenship recognized as legitimate under international law and global institutions.[23]

During the long period when Europeans were building modern nation states with the underlying institutions of modern citizenship they were also, and simultaneously, building these states as competing *imperial* modern nation states. As imperial states they built and

---

[23] Subsection 4 is based on the detailed studies and references to the scholarly literature in Tully, *Public Philosophy* II, chapters 1, 4, 5 and 7. I have not repeated all these references here except for a few cases.

defended vast overseas empires that colonized (in various ways) 85 per cent of the world's population by 1914. The imperial 'great game' of competing economically and militarily against other great European powers over the control and exploitation of the resources, labour and markets of the non-European world *and* the counter-actions of the non-European peoples co-created the modern West and the modern colonized non-West. After decolonization, this great game continues, between the former imperial powers (renamed the 'great eight'), exercising 'hegemony' rather than 'imperium' through the post–World War II Bretton Woods institutions of global governance, and over the renamed 'post-colonial' world of more than 120 nominally free and equal (sovereign), yet substantively still dependent and unequal, new modernizing nation states, constructed on the foundations of the former colonies and protectorates. The spread of modern citizenship and its institutional preconditions beyond Europe can be understood only in the context of this immensely complex contrapuntal ensemble of Western strategies of expansion and non-Western strategies of counteraction, and the effects of their interaction over the last half millennium.

The module of institutional preconditions of modern citizenship was implanted abroad, in the course of European expansion, by a deceptively innocuous apparatus that linked a right of global citizenship to imperial power in a circular relationship. Formulated and exercised in different ways by the different European powers in the early modern period, the imperial right of cosmopolitan citizenship for Europeans is called the right of commerce (*ius commercium*) or 'cosmopolitan' right. From the earliest phase of European expansion under Portugal and Spain to the present day the great powers have claimed the cosmopolitan right of their citizens, trading companies, monopoly companies and multinational corporations to travel to other countries and attempt to engage in 'commerce' in two early-modern senses of this term. The first is to travel the globe freely and converse with the inhabitants of other societies. This covers such activities as the right – and duty – of Western explorers, missionaries, religious organizations, voluntary associations and academics to travel to non-Western countries in order to, first, study and classify their different customs and ways into developmental stages of different societies and races, and, second, try to free them from their uncivilized ways and teach them the uniquely civilized ways of the West. This cosmopolitan right is the historical antecedent of the right of modern cosmopolitan citizenship of civil society associations (modern Non-governmental Organizations (NGOs)) to modernize and democratize people in the post-colonial world today. The second sense of this cosmopolitan right is to travel and attempt to engage in 'commerce' (trade) with the inhabitants. This includes such commercial activities as entering into contracts and treaties, gaining access to resources, buying slaves, hiring and disciplining labourers, establishing trading posts, making investments, establishing plantations and so on. At first it was used by the European powers to establish imperial monopolies over the exploitation of the resources and labour of non-European societies, but monopoly imperialism gradually gave way to 'free trade' or 'open door' imperialism in the nineteenth and twentieth centuries.

This cosmopolitan right correlates with the duty of 'hospitality' of the host country to open their doors to free commerce in this dual sense. If they inhospitably close the door to entry, break the contract or expropriate the property of a foreigner who has engaged in commerce, or if they expel the missionaries and voluntary societies, then the appropriate recognized legal authority – under the old law of nations, or imperial law of the respective empire or, later, international law – has a reciprocal right to open the door by diplomacy or military intervention (gunboat diplomacy), punish the violation of the cosmopolitan right and demand reparations or compensation. The correlative duty of hospitality – openness to free commerce – holds even if the cosmopolitan right was initially exercised unjustly: that is where a trading company used force and fraud to establish trade relations and contracts in the first place. The early-modern duty of non-European societies to open their resources to commerce dominated by the West continues to be one of the core duties of transnational trade law agreements today.

As with civil liberty within a modern state, this cosmopolitan right presupposes a number of institutions. The host country must have or adopt the legal, economic and cultural institutions that make possible commerce in this broad sense (private property, foreign corporations, contracts, wage labour, dependence on the international market dominated by the West, openness to cultural conversion, protection of foreigners and so on). The imperial power must either submit to and modify the local laws and institutions or impose a structure of commercial law that overrides and restructures them, such as Merchant's Law (*lex mercatoria*), the vast global system of trade law that developed in conjunction with Western imperialism.

We can see that this cosmopolitan right is a right of citizens of the civilized imperial states to exercise the first right of modern citizenship (civil liberties of private autonomy) and a version of the second right (to participate) beyond their nation state and to be protected from interference in doing so. The two rights – of the trading company to trade and the voluntary organizations to converse and convert – also fit together in the same way as within the nation state. The participatory right to converse with and try to convert the natives complements the primary right of commerce since the inhabitants are taught the requisite forms of subjectivity and modes of civil conduct that go along with the commercialization of their society and its gradual civilization. The discipline of slavery and indentured labour on the plantations, the various forms of religious and occupational education and the military and civil training of dependent elites at the top were seen as steps in the civilizing process. From the modern perspective, these two rights of cosmopolitan citizenship linked to imperial power appear to bring the gift of the civilizing institutions of law, commerce and Western civility to a closed, uncivilized or semi-civilized world, gradually removing all 'savage' (insubordinate) alterity and remaking it as the subordinate image of the modern West. From the perspective of non-Western civilizations and diverse citizenship this 'cosmopolitan' apparatus of free trade appears as the Trojan horse of Western imperialism.[24]

In practice, this apparatus was employed to globalize the underlying institutions of modern citizenship in three main strategies. First, settler colonies were established that *replicated* the basic legal, political and economic institutions of the imperial country in the Americas, Australia and New Zealand. The settlement of these 'new Europes' involved the dispossession of the indigenous peoples of their diverse civilizations, territories and resources, the genocide of 80 to 90 per cent of the population, the marginalization of those they could not enslave or assimilate (ethnocide), the transportation of 12 million Africans as slaves to plantations in the Americas and the imposition of Western institutions of property and rudimentary representative government (colonial legislatures). The colonies gained independence from their empires by revolution or devolution and developed the institutions of modern civil citizenship in ways similar to Europe.[25] After World War II they developed modern minority rights in domestic and international law as a tactic of 'internal colonization' in response to the continuing struggles of 300 million indigenous peoples for their unceded sovereignty over their traditional territories; the very territories over which these modern states claim to exercise unquestionable sovereignty.

Second, 'indirect' imperial rule opened non-Western societies to commerce by establishing a small colonial administration, often run by trading companies, to rule indirectly over a much larger indigenous population. A centralized system of Western colonial law was used to protect the commercial rights of their citizens and traders, while also preserving and modifying the local customary laws and governments so resources and labour were privatized and subject to trade, labour discipline and investment dominated by the Western trading companies. Local rulers were recognized as quasi-sovereigns in their

---

[24] See especially A. Anghie, *Imperialism, Sovereignty and the Making of International Law*, Cambridge: Cambridge University Press, 2007; and D. B. Abernathy, *The Dynamics of Global Dominance: European Overseas Empires, 1415–1980*, Yale: Yale University Press, 2000.

[25] As in Subsection 3.

regions and unequal treaties were negotiated. The local elites were made dependent on Western economic and military power, undermining their accountability to local citizens, and were employed to introduce modernizing techniques of governance and train the local army to protect the system of property, often against the majority of their own population. This was the main way the institutional preconditions of modern citizenship (and actual modern citizenship for European colonials) were introduced in India, Ceylon, Africa and the Middle East in the twentieth century.

The third and most recent strategy is informal or free trade imperialism. Here the imperial power permits local self-rule, and eventually self-determination, but within a protectorate or sphere of influence over which they exercise informal 'paramountcy' (now called hegemony and dominance). By informal means they induce the local governments to open their resources, labour and markets to free trade and liberalization by establishing the appropriate modern institutions. These provide the foundations for eventual modern citizenship with tier-one market liberties preceding and circumscribing the others. The means include: structural dependency on economic, military, technological and educational aid; the modernization of the population by Western experts and civil society organizations; bribes and threats; training and arming local militaries and counter-insurgency units (death squads) and low-intensity military interventions. This in turn requires small but effective military bases strategically located around the world, linked together by a global navy and (since World War II) air force. These bases, originally coaling stations for the British navy, are used to arm and train the local militias or to intervene whenever local citizens try to take control of their own economic and political affairs and thereby violate their duty of openness to free trade.

This strategy of informal intervention imperialism was developed by the British in the nineteenth century. However, it is the United States that has taken the global lead, first in Latin America under the Monroe Doctrine and then throughout the world by the end of the Cold War. Beginning with over 5,000 interventions in sovereign Latin

American countries in the nineteenth and early twentieth centuries and the establishment of military/training bases such as Guantanamo Bay (1901), the United States now has over 760 bases beyond its state borders. These are connected by a network of navy, air force, satellite systems and the weaponization of space that continuously surveils and patrols the planet. Similar to the pro-consuls of the Roman Empire and the governors-general of the British, the whole world is divided into four regions under the command of four regional Commanders in Chiefs (CINCs) who report directly to the Joint Chiefs of Staff. According to the Pentagon, this worldwide military empire exercises 'full spectrum dominance' over the informal global system of 'open commerce and freedom'.[26]

The cosmopolitan apparatus and its three strategies were gathered together and formalized as the 'standard of civilization' in the creation of modern international law during the nineteenth century. The European imperial nation states (and the United States after 1895) declared themselves to be 'civilized states' in virtue of their institutions of modern statehood and citizenship (the modern rule of law, openness to commerce, representative government and modern liberty were the main criteria). As such they were the sole bearers of sovereignty and subject only to the laws they could agree to among themselves, which they called modern 'international' laws. Their modern institutions provided a standard of civilization in international law by which they judged all other civilizations in the world as 'uncivilized' to varying degrees (depending on their stage of development) and thus not sovereign subjects of international law, but subjects of the sovereign imperial powers through colonies, indirect protectorates and informal

---

[26] Joint Chiefs of Staff, *Joint Vision 2010*, available at: www.dtic.mil/jv2010/jvpub.htm (Accessed 19 September 2007). See the discussion and references in Tully, *Public Philosophy* II, chapter 5, especially A. Bacevich, *American Empire: The Realities and Consequences of U.S. Diplomacy*, Cambridge, MA: Harvard University Press, 2002. For the most recent account see G. Grandin, *Empire's Workshop: Latin America, the United States and the Rise of the New Imperialism*, New York: Metropolitan Books, 2007. The classic is E. Galeano, *Open Veins of Latin America: Five Centuries of the Pillage of a Continent*, New York: Monthly Review, 1997. See Tully, *Public Philosophy* II, chapter 5.

spheres of influence.[27] They asserted a right and duty of civilization under international law. 'Civilization' referred to both the historical processes of modernization and the normative end-point of a modern civil state. The duty to civilize consisted in the consolidation and international legalization of the imperial strategies they began in the earlier period. The opening of non-European societies to European-dominated commerce and property law, the exploitation of their resources and labour and the removal of uncivilized customs that blocked progress were seen as the first steps of the civilizing mission. The second and equally important duty was to introduce into the colonies and protectorates more systematic and effective forms of colonial governance (or governmentalité) that would shape and form the dependent peoples and races into civilized subjects eventually capable of modern self-government.

This global civilizing project under international law lacked an enforcement mechanism and the civilizing duty was left to the sovereign empires and their voluntary organizations. The destruction, exploitation, oppression, despotism, genocide and wars of imperialism and anti-imperial resistance continued apace. They increased after the failure of the Berlin Conference (1884) and the 'scramble for Africa', cumulating in the barbarism of World War I – the 'great war of civilization'. In response to these horrors and to contain increasing demands for decolonization, the first concerted attempt to operationalize the civilizing duty under international law was set up under the Mandate System of the League of Nations. The League classified the subject peoples into three categories according to their aptitude for tutelage in modern citizenship and gave the respective imperial powers the mandate to civilize them as they increased their economic exploitation, especially in the oil-rich Middle East.[28]

---

[27] The classification of non-Western societies followed the subalternizing logic mentioned in Subsection 2.

[28] Middle Eastern peoples were classified as capable of modern self-government and citizenship after a period of 'tutelage', tropical Africans after a longer and more despotic period of 'guardianship' and South Western Africans, Pacific Islanders and Indigenous peoples were classified as too 'primitive' ever to be civilized. See Tully, *Public Philosophy* II, chapter 5.

This citizenizing project was interrupted by the decolonization movements of the mid-century. Although the overwhelming majority of people fought for freedom from imperial dependency on the West or the Soviet Union and for their own modes of government and citizenship, the Westernized and nationalizing elites (subject to intensified economic and military dependency) and the informal means of the great powers brought about the continuity of the imperial processes of development. During the Cold War and post-independence state formation in conditions of neocolonial dependency, the nation-building elites were constrained to destroy or subordinate local economies and governments, enforce the artificial colonial boundaries, centralize government, open their resources to free trade, accept constitutions designed by experts from the imperial metropoles and promise minimal institutions of modern citizenship, or face sanctions and military intervention. The result tended to be constitutional and institutional structures that either concentrated power at the centre or, as in Africa, in both the urban and rural regions, replicating the worst features of colonial administration in both types of the case.[29]

During the same period, the cooperating great powers set up the institutions of global governance through which informal imperial hegemony and post-colonial subalternity could be continued. These are the concentrations of power in the permanent members of the Security Council of the UN, the World Bank (WB), International Monetary Fund (IMF), General Agreement on Trade and Tariffs (GATT), the World Trade Organization (WTO) after 1995 and its transnational trade agreements (such as TRIPS and GATTS), modernizing NGOs, the North Atlantic Treaty Organization (NATO) and, emerging as the indispensable leader and guarantor after 1989, the United States with its global system of military dominance.

---

[29] M. Mamdani, *Citizen and Subject: Contemporary Africa and the Legacy of Late Colonialism*, Princeton: Princeton University Press, 1995. And for a comparative survey of constitutionalization since World War II, M. Schor, 'Mapping Comparative Judicial Review', *Comparative Research in Law and Political Economy Research Paper Series* 3 (4): 545–67, 2007. Available at: www.comparativeresearch.net.

At the request of the newly independent states, the language of
civilization was removed from international law and the UN.[30] However,
it was immediately replaced with the language of modernization,
marketization, democratization and globalization with the identical
grammatical structure, signifying universal processes of development
and a single endpoint of modern citizenship and its institutions, and
ranks all alternatives in relation to its regulative ideal. These processes
are now to be brought about, not by a civilizing mission, but by the 'global
governance' of the informal coalitions of the modern (or post-modern)
states and their multinational corporations imposing 'good governance'
through the global institutions (WB and IMF), and by modern NGOs
building civil societies and making civil subjects in the less-developed
states. This is all backed up by the US military networks and alliances,
for, as its neo-imperial proponents forthrightly explain, the 'hidden
hand' of the market, given its intolerable exploitations and inequalities,
always needs to be protected by the 'hidden fist' of the military, and the
'savage wars of peace'.[31] As the leaders of decolonization movements
recognized shortly after independence, they were conscripted into an
all-too-familiar script, but now in a new language of an abstract modern
world system of free and equal nation states and global governance that
was said to have come into being in 1648 (the Westphalian System),
thereby concealing the imperial construction of this world and its
persisting relationships of dependency, inequality and exploitation.

The difference from the old colonial strategies of spreading modern
citizenship is that the formerly colonized peoples are now seen as
active, self-governing agents in these processes at home and in the
institutions of global governance (the G120). They are now bearers
of modern civil and cosmopolitan citizenship, yet still under the

---

[30] See Anghie, *Imperialism*, pp. 196–235; and Tully, *Public Philosophy* II, chapter 5. However,
a reference to the authority of the 'general principles of law recognised by the civilized
nations' appears in International Court of Justice, *Statute of the International Court of
Justice*, §38.1.c., available at: www.icj-cij.org/documents/index.php?p1=4&p2=2&p3=0
(Accessed 30 July 2007).
[31] The 'hidden hand' and the 'hidden fist' are from T. Friedman, *The Lexus and the Olive
Tree*, New York: Farrar, Strauss, Giroux, 1999, cited in M. Boot, *Savage Wars of Peace*,
New York: Basic Books, 2003, p. xx.

enlightened leadership of the more advanced or developed peoples. International law provides the basis for this by promoting a 'right to democracy'. Democracy and democratization projects are equated with tier-one civil liberties (neoliberal marketization) and a short list of democratic rights (primarily elections). However, if citizens become too democratic and seek to exercise their right of self-determination by taking democratic control of their own government and economy, and thus violate their duty to open their doors to the global economy and its laws, multinational corporations and democratization from above, one of two strategies follow. They are repressed by their own dependent elites, democratic rights are further reduced or eliminated and the governments become more authoritarian. Or, if the people manage to gain power, the repertoire of covert and overt informal means available to the great powers are employed to destabilize and undermine the government, bring about regime change and institute neoliberal structural adjustment policies that promote tier-one civil liberties of individuals and corporations. As in the colonial period, the imposition of market discipline is said to come first and lay the foundation for democratic rights. The result in either case is the suppression or severe restriction of democratic citizenship, the corresponding rise of militarized rule and market freedoms on one side and increasingly violent and authoritarian resistance movements on the other. The countries that are subject to these horrendous oscillations are described as 'failed' or 'terrorist' states, covert or overt military intervention follows, resistance intensifies and instability persists.[32]

---

[32] The recent 'War on Terror' can thus be seen as the continuation of a much longer trend as many scholars have argued. See Tully, *Public Philosophy* II, chapters 5 and 7; R. Khalidi, *Resurrecting Empire: Western Footprints and America's Perilous Path in the Middle East*, Boston: Beacon, 2004; and R. Skidelsky, *The Prince of the Marshes and other Occupational Hazards of a Year in Iraq*, London: Harcourt, 2006, for the continuity with earlier British indirect rule in the Middle East. T. Smith, *A Pact with the Devil: Washington's Bid for World Supremacy and the Betrayal of the American Promise*, London: Routledge, 2007, for its continuity with Wilsonian intervention imperialism; Grandin, *Empire's Workshop*, for its continuity with US imperialism in Latin America and Anghie, *Imperialism*, for its longer continuity. Osama bin Laden also places the rise of Al-Qaeda in the broad historical context of Muslim resistance to Western imperialism: O. bin Laden, *Messages to the World: The Statements of Osama bin Laden*, London: Verso, 2005.

The consequence is that a restricted or 'low intensity' form of modern civil citizenship is promoted or promised at the national level with an equally low intensity form of modern cosmopolitan citizenship of individuals and NGOs at the international level. The first wave of international human rights after World War II sought to give protection to the individual person from the worst effects of these processes (civil liberties) and to elaborate a set of global democratic, social and economic and minority rights similar to those at the national level. However, these are hostage to implementation by nation states and thus subject to the processes described above. The second wave of international law brought into force a vast array of transnational trade law regimes (under GATT and the WTO) that override national constitutions and constrain the weaker and poorer countries (which contain the majority of the world's population) to open their economies to exploitation and pollution dumping in order to gain loans, aid and debt relief. The third wave of international law after the Al-Qaeda attack on the World Trade Centre and the Pentagon of 9/11/2001 consists of Resolutions of the Security Council of the UN promoting international security. These global securitization regimes, which protect the security and liberty of modern citizens, often override the first-wave international human rights, force national governments to enact security legislation that rolls back hard won democratic rights, thereby circumscribing democratic opposition to the War on Terror and neoliberal globalization, and securing civil and cosmopolitan market liberties of individual and corporate citizens in national and transnational law.[33]

This new articulation of the old cosmopolitan Trojan horse is now the major justification for the continuation of Western informal imperialism, as we see in Iraq and Afghanistan today. The opposition parties on the left criticize neoliberal and neoconservative policies and offer a more social democratic and multilateral alternative strategy,

---

[33] For these three waves of International law, see Ishay, *History of Human Rights*, pp. 173–356; K. L. Scheppele, *The International State of Emergency: Challenges to Constitutionalism after September 11*, Unpublished Manuscript: Princeton University, 2007; and Tully, *Public Philosophy* II, chapter 7.

yet they do so entirely within the shared languages and institutions of modern citizenship. The result is not only continued popular resistance, escalating militarization, and instability, as above, but escalating global inequalities between the West and the non-West that are worse now than at the height of the ruthless phase of Western imperialism at the turn of the nineteenth century.

Approximately 840 million people are malnourished. There are 6 million children under the age of 5 who die each year as a consequence of malnutrition. Roughly, 1.2 billion people live on less than $1 a day and half the world's population lives on less than $2 a day. Ninety-one out of every 1,000 children in the developing world die before 5 years old. Twelve million die annually from lack of water, and 1.1 billion people have no access to clean water. About 2.4 billion people live without proper sanitation, while 40 million live with AIDS and 113 million children have no basic education. One in five does not survive past 40 years of age. Of the one billion non-literate adults, two-thirds are women and 98 per cent live in the developing world. In the least developed countries, 45 per cent of the children do not attend school. In countries with a literacy rate of less than 55 per cent, the per capita income is about $600.

In contrast, the wealth of the richest 1 per cent of the world is equal to that of the poorest 57 per cent. The assets of the 200 richest people are worth more than the total income of 41 per cent of the world's people. Three families alone have a combined wealth of $135 billion. This equals the annual income of 600 million people living in the world's poorest countries. The richest 20 per cent of the world's population receive 150 times the wealth of the poorest 20 per cent. In 1960, the share of the global income of the bottom 20 per cent was 2.3 per cent. By 1991, this had fallen to 1.4 per cent. The richest fifth of the world's people consume 45 per cent of the world's meat and fish; the poorest fifth consume 5 per cent. The richest fifth consume 58 per cent of total energy, the poorest fifth less than 4 per cent. The richest fifth have 75 per cent of all telephones, the poorest fifth 1.5 per cent. The richest fifth own 87 per cent of the world's vehicles, the poorest fifth less than 1 per cent.[34] As a result of the globalization of modern citizenship and its underlying institutions, the majority of the world's population of landless labourers is thus at liberty to exercise their modern freedom in the growing sweatshops and slums of the planet.[35]

We can see that the globalization of modern citizenship has not tended to democracy, equality, independence and peace, as its justificatory theories proclaim, but to informal imperialism, inequality, dependence and war. This tendency is intrinsic to the modern mode of citizenship as a whole. From within its institutions, modern citizens see their citizenship as universal, superior and what everyone else would assent to if they were only freed from their particular and inferior ways. Accordingly, they see themselves as having the cosmopolitan right and duty to enter into other societies to free them from these inferior ways, impose the institutional preconditions of modern citizenship, which bring obscene profits to their corporations and unconscionable inequality to the people they are modernizing, and remove the obstacles and resistances to progress. The background languages of universal and necessary modernization and of universal and obligatory norms and institutions of the four tiers of modern citizenship that they project over the global field render the whole ensemble self-validating in theory and practice. In carrying it forward modern citizens are only doing what is both inevitable and right. When others resist, this proves that they are not yet fully civil and rational and legitimates the use of more coercion in response, thereby creating the conditions of its validation and expansion.

From the perspective of diverse citizenship, this mode of citizenship is neither freedom nor democracy but 500 years of relentless 'tyranny' against local citizenship and self-reliance. It is the undemocratic imposition of a low-intensity mode of citizenship over others, in which the people imposed upon have little or no effective democratic say as

---

[34] J. Seabrook, *The No-Nonsense Guide to World Poverty*, Toronto: New Internationalist, 2003, p. 53. See Tully, *Public Philosophy* II, chapter 7. For the measurement of global inequalities, see B. Milanovic, *Worlds Apart: Measuring International and Global Inequality*, Princeton: Princeton University Press, 2005.

[35] M. Davis, *A Planet of Slums*, London: Verso, 2005.

citizens, and under which they are not free and equal peoples but subjects of imperial relationships of inequality, dependency and exploitation.

Section Two: Diverse Citizenship

5. Diverse civic citizenship

I now want to move around and survey the same contested field of global citizenship from the orientation and practices of the other, diverse mode of citizenship. To begin this difficult movement I start from a brief synopsis of the globally predominant modern mode of citizenship we examined in Section One. I then show how diverse citizens apply their critical attitude to free themselves from taking its language as the comprehensive language of citizenship and thus enable us to move around to see the field of citizenship and the place of modern citizenship within it from the comparative perspectives provided by other disclosive languages of citizenship.[36]

Synoptically, modern citizenship is a status consisting of four ranked tiers of rights and duties that make sense and are exercised within a canonical set of underlying legal, political, economic, educational and military institutions of the modern nation state, international law and global governance. Modern citizenship is presented as the institutionalization of civil liberty or freedom (freedoms of the person and the market) and democracy (representative government and participation in the public sphere). It is universal in virtue of three constitutive languages: world-historical processes of modernization that bring these institutions into being through stages; the normative ideal of modern citizenship and its institutions presented as the universal form of citizenship for every human being and as the telos of the causal processes and the comprehensive disclosure and ranking of all other

---

[36] Subsection 4 draws on the detailed discussion of the civic tradition in all the chapters in Tully, *Public Philosophy* I–II.

modes of citizenship as either not really citizenship or historically and culturally inferior relative to modern citizenship. Because it is the universal form and as the Western states are closer to realizing its ideal form (more developed), they have a right and duty to bring its underlying institutions, beginning with tier-one institutions, to the less-developed by means of the 'civilizing apparatus' and its many strategies. They also have the duty to defend this unfinished project against those who fail to conform, for it is the mode of citizenship everyone would assent to if and when they exchange public reasons and reach agreement within the universal civil institutions of modern citizenship.

The discussion and criticism of citizenship takes place within these background languages of disclosure of the field of citizenship and the corresponding modern institutions. Questions of citizenship always lead back to the juridical subject with rights and underlying institutions, the social scientific theories of historical processes that bring them about and the normative theories of its ideal universal form and justifications for its globalization. As it is spread around the globe this particular world picture in all its complexity becomes the living identity of modern citizens and of those who see themselves as on their way to becoming modern. It is difficult to free moderns from this world picture, for it lies in the languages they use and the globalized institutions in which they use them and project them over others. One thinks that one is thinking and acting critically with respect to the very essence of citizenship, yet one is predicating over and over again the modern representation of citizenship onto the field of citizenship.

Members of the tradition of diverse citizenship see this self-described universalism and cosmopolitanism as one of the most dangerous forms of circular parochialism and fear of alterity. It appears as the prejudice of taking one's familiar form of national citizenship as the only acceptable form, projecting its hierarchical classifications over others, and trying to make them over in one's own parochial image, with the disastrous effects we have surveyed. How, then, do diverse citizens avoid being taken in by this captivating world picture, exercise their critical attitude on it and sustain a multiplicity of alternative forms of citizenship, thereby making the actual contrapuntal global field of citizenship qualitatively different from the subordinate mirror image of themselves that the modern mode of citizenship presents to its captivated citizens? I think the answer is a practical one. They avoid assimilation and sustain alternative worlds by *acting* otherwise – by participating in other practices of citizenship (often in the same institutions). I will try to elucidate these alternatives by comparing and contrasting diverse civic citizenship with modern civil citizenship in this section and diverse glocal citizenship with modern cosmopolitan citizenship in Subsection 6. Many of the aspects of civic citizenship are aspects of glocal citizenship as well.

1. The first and fundamental difference between the two traditions is their basic orientation. Rather than looking on citizenship as a status within an institutional framework backed up by world-historical processes and universal norms, the diverse tradition looks on citizenship as *negotiated practices*, as praxis – as actors and activities in contexts. Civic activities – what citizens do and the ways they do them – can be more or less institutionalized and rationalized (in countless forms), but this is secondary. The primary thing is the concrete games of citizenship and the ways they are played.[37] The modern tradition in social science and political theory overlooks these activities because it presupposes that the rights, rules, institutions and processes must be primary (the conditions of civilization) and human actors and activities secondary (what happens within the civil space constituted by the civilizing rights, institutions, rules and processes). The diverse tradition reverses this modernist, institutional orientation and takes the orientation of citizens in civic activities in the habitats they are enacted and carried on. Institutionalization is seen and analysed as coming into being in unpredictable and open-ended ways out of, and in interaction

---

[37] As I intimated in the Introduction, my formulations of several aspects of civic citizenship, including this one, draw on Wittgenstein's complementary work on explicating language from the perspective of the activities of language users in the *Philosophical Investigations*. His central insight that it 'is our *acting*, which lies at the bottom of the language game' is at one with the civic orientation (L. Wittgenstein, *On Certainty*, Oxford: Wiley-Blackwell, 1969, p. 204).

with, the praxis of citizens – sometimes furthering, strengthening and formalizing these activities while at other times dispossessing, channelling, dominating, cancelling, downsizing, constraining and limiting.

Civic citizenship does not take a 'practice' of civic activity as a *form* of organization within which civic activity takes place, for this would be to treat civic activity as resting on some proto-institutional background (rules, conditions, processes). Rather, civic citizenship consists of *negotiated* practices all the way down. It comprises civic activities and the ongoing contestation and negotiation of these practices by the participants and by those subject to and affected by but yet excluded from them, and so on in turn. There is never the last voice or word. The form of a civic practice is never closed by a frontier but always open to negotiation. The skills of civic citizenship consist not only in learning how to play by the given rules of a civic practice but also on how to enunciate a critical question about the rules (and their theoretical justifications) and to listen attentively for voices that are silenced or misrepresented by the official rules or the most powerful critics. These ongoing negotiations of practices of civic citizenship are themselves activities of civic citizenship that keep the internal organization of civic activities open and democratic. As we saw in the Introduction, this is just to acknowledge and build into the practice of citizenship a repressible yet irreducible feature of it.[38]

2. The second way the diverse tradition avoids the prejudice of mistaking one institutionalized form of citizenship as the model for all possible forms is to take any specific civic activity in context as one local negotiated practice of citizenship among many. The way diverse citizens do this is by always keeping the multiplicity of games of citizenship in view (even within their own civic organizations). This enables them to resist (and refute) the temptation to generalize or universalize from a small number of cases and the corresponding contempt for the particular case. They can thus avoid (and deflate) universalizing

---

[38] See Tully, *Public Philosophy* I, chapters 6 and 9 for how this is being done.

questions like 'What is citizenship?' and the presumption that there must be one general answer; usually, as we have seen, simply the projection of one's own familiar example. They take any example of citizenship – no matter how universal or global its own language of self-description and justification claims to be – *as an example*, a particular and local form of citizenship in its environs (as I have tried to do for modern citizenship). In contrast to the universalizing rationalities of modern citizenship, diverse citizens employ contextual and comparative genres of reasoning (Subsection 1). They start from the local languages and negotiated practices of citizens on location and compare and contrast their similarities and dissimilarities with each other from various standpoints, either by engaging in other forms of citizenship or by civic dialogues among diverse citizens. There is thus no comprehensive and universal language of citizenship that defines all others in relation to one ideal form, but, rather, a multiplicity of criss-crossing and overlapping partial and always-incomplete languages of similarities and dissimilarities woven into their practices, employed for various purposes and of which the language of modern citizenship can be seen to be one singular example masquerading as being comprehensive. By these situated alternative means, genres of comparative reasoning and critical dialogues citizens disclose the civic world as a diverse multiverse, and their civic attitude is one of diversity awareness.[39]

3. Since civic activities are primary, people do not become civic citizens in virtue of a status defined by rights and guaranteed by the institutions of the constitutional rule of law. From the civic perspective, civil citizenship indicates that one is a 'subject' of a system of laws and a 'member' of that association. Rather, agents (individual or collective) *become* civic citizens only in virtue of actual participation in civic activities. It is only through apprenticing in citizenship practices that one comes to acquire the characteristics of a citizen: linguistic and non-linguistic abilities, modes of conduct and

---

[39] For this mode of reasoning together, see Tully, *Public Philosophy* I, chapter 2, and for its history see Tully, *Strange Multiplicity*.

interaction in relationships with others, forms of awareness of self and other, use of equipment, the abilities of questioning and negotiating any of these features and of carrying on in new and creative ways. This distinction between citizenship as primarily an institutional status and as a negotiated practice is made in a number of different ways. Let me mention three.

The most familiar way is the linguistic distinction between 'civil' (law-based) and 'civic' (activity-based). Whereas civil citizens have the legally guaranteed opportunity to participate in the civil sphere if they chose, civic citizens engage in and experience 'civics' – the activities and practical *arts* of becoming and being a citizen, referred to as 'civicism'. Civic citizenry are not seen as the bearers of civil rights and duties but of the abilities, competences, character and conduct acquired in participation, referred to as 'civic virtues'.[40] Civil citizens are civilized by the institutional rule of law, commerce and anonymous processes of civilization, whereas civic citizens criticize and reject this disempowering picture that conceals the real world of histories of civic struggles. They 'civicize' themselves. They transform themselves into citizens and their institutions into civic spaces and free 'cities' by civic activities and the arts of citizenship, whether or not these activities are guaranteed by the rule of law or informal customs, or neither. Civic citizenship is not brought into the world by coercion, the institutions of law, the nation state or international law, but by citizens engaging in civic activities and creating civic worlds. As a consequence, participation in civic activities cannot be a duty enforced

---

[40] It is tempting to say that tier two rights of participation of civil citizenship might be thought of as 'equipment' *for* a certain type of civic citizenship (in the civil sphere of modern states and global civil sphere), and so they overlap to this extent. But, even here, this is not completely accurate, as you can have these rights and not be able to exercise them for all sorts of reasons (financial constraints, time constraints, lack of knowledge, fear of consequences, etc.) and thus not even reach the stage of developing the corresponding abilities through practice. And, of course, this particular equipment, as important as it is, is not necessary for participation, since millions participated and continue to participate in civic struggles for rights of this kind and for extending them without having them. Rights are neither necessary nor sufficient conditions of citizenship.

by a coercive authority, for this would be to put a civil institution prior to civic activities.[41]

One of the oldest distinctions is between 'libertas' – liberty and liberties – of civil citizens and 'freedom' of civic citizens. It is impossible to predicate 'liberty' of human action ('liberty action' makes no sense). Rather, the formal grammar of 'liberty' refers to a condition of being 'at liberty' (not under the will of another) that a subject has thanks to a law. The civil citizen is at liberty *to* participate or not as he or she wills. In contrast, the informal vernacular term 'freedom' (freo, das Frye) is predicated primarily of agents, action, activities and fields of activity throughout its long history.[42] The civic citizen manifests the freedom *of* participation. The free citizen is free in engaging in civic activities and, *eo ipso*, making these activities free. Civic freedom is not an opportunity but a manifestation; neither freedom *from* nor freedom *to* (which are often absent or suppressed), but freedoms *of* and *in* participation, and *with* fellow citizens. The civic citizen is not the citizen of an institution (a nation state or international law) but the free citizen of the 'free city': that is, *any* kind of civic world or democratic 'sphere' that comes into being and is reciprocally held aloft by the civic freedom of its citizens, from the smallest *deme* or commune to glocal federations. It is not a matter of official civil liberties and offices being open to participation, as civil theorists construe a free city, but of the citizenry *experiencing* the civic way of life that makes it a free city, including engaging in opening offices in the first place, as the civic theorists characterize it. Hence, the civic tradition finds one exemplar in the experience of Athenian

---

[41] I thus see the coerced duty to participate as an (optional) instrument of the civil tradition and incompatible with the civic, although some theorists who are classified as civic have seen it otherwise (see below). My understanding of these two intertwined traditions is indebted to the invaluable scholarship of John Pocock and Quentin Skinner and the wealth of study their work has inspired. For recent reflections, see A. Brett and J. Tully, eds, *Rethinking the Foundations of Modern Political Thought*, Cambridge: Cambridge University Press, 2006.

[42] H. Pitkin, *Wittgenstein and Justice: On the Significance of Ludwig Wittgenstein for Social and Political Thought*, Berkeley: University of California Press, 1973, pp. 10–11; and H. Pitkin, 'Are Freedom and Liberty Twins?', *Political Theory* 16 (4): 523–52, 1988. This distinction is at the heart of Arendt's history of freedom (see volume I, chapter 4).

democracy as a civic way of life reciprocally sustained by democratic citizenship as the freedom of participation (*isegoria*).[43]

Finally, the priority of civic activities to civil institutions is marked by one of the enduring conventions of Western law. This is the convention that long use (*usus*) and practice brings into the being the 'right' (*ius*) to engage in that activity, not vice versa. This is true not only of the origin of common and private property and of the rule of law itself but also of the right of people to govern themselves over a territory. This right of self-government – the very normativity we are trying to understand – comes from citizens governing themselves over a long period of time and being acknowledged by others. This sturdy structure of normativity is so indestructible that even conquest and usurpation by the most institutionalized imperial states in the world cannot extinguish it unless the citizens and descendents either consent to surrender the right (i.e. another citizen activity) or entirely give up *all* the activities of governing themselves after generations of repressive and assimilative occupation (which rarely happens).[44] Institutionalized rights come into being from the practice of corresponding activities and are continued and guaranteed in the final analysis by the ongoing activities. This is precisely the civic view of the relation between citizenship activities and citizenship rights.[45] As we have seen in Section One, the civil tradition reversed this orientation, for reasons we will see below (aspect ten).

Of course there is a Western tradition that also places a high value on civic activity but presupposes that it has to take place within a canonical institutional setting. The institutions of the Greek polis, the Renaissance city-state and the modern nation state are standardly taken as the institutional preconditions. This tradition can be seen as 'civic' in a narrow or circumscribed sense in contrast to the broad and extended sense that I am explicating. However, it also can be interpreted as a democratic wing of the civil tradition, since it takes an institutional

---

[43] For this interpretation of Athenian democracy, see M. I. Finley, *Democracy Ancient and Modern*, London: Hogarth, 1985.

[44] See Tully *Public Philosophy* I, chapter 8.

[45] See Tully, *Strange Multiplicity* for this convention.

form as primary and necessary, differing only over the importance of democratic participation (tier- two rights). Consequently it shares the civil tradition's commitment to the coercive imposition of institutional preconditions and myths of founding.[46] This latter interpretation thus seems more apt, since this tradition contradicts the primacy of practice and the commitment to a plurality of forms of political organization of the civic tradition (aspects one and two). As we proceed we will see that such attempts to circumscribe civic activity in canonical institutions are continuously undone by the democratic activities of civic citizens and the institutions reformed by the activities.

4. Whereas civil citizenship always exists in institutions, civic citizenship always exists in relationships. There are of two general kinds of civic being-with relationships: (1) relationships among roughly equal citizens exercising power together in citizen–citizen relationships of solidarity, civic friendship and mutual aid (citizen relationships); and (2) relationships between citizens and governors (citizen/governance relationships). To see the importance of this aspect we have to set aside the dominant institutional language of the civil tradition (constitutions, rights, autonomous rules, jurisdiction, states and sovereignty) and look at what goes on before, within, beyond and often in tension with these institutions. What we see are individual and collective actors in citizen and citizen/governance relationships. I will treat citizen/governance relationships first, in which civic citizenship is the vis-à-vis of government, and then turn to citizen relationships (aspect eleven).

The language of relationships between governors and the governed (the people) developed alongside the juridical and institutional language of modern citizenship in Europe as a way of describing government from a more practical and interactive perspective (in contrast to the institutional language of sovereignty, rule and obedience), yet still from the perspective of the governing class.[47] That is, it characterizes the citizenry in the first instance as the subject and object of the arts and

---

[46] This is the tradition mentioned above that often endorses a coerced duty to participate.
[47] See Tully, *Public Philosophy* I, chapter 3, and *Public Philosophy* II, chapter 2 for the language of governors and governed.

sciences of government, namely, as 'the governed' (or 'all affected'). In the early modern period, the language of governor–governed was used very broadly to characterize any relationship of power and authority in which one actor seeks to govern – to guide – the conduct of another actor: parents–children, master–slave, master–servant, company–employees, sergeant–soldier, teacher–pupil, government–people, colonial administration–colonies, priest–flock, master–apprentice, protégé–mentor, older and younger friends, dance partners and an individual governing his or her own thoughts, desires, will and comportment. Since the phenomena of some agents 'guiding' the actions of others in all these vastly different ways are co-extensive with living in society and interacting with others, relationships of governing and being governed were taken to be the basic unit of analysis, beneath, within and beyond the more formal institutionalization and rationalization of these relationships in the centralizing institutions of modern European societies.

As the modern nation state consolidated and brought many relationships of governance under its direct or indirect auspices, the terms 'government' and 'the governed' came to be restricted to the formal institutions of 'representative government' and its civil citizens in the official public sphere. Modern political science and theory restricted its focus to these institutions, as we have seen, leaving the other relationships of governance in the official private sphere to other specialized disciplines. However, since our conduct is governed in a multiplicity of overlapping ways in contemporary societies and global networks that do not all pass through legal and political institutions, the language of governance in its broad sense has been rediscovered and used anew to analyse in detail the actual workings of contemporary relationships of power, knowledge and subjectification by the governmentalité and 'global governance' schools (among others). These two schools can analyse anything from the most specific forms of face-to-face power relationships or the ways media conglomerates govern our thoughts and desires in detail to the most general modes of informal power through which multinational corporations and coalitions of great powers informally govern the conduct of subaltern states and populations in relation to production, consumption and the environment, through global relationships that bypass, outrun or manipulate traditional legal and political institutions. No matter how anonymous these relationships may appear, especially from an institutional perspective, and no matter how clever those responsible are in evading their responsibility, a relationship of governance can almost always be traced back to identifiable agents who govern (directly or indirectly) on one side and agents who are governed on the other (as environmental movements have shown time after time).[48]

Civic citizens share the view that humans are always already in relationships and that *many* are relationships of this general governance kind (in both its restricted and broad sense). However, while all relationships can be said to 'guide' the partners in some way or another, only a large subset of these can be characterized as 'governing' the partners, in the sense of 'directing', in some more or less calculated way.[49] They also realize that the practical arts and sciences of government (restricted and broad) consist in a wide variety of knowledges, means and strategies. The bodies of knowledge under which people are picked out and governed comprise the range of human, environmental, policy and administrative sciences that modern governments and governing organizations in the private sphere employ to govern their members, 'all affected' and their relationships with each other. The means can range from the mobilization of the consent of the governed on one side to the use or threat of violence and force on the other. The strategies can range from the most detailed governance of individual preference and character formation through techniques of consultation and deliberation to the global use of sanctions, financial manipulation and military manoeuvers. However, this is where the civic school parts company with the governmentalité and global governance schools.

---

[48] I discuss these two schools in Tully, *Public Philosophy* II, chapters 2 and 4.
[49] Citizen relationships, for example, guide but do not govern (see below under aspect 11). Relationships of love and of friendship are other examples, even though they can involve episodes of governing one another.

Civic citizens rotate the whole orientation around the axis of their real need and examine governance relationships from the standpoint of the partner who is governed – not *as* a governed subject but *as* an agent, a civic citizen.

5. Accordingly, the fifth aspect is the characterization of governance relationships as relationships between citizens and governors. At the heart of any governance relationship and constantly animating it is the freedom of the governed *as* citizens. A relationship of governance does not act directly on the body or mind of the governed, determining the behaviour in detail (or it would be a relationship of force and determination). Rather, it acts on and conducts the 'conduct' of the governed partners (their actions, thoughts, expectations, comportment) to induce them to acquire a predictable form of subjectivity (to become self-governing subjects in the relationship). In this sense, governance always presupposes and acts on subjects who are 'free'. That is, they are individual or collective agents who are faced with a limited field of possible ways of thinking, speaking, acting, organizing and conducting themselves *within* the (rules of the) relationship, including the many arts of appearing to conform while acting otherwise within. And, second, if they refuse to be governed in this way and work within the relationship, there is also a range of possible ways of directly confronting and negotiating the limits of the relationship itself, from the acceptable procedures of grievance and negotiation, strike and direct action to strategies of disobedience, revolt and revolution or escape. The aim of governance is to try to guide (induce, disallow, anticipate and respond to) the freedom of the governed in their activities so they disclose and act on the field of possibilities open to them in predictable, utile and productive ways.[50]

Freedom in the field of a relationship – *Spielraum* or free play – is both the existential field – the room or space of manoeuverability

---

[50] This specific description of situated freedom in governance relationships draws partially on the late Foucault, who introduced it into his own work only in 1980. See Tully, *Public Philosophy* I, chapter 3. My development of it departs from Foucault in a number of ways.

(the range of possible moves) – and the experiential ways the partners can and do disclose and act on their possibilities – the games (*Spiel*) they play *in* the relationship or in the confrontation of its limits. This twofold freedom is the 'field freedom' of human beings insofar as they are 'field beings' in relationships. 'Field' refers to both the broad sense introduced in the Introduction and the primary sense of the field in the natural world where freedom takes place. It is irreducible, exists and is enacted to widely varying degrees in different relationships.[51] It exists in the playful 'guidance' relationship between parent and child long before language acquisition, between pupil and teacher in pedagogical relationships, in linguistic relationships,[52] to a narrow degree in tightly governed institutions (prisons) and more broadly in informal imperial relationships. The governed partner is thus always an active agent – an apprentice player who must learn how to navigate and negotiate his or her way around the field and how to play the game through acting and interacting with the governing partner. The governor is always an interactive partner to some extent, drawn into the game of giving further instructions, answering questions, correcting conduct, responding to seemingly untoward rule following and so on. Humans are always unavoidably *homo ludens*, creative game players and prototypical civic citizens in the dialogical relationships of their cultures and civilizations before and *as* they take on any other identities.[53]

Since the 'governed' in any relationship are always already active agents partaking in guiding and being guided in countless ways, they have to engage in practices of self-formation by which they develop the abilities to act and interact in the relationship. These embodied or

---

[51] This way of describing freedom in a field draws on Maurice Merleau Ponty. An influential use of Spielraum in a somewhat similar way is M. Heidegger, *Being and Time*, New York: Harper and Row, 1962, p. 185 (I.5.31). However, I have learned more from Martin Buber's innovative attempts to place this field freedom in dialogical relationships and link it to a concrete global politics of non-violence and peace, as I am trying to do as well. See M. Buber, *I and Thou*, New York: Scribner, 1970 and M. Buber, *Between Man and Man*, London: Routledge, 2002.

[52] As we saw in the Introduction.

[53] J. Huizinga, *Homo Ludens: A Study of the Play Element in Culture*, Boston: Beacon, 1955; J. Carse, *Finite and Infinite Games: A Vision of Life as Play and Possibility*, New York: Ballantine Books, 1986. See Tully, *Public Philosophy* I, chapter 4.

phenomenological abilities of knowing how to mutually acknowledge and interact with self and others in intersubjective relationships begin to develop in the earliest days of childhood, long before language use and training for specific roles. Apprentices for specific roles usually initially engage in these practices under the direction of the governing partner or peers, and then gradually develop the abilities to perform the role self-critically, creatively and without further direction, but never without further negotiation. One does not become a practitioner blindly. The requisite abilities are acquired in pre-linguistic interaction and by more or less elaborate and reflective practices of the self and on the self in the course of learning one's way around in a specific relationship. Language-learners and novitiate students, for example, gradually become self-critical and self-educating language-users and competent students, each with their own individual and distinctive style, through years of study, practices and exercises of self-formation. The explicit practices of self-formation in any relationship and the more general phenomenological practices that underlie these are the basis for the whole array of more complicated practices of self-formation of civic citizens in citizen/governance and citizen relationships.[54]

No matter how relentlessly domineering governors try to implant and internalize these role-related abilities without the active interplay of the patients, as if they are blank tablets, in behavioural modification experiments, repetitious advertising and total institutions of colonial and post-colonial discipline (such as internment camps and residential schools), they invariably fail to 'construct' the other all the way down. They cannot completely eliminate the interactive and open-ended freedom *of* and *in* the relationship or the room to appear to conform to the public script while thinking and acting otherwise, without

---

[54] For background embodied phenomenological dispositions and their development into abilities pre-reflectively and reflectively, see J. Searle, *The Construction of Social Reality*, New York: Free Press, 1995; S. Gallagher, *How the Body Shapes the Mind*, Oxford: Clarendon, 2005; Medina, *Language*; M. Foucault, *Hermeneutics of the Subject: Lectures at the Collège de France, 1981–1982*, New York: Palgrave, 2005; H. O'Grady, *Woman's Relationship with Herself: Gender, Foucault and Therapy*, London: Routledge, 2005 and Tully, *Public Philosophy* I, chapter 2.

reducing the relationship to one of complete immobilization. As we have seen, they are reduced to trying to induce and then respond to and work on the ways the governed conduct themselves in the sparsely limited Spielraum open to them. This is the constrained space in which indigenous peoples and others have exercised the arts of resistance and survived centuries of imperialization.[55]

If, therefore, we analyse a governance relationship from the side of the governed *as* the citizenry, we can see that the free play of negotiation in relationships is the ground of the civic freedom that manifests itself in civic activities and to which governments respond. So, a relationship of governance is always a relationship of prototypical civic citizenship negotiation to some degree, from the side of the governed. It is not a phenomenon of unilateral control of the conduct of the other, but a much more complicated and open-ended game of interplay and interaction between the arts and practices of proto-citizens and governors. While governors, by their free actions try to structure the field of possible actions of the governed, the governed, by their actions and insofar as they are citizens, try to govern or, rather, 'citizenize' the actions of their governors. If a defining characteristic of governance relationships is the 'conduct of conduct', it must always be read contrapuntally: as governors and citizens reciprocally conducting the conduct of each other and being conducted by their ongoing interaction in and over the relationships between them.

6. I am saying that we are always and everywhere proto-civic citizens, engaged in practices of negotiating the fields of possibilities in the relationships in which we find our feet and learn to walk. This overlooked everyday, grass roots world of proto-civic freedom in which the official and more familiar activities of citizenship are nurtured and grow is perhaps the greatest discovery of civic practice and philosophy. It

---

[55] See J. Scott, *Domination and the Arts of Resistance: Hidden Transcripts*, Yale: Yale University Press, 1990; Tully, *Public Philosophy* I, chapters 7 and 8, and Subsection 6. For the counter-argument that humans are constructed all the way down in power relations and the difficulties in accounting for critical freedom on this view, see Hoy, *Critical Resistance*. It is perhaps noteworthy that several of the authors Hoy discusses moved to a view closer to the one advanced here.

is first and foremost a discovery of feminist movements and of feminists reflecting on this experience in a number of different disciplines. They have transformed the civic tradition.[56]

To survey the field of civic citizenship practices we need to differentiate different types of cases that evolve out of this broad and so far undifferentiated field of proto-civic activities and cross the threshold to civic activities of civic citizens. I want to say that there is no single answer to the question of what makes negotiation in a governance relationship 'civics', the negotiators 'citizens' and transforms the governance relationship into a citizen/governance relationship (or a citizen relationship). Rather, there are family resemblances among cases that give us good but not incontestable reasons for calling a particular case 'civic'. These similarities and dissimilarities relate to: the nature of the activities, the locations they take place, the specificity of citizen relationships, the goods for the sake of which the activities are undertaken, the relationship of the activities to the natural world and the means employed. I will now take up each of these in turn in the following aspects.[57]

For our purpose of introducing the field of civic (and glocal) citizenship by beginning with activities, we can disclose the field under four general types of civic activities. The first is the wide or narrow range of activities recognized by and available to citizens under their existing system or multilayered systems of government. These constitute the official field of civic activities that each generation inherits and carries on from their forebears. Second, within these official fields there is a range of ways of 'acting otherwise' than the dominant norms of civic conduct without challenging the official rules governing citizen activity. This Spielraum of acting on the given possibilities in creative ways

---

[56] For feminist works on freedom in relationships to which I am particularly indebted see A. J. Norval, *Aversive Democracy: Inheritance and Originality in the Democratic Tradition*, Cambridge: Cambridge University Press, 2007; L. Zerilli, *Feminism and the Abyss of Freedom*, Chicago, University of Chicago Press, 2005; C. Heyes, *Line Drawings: Defining Women Through Feminist Practice*, Ithaca, NY: Cornell University Press, 2000; P. Bowden, *Caring: Gender-Sensitive Ethics*, London: Routledge, 1997; K. Anderson, *A Recognition of Being: Reconstructing Native Womanhood*, Toronto: Sumach, 2000.

[57] For the disclosure of the field of civic activity from a civic rather than civil perspective, see N. Kompridis, *Critique and Disclosure: Critical Theory between Past and Future*, Cambridge, MA: MIT Press, 2006.

and 'playing the civic game differently' within the official rules is, as we will see, a world of civic pluralism and cultural diversity unseen by approaches that presume rules determine rule-following.[58] The third and classic field comprises the activities by which citizens no longer act within the field of a governance relationship but turn and negotiate some aspect of that relationship. Finally, when citizen activities run against unjustifiable limits of the fields in which they act, act otherwise and negotiate, they turn to civic activities of directly confronting the limits. This range of activities from protests to revolutions comprises the field of civic confrontation strategies.[59] I discuss examples of these four types *en passant*, beginning with the third: negotiation.

One of the classic features that render an activity 'civic' is when the agents in a governance relationship not only negotiate how to act in accord with it but negotiate the relationship itself. This consists in (but is not restricted to) calling some aspect of the relationship into question and demanding that those who govern enter into negotiations, either within, over or without the acceptable procedures of negotiation (including litigation). This is a demand literally to *civicize* the relationship: to bring it under the shared negotiation and authority of the partners subject to it. If successful, the governance relationship is no longer imposed monologically over the governed who are constrained to negotiate their activities within its prescribed limits. It becomes a more cooperative, dialogical or citizen/governance relationship worked on by both partners through ongoing phases of 'negotiation' in the broad sense: contestation and critique, specific negotiations (arguing and bargaining), modification or transformation, implementation, review, renegotiation by future generations and so on, world without end. To civicize governance relationships is – eo ipso – to 'democratize' them, for one of the oldest and most ordinary meanings of 'democracy' is that the

---

[58] See Tully, *Public Philosophy* I and *Public Philosophy* II, chapter 8 for this type of civic activity. For an excellent introduction to the whole field, see A. Wiener, *The Invisible Constitution of Politics: Contested Norms of International Encounters*, Cambridge: Cambridge University Press, 2008. I discuss it further under the tenth aspect and in Subsection 6.

[59] These four types are distinctions within the field introduced under aspect five.

people have an effective and ongoing say in and over the relationships (rules) to which they are subject. The 'arts of citizenship' are precisely the democratic arts of critique, negotiation and transformation of the governance relationships we bear into citizen/governance relationships. This whole world of democratic negotiation in the broad sense is the classic world of *negotium* (civic action) as opposed to *otium* (the non-civic life of contemplation).[60]

7. In contrast to the processes of *civilization* and *democratization* in the civil tradition, *civicization* and *democratization* are not identified with a set of Western institutions and processes of often coercive imposition over other practices, but with citizens non-violently negotiating and transforming the governance relationships in which they find themselves into citizen/governance relationships (or citizen relationships) from the ground up. This is the heart of civic citizenship. As we have just seen, this activity flows out of the proto-civic negotiated practices on the field of possibilities within the relationship. Both partners (governors and governed) enter into and subject themselves to the give and take of negotiation in and over the relationship they share. The governed *become* 'good citizens' only by exercising their civic freedom of entering into these kinds of negotiation in all their complex phases (above): of listening to the other sides and for silenced voices, of responding in turn, negotiating in good faith and being bound by the results, experimenting with the amended or transformed relationship and so on. Reciprocally, governors become good governors only by doing the same: listening to what the citizens have to say, responding and being held accountable by them. A citizen/governance relationship is an interdependent, interactive and open-ended partnership of mutual enabling, nurturing and reciprocal learning. The unpredictable evolution of the relationship and of the identities of the partners over time is what the civic tradition calls progress. If the governed fail to exercise their freedom of having a say in and over the governance relationships they bear and speak truthfully to power, they never become citizens. They remain unfree and

---

[60] Tully, *Public Philosophy* I is a series of surveys of this whole field.

servile 'slaves': that is, subjects of monological or 'despotic' relationships of command and obedience. It is like the life of 'exile', where one may have negative freedom but not civic freedom. Reciprocally, if the governors refuse to listen and enter into negotiations, and either silence citizens or treat their demands as free speech to which they have no obligation to respond, they never become good governors. They remain unaccountable 'tyrants', independent and subject only to their own arbitrary will and appetites. Neither becomes a mature human being.

A superb presentation of the civic relationship of reciprocal enlightenment between free governors and free citizens, where there is neither master nor slave but only free and frank speaking relationships (*parrhesiastic* dialogues) between partners, is the dialogue between Jocasta and Polyneices on the value of citizenship in Euripides's *The Phoenician Women*. The two previous paragraphs are a gloss of this crystallization of civic freedom. Polyneices, who represents democracy, is returning from exile to free Thebes from his brother, Eteocles, who broke the pact to share rule on an annual basis and thus represents tyranny. He is speaking to his mother, Jocasta:[61]

JOCASTA:	This above all I long to know: What is an exile's life? Is it great misery?
POLYNEICES:	The greatest; worse in reality than in report.
JOCASTA:	Worse in what way? What chiefly galls an exile's heart?
POLYNEICES:	The worst is this: the right of speaking freely [*parrhesia*] does not exist.
JOCASTA:	That's a slave's life – to be forbidden to speak one's mind.
POLYNEICES:	One has to endure the idiocy of those who rule.
JOCASTA:	To join fools in their foolishness – that makes one sick.
POLYNEICES:	One finds it pays to deny nature and be a slave.

---

[61] Euripides, *The Phoenician Women*, New York: Penguin, 1983, lines 386–94. For the context of practices of free speaking in unequal relationships of governors and governed, see M. Foucault, *Fearless Speech*; J. Pearson, eds, Los Angeles: Semiotexte(e), 2001. For my interpretation and extension see J. Tully, 'La liberté civique en contexte de globalisation', *Les Cahiers du Juin 27* 1 (2): 1–10, 2003.

This account of interdependence and civic freedom in relationships also stands as a critique of the priority and adulation of independence and negative freedom in the civil tradition (as in tier-one civil rights). Agents who are independent and free of interdependent relationships, subject only to their own will, are on the road to becoming arbitrary tyrants, disposed to lording it over others and enslaved to their own whims and desires, as we have seen with the history of Western imperialism. It is only by being subject to democratic relationships with others and the practices of self-formation these require that those who govern can learn to discipline themselves and serve the civic good. Reciprocally, if citizenship is only a status, 'guaranteed' by institutions, then citizens tend to become either servile subordinates or arbitrary bosses in the vast sea of non-democratic, hierarchical relationships in which they find themselves for most of their lives. They tend to become unaccustomed, unable and too submissive to exercise their civic freedom in the official public sphere, let alone in the private sphere, and prone to submit uncritically to the socialization and media glorification of a life of negative freedom and private consumption that accompanies tier-one liberty and free trade.[62] The powerful then dismantle the democratic rights that earlier generations of civic activists fought and died for.

As Jocasta and Polyneices agree, far from seeing dialogical relationships with governors and fellow citizens as interference with their negative freedom, they identify with these free-speaking relationships, as the enabling and nurturing conditions of their civic freedom and maturity. The crucial kind of freedom is thus neither the freedom from relationships of interdependency (negative freedom) nor the freedom of acting in conformity with allegedly ideal and universal legal relationships that 'we' impose on ourselves (positive freedom). It is the proto-civic and civic freedom of negotiating and democratizing

---

[62] See B. Barber, *Consumed: How Markets Corrupt Children, Infantilize Adults, and Swallow Citizens Whole*, New York: Norton, 2007. For the pathological aspects of a relentless drive for negative freedom, see F. Bergmann, *On Being Free*, Notre Dame: University of Notre Dame, 1977.

in/over the always less-than-ideal relationships in which we live and breathe and become who we are. The only guarantee of freedom and democracy is, not surprisingly, the daily cooperative practices of democratic freedom in webs of relationships and on the fields of possibilities they disclose.[63]

8. Civic activity is not restricted to the official, institutionalized civil public sphere of the modern nation state and the global civil sphere of cosmopolitan globalization. One does not have to be a civil citizen to engage in civic activity. Insofar as an individual or group is subject to the effects of a governance relationship, no matter how local or global, they have for that very reason a civic right to act civically in relation to it. A non-violent activity by the governed that brings the relationships they bear into the open space of questions and negotiations is an instance of the civic activity of citizens, no matter where it takes place, whether in the official public or private spheres. A civic public sphere, in contrast to the civil public sphere, comes into being whenever and wherever those who are subject to a closed governance relationship take it out of the darkness of the 'private sphere' of being unquestioned, either in the sense of being taken for granted and coordinating our interaction behind our backs or of being explicitly placed off limits. They do this by calling it into question (speaking truth to power), subjecting it to the light and enlightenment of public scrutiny, and opening it to negotiation with the powers-that-be. They become citizens, the space of negotiation becomes public and the relationship itself becomes civicized and democratized just insofar as the governors enter into, and are subject to, the ongoing negotiation of the relationship between them. Hence the popular slogan 'we are everywhere'.[64]

---

[63] For a history of civic freedom in the narrow sense vis-à-vis the more familiar traditions of negative and positive freedom in the West see O. Patterson, *Freedom in the Making of Western Culture*, New York: Basic Books, 1991.

[64] As Nancy Fraser stresses, these unofficial public spheres are often more open and innovative than the elite-dominated official public sphere: N. Fraser, 'Rethinking the Public Sphere: A Contribution to the Critique of Actually Existing Democracy', in C. Calhoun, ed., *Habermas and the Public Sphere*, Cambridge, MA: MIT Press, 1992. For an introduction to this aspect of the field see R. Coles, *Beyond Gated Politics: Reflections for the Possibility of Democracy*, Minneapolis: University of Minnesota Press, 2005.

These civic and publicizing activities are not seen as acts of 'resistance' or 'rebellion', as they are seen from civil and governmental perspectives. It is rather the powers-that-be who refuse to enter into civic negotiations and be held accountable that engage in resistance and rebellion against civicization and democratization. They are also not seen as heroic acts of resistance by great leaders and writers overcoming the habituation, interpolation, conditioning or internalization that construct the very consciousness and body of the assimilated and colonized majority, as they are often portrayed in the critical tradition.[65] They are understood as the certainly courageous yet non-heroic extension of everyday practices of negotiation in which ordinary citizens are already engaged into the civic sphere. They consist in nothing more (or less) than disclosing the field of possibilities within the relationship from the standpoint of concerned citizens and acting on it.[66] Finally, they are not seen as the spontaneous irruption of unformed constituent power, for the civic powers are already exercised in, and extend out from, everyday practices and relationships of governance.[67]

9. Why does the civic tradition construe cases of citizenship so broadly, as participation in activities of negotiating the arbitrary constraints of a field in governance or citizen/governance relationship at the most appropriate and effective sites by those affected? In contrast to the civil/cosmopolitan tradition this seems too unruly. Civil law circumscribes the exercise of democratic rights (tier two) to official citizens negotiating or litigating the law in the official institutions of civil/cosmopolitan society and in accord with their procedural rules, and, if necessary, their institutions of amendment of these rules. Members of the civic tradition agree that these are exceptionally important citizenship practices; noting as well that they have been fought for, institutionalized, extended and defended by civic citizens who did not initially have a right to them. But, they argue, to place these institutional limits on citizenship is to impose limits on democratic

---

[65] See note 54 for this view.
[66] Norval, *Aversive Democracy*, chapter 3.
[67] For these alternatives, see Tully, *Public Philosophy* II, chapter 7.

citizenship that are unsustainable in practice and unjustifiable in a free and democratic society. This follows from everything we have already said about the open-ended character of negotiated practices since the Introduction. However, it can be seen most clearly by comparing the civil and civic conceptions of law: the (civil) rule of law as an institution and the (civic) rule of law as a practice.

The civil tradition makes a fundamental distinction between the institutional rule of law and the citizen activities that take place within the boundaries of these institutional settings. The institutionalized rule of law exhibits a systemic or functional quality of formality and independence from the agents who are subject to it and act within its boundaries. This picture is encapsulated in the mantra, 'rule of law not of men'. The features of institutionalization and rationalization that establish the independence of the rule of law from the rule of men and women consist in the definite rules, procedures and training of the institutional offices, the hierarchical, command–obedience relationships among the members, the specialized division of labour, the separation of knowledge from use, reflexive monitoring and the systematic application of coercion to align behaviour with rules. That is, it is the non-democratic and procedural character of the relationships within an institution that give it its formality and independence from the informal rule of men. The language of governance is replaced by that of administration, management, control, discipline, procedure, direction and monitoring. As a consequence, the rules and procedures of an institution are conceptualized as 'rails' that the officeholders follow, like the operation of an adamantine calculus according to definite rules. The roles of humans seem to disappear.[68] While there may be some room for manoeuver in individual cases of decision making by an errant officeholder, this foreground indeterminacy is absorbed by the systemic operation of the vast background rules, procedures

---

[68] For the misrepresenting role of the metaphor of the 'rule of law not of men' and the calculus conception of rule following, see G. P. Baker, 'Following Wittgenstein: Some Signposts for Philosophical Investigations 143–242', in S. Holtzman and C. Leich, eds, *Wittgenstein: To Follow a Rule*, London: Routledge, 1981, pp. 48–58.

and hierarchical relationships of the institutions as a whole that are untouched. If a background rule is challenged and negotiated, then this proceeds as well within institutionalized rules and procedures. Democratic rights (tier two) have their foundation in the institutional rule of law, are protected by it and exercised within its boundaries. This is the separation or disembedded thesis of the civil institutionalized rule of law.

In contrast, the civic understanding of the rule of law is of a network of relationships of negotiated practices. Law is a craft or practical art rather than a science. For example, men and women in ministries draft rules to govern the relationships of their political association as Bills; legislators debate, negotiate and vote on enacting them as laws; lobbyists lobby; administrators struggle to translate them into executable legislation and rules for application; civil servants apply them and officers enforce them, subjects try to figure out how to obey them in individual cases; experts advise them; ordinary citizens, corporate citizens, civil society organizations and media discuss and challenge them and take them back to their representatives or to the courts; lawyers argue pro and contra; judges discuss, interpret, judge, write majority and minority decisions; the legislatures respond and so on. At each of these site-specific practices men and women not only negotiate the particular law in question (which is just another rule) but they do so by acting in accord with the rules and procedures that govern the relationships of their office. As we have seen, the differentially situated players negotiate the Spielraum that the rules and procedures disclose to them, no matter how explicit the rules are and how many recursive sets of rules exist for the application of the rules.[69]

This is not to deny the importance of institutionalized procedures. It is rather to observe that the way a person 'grasps' a procedural rule is not itself a procedure but a negotiated practice. The practical, know-how attitude underlies the institutional know-that orientation and is

---

[69] See Wittgenstein, *Philosophical Investigations*, §§82–7, 198–201; and Tully, *Public Philosophy* I, chapter 2.

ineliminable. From this rule-maker, rule-enforcer, rule-follower, rule-challenger and rule-interpreter perspective, an institutionalized rule is neither a rail nor a calculus. It is more like a signpost. It points us to the complex network of negotiation practices going on under its sign. Both our understanding of the rule and the actual rule itself are immanent in the negotiated practices that cannot be circumscribed. The living rule of law is the pattern of interplay and interaction of the negotiated practices. This is the immanent or manifestation thesis of the civic rule of law. The unfolding of the rule of law, no matter how institutionalized and rationalized, is internally related to the indeterminate negotiated practices of the law.[70] In a word, civic citizens are 'constructivists'.[71]

If the civic thesis is plausible, there should not only be proto-civic negotiation practices within the institutions of the rule of law but these practices should extend in the course of things into demands for onsite civic negotiations, just as we have seen in the similarly institutionalized corporations of the official private sector. Historically, union movements and collective bargaining associations have been the agents of such sporadic civicization of institutions. Over the last 30 years there has been an explosion of new demands for ad hoc practical negotiations of the rules and procedures within the legal and political and administrative institutions of contemporary societies. Public and private sector employees demand a direct and effective say over the rules and covert conventions of the relationships they bear: hiring procedures, discriminatory practices, equity the organization of work and time-off, environmental practices, the right to disclose and make public information and bad practices, whistle blow and so on. These activities dissolve the distinction between the civil institutions

---

[70] See Medina, *The Unity of Wittgenstein's Philosophy*, p. 179. For a detailed presentation of this pragmatic view of normativity, see R. B. Brandom, *Making it Explicit: Reasoning, Representing, and Discursive Commitment*, Cambridge, MA: Harvard University Press, 1998, pp. 3–66.

[71] See A. Wiener, 'Constructivist Approaches in International Relations Theory: Puzzles and Promises', *Con.WEB* 5, 2006. Available at: www.qub.ac.uk/schools/SchoolofPoliticsInternationalStudiesandPhilosophy/FileStore/ConWEBFiles/Filetoupload,52215,en.pdf (Accessed 30 August 2007); and Tully, *Public Philosophy* II, chapter 5.

inhabited by civil servants and the exercise of democratic rights in civil society by civil citizens. Civil servants demand to be civic citizens within and over civil institutions, civicizing their governance relationships at work into citizen/governance relationships through the creation of tailor-made alternative dispute resolution practices. New departments, disciplines and epistemic communities of dispute resolution have sprung up in universities and policy communities throughout the world and the courts have supported this revolution on the grounds that its curtailment is unjustifiable and unsustainable in a free and democratic society.[72]

10. We can now place the separation thesis of civil institutionalization in the broader canvas of Section One and see the two major roles it has played. In the early modern period the civil theorists argued that the existing practices of governance and citizenship constituted an informal, haphazard, conflict-ridden, uncertain and insecure crazy quilt of overlapping jurisdictions that gave rise to the Thirty Years War. Civil philosophers, lawyers and administrators explained that only centralization and institutionalization would resolve these problems of informal (underinstitutionalized and underrationalized) practices of law, governance and citizenship.[73] The modern contract tradition of political and legal theory rose to prominence by portraying this dispossession of local 'uncertain' practices of self-government in terms of a hypothetical contract or agreement. Despite the empirical evidence to the contrary, the recalcitrant local peoples could nevertheless be seen to be individuals (or a collective people) who would consent to delegate or alienate their powers and rights of local self-government to their new centralized and incorporated governors, if they only knew their best interests, in much the same way as they were contractually alienating their labour powers (formerly exercised in the local governance relationships of guilds, crafts, commons and so on) to the new

---

[72] See Tully, *Public Philosophy* I, chapter 6.
[73] See I. Hunter, *Rival Enlightenments: Civil and Metaphysical Philosophy in Early Modern Germany*, Cambridge: Cambridge University Press, 2001; and J. Tully, 'Diverse Enlightenments', *Economy and Society* 32 (3): 485–505, 2003.

institutions of private corporations. In exchange, they received from the institutions of government the security, certainty and enforceability of modern civil liberties and democratic rights at the national level. Their erstwhile local practices were portrayed in theory as a pre-political state of nature or war and their new institutions as the embodiment of the rule of law, not of men.

The idea that governors and citizens should exist in relationships of mutual subjection was not abandoned but applied exclusively to political relationships of representative government, where the elected government governed the population and the opposition party governed the government in a system of competing parties (organized internally along institutional lines). Citizens could play a role in this by exercising their democratic rights, but only in institutional elections and the civil sphere. This sphere of representative government was surrounded by and anchored in the new, administrative institutions of rule of law that provided the non-democratic basis of representative democracy. The prestige of the institutional mode of organization increased as more and more activities were organized accordingly: new model armies and navies, workhouses, public schools, factories, prisons, colonial plantations, labour discipline and the bureaucracies of the modern national and imperial states. In short, it became the favoured organizational form of the modern mode of citizenship and its constitutive institutions.[74]

This transition to the modern institutional orientation undermined and reversed the old civic law convention that authoritative rights and government derive from long use and practice. Political authority was defined as an authority that was independent of relationships of interdependency and called 'sovereignty'. Sovereignty and right were now said to be above and behind 'government'; located in the central institutions of the modern state and placed there by the agreement of the people themselves precisely because it constituted

---

[74] J. Tully, *An Approach to Political Philosophy: Locke in Contexts*, Cambridge: Cambridge University Press, 1993, pp. 9–70, 179–261.

a superior and uniquely modern form of rule, combining a sea of institutionalization with an island of representative governance.[75] The civil thesis of the superiority of institutional rule was the hinge of the whole transition.

The second role of the civil institutionalization thesis was to justify the dispossession of the non-European world of their local forms of government and citizenship. Under the civic convention that authority and right derive in endless forms from long use and negotiated practices the world was already full of authoritative governments and citizenship practices and thus there was no legal justification for Western imperialism. The way around this 'obstacle to progress' was to discredit it in the same manner as local governments were discounted within Europe, as not sufficiently institutionalized and independent of practice to be the bearers of formal law and sovereignty. Their laws were classified as informal and customary, still internally related to the vagaries of everyday practice, and the authority of their governors, if they were seen to exist at all, was non-sovereign or, at best, quasi-sovereign, still directly dependent on ongoing agreement of the governed who could dissolve authority by walking away from it. There was either no coercive mechanism in 'primitive societies' or the arbitrary exercise of coercion by men in the more advanced stages, but not the systematic application of coercion through the law characteristic of the West. The more sophisticated theorists allowed for lesser degrees of law and sovereignty, but mostly for the purpose of entering into treaties that extinguished or subordinated that sovereignty, and for a degree of continuity of indigenous self-government after conquest, yet under the sovereignty of European states. Non-Europeans thus were pre-emptively misrepresented as lacking precisely what Europe claimed to have in virtue of its recent institutionalization: the integration of

---

[75] J. Tully, *On the Duty of Man and Citizen According to Natural Law*, Cambridge: Cambridge University Press, 1991, introduction; Q. Skinner, *Visions of Politics, Volume II: Renaissance Virtues*, Cambridge: Cambridge University Press, 2002, chapter 14; Q. Skinner, *Visions of Politics Volume III: Hobbes and Civil Society*, Cambridge: Cambridge University Press, 2002, chapter 6.

law and coercion separate from the ruled. Once the civic thesis was relegated to the pre-modern and non-European by this sleight-of-hand, the imperialism of modern, institutionally sovereign states could be justified by the Trojan horse that claims to bring the institutional preconditions of modern law, government and citizenship to a world devoid of them.[76]

Given the pivotal justificatory role of the civil/institutional conception of the rule of law in the global spread of the institutional form of organization it is scarcely surprising that it is difficult to dislodge it even after it has been shown to be untenable in theory. Although it has been shown that no system of rules could possibly be as autonomous as the civil thesis requires, that there are differences of degree but not of the formal/informal kind among Western and non-Western legal and political orders, that negotiated practical know-how grounds procedural competence and that normativity remains related to use and negotiated practice in complicated ways, nevertheless, the background picture continues to prevail. But, as always, the most effective disprove is the pragmatic one. It includes the examples of the civicization and democratization of civil institutions by their own members that are so prominent today (above) and the obvious ability of non-Western peoples to govern themselves by their own distinctive laws and ways.[77]

11. I want to turn to the other general type of civic relationship that I set aside above: the citizen relationship. These are relationships among fellow citizens as equals in which there is no citizen/governor distinction. For the civic tradition this is the more important type of civic relationship. These are the relationships citizens form whenever and wherever they 'act together' *as* citizens in various activities. The relationships are civic and democratic partnerships among equals negotiating and acting together. These are relationships of trust, conviviality or solidarity and civic friendship across identity-related

---

[76] Tully, *Strange Multiplicity*, pp. 58–98, and *Public Philosophy* II, chapter 7.
[77] See Subsection 6.

differences and disagreements of various kinds. This is the realm of civic freedom as *isegoria*, citizens speaking to each other in equal relationships about their common concerns, rather than *parrhesia*, speaking to their governors in unequal relationships. On occasion one partner may take the lead and the others follow, especially when the task at hand requires specialized skills, but it does not become a citizen/governance relationship, let alone a governance relationship, because the leader ceases to be a leader whenever the followers cease to follow. It then automatically becomes a relationship of equals acting together again and they co-organize or 'coordinate' their interaction co-equally. It is tempting to say that they 'govern together' or are 'self-governing', but they are not 'governing' insofar as this term entails the correlate of the 'governed'. They are neither governing and being governed in turn nor simultaneously governing others and being governed by them. They are exercising power *together as* citizens all the way down. The citizenry cooperatively 'citizenize' rather than 'govern' the association composed of their citizen partnerships. They are literally 'doing democracy'. This is a distinct mode of exercising power different from governance and institutionalization.[78]

There are two main families of citizen partnerships. One is when citizens organize themselves in order to negotiate in or over a citizen/governance relationship, as in deliberative fora, collective bargaining, negotiating NGOs, social movements and non-violent revolutionary movements insofar as their internal relationships are citizen partnerships. The other is when citizens organize and run an entire activity on the basis of citizen partnership, not in relation to a government, but to citizenize the activity for its own sake (rather than submit to institutionalization or governance). The classic examples of citizen partnerships are the celebrated practices of direct democracy, village commons and urban communes throughout history and today, such as Porte Allegro, autonomous communities in the North and

---

[78] The verb 'citizenize' first appeared in 1593.

South and the Zapatista. However, the most ubiquitous and familiar example is the vast array of civic 'cooperatives' in the broad sense of civic organizations comprised of citizen relationships.

If the private corporation is both the basis and flagship of modern citizenship – the institution in which moderns exercise their civil liberties in competing, working, shopping and consuming – then the commonplace cooperative is the comparative organization of the civic tradition. Here citizens ignore the civil division between (non-democratic) private and (representative) public spheres, between civil liberties and democratic rights. They participate as democratic citizens governing themselves directly in the economic sphere (and other spheres), citizenizing the same kinds of activity that corporations privatize. In contrast to individual and corporate competition in market relations, cooperatives are founded on the ethics of cooperation. In the place of competitive free trade, they practice fair trade: trade relationships based on non-violent democratic negotiations among all citizens affected. In contrast to the goal of profit, many coops are not for profit but for living democracy and mutual aid. Instead of globalizing from above, they are grounded in the local first and foremost. All the human creativity that is channelled into the world of commerce and private profit by corporations is poured into experimentation with forms of democratic cooperation by the cooperative movements.[79] The most astonishing feature of the countless cooperatives on the planet is that they manifest, in concrete and practical forms, actual alternative worlds of democratic citizen partnerships *within* the interstices of the globally dominant political, legal and economic institutions of modern citizenship. They do not organize to overthrow the state or the capitalist mode of production, or to confront and negotiate with governors to change this or that regulation. They simply *enact* alternative worlds

---

[79] For the contrastive dimensions of the private corporation listed in this paragraph, see J. Bakan, *The Corporation: The Pathological Pursuit of Profit and Power*, London: Penguin, 2004.

of citizen relationships around various activities, refusing to abjure
their civicism to privatization or governmentalization. Cooperatives
are thus classic examples of 'acting otherwise'.[80]

12. A civic activity also has another important aspect, the telos or
good towards which the activity is oriented and which the activity
upholds and manifests. It gives the activity its civic character or ethos.
A civic telos is thus a 'civic good'. Modern citizenship is 'egocentric',
oriented towards the protection of the liberty of individuals to be
free from interference and to be free to exercise their autonomy in
the private sphere (tier-one rights) or in the official public sphere
(tier-two rights). In contrast, diverse citizenship in both citizen and
governance/citizen relationships is ecocentric and human-centric (or
relationship-centric in both cases). Civic activities are oriented towards
caring for the public or 'civic goods' of the correlative 'city': namely, the
community and its members bound together by citizen/governance
and citizen relationships in interdependency relationships with non-
human animals and the environment they bear as inhabitants of the
natural habitat.[81] Civic goods are multiplex and they too are subject
to ongoing democratic negotiation. They include such democratic
goods as civicizing relationships in many spheres and the character
development and conviviality that come from participation; and such
substantive goods as caring for the environment, economic self-reliance,
mutual aid, fair trade, equality among citizens and so on. When civic
citizens call a particular governance relationship into question they do
so under the general critical ideal that it fails to realize civic goods in

---

[80] For an introduction to cooperatives and cooperative democracy in this broad sense, see
the global survey www.WiserEarth.org under *Civil Society Organizations*. For the history
of consumer and producer cooperatives respectively, see E. Furlough and C. Strikwerda,
eds, *Consumers against Capitalism? Consumer Cooperation in Europe, North America,
and Japan 1840–1990*, Lanham: Rowman and Littlefield, 1999 and K. M. Grimes and
L. Milgram, eds, *Artisans and Cooperatives: Developing Alternative Trade for the Global
Economy*, Tucson: University of Arizona Press, 2000. For autonomous movements in
Europe, see G. Katsiaficas, *The Subversion of Politics: European Autonomous Movements
and the Decolonization of Everyday Life*, New York: Humanities, 2007.

[81] See Bowden, *Caring*, pp. 141–82; Anderson, *Recognition of Being*, pp. 194–229.

some specific way or another. These are goods that make possible and enhance civic forms of life.[82]

13. Civic citizens are thus 'care takers' of the goods of the dwelling places in which they live in this broad sense that dissolves the modern distinction between culture and nature. Every locale and network of locales of civic activity is not only culturally diverse but also a place in the natural world with its web of relationships of biological and ecological diversity. They see the interactive and interdependent relationships between humans and nature as similar in kind to human relationships and they attend to and care for them in similar ways. They listen and respond carefully to nature as a living being (Gaia) in their ecological sciences and daily practices of treading lightly. Civic citizens realize that this non-metaphorical field of possibilities in human/natural relationships and its limited Spielraum is the ground of all others. They are Gaia citizens.[83]

They also take their civic responsibility of caring for the good of communities and members *in* dwelling places and placeways to be prior to protecting the liberty rights of abstract individuals. They translate the latter back into one important civic good (negative freedom), detach it from free trade and place it among other goods that vie for attention in civic deliberative practices. They also reply that, in many cases, what oppressed individuals and minorities say they want is not protection from their own communities by a tier-one right enforced by a distant national or international court, but democratic empowerment in their local communities (civic freedom). In theories of modernity, this grounded civic ethic is discredited by redescribing it as a pre-modern

---

[82] In his global survey of civic organizations, Paul Hawken classifies these goods into two main categories, social justice and the environment: P. Hawken, *Blessed Unrest: How the Largest Movement in the World Came into Being and Why No One Saw it Coming*, New York: Viking, 2007. For the contrast between ego-centric and eco-centric ethics, see Tully, *Public Philosophy* II, chapter 3.

[83] For a historical and interdisciplinary introduction to this ecological dimension of citizenship, see E. F. Moran, *People and Nature: An Introduction to Human Ecological Relations*, Oxford: Blackwell, 2006. See also J. Borrows, *Recovering Canada: The Resurgence of Indigenous Law*, Toronto: University of Toronto Press, 2002; F. Capra, *The Web of Life: A New Synthesis of Mind and Matter*, New York: Anchor Books, 1996; J. Lovelock, *The Revenge of Gaia: Why the Earth Is Fighting Back – and How We Can Still Save Humanity*, London: Penguin, 2007, chapter 6; Hawken, *Blessed Unrest*.

stage of historical and moral development and as a particular ethics of care in contrast to the allegedly higher and universal theory of morality and justice for the abstracted and independent individuals of modern citizenship. And the public good is redescribed as the spread of modern liberties and their underlying institutions of economic growth.[84] Notwithstanding the hegemony of this egocentric worldview with the rise of Western imperialism, multilayered ethics of civic freedom and care in human and natural relationships have been and continue to be the more basic and widely endorsed orientation of the world's peoples in their diverse cultures and traditions for millennia.[85] Moreover, the dawning awareness of the destruction of local communities, environmental devastation, global warming and climate change brought about by four centuries of expansion and exploitation under the sway of this modernizing orientation, in which these public bads are concealed as 'externalities', is gradually undermining its credibility and paramountcy. Not only environmental and climate scientists of the world community and millions of citizens but even former modernizers and globalizers are quietly walking away from it and coming around to see the good of this alternative way of being a citizen *in* the world.[86]

14. Civic citizens are learning to be non-violent game players and one of their most important civic activities today is the teaching and practice of non-violent dispute resolution and disarmament. As we have seen, the institutions of civil citizenship are spread and enforced by coercion. The justification for this is that people without the canonical civil institutions are not civilized and thus are not trustworthy. It is rational to distrust and fear them in their state of lawlessness and insecurity.

---

[84] As we have seen in Subsection 4 and Tully, *Public Philosophy* II, chapters 1, 4, 5 and 7.

[85] For the anthropological and interdisciplinary literature on this claim see Moran, *People and Nature*.

[86] For examples of this turn in the World Bank, see H. Daly and J. Cobb, *For the Common Good: Redirecting the Economy Community, the Environment, and a Sustainable Future*, Boston: Beacon, 1994 and J. Stiglitz, *Globalization and its Discontents*, London: Allen Lane, 2002. Hawken, *Blessed Unrest*, dates the transitions to an ecological orientation among civic activists in non-indigenous North America to the influence of Thoreau and Emerson in the mid-nineteenth century, Rachel Carson's *Silent Spring* in the 1960s, the environmental and social justice movements and climate change and global warming. In Canada one would add the name of David Suzuki.

Only the civilizing force of institutionalized modern law and capitalism can render them civilized, predictable and trustworthy. If they do not submit or remove themselves, coercion can and should be used. Not surprisingly, the peoples in their own civilizational relationships who are approached, occupied and continuously patrolled by armed foreigners with this aggressive superior/inferior attitude and conduct respond by fearing and distrusting *them*, and trying to protect themselves and expel the uninvited and uncivicized guests. The dynamics of fear and hatred and war preparation and war ensue.[87]

Democratic citizens have learned from this depressing history that distrust and violence beget distrust and violence and from the history of non-violence that there is another more powerful way that leads to peace. They start from the simple premise that humans in all civilizations are already familiar with proto-civic and civicizing relationships, even imperialistic Westerners, and thus already able to recognize and enter into others. Accordingly, they approach others unarmed and with the embodied attitude and comportment of openness and trustworthiness. This takes the phenomenological form of the extended open hand, which says 'I trust you and come in peace, please reciprocate' in almost all cultures, in opposition to the closed fist. Only this vulnerable yet courageous and disarming comportment of groundless trust can initiate the reciprocal, pre-linguistic response and begin to weave a negotiated relationship of grounded mutual trust one strand at a time, civicizing the partners as they interact, just as one does across differences in one's own neighbourhood. Democratization cannot be spread by imposing institutional preconditions because non-violent grass roots democratic relationships are the preconditions of democratization. Consequently, peace cannot be the end of a long historical process of war and the spread of Western institutions. Peace is the *way*.[88] This commitment

---

[87] As we saw in Subsection 4.
[88] This view, which is antithetical to modern imperial citizenship, is widely recognized in different ethical and spiritual traditions. For example, M. K. Gandhi, *All Men are Brothers: Autobiographical Reflections*, New York: Continuum, 2005; J. Vanier, *Finding Peace*, Toronto: Anansi, 2003; T. Hanh, *Keeping the Peace*, Berkeley: Parallax, 2005; D. Chopra, *Peace Is the Way: Bringing War and Violence to an End*, New York: Three Rivers, 2005.

to non-violent democratic foreign policy is simply the extension of the non-coerced first step into civic citizenship (under aspect three).[89]

15. The final aspect of civic citizenship arises when citizens run up against unjustifiable limits to the civic activities in citizen/governance and citizen relationships that we have been discussing. In any of these activities there is always a vast ensemble of relationships that are not open to negotiation in the course of the activities. These background non-negotiable relationships 'structure' and limit the foreground field of possible actions in citizen/governance and citizen relationships. I will call these discursive and non-discursive relationships 'structural' relationships. If citizens try to bring these into the space of negotiation they are met with refusal, often because the structural relationships are the very basis of the unequal power and universal claim to authority of the hegemonic partners with whom they are negotiating. When, for example, a network of citizens negotiates with a multinational corporation over the sweatshop conditions under which their products are made, the multinational corporation and the global legal, economic and military relationships that support it remain immovably in the background, structuring the limited and unequal field of negotiable relationships. If citizens attempt to 'overcome' these background structural relationships, either by bringing them into the field of foreground negotiations (thereby transforming them into governance and citizen/governance relationships) or by overthrowing them entirely, as in a revolution, they move beyond negotiation to 'strategies of confrontation'. Confrontation strategies comprise the fourth type of civic activities.[90]

The problem (from a civic standpoint) is not only that there are such background structural relationships to any local negotiation, but that, as we saw in Section One, local structures are embedded in complex layers of

---

[89] For the civic tradition of non-violence, see P. Ackerman and J. Duvall, *A Force More Powerful: A Century of Non-Violent Conflict*, New York: St Martin's, 2000; M. Kurlansky, *Nonviolence: Twenty-Five Lessons from the History of a Dangerous Idea*, New York: Modern Library, 2006 and Transcend International, *Transcend: A Peace and Development Network for Conflict Transformation by Peaceful Means*, www.transcend.org.

[90] See under aspect six.

national and imperial structural relationships of inequality, dependency and exploitation that have been built up over half a millennium. This vast network of multilayered structuration appears to be a 'world system' capable of *integrating* the foreground play of specific civic negotiations into its daily reproduction and expansion.[91] In many theories this is precisely what is meant by 'globalization'. No responsible account of civic citizenship can avoid the question of how citizens can confront, de-imperialize and civicize this imperial leviathan, which seems able to make playthings out of the other three types of civic activity. All of Subsection 6 addresses this question. However, to make the transition I want to clarify the terms of structure (structural relationships) and agency (confrontation strategies) that disclose the field.

It is important to note first that all forms of civic activity take place within background structural relationships that are not open to negotiation *in the course of* the foreground negotiations. They are background enabling conditions that facilitate negotiations while foreclosing infinite regress. In the sweatshop example, the citizens appeal to sections of the background transnational trade law and international law to bring the multinational to the table. Civil citizens interpret them as the very 'conditions of possibility' of civic engagement and the grounds of universalizable citizenship, whereas civic citizens interpret them as singular and contingent enabling conditions of a particular form of civic engagement with a history of struggles behind them, but they both agree on their role in civic activities. They have to be held firm for the negotiations to take place, or, from the civic orientation, the activity of negotiating holds them in place. Thus, it is not the structural role of such relationships that makes them objectionable, as long as they are open to civic questioning and negotiations under other circumstances.[92]

Rather, what makes structural relationships objectionable from the civic perspective is when they do not enable civic citizens to care for

---

[91] The classic presentation of this is Immanuel Wallerstein's world systems theory. See the *Journal of World Systems Research* for this approach.
[92] As we saw in aspect nine.

civic goods but disable them in some way. They suppress, disallow, block, arbitrarily constrain, misrecognize, render negotiators unequal, include and assimilate, co-opt and enable the powerful to bypass the democratizing negotiations of citizens. Structural relationships that play these anti-democratic roles are structural relationships of 'domination'. They are the target of confrontation strategies.

If we focus on the classic modern revolutions against a state system of domination as the abstract paradigm of confrontation then there appears to be a sharp binary distinction between negotiation and confrontation. In confrontations 'revolutionary' citizens 'liberate' themselves from a structure of domination, whereas in negotiations 'reforming' citizens exercise their limited civic freedom within it. But this unsituated picture obscures the complexity of real-world civic struggles in locales. From the situated perspective of civic citizens engaged in concrete civic activities, confrontation strategies form a continuum from refusing to negotiate in accordance with the rules to revolution. It is difficult to draw a sharp distinction between negotiation and confrontation. When does a negotiating tactic become an act of confrontation: refusal to follow an order, speaking truth to power, walk out, witnessing, sit in, protest, strike, general strike, picket line, road block, local or global boycott, coordinated uprising, rebellion or revolution? In each case, the citizens are refusing to negotiate and confronting what is, from their local perspective, a structural relationship of domination. On what grounds, other than the binary paradigm, could one say that a reforming negotiator who takes this courageous step within the negotiations is necessarily co-opted and ineffective, whereas the citizens who refuse to enter into negotiations and organize for the revolution from the outside are necessarily confrontational and effective? Even retrospectively it is difficult to say which confrontation activities precipitated an overall change or transformation.

Confrontational strategies are multiplex not only in their tactics but also in the civic activities they initiate. Think of these examples. Citizens who have no civil right to protest or demonstrate against harms to civil goods do so anyway, not simply to protest monologically, but to force the powers-that-be to enter into negotiations, and they see this as a success only if mutually binding negotiations transpire. In other cases, citizens bypass protests and simply engage in a form of civic activity even though they do not have the civil right to do so and on the ground that it needs to be done. *Médecins sans Frontières* (Doctors without Borders) is a global example of this phenomenon of 'acting otherwise' without a civil right but not without civic right.[93] If these sorts of confrontation turn out to be successful, the initiatory precedents often harden into a customary or institutionalized civil right to continue to engage in them (as in aspect 3, pp. 37–41). They are exemplars of extending the use of 'citizenship' by enacting it that we discussed in the Introduction. Neither case fits the revolutionary model yet each may well be revolutionary in its consequences. Conversely, neither is a case of lawlessness or 'anything goes' for both are undertaken for the sake of civic good and to bring the activity under civicizing relationships. As we saw in Subsection 3, such confrontational precedents are often absorbed into the civil institutions and their civic history forgotten.

Correlative with the tendency to construe confrontation in terms of revolution is the tendency to view structural relationships of domination through the paradigm of a bounded system like a state or a system of states (as is presupposed in the use of 'inside' and 'outside' above). Yet, from the civic standpoint, structural relationships of domination are neither bounded nor systemic. The common experience of confrontations suggests otherwise. When citizens overthrow a local structural relationship or convert it into a citizen/governance relationship (or a citizen relationship in cases of cooperatizing private corporations), they find a further layer of dominating structural relationships behind it, and so always have to begin again the next morning.[94] The decisive example is the decolonization revolutions of the mid-twentieth century and the de-imperialization revolutions in the

---

[93] *Médecins sans Frontières*, www.msf.org. For an analysis of this example from a civic perspective see M. Foucault, 'Confronting Governments: Human Rights', in J. B. Faubion, ed., *The Essential Works*, Volume III, New York: New Press, 2000.

[94] See Tully, *Public Philosophy* II, chapter 4.

new world order today. As we saw in Subsection 4, citizens of the colonies were able to overthrow structural relationships of *political* domination (colonialism), by a complex repertoire of confrontation strategies, but they found the political powers they (or their elites) acquired deeply embedded in further layers of background imperial structural relationships of domination. The revolutionary anti-imperial struggles since the end of decolonization have confirmed this complex situation. A successful revolution against the local dependent elite is followed by financial boycotts, economic pressure, tactics of destabilization, covert and proxy military operations and, if necessary, the overt fist of US military intervention in order to 'overthrow' the popular government.[95] The classic picture of a bounded people overthrowing their unjust regime and setting up a new government as they see fit within bounded states has quite limited application, yet it continues to prevail, perhaps because it hides the unjust reality.

These examples, and others to follow, also illustrate what we saw in Subsection 4. The structural relationships of domination are not only layered rather than bounded but also networked rather than systemic. What holds structural relationships of domination in place and integrates both civic negotiations *and* confrontations into an ongoing global organization is neither a functional property of a world system nor a hidden hand, as it appears from the theoretical gaze. Rather, it is the actual contingent exercise by humans of all the considerable means available to the hegemonic partners in the layers of informal imperial networks that encircle the globe. The networkization of informal imperialism beginning in the 1970s consists in linking together the various unequal nodes (communicative, economic, financial, military,

---

[95] In addition to the literature referred to in *Volume II*, in chapters 5 and 7, see S. Kinzer, *Overthrow: America's Century of Regime Change from Hawaii to Iraq*, New York: Holt, H, 2006; J. Carroll, *House of War: The Pentagon and the Disastrous Rise of American Power*, New York: Houghton Mifflin, 2006; C. Johnson, *Nemesis: The Last Days of the American Republic*, New York: Metropolitan, 2006; for the early history of intervention, see R. Kagan, *Dangerous Nation: America's Foreign Policy from its Earliest Days to the Dawn of the Twentieth Century*, New York: Vintage, 2007. The imperialists celebrate these overthrows. See, for example, R. D. Kaplan, *Imperial Grunts: The American Military on the Ground*, New York: Random House, 2002.

legal, educational and so on) in structural and governance relationships that make up the network. For our purposes, the crucial feature of this non-systemic form of organization is that the nodes are composed of humans networking in a variety of different forms of association, yet all of which rest ultimately on the negotiated practices of the participants in their relationships with each other.[96] At the end of the day, therefore, what keeps the imperial network going and the structural relationships of domination in their background place, is nothing more (or less) than the activities of powerfully situated actors to resist, contain, roll-back and circumscribe the uncontainable democratizing negotiations and confrontations of civic citizens in a multiplicity of local nodes. These sites of civic activity are the Achilles Heel of informal imperialism. To see them as a systemic structure and to organize confrontation accordingly is to misrepresent the field of local and global citizenship and to overlook the concrete possibilities available on it for creative and effective negotiations and confrontations of civicization and de-imperialization.

With this more accurate survey of the field in hand we are now in a position to turn to glocal citizenship practices.

6. The glocalization of civic and glocal citizenship

I want now to examine two main ways diverse citizenship spreads around the globe. The first is the persistence and recent renaissance of local forms of civic citizenship practices despite the globalization of modern citizenship. The second is by the global civic federation and networkization of local diverse citizenship practices. I call this global networking 'glocalization' and the networkers 'glocal citizens' because they are grounded in and hyperextend the civic features of local citizenship.[97]

---

[96] For the networkization of informal imperial governance see Tully, *Public Philosophy* II, chapter 6. See also *Public Philosophy* II, chapter 3 for another argument for the non-systemic character of large historical concatenations of practices.

[97] Subsection 6 draws on the chapters and literature referred to in Tully, *Public Philosophy* II.

I will also discuss these two ways of glocalizing civic citizenship in relation to the global crisis of citizenship we examined in Subsection 4. To recollect, the formal and then informal imperial spread of modern citizenship and the underlying institutions it sends on ahead to lay the foundations of civilization has led in many cases, at best, to a form of global cosmopolitan citizenship for official NGOs and multinational corporations, low-intensity citizenship for dependent elites of the former colonies, the dispossession or marginalization of local citizenship and governance, the subordination of local economies and polities to global corporations and trade regimes, enormous inequalities, violent cycles of repression and resistance and increasing environmental destruction. This crisis of modernity/coloniality has coincided with a crisis of democratic deficits in the representative democracies of the hegemonic states. The informal imperial networks of economic, legal, cultural, media, security and military relationships not only bypass and undercut the diverse citizenship of billions of people who are governed by them, they also manipulate, downsize and disregard the representative and legal institutions of modern citizenship that are supposed to bring them under representative authority. These trends of globalization constitute a crisis of global citizenship that, viewed in isolation, fosters a pervasive sense of disempowerment and disenchantment. I want now to move around and re-interpret them from the standpoint of glocal citizenship.

First, despite these devastating trends, another world of legal, political, ecological and even economic diversity has survived and continues to be the *loci* of civic activities for millions of people. The reason for this remarkable survival and renaissance in the post-colonial world, unknown to the dominant debate over global citizenship, is that Western imperialism governs through indirect or informal means and thus depends on the active collaboration of imperialized peoples exercising constrained local self-government in their own cultural ways. Those who are not part of the Westernized elite have been able to keep their diverse practices and forms of life alive to some extent within the considerable Spielraum of informal dependency relationships. Another world of pluralism exists in the interstices of globalization.[98] One of the most astonishing examples is the survival and resurgence of 300 million indigenous peoples with their traditions of governance and Gaia-based citizenship after 500 years of genocide, dispossession, marginalization and relentless assimilation.[99] The lived experience of citizenship in the present age is thus different from and more multiplex than it is portrayed through the sweeping generalizations of globalization theories of both defenders and critics.[100]

Many existing diverse practices of governance have been corrupted into exploitative and despotic relationships by their dependency on indirect rule and others were non-civic from the get go.[101] The point is neither to reject them simply because they are non-modern nor to uncritically accept them because they are different or traditional. It is rather to bring them into comparative and critical discussions with other forms of governance and citizenship and to explore ways citizens can civicize them by speaking and acting within them.[102] In the modernized West a vast repertoire of local citizenship practices have also survived within the interstices of state-centric modern citizenship, such as traditional working-class organizations and new and creative forms of coops and networks linking rural and urban citizens in countless ways and around various civic goods (the environment, non-violent dispute

---

[98] See Tully, *Public Philosophy* II, chapters 5 and 7; for an introduction to this historical field, see L. Benton, *Law and Colonial Cultures: Legal Regimes in World History*, 1400–1990, Cambridge: Cambridge University Press, 2002.

[99] J. Mander and V. Tauli-Corpuz, eds, *Paradigm Wars: Indigenous Peoples' Resistance to Economic Globalization*, San Francisco: International Forum on Globalization, 2005.

[100] V. Shiva, *Earth Democracy: Justice, Sustainability and Peace*, Cambridge: South End, 2005; D. McNally, *Another World is Possible: Globalization and Anti-Capitalism*, Winnipeg: Arbeiter Ring, 2006.

[101] As we have seen in Subsection 4, the role of the United States' military and multinational corporations in countries in Latin America and Saudi Arabia (and other petrotyrannies) are examples of how informal imperialism (by a low intensity civil democracy) corrupts local governments, props up the most repressive regimes and subverts grass roots democracy. For Latin America, see Grandin, *Empire's Workshop*. For Saudi Arabia, see R. Vitalis, *America's Kingdom: Mythmaking on the Saudi Oil Frontier*, San Francisco: Stanford University Press, 2007. For a general survey of the petrotyrannies under informal imperialism, see J. Bacher, *Petrotyranny*, Toronto: Dundurn, 2000.

[102] M. Mamdani, 'Beyond Settler and Natives as Political Identities: Overcoming the Legacy of Colonialism', *Comparative Studies in Society and History* 43 (4): 651–64, 2001.

resolution, low-cost housing, anti-racism, organic farming, place-based pedagogy, neighbourhood security and so on). These old and new citizenship practices and improvizations are multiplying rapidly today in the 'return to the local' of a new generation disenchanted with the elite manipulation of representative citizenship, the destruction of local communities by a half millennia of globalization from above, and moved by the ecological revolution of the last century.[103]

The second example of glocalizing civic citizenship is the array of movements to 'democratize democracy' we touched on in Subsection 5. The aim of these movements is to democratize the legal, political and bureaucratic institutions of modern representative democracy so that the people who are subject to them are consulted and have an effective negotiated say within them *wherever* power is exercised non-democratically and unaccountably, in ad hoc confrontations of speaking out and 'going public' or in more formal modes of negotiation in which those who govern must listen and give an account. These are thus movements to 'civicize' the civil institutions of modern citizenship. Here civic citizens join hands with civil citizens engaged in the same projects from within – such as proportional representation, deliberative democracy, democratic constitutionalism, legal and political pluralism and civic *versus* civil security. Globally, they include the movements to democratize the institutions of global governance and to establish the UN as an effective democratic forum that represents the majority of the peoples of the world who are subject to the relationships of inequality, dependency and exploitation.[104]

Third, since decolonization and the triumph of informal imperialism, millions of the world's poor have been forced to migrate from the

---

[103] C. Hines, *Localization: A Global Manifesto*, London: Earthscan, 2000.

[104] B. de Sousa Santos, eds, *Democratizing Democracy: Beyond the Liberal Democratic Cannon*, London: Verso, 2005; I. Loader and N. Walker, *Civilizing Security*, Cambridge: Cambridge University Press, 2007; D. Archibugi, D. Held and M. Köhler, eds, *Re-imagining Political Community: Studies in Contemporary Democracy*, Cambridge: Polity, 1998; and Volume II, chapters 2 and 4. Bronsilaw Malinowski called for the democratization of the United Nations at its inception and predicted the imperial and violent consequences of the control of the great powers, in B. Malinowski, *Freedom and Civilization*, Bloomington: Indiana University Press, 1944, pp. 1–16.

colonized world to the imperial countries to find work in a closely controlled global labour market.[105] Despite the hardships of poverty, slavery, exploitation, racism, xenophobia and second-class or non-citizenship, they refuse to be servile subjects. Instead, they exercise their civic citizenship in new and untoward ways, negotiating their diverse cultural ways into the public and private institutions of modern citizenship. This 'journey back' or 'boomerang effect' of formerly colonized peoples now civicizing the imperial countries challenges the dominant imperial, nationalist and racist cultures encoded in modern citizenship institutions and creates new forms of multiculturalism and multi-civilizationalism on the ground, both in the urban centres and the diasporic relationships (transnational civicscapes) they sustain with their former countries. These grass roots multicultural communities in 'mongrel cities' generate new kinds of citizen relationships of conviviality among their members and supportive local civic citizens groups which are often overlooked by, or poorly integrated into, the official policies of respect for diversity.[106]

These three examples and many others similar to them are existing practices of local civic citizenship. These worldwide local sources and resources of civic citizenship are much stronger and resilient than we think. They are the bases of glocal citizenship. NGOs, social movements, networks, informal civic federations and similar creative improvizations are the means by which glocal citizens link together and so glocalize these local civic bases. These networks are civic and glocal just insofar as they (1) are grounded in and accountable to the local civic nodes, and (2) hyperextend civic relationships (citizen and citizen/governance) and other civic aspects in their own organization and their relationships with others. Of course not all networks are composed of citizen and citizen/ governance partnerships. Many are institutional and governmental in form. They 'mobilize' rather than civicize. However, the network mode

---

[105] A. Richmond, *Global Apartheid: Refugees, Racism, and the New World Order*, Oxford: Oxford University Press, 1994.

[106] L. Sandercock, *Cosmopolis II: Mongrel Cities in the Twenty-First Century*, London: Continuum, 2003; and Tully, *Public Philosophy* II, chapter 8.

of organization has the flexibility and potential to be organized civically and democratically all the way down. This mode of being-with is within its field of possibilities.[107] If, in contrast, networkers are organized institutionally and/or governmentally, and if they see themselves as the bearers of the gifts of civilization and modern citizenship to the less-developed, then they are modern (civil and cosmopolitan), imperial networks.[108] In addition to providing mutual learning and aid to their member civic nodes, glocal networks also crucially provide the civic means of democratizing the persisting global imperial relationships of inequality, exploitation and dependency that are the major causes of the crisis of global citizenship. Glocal networks do this counter-hegemonic work of de-imperializing the world in two main ways.

First, as we have seen in Subsection 4, the persisting economic, legal, political, debt, media, educational and military relationships of informal imperialism are so unequal that, although the elites within the former colonies are able to have a say and negotiate (in global governance institutions and elsewhere), they (the G120) are barely able to modify these governance relationships, let alone transform them into governance/citizen relationships, and they are in turn scarcely in civicized relationships with their own people (the majority of the world's population). Similarly, the hegemonic partners in the relationships – the great powers and their multinational corporations – are not held democratically accountable by their own citizens. Even where there are well-defined international laws and rights, the more powerful bypass or manipulate them to their advantage so they function as a legitimating façade rather than an effective guarantee.[109] As we have

---

[107] Tully, *Public Philosophy* II, chapter 6.

[108] A. Ayers, 'Demystifying Democratization: The Global Constitution of (Neo) Liberal Polities in Africa', *Third World Quarterly* 27 (2): 312–38, 2006; T. Evans and A. Ayers, 'In the Service of Power: The Global Political Economy of Citizenship and Human Rights', *Citizenship Studies* 10 (3): 289–308, 2006.

[109] See Tully, *Public Philosophy* II, chapter 4. This is also the conclusion of Ishay, *History of Human Rights*, and she recommends glocal citizenship networks as the most effective response (pp. 348–9). This is also the view of V. Shiva, 'The Greening of Global Reach', in S. Daly and P. Routledge, eds, *The Geopolitics Reader*, London: Routledge, 1998; and A. Dobson, 'States, Citizens and the Environment', in Skinner and Ström, eds, *States and Citizens*.

seen in the domestic context, the only guarantee of democratic rights is the concrete exercise of civic freedom. Accordingly, the first role of a glocal network is to glocally link together enough local citizenship practices of those who are governed by any of these relationships to single it out and contest it: to call its existence and privacy into the space of public questioning and put enough soft power pressure on the responsible powers-that-be to bring them to negotiations in the most effective place or places. It is thus the glocalization of the whole practice of civic negotiation and confrontation vis-à-vis unequal global governance relationships outlined in Subsection 5.

Networked contestation, negotiation and confrontation can take place anywhere and by anybody in the relationships (e.g. in sweat shops and/or consumer boycott of sweatshop products, in the WTO or in protest against the WTO). It should not be the burden of the wretched of the earth to refuse to submit and act otherwise, as in the dominant theories of resistance, but of the most powerful and privileged to refuse to comply and engage in the work of glocal citizenship. In doing this, citizens in glocal networks are engaged in civicizing and democratizing these imperial relationships by bringing them under the shared authority of all those subject to them *in* their local places and ways. They can steer the negotiations into the civil, legal and political institutions of the most effective nation state or of global civil society, or they can negotiate directly in civic society, or they can pursue both strategies at once. If the negotiations take hold, the subaltern partner ceases to be 'dependent' but also does *not* become 'independent' (as was imagined in the unsuccessful theories of decolonization). Rather, the partners gradually become 'interdependent' on the ongoing democratic relationships between them.[110] These innumerable practices of glocal negotiation and confrontation comprise one non-violent path of de-imperialization and democratization characteristic of the civic tradition.[111]

---

[110] As we saw for the local examples in Subsection 5, aspect 7.
[111] See I. M. Young, *Global Challenges: War, Self-Determination and Responsibility for Justice*, Cambridge: Polity, 2007, especially pp. 137–9; and Tully, *Public Philosophy* II, chapter 4.

The second way glocal networks work to transform imperial relationships into democratic ones is through the spread of cooperative citizen relationships between partners in the North and Global South. These cooperative informal federations are not strategies of contestation and negotiation, but of directly acting otherwise: of creating non-violent civic relationships between partners in the North and the Global South. The relationships among all the partners in the network, and within each partner's local community association, are worked out civically and democratically as they go along.[112] Although there are thousands of examples, perhaps the best known are glocal cooperative 'fair trade' and self-reliance relationships, such as the specific Fair Trade and Level Ground cases, in contrast to competitive free trade; glocal networks of non-violent dispute resolution in contrast to war, militarization and securitization and deep ecology networks in contrast to (oxymoronic) sustainable development.[113] Like their local cooperative partners, these glocal cooperative citizens work within the Spielraum of existing global rules in each case, yet they play a completely different game with different goods. They create and live 'another world' in their civic and glocal activities.[114]

The World Social Forum has emerged as an important place where civic and glocal citizens can meet each year. It is to glocal citizenship as the World Economic Forum is to modern citizenship. The forum does not take a position, but, rather, provides a civic space in which participants from diverse citizenship practices can enter into civic dialogues of translation, comparison, criticism, reciprocal learning and further networking. They share the knowledge of their different arts of citizenship with each other without granting modern citizenship the

---

[112] They build on the local coops of Subsection 5, aspect 11.

[113] For fair trade and mutual aid as the antidote to free trade, see G. Dunkley, *Free Trade: Myth, Reality and Alternatives*, London: Zed Books, 2003. For examples see Tully, *Public Philosophy* II, chapter 8.

[114] For a global survey see Hawken, *Blessed Unrest*, and his website of civilizing networks around the world at www.wiserearth.org; Grimes and Milgram, *Artisans and Cooperatives* and Tully, *Public Philosophy* II, chapter 8. For the primary importance of building webs of nurturing relationships among local ecologies, food producers, food consumers and waste recyclers, see Moran, *People and Nature*.

universal and superior status it claims for itself and on the presumption that each mode of citizenship is partial and incomplete, so each can learn its limitations from others. The forum also hopes to develop closer links of reciprocal learning between academic research and the practices of citizenship we have been discussing, perhaps setting up popular universities of the social movements for this purpose.[115]

Relationships of reciprocal elucidation between academic research and civic activists, of which the popular universities is only one example, bring into being yet another kind of glocal partnership. These are glocal pedagogical partnerships that aim to challenge the institutional separation between university education and its 'fields of study' that is characteristic of the modern university.[116] They also challenge the current privatization and globalization of this institutional model of the university. Glocal pedagogical relationships aim to bring university learners, teachers and researchers into a more practical and mutually edifying relationship with the activists and activities studied, as well as to encourage universities to become good, responsible civic citizens of their own locales, sharing their knowledge with local communities and becoming exemplary glocal citizens. This is a civicizing revolution in the way we think of and practice higher education in relation to public affairs.[117]

Finally, all these examples illustrate one of the most fundamental practical advantages of a civic/glocal orientation. Many if not most of the global harms to public good we have discussed, from inequality, exploitation and war to climate change and global warming caused by imperial competition over scarce resources, cross the jurisdictional boundaries of the institutions of civil and cosmopolitan citizenship.

---

[115] B. de Sousa Santos, *The Rise of the Global Left: The World Social Forum and Beyond*, London: Zed Books, 2006; J. Conway, 'Citizenship in a Time of Empire: The World Social Forum as a New Public Space', *Citizenship Studies* 8 (4): 367–81, 2004.

[116] This particular institutional separation of university education is part of the more general modern trend discussed in Subsection 5, aspect 9.

[117] M. R. M'Gonigle and J. Stark, *Planet U: Sustaining the World, Reinventing the University*, Gabriola Island: New Society Publishers, 2006; and Tully, *Public Philosophy* I, chapter 1 for this pedagogical relationship between academic research teams and civic citizens.

There is thus a series of disempowering 'disjunctures' between the agents who cause the harm and the people who are affected by them, for the agents responsible are often not subject to the jurisdiction of the civil institutions in which those affected have the status of civil citizens.[118] This is a critical problem of civil citizenship organized within nation states and an international law system of formally equal yet substantively unequal and dependent nation states. It can be addressed within the civil tradition only by the establishment of something like a world state or its negative surrogate (an alliance of powerful states) to enforce the empire of rules of modern cosmopolitan citizenship and its underlying institutions. Yet, as we have seen, this further and perhaps ultimate projection of this imperial model would bring with it all the preconditions of the global harms in the first place.[119] The civic tradition simply does not have this disenfranchising disjuncture problem. By starting from the premise that any community subject to and affected by a relationship of governance that harms a public good is for that very reason a citizenry with the civic right to hold the responsible party accountable through civic negotiations, it links democratic organization, networkization and civicized institutionalization directly to the specific power relationship at issue and at the most effective sites.

7. Conclusion: Exemplars

If all the millions of examples of civic and glocal citizenship practices could be taken in a single view, as the tradition of modern citizenship and globalization presents its inexorable progress, perhaps this would help to dissipate the sense of disempowerment and disenchantment the present crisis induces. But, from the situated standpoint of diverse

---

[118] David Held introduced this 'disjuncture' problem (see Tully, *Public Philosophy* II, chapter 2).

[119] For my objections to various plans to extend the imperial project, see Tully, *Public Philosophy* II, chapters 5, 7 and 8. For another example, see J. G. Ikenberry and A. Slaughter, *Forging a World of Liberty under Law: US National Security in the 21st Century*, The Princeton Project on National Security, The Woodrow Wilson School of Public and International Affairs: Princeton University, 2006.

citizenship, this cannot be done and the attempt would overlook the very diversity that the civic approach aims to disclose, keep in view, learn from and work with. Civic empowerment and enchantment do not come from grand narratives of universal progress but from *praxis* – actual participation in civic activities with others where we become the citizens we can be. But this response raises the question of the motive for participation in the first place. The civic answer has always been the motivating force of examples of civic activities and exemplars of civic citizenship. Since the civic tradition has no place for the cult of great leaders and leadership but only for citizens linking arms and working together in partnerships, it turns once again to everyday practice for these motivating stories.

Fortunately today there are over one million examples of civic and glocal networks and cooperatives and millions of exemplary ordinary citizens from all walks of life in all locales that move potential citizens of all ages to participate. They arguably make up the largest non-centralized and diverse movement of movements in the world.[120] But perhaps an illustrative exemplar for our dark times of the kind of glocal citizenship I have sketched is Mahatma Gandhi and his lifelong activities to rid the world of imperialism. His ordinary civic and glocal life continues to move millions of people to begin to act. The reason for this, I believe, is the simplicity of the four citizenship practices his life of *Satyagraha* manifests.[121]

The first is active non-cooperation vis-à-vis any imperial (non-civic) relationship and its corresponding idea of one universal civilization or cosmopolitanism for all. The second is the way of peace. For Gandhi this consists in civic organization and uncompromising non-violent confrontation and negotiation with those responsible for imperial relationships with the aim of converting them to non-violent, democratic and peaceful relationships. Third, for these two activities to be effective they have to be grounded in the local field and practices of the alternative

---

[120] Hawken, *Blessed Unrest*, makes this argument.
[121] For Gandhi's life and influence, see T. Weber, *Gandhi as Disciple and Mentor*, Cambridge: Cambridge University Press, 2004.

world you want to bring about. For Gandhi this consists of 'constructive work' in local, self-reliant, civically organized Indian villages and respectful participation in their ways. Like millions of glocal journeyers, Gandhi started from and returned home to the close and closest things after a sojourn in the transcendent world of modern citizenship, seeing these homespun activities in a new and enchanting light. 'Where have I been?' one often exclaims at this moment of insight and transformation into a citizen who sees, thinks and acts glocally.[122] Fourth, the first three practices are integrated into a singular style of civic life by the more personal practices of self-awareness and self-formation.[123] For Gandhi these arts and exercises comprise a spiritual relationship to oneself in one's relationships with others and the environing natural and spiritual worlds.[124] This is a meditative relationship of working truthfully on oneself and one's attitude to improve how one conducts oneself in the challenging yet rewarding civic relationships with others. These are daily practices of becoming an exemplary citizen.

8. Afterword – The crisis of global citizenship: Civil and civic responses

The crisis of global citizenship

This afterword expands on the crisis of global citizenship and democratic deficit referred to in *On Global Citizenship*. The objective is to show more specifically how practices of civil and civic citizenship can be seen as democratic responses to the insufficiency of participation within the

---

[122] A moving rendition of such a journey of self-discovery, which walks us through many of the steps of this chapter, was written by Nietzsche in Nice in the summer of 1886 when he was composing the life-affirming fifth book of the *Gay Science*. See F. Nietzsche, 'Preface 1886' in *Human, All too Human: A Book for Free Spirits*, Cambridge: Cambridge University Press, 1986. For an analysis of experiences of transformation from subject to active citizen, see Norval, *Aversive Democracy*.

[123] For the place of practices of the self see Subsection 5.

[124] Similar practices are available in every culture. See D. Fontana, *The Meditator's Handbook: A Complete Guide to Eastern and Western Meditation Techniques*, London: Thorsons, 1992.

institutions of modern civil citizenship. The afterword incorporates the main arguments in 'A Dilemma of Democratic Citizenship' referred to by the contributors, and some further arguments.[125] It thus provides a necessary background for understanding several of the arguments of the contributors and my responses to them.

The crisis of global citizenship refers to the difficulties citizens have in trying to respond effectively to the global problems outlined in *On Global Citizenship*. Let us take four local-and-global injustices as examples. These are: (1) the horrendous inequalities, poverty and exploitation of the Global South, and, increasingly in the Global North; (2) climate change and the destruction of the environment; (3) global wars, the militarization of conflicts and their collateral and blowback effects and (4) unjust forms of recognition and non-recognition.

These problems are interconnected. The historical processes of modernization, industrialization, Western expansion, exploitation of the world's resources and economic globalization that are the major cause of the ecological crisis are also the major cause of the inequalities between the Global North and South, and within the Global North. And, the primary role of the huge global military empire of the Great Powers is to protect and expand the very processes of economic globalization that are deeply implicated in the ecological and inequality problems. Moreover, the unjust forms of recognition of individuals, groups, peoples and civilizations are often closely related to their nonconformity to the institutions and processes of modern development.

Many social and ecological scientists argue that the apparent trend of these four complex processes is the gradual destruction of life on earth; through starvation, hunger and poverty; ever more destructive wars, war-preparation and their collateral effects; the destruction of biodiversity and the environment and greenhouse gases, global warming and massive climate change. From 1992 to the latest report of the Intergovernmental Panel on Climate Change, over 1,000 climate scientists warn that, if humanity does not change this destructive way

---

[125] Also see J. Tully, 'The Crisis of Global Citizenship', *Radical Politics Today*, July 2009 at www.spaceofdemocracy.org.

of life, then the planet will become uninhabitable for most forms of life. This is called the Medea Hypothesis.[126]

When citizens engage in the institutions of modern civil citizenship to address these problems, they find that the effective exercise of their democratic capabilities is limited. The ineffectiveness of and limitations on the exercise of global citizenship through official channels is a fifth injustice of our age. This 'incapacitation' of practices of democratic citizenship in response to local and global injustices is a global democratic deficit. My thesis is that the democratic deficit is a structural feature of the institutions of modern civil module and its four tiers of rights and duties.

As we have seen, the module limits democratic participation in the following ways. First, the anti-democratic ways it is spread around the world and the ways it limits or eliminates other forms of government and participation are unjust. Second, it limits participation to the exercise of communicative capacities in official public spheres and parties with the hope of influencing electors and representatives. Third, by placing the organization, exercise and development of the productive capacities of human beings in the private sphere, it shields them from 'democratization': that is, from bringing these social and economic activities under the democratic authority of those who are subject to them. This is done by placing the commodification of labour power and resources under the protection of the tier-one right of non-interference of individuals and corporations. Yet, these privatized activities are the major interconnected cause of the local-and-global problems citizens are trying to address. These three limits incapacitate citizens from addressing the global problems effectively and thus give rise to the crisis of global citizenship. From a democratic perspective, this could be called 'the tragedy of privatization' in contrast to the dominant thesis of the 'tragedy of the commons', which has served to legitimate the spread of the institutional structure of privatization and low-intensity democracy since Hobbes.

[126] T. Flannery, *Here on Earth: A Natural History of the Planet*, New York: Atlantic Monthly, 2010.

Reform from within: The civil and civic response

The first response to the crisis of global citizenship by both civil and civic citizens is to try to reform the institutions of participation from within. Theorists from Rousseau to Rawls argue that a necessary feature of a free society is that citizens not only participate within the institutional structure available to them, they must also be free to exchange public reasons over the justice or injustice of the basic institutional structure they have inherited. Accordingly, faced with the limits on participation and the tragedy of privatization, democratic citizens around the world enter into the official and unofficial public spheres, parties and reform movements within states, at the UN and institutions of global governance, and through the human rights available in International Law, and seek to bring this diagnosis to the attention of fellow citizens and elected officials. These are the practices of 'democratizing democracy' mentioned in *On Global Citizenship*.

Many important reforms have been achieved: the extension of the franchise, feminist movements, the struggles for social and economic rights by labour organizations, struggles for minority rights and the recognition of indigenous peoples, the demands for legal and political pluralism, the formation of green parties, rights to clean water and environmental protection, initiatives to improve representation at the UN and institutions of global governance and struggles to make local, national and global public spheres and governments more inclusive, proportional and pluralistic.

Yet, the institutional limits on democratic participation and in relation to privatization are so powerful in law, practice and modern theories of negative freedom that it is exceptionally difficult even to regulate economic activities to some modest extent through the official channels of public deliberation, representative government and legislation, as we have seen again in the financial crisis and responses to it.

Elected officials are dependent on corporate campaign funding; governments are dependent on corporate taxes; access, voice and communicative power in public reasoning are radically unequal and powerful corporations and ministries are able to influence legislation and exert control over the framing of issues in public spheres and over the 'influence power' public deliberations are said to have. Powerful multinational corporations can hide behind their tier-one rights, bypass or bribe impoverished local governments, intimidate sweatshop workers, influence the institutions of global governance and invoke transnational trade laws that protect free trade from democratic scrutiny. Finally, while the free press and media that accompany the spread of the basic institutions *can* assist public reasoning, they can also come under the hegemony of concentrations of private, government and military power beyond the reach of democratic participation.[127]

Four civic responses

When civic citizens run up against the limits of reform they turn to practices of cooperative citizenship. They begin to extend practices of citizen participation beyond the reforms of the official spheres of representative democracy. They do so in a multiplicity of ways. I would like to sketch four practices of cooperative citizenship that are responses to the crisis of global citizenship. In the theories of modern representative government, these citizens are said to have conditionally delegated their capacities of self-government to their representatives and to have retained only the communicative capacities they exercise in voting and exchanging public reasons in public spheres. In each of the types of cooperative citizenship, they re-appropriate these capabilities of self-organization and self-government and exercise them directly in concert. In so doing, cooperative citizens are revolutionary in weaving together as tightly as possible speaking together and acting together as citizens – public reasoning and public acting. This re-integration

---

[127] See J. Tully, 'On the Multiplicity of Global Public Spheres', in C. Emden and D. Midgley, eds, *Beyond Habermas: Democracy, Knowledge and the Public Sphere*, New York: Berghahn Books, 2012; Also the other chapters in this volume. For the limits to reform from within I am deeply indebted to the work by Michael M'Gonigle from a green legal perspective. In particular, see the devastating critique of M. R. M'Gonigle and L. Takeda, 'The Liberal Limits of Environmental Law: A Green Legal Critique', *Pace Environmental Law Review*, 30, 2013.

of the capacities of self-government is literally impossible within the institutions of modern representative democracy. They are designed to dis-embed these capabilities from situated practices and differentiate their exercise into separate spheres.

Practices of negotiation

The first re-appropriation is to take back the democratic capacities of negotiating with the actors who they believe are responsible for the global problems. These are the negotiation capabilities that are delegated to legislatures and courts in the representative module. These citizens organize democratic negotiation networks locally and globally around a specific activity that is argued to be a cause of inequality and exploitation, environmental damage, militarization and authoritarian rule. They then use non-violent networks of public education, persuasion and pressure to bring the powers-that-be to the negotiating table, whether this is an official table or an ad hoc table, as I outline in *On Global Citizenship*.[128] These arts have been developed in response to the failure of institutional reform: that is, as states, political parties and global institutions promoted neoliberal globalization and coercive structural adjustment, and ignored the democratic protests of the millions of people subject to these policies. These kinds of activities bring the actor in question to the negotiation table and to democratic practices of arguing and bargaining, alternative dispute resolution and methods of transformative justice.

Notice that these democratic practices of negotiation are closely related to the movements for reform of the official institutions. For, the moment a reform movement calls into question a limit on official participation and seeks to change it through unofficial forms of protest, boycott and negotiation, it is beginning to engage in this civic kind of negotiation as well. The great reforms of the institutional structures of modern states and international law by women, labour movements, minorities, immigrants, community-based organizations

---

[128] Tully, *On Global Citizenship*.

and indigenous peoples are often examples of this type of democratic citizenship – combining civil and cooperative.[129]

Practices of social and economic cooperation

In the next two types of civic citizenship citizens extend the practices of democratic participation into the private economic sphere: into the activities of resource extraction, production, distribution, consumption and recycling that underlie the tragedy of privatization. They do this by re-appropriating their capacities of social and economic organization and exercise them in common. One way to see the participatory practices of cooperative citizenship in this light is through the analysis of the privatization tragedy first given by Karl Polanyi and continued in the recent work on alternative globalization from below and reclaiming the commons. I did not see cooperative citizenship in the light of Polanyi's analysis when I wrote *On Global Citizenship*. I hope this perspective shows more clearly and specifically how civic practices of cooperation are effective responses to two structural features of the crisis of global citizenship.

Polanyi diagnosed the way that the private sphere was constructed in modern societies in the nineteenth century so as to place limits on democratic participation in the economic sphere. He argued that these limits were unique to nineteenth-century capitalist markets in contrast to all other forms of markets he studied. He singled out two unjustified and destructive limits in particular.[130]

The first limit according to Polanyi is to privatize the producing and consuming capabilities of humans as if they were commodities like any other. This kind of commodification dis-embeds the producing and consuming capabilities and activities from the surrounding social relationships in which they take place and re-embeds them in abstract,

---

[129] See, for example, de Sousa Santos, *Democratizing Democracy*.
[130] K. Polanyi, *The Great Transformation: The Political and Economic Origins of Our Time*, Boston: Beacon, 2004. Three unjustifiable limits or fictitious commodities are set out in chapter 6, 'The Self-regulating Market and the Fictitious Commodities: Labour, Land and Money'. I do not discuss money here. For a contemporary restatement of his thesis, see P. Evans, 'Is an Alternative Globalization Possible?', *Politics and Society* 36 (2): 271–305, 2008.

competitive and non-democratic global market relationships. The surrounding social relationships in which producers and consumers live are treated as externalities. As a result, the exercise of human capabilities in these abstract and competitive economic and legal relationships gradually undercuts the webs of interdependent social relationships and social capital on which humans depend for their well-being.

The remedy to this injustice is not only to exchange public reasons in hopes of influencing governments, for this has its limits. For cooperative democrats, the response is to non-cooperate with this undemocratic mode of production and consumption, to withdraw one's producing and consuming capabilities from commodification and to exercise productive and consumptive capabilities 'in common' in democratically run cooperatives and community-based organizations that are re-embedded in social relationships. Such grass roots democracies then produce and distribute the basic public goods that are privatized under the dominant form of democracy: food, shelter, clothing, health care, clean water, security and so on. These social and economic democracies are linked together by global networks of fair trade relationships that are also under the democratic control of the producers and consumers subject to them. This famous response to the injustices of the privatization of labour power gave rise to the tradition of cooperative democracy throughout the world. From Robert Owen, William Thompson and Peter Kropotkin in Europe, to Gandhi, Schumacher and the Swaraj and Swadeshi movements across Asia and Africa, to food sovereignty in Latin America, the turn to local food production, microcredit, democratic cooperatives and indigenous and non-indigenous community-based organizations of diverse scales and types, these are linked together by global networks of fair trade and self-reliance.[131]

These cooperative practices generate social capital and realize social and economic justice directly by bringing the local and global organization of economic activities under the democratic cooperation

---

[131] J. Restakis, *Humanizing the Economy: Co-operatives in the Age of Capital*, Gabriola Island: New Society, 2010.

and mutual aid of all subject to and affected by them. This is the cooperative citizenship response to the global problem of economic inequality and exploitation. It is important to note that despite the global spread of the institutional module of modern representative government and civil citizenship, poverty and hunger persist:

> 963 million people go to bed hungry every night. One billion people live in slums. One woman dies every minute in childbirth. 2.5 billion people have no access to adequate sanitation services and 20,000 children a day die as a result.[132]

Cooperative democrats offer a response to this glocal injustice that is more immediate and perhaps more lasting than representative responses because the victims of hunger, starvation and poverty become the agents of grass roots democracy and economic self-reliance.

Practices of ecological cooperation

The second unjust and destructive limit according to Polanyi is the privatization of land and natural resources as if they are commodities like any other commodity. Yet, he argues, natural resources are not commodities like any other. This global enclosure of natural resources and biological diversity dis-embeds natural resources from the interdependent ecological relationships in which all forms of life live and breathe and have their modes of being; and it re-embeds them in abstract and competitive global market relations of development. The enveloping ecological relationships are then treated as externalities. The result of 'development' under this privatized system is the destruction of the webs of interdependent ecological relationships that make up and sustain the natural and human world, giving rise to the environmental crisis and climate change. This form of privatized development gradually eats away the ecological relationships or ecological capital on which life on earth depends.

---

[132] I. Kahn, *The Unheard Truth: Poverty and Human Rights*, New York: W.W. Norton, 2010.

The response to this injustice by actors in the cooperative tradition is to withdraw their capacities from activities based on the commodification of the environment and to develop a responsible way of relating in and to it. They re-embed natural resources and their use by humans into their place within ecological relationships. Following Albert Schweitzer, they see the webs of ecological relationships as a 'living commonwealth of all forms of life'. They derive the fundamental duties and rights of democracy in the first instance from their membership in the webs of ecological relationships in which democracy takes place and on which all forms of life depend. This natural gift economy is for them the true mother of democracy. The norms of ecological well-being govern economics, not the other way round. They are Gaia citizens.[133]

This revolutionary response to the injustice of privatization of the natural world has given rise to the great cooperative and community-based ecology movements. From Aldo Leopold, Rachel Carson and Vandana Shiva to the Chipko Movement in India and Asia, and on to Japanese fishing cooperatives, the water justice movement, Food Sovereignty and everyday ecological footprint initiatives, millions of Gaia citizens are reclaiming the commons and exercising their capabilities democratically in ethical relationships of stewardship in the commonwealth of all forms of life. These experiments in eco-democracy are responses and alternatives to the idea of development that gives rise to the tragedy of privatization and the environmental crisis.[134]

As we have seen, the two premises that underlie the institutions of modern civil citizenship are that humans are naturally antagonistic and thus that they need an authoritarian master who coercively imposes a structure of law over them as a socializing precondition of peace and democracy. These are the two premises of processes of civilization and modernization.[135] As we can also see, civic citizens reject these

---

[133] Tully, *On Global Citizenship*.
[134] See, for example, Shiva, *Earth Democracy*, and earlier, E. F. Schumacher, *Small Is Beautiful: A Study of Economics as if People Mattered*, Tiptree Essex: Anchor, 1973.
[135] For the rise of these two modern premises, see T. Todorov, *Life in Common: An Essay in General Anthropology*, translated by K. Golsan and L. Golsan, London: University of Nebraska Press, 2000.

premises. They argue that humans are basically self-organizing and self-governing beings. Autopoiesis – self-organization, cooperation and non-violent contestation and dispute resolution – are more basic conditions of human evolution than violent conflict and command relationships.[136] If this were not the case, if Kantian antagonism and Hobbesian war of all against all were primary, the human species would have perished long ago. We overlook this pacific feature of our everyday activities precisely because it is so commonplace and familiar.[137] Humans are not unique in this respect. The hypothesis holds for all forms of life and for the ecological relationships in which they all live. This was put on scientific footing in the 1960s by Sir James Lovelock and given the names Gaia hypothesis and Gaia theory in the 1970s. It is widely endorsed by biological, ecological and climate scientists today.[138] This view that the ground of our being as earthlings is relationships of mutual interdependence and support – of biophilia or love – is also widely endorsed by many of the spiritual traditions of the world. This helps to explain the powerful attraction of cooperative citizenship to people from such different secular and spiritual traditions. Cooperative citizens, one might say, act in and for the love of the world.[139]

Practices of non-violent ethics and agonistics

Cooperative citizenship is the manifestation of a distinctive ethical norm: citizens should 'be the change'. To be citizens, citizens should embody in their everyday activities the change they wish to see in

---

[136] For example, this cooperative working hypothesis was put forward by Johann Herder in response to Kant, Peter Kropotkin in response to T. H. Huxley's interpretation of Darwin and Ashley Montagu during the Cold War. For a comprehensive restatement of it, see E. Thompson, *Mind in Life: Biology, Phenomenology and the Sciences of Mind*, Cambridge, MA: Harvard University Press, 2007.

[137] M. K. Gandhi, *Gandhi: Hind Swaraj and Other Writings*, A. Parel, ed., Cambridge: Cambridge University Press, 2007, 88–99.

[138] J. Lovelock, *Gaia and the Theory of the Living Planet*, London: Gaia Books, 2005. For an introduction to Lovelock's theory in relation to other traditions of thought, see S. Harding, *Animate Earth: Science, Intuition and Gaia*, White River Junction Vermont: Chelsea Green, 2006.

[139] See, for example, Dalai Lama, *Beyond Religion: Ethics for a Whole World*, Toronto: McClelland and Stewart, 2011. Eric Fromm introduced the widely-used term 'biophilia' in 1956.

the larger society and argue for in the public sphere. It is not enough to present arguments in the public sphere in hopes of influencing voters and governments, and on the assumption that it is the role of government to bring about the corresponding change. It is also necessary ethically to practice what one preaches in one's conduct: to perform the duties that bring about the results one advocates. If you argue publicly for democracy, then act democratically in relationships with others, always relating to them as co-agents, never as things to be unilaterally commanded or killed. That is, relationships of power and governance in any sphere should always be open to the ongoing questioning, negotiation and transformation of those who are subject to and affected by them: if you advocate a stewardship relationship to the environment, then care for the environment in your everyday activities; if you argue for democratic and egalitarian relationships between the Global North and South, then enter only into this kind of negotiated and fair trade relationship and refuse unequal and non-democratic free trade relationships; if you argue for just forms of recognition then recognize and relate to others accordingly in your everyday activities and if you argue publicly for world peace, then act peacefully in every breath and step you take and refuse to support violent relationships.[140]

The result of enacting this ethical norm is that cooperative citizens begin to bring the other world of change into being here and now, step by ethical step. This is the meaning of grass roots democracy or democratic-globalization from below. It is the way to bring about radical and lasting change. On this civic view, the great changes in the ethico-political conduct of citizens are what move governments to end slavery, enfranchise women, enact environmental legislation, end unjust wars, adopt effective human rights, support economic self-reliance and self-government and pass climate change legislation.

---

[140] For example, see T. Nhat Hahn, *Peace is Every Step: The Path of Mindfulness in Everyday Life*, New York: Bantam Books, 1992. For a defence of this way of thinking about ethics as ethos, in contrast to deontology and utilitarianism, see P. Curry, *Ecological Ethics: An Introduction*, Cambridge: Polity, 2011.

The ethical norm of being the change is also the expression of the organic relationship between means and ends. For cooperative citizens, means and ends are internally related, like a seed to the full-grown plant, as Gandhi put it.[141] They are pre-figurative or constitutive of ends. Consequently, democratic and peaceful relationships among humans are brought about by democratic and non-violent means. Conversely, the means of violence and command relationships do not bring about peace and democracy. They too are constitutive means. They bring about security dilemmas and the spiral of the command relations necessary for war preparation, arms races and more violence. Democracy and peace, on this civic view, do not grow out of the barrel of a gun or the imperatives of an authoritarian government, but despite and in the interstices of their presence.[142]

These three ethical, existential and social scientific arguments for the primacy of democratic and non-violent ways of being in the world bring us to the fourth example of cooperative citizenship, the democratic, non-violent movements of the last 150 years. Their aim is to replace the power politics of violence and command with the global politics of non-violence and negotiated relationships of civic and civil freedom. Although these three arguments were well-developed and widely supported by the early twentieth century, the peace movements lacked a substitute or equivalent for war and violence as the means to settle disputes among and within states and to bring about regime change.[143] These arguments seemed to lead to non-resistance or pacifism.

The revolutionary solution to this problem came from the life-long practice and writing of Mohandas Gandhi. He developed a whole repertoire of very active non-violent, agonistic arts for confronting and transforming the most powerful empire in the world (the British

---

[141] M. K. Gandhi, *The Essential Writings*, J. Brown, ed., Oxford: Oxford University Press, 2008, p. 58.

[142] H. Arendt, *On Violence*, New York: Harcourt Brace & Company, 1970. The most systematic treatment of violent and non-violent means and ends is J. V. Bondurant, *Conquest of Violence: The Gandhian Philosophy of Conflict*, Princeton: Princeton University Press, 1989.

[143] W. James, 'The Moral Equivalent of War', *McClure's Magazine* 35: 463–68, 1910. For the background to James's challenge to the peace movement, see Kurlansky, *Nonviolence*.

Empire in India) and for constructing non-violent collective self-government (swaraj) and economic self-government (swadeshi).[144] These obstructive and constructive arts of non-violent self-government reach from individual and local self-government to global federalism. The aim of non-violent agonistics of confrontation and negotiation is neither to defeat the enemy and impose an institutional structure over them nor to bring an end to conflict and contestation over justice and recognition. Rather, it is to convert the adversary to non-violent and creative ways of negotiating and overcoming differences, on the one hand, and to transform the relationship between adversaries to a democratic one that is open to this kind of ongoing negotiation, on the other. It is to integrate all the energy expended in violent conflict into a non-violent search for creative solutions that the partners cannot even begin to see until they enter into the inter-subjective space of the critical exchange of words and deeds over the injustice in question between them. The revolutionary arts of non-violent self-government and citizenship are less than 100 years old. Yet, they are now used around the world, tested and improved in practice and theory, and new techniques added to the repertoire. As a result, practitioners and social scientists are beginning to appreciate the transformative power of participatory non-violence and the futility of war in comparison.[145]

Joining hands and working together

I began by mentioning how civil and civic citizens work together to reform the institutions of representative government and global governance from within. I now wish to suggest the ways in which civil and civic reform movements within and the four practices of cooperative citizenship without can join hands, work in mutually supportive ways and change the world. I did not see these connections when I was working on *On Global Citizenship* and *A Dilemma of Global*

---

[144] M. K. Gandhi, *Nonviolent Resistance* (Satyagraha), Boston: Schocken, 1961.
[145] I discuss the techniques of non-violent agonistics and participatory democracy in my responses to the contributors. For a general introduction, see Ackerman and DuVall, *A Force More Powerful*.

Citizenship. The connections between the two traditions of citizenship were the dilemma that remained unanswered. However, when I began to study the civil research of Amartya Sen and the civic and cooperative research of Elinor Ostrom, the connections of complementarity became obvious.[146]

First, by 'being the change', cooperative citizens put into practice the arguments for democracy and justice that deliberative democrats argue for in the public sphere. They realize in their everyday activities the ideals that the democratic reformers share.

Next, cooperative democrats benefit from robust and responsive public spheres and discussion-based governments that are open to and supportive of their concrete experiments in making another world of democracy actual. Reciprocally, to be able to hear and understand the voices of the oppressed, to be able to scrutinize the various responses and counter-responses and to be able to advance comparative and effective recommendations in public reasoning, reform-minded civil democrats need to have the experiential knowledge of living democratically that participation in local cooperative democracies can provide. Democratic knowledge is practical knowledge: acquired in practice, studied in academic research and returned to practice for testing.[147]

Similarly, academic researchers in both traditions can also join hands and work together. They need to find ways to work more closely with citizens engaged in practices of democratic citizenship of both types. This form of research is based on the realization that practices of democratic citizenship are epistemic communities in their own right and from which they can learn. This is a way to overcome the tendency to approach these forms of citizenship with the conceptual frameworks of citizenship that developed along with the dominant institutional structure, and thus to discount, obscure and misrecognize alternative

---

[146] See J. Tully, 'Two Ways of Realizing Justice and Democracy: Linking Amartya Sen and Elinor Ostrom', *Critical Review of Social and Political Philosophy* 16 (2): 220–32, 2012. For a complementary analysis in Latin America, see A. Escobar, 'Latin America at a Crossroads', *Cultural Studies* 24 (1): 1–65, 2010.

[147] For an example, see C. Barlow, *Blue Covenant: The Global Water Crisis and the Coming Battle for the Right to Water*, Toronto: McClelland and Stewart, 2007.

practices of citizenship. Just as researchers can learn from democratic practices of citizenship, cooperative citizens have much to learn from academic research. Thus, relationships between research communities and citizenship communities can also be relationships of reciprocal support and enlightenment.

Last but not least, civil democrats need the mutual aid of cooperative democracy whenever they run up against the limits of public reasoning with an unjust government and whenever a whole people are told that they require authoritarian rule until they are 'ready for democracy'. Rather than turning to self-defeating violent means, reform democrats require the existing social capital and non-violent democratic skills of cooperative democrats to organize protests and widespread non-cooperation to move the unjust government to negotiate or to undermine its authority and to build a more democratic one from the ground up. This is the lesson of Gandhi, Martin Luther King Jr and the non-violent democratic social organizations in the Egyptian revolution in 2011. It may be the lesson of every successful non-violent revolution of and for democracy in our time.[148]

The life of Gandhi provides an example of how these two modes of citizenship can complement each other. As a representative democrat he supported the Congress Party and representative government, and he reasoned and negotiated endlessly in the official public spheres available to him.[149] Yet, he also grounded himself in cooperative citizenship practices of non-violent agonistics and regime change, and in alternative practices of social, economic and ecological self-government. He organized movements of non-cooperation with rule,, organized self-reliant and self-governing ashrams and worked with self-reliant villages. Furthermore, he also engaged in daily spiritual practices of cultivating non-violent relationships to oneself, other living beings and the spiritual realm. Finally, he also saw all these practices as

---

[148] For the example of the non-violent Egyptian revolution of 2011, see J. Tully, 'Middle East Legal and Governmental Pluralism: A View of the Field from the Demos', *Middle East Law and Governance*, 4: 1–39, 2012.

[149] This did not stop Gandhi from writing a thoroughgoing criticism of the British system of representative government in Hind Swaraj.

'experiments in truth' that enabled him to test and revise his modes of civil and civic citizenship as he went along. In concert, these practices realize a comprehensive way of life he called Satyagraha (soul power). It consists in striving to be truthful to the ground of being in everything we say and do. And the ground of our being is relationships of ahimsa (non-violence or love).[150]

---

[150] For an excellent selection of Gandhi's writings on this theme, see T. Merton, ed., *Gandhi on Non-violence*, New York: New Directions, 2007. For an introduction to recent scholarship on Gandhi, see J. M. Brown and A. Parel, eds, *The Cambridge Companion to Gandhi*, Cambridge: Cambridge University Press, 2011.

Part Two

Responses

2

The Authority of Civic Citizens*

Anthony Simon Laden

In the course of his survey of the field of citizenship and globalization, James Tully brings two forms of citizenship into view: 'modern' or 'civil' citizenship and 'diverse' or 'civic' citizenship:

> Whereas modern citizenship focuses on citizenship as a universalizable legal status underpinned by institutions and processes of rationalization that enable and circumscribe the possibility of civil activity (an institutional/ universal orientation), diverse citizenship focuses on the singular civic activities and improvizations of the governed in any practice of government and the diverse ways these are more or less institutionalized or blocked in different contexts (a civic activity/contextual orientation). Citizenship is not a status given by the institutions of the modern constitutional state and international law, but negotiated practices in which one becomes a citizen through participation. (p. 9)[1]

In this chapter, I offer a survey of a field that intertwines with those of citizenship and globalization: the field of 'authority'. This survey adds a further dimension to the contrast between the activities of civic and civil citizens, one that I hope not only enriches our understanding of civic citizenship but helps to see both why it is a distinctive form of *citizenship*, and why those thinking about citizenship have so often failed to see it as a possibility. At the same time thinking about the varieties of

---

* This essay is based heavily on chapter 2 of A. S. Laden, *Reasoning: A Social Picture*, Oxford: Oxford University Press, 2012.

[1] Unless otherwise noted, all parenthetical page references in the text are to Tully's chapter in this volume.

authority in the context of Tully's distinction helps to bring into relief a form of authority that is often overlooked by political philosophers. The crux of my claim will be that whereas civil citizens invoke what I call the authority of command, civic citizens invoke and construct what I call the authority of connection. Since the authority of connection has not been properly recognized as a form of authority at all, it has been hard to understand the activities that Tully describes as central to civic citizenship as really deserving the name of political and thus of citizenship at all.[2] Once we grasp the possibility of the authority of connection, it may be easier for some who are not convinced by Tully's survey to see why civic citizenship is really a distinctive and attractive form of civic action.

I begin with a familiar enough contrast: between dictatorial and democratic authority (Subsection 1). Though familiar, it occludes the distinction I will go on to draw between democratic and civic authority (Subsection 3). Since civic authority turns out to have a number of features that seem to contradict what are often thought to be essential features of any form of authority, drawing that distinction will require some preparatory work in broadening our understanding of the nature of authority (Subsection 2). Before drawing distinctions, I make some prefatory remarks about authority more generally.

Authority, unlike power or force, involves normative rather than casual relationships. Even in the most unambiguous and unilateral authority relationships, what is done in virtue of having authority is not causal. The commander issues a command. The command does not actually cause the commanded person to act a certain way. Nor do laws actually make people behave in accord with them. In each case, what the command or law does is change what might be called the normative environment by altering the significance of certain actions. If you command me to stop and I nevertheless keep going, then this

---

[2] The closest major discussion of what I am calling the authority of connection is in Hannah Arendt's work on power as the result of speaking and acting together. But Arendt sharply distinguishes power from authority in ways that hide from view the possibility of the move I make here.

now counts as disobeying you, and depending on the nature of your right to command me, may also be insubordination or treason. If the legislature passes a 55mph speed limit, then my driving at 65mph becomes speeding.

Nevertheless, though authority concerns normative relationships, the concept of 'authority' is itself descriptive, rather than normative: to say that a given situation is one where someone has authority, or that a relationship grounds a particular form of authority is to describe something, to make a claim which can be true or false, albeit to make a claim that is about something normative. It is not, however, to say that the world or the normative order should be that way. So we can simultaneously deny that some group of people have authority in virtue of the structure of institutions or their fellow citizens' attitudes and behaviours and conclude that their lack of authority is one of the things that renders their society unjust.

Finally, one of the effects of focusing on authority as we investigate political relationships and activities is that our attention is drawn to relatively stable features of our normative orders. That is, authority seems to have a kind of solidity that action and power can appear to lack. This is especially true if, like Tully, one is drawn to Arendt's analysis of politics and power in terms of action. For Arendt, power is something that comes into being in the course of acting together, but there is an open question of whether it endures beyond its creation.[3] In contrast, we tend to think of authority relations as grounded in something more lasting.[4] If we can capture an idea of authority that is closely tied to the kind of Arendtian action that Tully connects to the civic action of citizens, then we may also be in a position to understand how civic action not only brings new worlds into being, but sustains

---

[3] For the classic discussion of the creation of power through acting together, see H. Arendt, *The Human Condition*, Chicago: University of Chicacgo Press, 1958. Patchen Markell argues for a reading of Arendt which makes possible a more lasting creation as a result of action, what he calls 'after-power' (as in 'after-image'); For example, paper given at Political Power and Citizenship Symposium, University of Utrecht, May 2011.

[4] Arendt certainly did. H. Arendt, 'What is Authority?', in *Between Past and Future: Eight Exercises in Political Thought*, Harmondsworth: Penguin, 1977.

them, and thus appreciate why Tully describes the telos of civic action as caretaking (pp. 64–6).

1. Dictatorial versus democratic authority

If we begin an investigation into the authority of citizens with a standard definition of authority as the right to rule, then it appears that our main task is to distinguish the democratic authority of citizens from the undemocratic rule of dictators. Doing so leads us to focus on three features of democratic authority that distinguish it from dictatorial authority: it is norm-governed, reciprocal and revisable. These three features pertain to laws passed by a legitimate democratic government. In order to legitimately legislate, a democratic body must follow a set of procedures and stay within prescribed limits. Not every utterance of the US Congress has the status of federal law. It must be duly passed by the chamber in accordance with its rules, passed by the Senate, signed by the president and not violate any of the strictures of the US Constitution as interpreted by the federal courts. Second, among the norms that govern democratic legislating are norms of reciprocity and revisability. There are two senses in which we might describe a legislative body as democratic: it might be democratically elected or chosen and it might operate according to democratic principles. In either case, however, one of the features that makes it democratic is that it embodies a form of reciprocity: no one has more say than anyone else, and everyone who has a say in determining legislation is also subject to it. In order to combine reciprocity with the capacity to obligate another, thinkers who follow this line of thought analyse democratic governance as involving what we might call mutual hierarchy. A relationship between two people is reciprocal in this sense if each has equivalent command authority over the other one, so that each is both sovereign and subject. Modern democratic legislatures are democratic in both the senses above, and thus are characterized by two sets of mutual hierarchical relationships. Though elected lawmakers command citizens by making the laws that govern them, citizens command their legislators by periodically electing them, and both legislators and other citizens are subject to the laws so passed. Moreover, within a legislative body, each member, in having the right to vote, has a conditional authority to decide for the body, and thus command what it does. The condition of wielding such authority is being in a position to cast the deciding vote on a given matter. In casting the deciding vote, I determine what the legislature does, but I only have that conditional authority if all members of the legislature do, and so it also amounts to a kind of symmetrical command structure.[5]

Finally, though both a commander and a legislature can revise their directives, there is a distinctive sense in which democratically passed laws are in principle open to revision. The difference lies in the source of the impetus to revise. When a dictator issues an order, it is, in general, not open to those being ordered to challenge the order or the dictator's authority to issue the order. In contrast, part of the procedure of democratic lawmaking includes an openness to challenge by the subjects of the law. This does not mean that those subject to a law are free to decide whether or not it has authority over them, but that the authority the law wields must be open to challenge from below.

Notice, however, that allowing authoritative laws to be revisable puts pressure on the requirement that authority structures be stable and thus in a position to rule. Insofar as I am still entertaining possible objections to a decision I am considering, I have not yet made that decision. Decisions bring conversations to an end, it would seem, precisely by closing off the opportunity to raise objections or reasons for revision. In order to square this circle, we can distinguish between two means of remaining open to criticism. On the first, a matter can be closed in a way that allows for reopening. On the second, a matter is never fully closed to begin with. If we want to hold on to the model of stable, decisive laws and institutions of government, and yet insist that democratic authority is always subject to challenge, then it appears that we must adopt the

---

[5] Tully discusses this mutual command structure of modern democracy at 12–15 and 41–2.

first of these means. Thus, we are led to a view of democratic citizenship and lawmaking where the deliberations of a democratic legislature lead to a final decision and a closure of the matter, but, in doing so, they leave open the possibility of revisiting the question should objections or further evidence be brought forward.

But now note that in distinguishing between democratic and dictatorial authority, we have vested the particular features of democracy in the institutions of law and representative government, and thus tied the special features of democracy to what Tully describes as the civil conception of citizenship (pp. 11–19). This suggests that if we want to be able to grasp the activities of civic citizens as not only democratic but also political in the sense of constructing and invoking forms of authority, we need to broaden our understanding of authority, so that we can describe democratic authority which is norm-governed, reciprocal and revisable in a way that does not yield the central features of civil citizenship.

2. In authority's family

In distinguishing the authority of democratic legislatures from the authority of dictators, we have already broadened our conception of authority to admit of certain variations. But we can loosen things up even further. Sometimes authorities do not command or legislate or otherwise direct what we do and think, but rather stand in judgement over it. The idea of authority as the right to pass judgement is implicit in the idea of the *authority* of law or command. If a law has authority over me, then I am accountable or answerable or responsible to it. It does not so much direct my action as stand in judgement over it.[6] So we can analyse the right to rule or legislate as the right to appoint and guide a judge on whom is conferred the right to pass judgement.

---

[6] Robert Brandom talks of authority this way in R. B. Brandom, *Reason in Philosophy: Animating Ideas*, Cambridge: Harvard University Press, 2009.

Thinking of authority as the right to pass judgement also clarifies a further kind of authority, that of the expert. The expert's claim to authority can also be understood as a right to pass judgement over her field of expertise. Being an expert does not give someone the right to rule or legislate the behaviour or thoughts of others, and while we may want to consult experts and follow their guidance, their authority ultimately consists in their capacity to determine whether what we do is correct by passing judgement on it.

We can also broaden our sense of what authority can do by recognizing that the authority to command or obligate brings with it the authority to issue permissions, insofar as permission involves not being obligated not to do whatever one has permission to do. Thus, authoritative bodies cannot only direct and command, but license and entitle. And these capacities can flow from the right to pass judgement as well. The expert can rule authoritatively on whether a judgement made within her domain is correct, but she can also accept it as not incorrect and thus as permitted.

There are, I think, a number of other familiar uses of authority that would further widen its conceptual boundaries (think about the moral authority of a certain kind of moral exemplar or leader), but rather than survey these, I want to take the material so far gathered and come at it from a somewhat different angle. Thinking about authority in the context of describing various activities can lead us in two different, though related, directions. First, we can attend to the credentials of the person or principle or agency claiming authority. The credential of one's authority is the condition for being invested with the authority, not the source or authoritative body that hands out the credential. So, for instance, the source of a legislature's authority may be a Constitution and behind that 'we the people', but the credential of any sitting legislature is its having been duly elected in accord with the procedures laid out in a constitution. In asking for the credentials that yield a certain form of authority, then, we are asking 'Who must one be to do that? On the basis of what authority can we so act?' And of course, the answer will depend on what 'that' is.

So, second, we can attend to the activities our authority authorizes: passing laws in the case of a legislature, rendering judgement in the case of a judge. As I suggested above, having authority involves the capacity to change the normative environment. We can thus call this aspect of authority, 'normative capacity'. So, the police officer's authority to arrest those suspected of crimes is not merely a permission or ability to interrupt their activities, put them in handcuffs or transport them to a court or a jail. It involves changing their status by putting them under arrest. To understand the police officer's authority in this sense, then, we have to know what this normative capacity amounts to, which may require knowing what the relation of arrest to punishment is, what counts as resisting arrest and what sort of record is made of arrests and how that affects one's civil and social status.

Part of the structure of authority, then, is a pairing of credential and normative capacity, along perhaps with some connection between the two, some explanation of why this credential should entitle its bearer to wield this normative capacity. Passing judgement, ruling, commanding, licensing, entitling and legislating are all kinds of normative capacity, and depending on their extent and scope, can be acquired through a variety of credentials. But now note that the list of normative capacities listed above is incomplete, and that there are a number of activities we engage in that involve a normative capacity which we have in virtue of some credentials that are not well captured by the canonical examples of authority canvassed above. Consider, for instance, the following list of activities that at least some people engage in legitimately: arresting someone, performing a legal marriage ceremony, voting in a municipal election, voting in Congress, conferring a degree, giving a grade on a term paper, giving you a reason to get off of my foot, assuring you that a mathematical proof is correct, showing you that a mathematical proof is correct, offering an idea in a brainstorming session, offering an idea in a joint deliberation, inviting you to join an organization of which I am a member, inviting you to dinner, inviting you to my wedding, proposing marriage, licensing you to attribute a belief to me or saying something to you by way of continuing or initiating a conversation. What I think unifies this disparate list is that in each case, one requires some form of credential to legitimately perform the action, and as a result of the action, some normative environment is changed. To see that some credential is required, note that in all cases, there are people who would be so ill-positioned to perform each action that we would say that they were doing so illegitimately. Thus, while anyone can, technically speaking, invite me to dinner, there are a fairly limited number of people who could appropriately do so. So, even if the credential here is vague and its boundaries less well-defined than those necessary to pass a law or arrest someone, there are some credentials nevertheless. Similarly, while it is clear how passing a law changes the normative environment, there is also an important way that a normative environment changes as a result of the cases that involve inviting or offering. In these cases, once a legitimate offer or invitation has been made, though one may be free to turn it down, one has nevertheless been called on to respond, and, under normal circumstances, one's failure to respond counts as a snub or a denial of the invitation's legitimacy.

Even if these cases share this basic structure, it would be an important mistake to try to assimilate the cases of inviting and offering and proposing to those of ruling and directing and licensing. And because these are fundamentally different kinds of normative capacity, we should not be surprised if the credentials they require are also fundamentally different. What this suggests, then, is that there is a family of such activities. It is, I think, a purely terminological matter whether we want to call all members of this family forms of authority and thus broaden our concept of authority, or keep the concept of authority narrow and admit that it has an interesting set of cousins.

Broadening our vision of the conceptual terrain inhabited by 'authority' has important effects when we return to the question of the authority of citizens. As we saw above, the standard moves involved in distinguishing democratic from dictatorial authority focuses our attention on legislation and thus on the credentials citizens must have as legislators. In doing so, however, we lose sight of precisely the kind of activities that are characteristic of civic citizens, perhaps also losing sight of the possibility that such action is also invested with authority and thus genuinely political. So opening up the concept of authority makes room for thinking about the authority of civic citizens.

Moreover, if we start with an assumption that we know what it is that citizens do as citizens, then the questions that remain about political authority will be about what grounds citizens' right to legislate to one another, and thus we will be focused on the search for adequate credentials for this capacity. So conceived, the problem looks ontological or at least theoretical: working out the conditions under which a certain kind of person has a certain property.

But if we want to take seriously the idea that citizenship is, fundamentally, an activity, then framing the problem this way leads us to grasp the wrong end of the stick, and ask the wrong question. Rather, as Tully argues, for civic citizens, citizenship is the name we give to our interactions when we claim they have a certain kind of structure, and in doing so, we also claim that what emerges from that interaction has a certain kind of authority insofar as it shapes our normative environment (p. 54). This means that the question we need to ask is not, 'how could our collective decisions have the legislative authority of commands or the right to pass judgement on us?' but 'how could our civic activities have the authority that would lead us to call them, and acknowledge them as, political?' Once we broaden the conceptual terrain of authority, it becomes a more open question of what makes an activity political, authoritative; and so merely calling our activity political is not doing much work, since it does not specify the nature of the normative capacity that we claim our actions have. And so, instead of the theoretical question about proper institutional conditions, we are left with a practical question about what sorts of capacities we need.

The answer to this question turns not on the nature of authority or action, but on what it is we want and need to do, what problems we face that might be solved through working and living together, by civic action. Rather than focusing on our credentials as citizens, understanding the authority involved in civic action requires a focus on the capacities we need to engage in civic action as the picture of civic citizenship that Tully sketches conceives of it. Doing so requires, however, that we have on hand a broader range of conceptions of authority so that we do not need to shoehorn the activity of civic citizens into the framework provided by the model of authority tied to civil citizenship. In the rest of the paper, I offer a characterization of a type of authority that captures some of the central features that Tully ties to civic citizenship, and show why it belongs within authority's family. The authority I bring into view is that displayed when the normative capacity in question does not involve commanding or directing, but inviting and calling for a response. Since invitations either rest on or try to bring into being connections between people, I call this type of authority the authority of connection. To bring out its distinctive features, I contrast it with the more familiar authority of command (whether dictatorial or democratic) along five axes, and show how it illuminates civic activity.

3. Authority of command versus authority of connection: Five differences

Normative capacity: Unilateral versus mutual

The first and clearest difference involves, as I suggested above, the particular normative capacity that each involves. The authority of command gives me the right to issue commands (including in the form of granting permissions and licenses). This right is a capacity to determine unilaterally some piece of the normative environment of those I command. This has two related dimensions: my commands, in general, alter the normative environments of my subordinates independently of what they do or think or say. It may be, of course, that my right to command depends on their prior agreement to place themselves under my command, but once my authority is established, I do not need further contributions from those I command to effectively shape their normative environment. Second, the unilateral character of the capacity requires a credential that rests on a similarly asymmetrical relationship: the commander's capacity to effectively shape his subordinate's normative environment does not entail and may even preclude that his subordinate have a similar capacity vis-à-vis the commander. As we will see below, there are cases where each of us is the other's commander, but in this case, there are two separate asymmetrical relationships in place, not one reciprocal one.

When we converse with each other on the basis of our connections, on the other hand, our capacity is a capacity to try to shape a normative environment we share, that we inhabit together. There are two features of this description that bear further discussion. First, the capacity here is essentially mutual: we are both entitled to try to shape each other's normative environment in part because we are each shaping a normative environment we share. Moreover, my credential to shape our normative environment in these cases (membership in a 'we' of which we are both a part) necessarily applies to you as well. So, in trying to shape that environment, I also accept that you can as well. Thus, the authority of connection is essentially reciprocal. It is also in evidence in the 'civicizing' practices of the civic citizen, whose demands to negotiate governance relations are 'demands to "civicize" the relationship: to bring it under the shared negotiation and authority of the partners subject to it' (p. 49).

Second, the capacity in question here is a capacity to try something, and this brings out another way that the capacity is mutual. I have the capacity to call forth some response from you but no particular response, so that while my speaking changes your normative environment in one sense, it only changes our normative environment if you respond to what I say by accepting it. That means that the capacity I have in virtue of the authority of connection is, in part, answerable to you. Your response to what I say plays a role in determining what I have managed to do. In many accounts of authority, the fact that I am answerable or accountable or responsible to you amounts to saying that you have authority over me. And so the fact that my normative capacity here is both a capacity of mine and answerable to you will mean that the authority of connection is not something that can be wielded or established unilaterally or asymmetrically. In claiming the normative capacity at issue here, it turns out that I acknowledge yours as well. This helps to explain and support the fundamental commitment to non-violence in the civic tradition. Civic citizens, Tully claims

> approach others unarmed and with the embodied attitude and comportment of openness and trustworthiness. This takes the phenomenological form of the extended open hand, which says 'I trust you and come in peace, please reciprocate' in almost all cultures, in opposition to the closed fist. Only this vulnerable yet courageous and disarming comportment of groundless trust can initiate the reciprocal, pre-linguistic response and begin to weave a negotiated relationship of grounded mutual trust one strand at a time, civicizing the partners as they interact, just as one does across differences in one's own neighbourhood. (p. 67)

Although it is easiest to picture relations structured by the authority of connection that are already established and perhaps supported and constrained by existing institutional structures, nothing in the capacities involved in the authority of connection requires such credentialing. We can also imagine relationships that are neither formalized nor fixed, where this standing is not assured ahead of time. If we are in the process of becoming friends, for instance, then not only may it be uncertain whether you will agree to my suggestions and invitations, but it may also not be a determined matter whether in even trying to make them I am presuming a level of relationship that does not yet exist. In such a case, my presumption as well as my suggestion will be answerable to you and you can legitimately deny both what I say and my right to say it. This possibility then allows that the civic actions of civic citizens might also be constructive and self-constructed: 'agents (individual or collective) *become* civic citizens only in virtue of actual participation in civic activities' (p. 37).[7]

---

[7] Note here also the connection to Arendt's contention that acting together brings new things into being. For a discussion of Arendt's conception of rule that shares a lot with Tully's conception of civic citizenship and the authority of connection, see P. Markell, 'The Rule of the People: Arendt, Archê, and Democracy', *American Political Science Review* 100 (1): 1–14, 2006.

Relationship: Hierarchical versus reciprocal

The second difference involves the nature of the relationship on which our authority rests. To command another, I need to stand in a hierarchical relation to him, to be in a superior position that gives me the right to command. This is true even if we accept that the only thing that can legitimately grant the right to command is the acknowledgement of the one commanded. For in such a case, even though there is no prior hierarchy, the acknowledgement establishes one. But to speak for another from the authority of connection does not require hierarchy; only our standing in a relationship that creates an 'us' that can be spoken for, about this, in this way.

The reciprocity required to construct the authority of connection is not the mutual hierarchy characteristic of democratic legislatures and voting. As I suggested above, two people stand in a relationship of mutual hierarchy if each stands to the other in a hierarchical relationship where she commands the other. The possibility that I can command you while at the same time you can command me is made possible by considering each member of such a relationship under at least two aspects: as both sovereign and subject, to use Rousseau's terms.[8] Contrast this with a relation of reciprocal connection. Our reciprocal connection consists in our capacity to respond to one another and to call for such responses. In a reciprocal relationship, what we suggest to or urge on each other is fully answerable to that other person's uptake or rejection of it. In virtue of such a relationship, either party can demand to be given a hearing, but cannot issue a command. Calling for a response goes beyond calling for a reaction. It requires that one heeds that response, which in turn requires that the other's response itself calls for a response. Thus in calling for a response from someone, I must simultaneously acknowledge their capacity to call for a response from me. Moreover, in acknowledging that, I do not

---

[8]   J. J. Rousseau, 'The Social Contract', in V. Gourevitch, ed., *Rousseau: The Social Contract and Other Later Political Writings*, Cambridge: Cambridge University Press, 1997.

acknowledge an additional relationship in which we stand, but merely the features of this one.[9]

One of the key differences between civil and civic citizens is the relationship they stand in to one another. Civic citizens develop and maintain relations of reciprocal connection, whereas civil citizens relate on terms of mutual command (see pp. 58–64). As civic citizens, we thus partake of our reciprocal relationship when we deliberate and act politically and reasonably, rather than when we vote. Reasonable deliberation requires that each participant be properly responsive to the rejection of his reasons by his fellow deliberators.[10] Such deliberation does not work by each party issuing conditional commands and waiting to see if the commands of others serve to satisfy the conditions. Deliberation on its own does not yield laws or decisions. So when I offer reasons in the course of deliberation, I am not commanding anyone or (even conditionally) determining the law. That would be to regard deliberation on the model of voting. Rather, I invite my fellow citizens to accept what I say and must be responsive to their rejection of my proposals. Authority in such a relationship is only eventually constructed when all come to agreement, rather than when a set of conditions on conditional commands are met.

The point of distinguishing relationships of mutual hierarchy from those characterized by reciprocal connection is to make clear that the authority of connection requires more than mere symmetry in our relationships, and that relationships can be symmetrical while still being hierarchical. Although symmetrical relationships of command are not hierarchical in a straightforward way, they must, nevertheless, rely on an existing hierarchical structure, a structure that is not

---

[9] Relations of reciprocal connection thus share fundamental features with the relations of reciprocal recognition that are central to Hegel's account of normativity, and the work of contemporary Hegelians. For discussions of recognition, see Brandom, *Reasons in Philosophy*, chapter 2; A. Honneth, *The Struggle for Recognition*, J. Anderson, trans., Cambridge, MA: MIT Press, 1996; R. Pippin, *Hegel's Practical Philosophy: Rational Agency as Ethical Life*, Cambridge: Cambridge University Press, 2008.

[10] I discuss reasonable deliberation and other activities of reciprocal and responsive interaction in more detail in Laden, *Reasoning*.

necessary to generate the authority of connection. This feature makes civic citizenship truly democratic from the ground up (pp. 53–4).

Credentials: Backward-looking versus forward-looking[11]

From these first two differences follow two further ones. The third difference involves the nature of the credentials needed for each kind of authority. In the case of the authority of command, credentials must be 'backward-looking' in the sense that whatever it is that establishes them must be prior to the exercise of the capacity they authorize: do we already stand in a relationship that gives me the authority, the superior position, to command you? One reason the source of my authority to command must be backward-looking is that only then can the question of my authority remain properly normative, by being independent of its being effective. If I try to establish my authority to command by commanding you and take my authority to have commanded you to depend on my success, then my command has no normative effect. Your failure to follow my command in this case would not count as disobedience, but rather would show that I lacked the capacity to command you in the first place. The backward-looking nature of democratic credentials leads civil citizens to refer to laws and other stable political institutions of government as warrant for their political activity, which then is confined to the space that these institutions create (pp. 11–12). It also explains why law and other institutions of the modern state are seen as the conditions of civil status: they establish the credentials of civil citizens to exercise their rights.

In the case of the authority of connection, however, things are different and more complicated. When I attempt to alter our normative environment by issuing an invitation, I rely on my understanding of the relationship between us. But whether or not our relationship is such as to support my capacity to alter it, or alter it in this particular way,

---

[11] I have drawn the contrast between backward-looking and forward-looking conceptions with regard to democratic legitimacy in A. S. Laden, 'Democratic Legitimacy and the 2000 Election', *Law and Philosophy* 21: 197–220, 2002.

may depend not merely on my understanding of our relationship or on firmly established, verifiable facts, but also on your understanding of our relationship and thus your response. Furthermore, the status and content of my authority may depend not only on whether I have the right to try to alter your normative environment, but whether my attempt actually succeeds. Even if there are definite facts that establish our positions vis-à-vis one another in a way that grounds my right to call for a response, these facts may very well not fully determine whether I should succeed in eliciting the response I hope for. Thus, the question of whether I have changed our normative environment as I intended may not be settled until after I have spoken because it may depend on whether you acknowledge what I say as what you would say as well.[12] And so my normative capacity can at times remain indeterminate until you either acknowledge or refuse what I said. But that means that in an important sense, my authority to speak this way, at least here and now, need not be something that is established ahead of time, but can be constituted, as it were, after the fact.[13] Thus, it must at least be possible for the credentials that ground the authority of connection to be forward-looking.

The distinction between the capacity to call for a response and the capacity to elicit the response I wish and thus the capacity to change our normative environment in this way can help make sense of some of the particularly civic features of citizenship by helping us disentangle the

[12] And given that intentions are not always fully formed prior to what we say and do but often only become fully formed as we act, it may be the case that what I intended to do will depend on what happens after I speak. On this general point about intentions, see Pippin, *Hegel's Practical Philosophy*; T. Brewer, *The Retrieval of Ethics*, Oxford: Oxford University Press, 2009. Thanks to David Owen for pointing out its relevance here.

[13] More needs to be said about this point to make it fully precise and convincing. By making the establishment of the authority of connection forward-looking I do not mean to rule out the possibility that some failures to acknowledge connection are wrong, inappropriate or unreasonable. But, even in such cases, it will be the case that in dismissing the connection, one breaks or alters it. Also, in some cases, invocations of connection will also rest on fixed norms or status, such as legal status that is established ahead of time. Nevertheless, there is plenty of room between allowing another to speak and taking seriously what they say. I can invoke the authority of command of the law to make you let me speak, but I cannot so force you to take what I say seriously. There I am dependent on your attitude towards me and what I say.

legal and civic or social features of our relationship as citizens. Thus, it is in virtue of our legal relation as citizens, a relation that is established ahead of time, that we have the credentials and thus the right to speak to one another on political matters, whether through deliberating or voting. But this legal status may not on its own establish a social and political relationship wherein one can fully reciprocally speak for and be spoken for by one's fellow citizens. Groups that are legally granted citizenship but are stigmatized or marginalized in various ways will often have the legal right to speak and be heard, but not the social authority to be heeded as representative of the whole. Whatever such citizens say will be taken as articulating their particular group interests or viewpoint, and not as possibly speaking for other citizens outside their group. They will be heard, for instance, as raising 'women's issues' or 'black issues' or 'gay issues' rather than as raising questions of equality, fairness or justice, or of social and economic organization more generally. In those cases, though they may invoke the commanding authority of the law to be able to give voice to their positions, their fellow citizens prevent them from also having the authority of connection. This, then, points to one of the ways that modern democratic states can broaden civil citizenship without thereby broadening civic citizenship (Tully makes a similar point at p. 59).

Loci of authority: Internal versus distributed

The fourth difference between the authority of command and the authority of connection concerns where authority resides. I label it by saying that whereas the authority of command is lodged in the hands of the commander, the authority of connection rests in part in the hands of the listener. This point is somewhat tricky but vitally important if we are to understand why the authority of connection is fundamentally different from the authority of command, and how it might thus alter our picture of citizenship.

Imagine that when the sergeant orders one of her soldiers to scout on ahead, the soldier, or someone watching the scene, questions the sergeant's authority. What kinds of facts might establish that the sergeant had the authority to issue this order? We would first need to look to facts about the sergeant: that she is in fact the commanding officer, that she has a right to order her soldiers in this way in these circumstances. This might, admittedly, require looking to the general context that places the sergeant in the position of authority: the military code, the authority of whoever placed her in command and so forth. And it might also require answering questions about the soldier's standing: that he is under the sergeant's command, that there are no extenuating circumstances that block such command and so forth. Nevertheless, what we are trying to ascertain in establishing the sergeant's authority to command is that here and now, giving this order, the final decision of what order to give and whether or not, in speaking, to give an order, are hers to make. It is in this sense that the authority lies, as it were, in her hands. Again, this feature of the authority of command is a result of the unilateral nature of the normative capacity it involves. Once I am entitled to issue commands, then whether or not my words count as commands depends entirely on me.

Now take the case where I make a suggestion to you about how to spend the afternoon, and rather than acknowledging my suggestion by either endorsing it or responding to it, you question my authority to make it. There are at least two ways you might issue such a challenge. First, you might question whether we stand in the kind of relationship that would entitle me to make suggestions to you on this matter. If a stranger joined our discussion about where to have dinner we would question his authority thus. In this case, a response would have the same structure as the one above: I would need to point to our relationship (or lack thereof) and thus to where each of us stands vis-à-vis the other. Even here, however, there is another possibility. Not all of the relationships that ground the authority of connection are firmly and publicly established ahead of time. So there is the possibility that in making my suggestion I am also at the same time inviting you to understand our relationship in a new or not yet fully established manner. Whether I have the authority is not yet settled, but open to you to accept or reject.

Second, you can also challenge the authority of what I say by challenging not my right to make suggestions about this to you but rather what I have suggested. Here you challenge, as it were, not the existence of our 'we' but its intimacy, its scope. In political contexts, this might happen when you reject my proposal on the grounds that it is not based in what John Rawls calls 'public reason', but instead on the basis of religious beliefs that we do not share.[14] In doing so, you accept that our status as fellow citizens entitles us to try to speak politically for one another. But you object to my proposal because it presumes that we form a kind of community of believers that we do not form. By denying that we form a 'we' in the way I imply, you reject my capacity to shape this part of our normative environment. It is not just that you disagree with the content of what I say but rather that you reject the extent of the authority I am presuming in saying it here. To see this, note that you might also so object to a fellow citizen who makes a non-public reason argument you think is sound for a position you agree with because it rests on a presumption about the scope of the 'we' we form as citizens. The objection, then, is not to the proposal itself, or even to the argument for it, but to my authority to make this argument in this context. These are the sorts of challenges that civic citizens raise to established orders of legal and political governance in the course of their political activities, contesting the authority of an institution or agent to determine the conditions of their subjection (pp. 68–73).

Faced with these sorts of challenges to my authority, what sort of facts would determine whether our relationship supported the authority I have implicitly claimed? Unlike in the case of commanding, they are not primarily about me. If my attempt to alter the normative environment rests on the authority of connection, then it rests on there being a 'we' whose environment can be changed in this way. What does there being such a 'we' depend on? Among other things,

---

[14] See J. Rawls, *Political Liberalism*, New York: Columbia University Press, 1996, especially pp. 212–54; J. Rawls, 'The Idea of Public Reason Revisited', in S. Freeman, ed., *Collected Papers*, Cambridge, MA: Harvard University Press, 1999, pp. 573–615.

it depends on us, on our acknowledgement of such a unit. In relying on what I take to be our connection, I have acknowledged it, and so what is left to determine is whether you, too, will acknowledge it. Thus, in order to establish my authority in this case, we need to determine something about you, not me. It is in this sense, then, that the authority of connection rests not entirely in the hands of the one speaking, but also in the hands of the one being spoken for: at the moment when I make my suggestion of how we should spend the afternoon, the final decision of whether or not I have the capacity, here and now, to alter our normative environment with this suggestion is no longer mine to make but yours to acknowledge or refuse or even ignore. This means that particular instances of the authority of connection are not wielded like a sword, but jointly constructed like a bridge. This is why the practices of contestation of civic citizens are misunderstood if they are interpreted merely as rebellion. They are, rather, a demand to understand the very relationship of authority differently (pp. 36–7, 68–73).

Now, suggesting that there is a form of authority whose status can be determined after its invocation by those over whom it is invoked will and should raise eyebrows. How, it will be asked, could such a form of authority be normative at all and thus how could it be a genuine form of authority? If every failure to acknowledge an attempt to speak for another, or to respond to a call for response dissolves the basis of that authority, then it will be impossible to rebel against such authority, which is to say that it will not be normative at all. Note that something like this thought stands behind at least one argument for dismissing the civic activities that Tully describes as not really political at all, but merely social or voluntary or otherwise lacking in authority (pp. 53–8).[15]

To respond to this concern, note that the authority of connection differs from the authority of command in terms of the options it leaves

---

[15] For a complementary point made in the course of a discussion of a debate between Hannah Arendt and Ralph Ellison about the borders between the social and political, see D. Allen, 'Law's Necessary Forcefulness', in A. S. Laden and D. Owen, eds, *Multiculturalism and Political Theory*, Cambridge: Cambridge University Press, 2007, pp. 315–49.

open to the recipient of the authoritative statement. Refusing my suggestions does not involve rebellion but a failure of acknowledgement, a kind of dismissal. Furthermore, I can reject what you say either by denying there is any kind of an 'us' whose normative environment you have the capacity to alter or by merely denying that what you have said does alter that environment. In the latter case, I reject your suggestion but accept our connection. I do not undermine your authority but (re)constitute it, by acknowledging that you have the capacity to change our normative environment, even though you have failed this time to exercise it effectively. Put differently, in responding to you, I answer your call and thus acknowledge its authority, while at the same time denying you the capacity to elicit the particular response you were hoping for. The civic process Tully describes as 'civicization' begins, in effect, with the issuance of such a call. We become civic citizens together by making and responding to such calls: 'The governed *become* "good citizens" only by exercising their civic freedom of entering into these kinds of negotiation in all their complex phases . . .: of listening to the other sides and for silenced voices, of responding in turn, negotiating in good faith and being bound by the results, experimenting with the amended or transformed relationship and so on. Reciprocally, governors become good governors only by doing the same: listening to what the citizens have to say, responding and being held accountable by them' (50).

Finally, to say that the authority of connection has forward-looking credentials and a distributed location does not imply that its invocation is not norm-governed. That is, even if you can undermine my authority through your response or lack of it, not everything you do to ignore me will have that effect. Just as not every utterance in the imperative mood is an authoritative command, not every failure to respond is an authoritative denial of authority. These considerations mean, then, that even if civic action is not officially authorized by extant legal and political institutions, it can construct a form of authority that would make it genuinely political.

What authority does: Ending versus continuing conversations

The fifth difference between the authority of command and the authority of connection has to do not with what they are but with what they do. Whereas the authority of command serves to end our conversations, the authority of connection leaves room for them to keep going. That commanding another serves to end a conversation should be clear enough. After all, the only appropriate response to a legitimate command is to carry it out, perhaps adding in a 'yes, sir' by way of acknowledgement that the command has been heard and will be obeyed. Commanding is not a way of initiating or continuing a conversation but of bringing about action. What is perhaps less obvious but no less important is that the issuing of commands cannot serve to prolong a conversation. Questioning a command itself, and not merely how to implement it, is questioning its authority and thus a form of rebellion. Of course, rebellion need not be violent, and it can be carried out with words, so that in rebelling against an authoritative command I can engage the commander in a conversation. But even when I do this, I am engaging the commander in a *different* conversation than the one that issued the command, a conversation about the extent of his authority, not about the considerations that went into the decision to issue the order in the first place.[16] The command has not prolonged the initial conversation but rather set the stage for a new one.

When I make a proposal or offer an invitation with the authority of connection, however, things are rather different. First of all, the capacity I exercise is a call for a response, and as we have seen, calling for a response as opposed to a mere reaction is to call for something

---

[16] That is not to deny that among the things I might raise in the conversation that follows my refusal to obey are criticisms of the commander's decision and questions about what considerations went into that decision. But the point of raising these at this point in the story is not to figure out what the commander should have commanded, but to show that his incompetence unfits him for his authority, at least in this instance. In that sense, they form, as I say above, part of a new conversation about the extent of the commander's authority.

that requires a response in turn. Moreover, since among the things your response may do is confirm or challenge or reconfigure my authority, there is ample opportunity for my invocation of authority to open space for our conversation to continue in any number of new ways. Calling for a response in this sense is not merely initiating a final sequence of words in the way that issuing an order that calls for a 'yes, sir' is.[17]

Moreover, it turns out that I cannot bring conversations to a close by invoking the authority of connection. This is obvious in the cases where I aim to alter our normative environment by making suggestions or offering criticisms as in the examples with which I began. In response to a suggestion whose authority you recognize, you need to make some sort of response, even if only to accept it. If I say, 'I think we should clean up the house this afternoon because it's a mess,' you can't just go and get the vacuum cleaner without somehow signalling your agreement. Since against a wide background of shared understandings, one way to accept a proposal is to begin wordlessly begin to act on it, you may be able to signal your agreement by getting the vacuum cleaner. But there is nevertheless an important difference between assenting to a proposal and obeying an order, and I mistreat your suggestion if I treat it as calling for obedience and not assent. We can make this clear by making explicit what will, in the normal course of things, often go unsaid: in response to a suggestion made and heard as a suggestion, you need to at least express agreement and issue a judgement: 'Yeah, you're right. Why don't I go get the vacuum cleaner while you start picking up the dirty clothes.'

But, even in the case where I try to decide for us on the basis of our connection, rather than just try to speak for us, there is an important sense in which this does not end our conversation so much as put it on hold. Because my authority in trying to decide for us in this case is established in part by being answerable to your acknowledgement of it, you must be free to withdraw that acknowledgement in the future. So

---

[17] The connection of authority and beginning as it figures in Hannah Arendt's work is the focus of Markell, *Rule of the People*.

my authority, even if accepted for the moment, is not thereby established once and for all. There is still room for it to be challenged or denied, and so the conversation in which I attempted to speak authoritatively is not closed, even if we have stopped talking for now. If I am authorized to make suggestions, but not to command you, I overstep that authority if I try to speak for you in a way that leaves no room for you to criticize what I say. I also overstep my authority if I try to close off room for later criticism for good.

Speaking in a manner that ends our conversation would require declaring that the time for objections and criticisms is over, and thus fail to give others a chance to express their reservations or veto. But that would be to undermine the reciprocal nature of our relationship that establishes and maintains the connection that credentialed my initial capacity to affect our normative environment. A definitive ending of the conversation, then, whether in the form of a command that no more be said, or, in an unwillingness to hear any objections as more than 'merely words' does not protect and establish once and for all my authority. Rather, it undermines that authority.

There are at least two ways that a conversation may stop and begin again. In the first, the conversation is in a kind of lull. Neither party has anything to say, but the conversation has not come to a stop, even if it is not continued here and now. If, during the current lull, one of the participants was called away or engaged on another topic (even by the same people), we would say that the first conversation had been interrupted, and were one of us to try to pick up the original thread later on, we might say that we were hoping to continue our earlier conversation. All this suggests that the conversation has not come to an end but was still open.

Contrast this with a case where a conversation comes to an end, but nothing in the way it ends prevents one of the participants from reopening it later. In such a case, we stop talking not because we have nothing more to say here and now, but because we have reached a kind of accord or agreement. If another person or topic were to be introduced at this point, it would not count as an interruption. In fact, if a person intruded and asked if it was alright to join us or take one of us away, we might reply that it was fine, as 'we were finished talking'. Such a conversation may be something we can revisit or reopen later. I may change my mind about its topic or come to have new information. This may prompt me to suggest that we return to the topic, rather than continue discussing it. This suggests that the conversation had indeed come to an end, and that we would now be reopening it.

As with the discussion of symmetrical relationships above, the foregoing point helps to clarify the difference between civil and civic democratic activity. When civil citizens have voted, then, barring irregularities, the decision has been made and the activity of deciding by voting is finished; their work as citizens is, for the moment, done. This need not preclude their returning to the question later on and reopening their consideration of it, but barring that, the thing is at an end. In the case of deliberation among civic citizens, however, though we may run out of things to say on a given topic, we cannot thereby declare the matter closed, only leave off discussing it (perhaps to now call a vote). In fact, if we are to maintain our authority as civic citizens, then we must continue to engage with one another, whether on this topic or another one. Because the work of civic citizens involves not only deploying and navigating existing institutional structures but constructing our political authority together and, more importantly, sustaining that authority over time, the work of civic citizens is never done (see p. 36 of Tully's essay for a similar point).

4. Conclusion

At the beginning of this chapter, I suggested that democratic authority has to be norm-governed, reciprocal and revisable, and I laid out how these features figure in the democratic activity of civil citizens, and how a focus on these features pushes our conception of citizenship into the civil frame. Now, however, we are in a position to appreciate from another perspective, the democratic possibility of civic citizenship that

Tully's essay holds out to us. Civic citizens construct the authority of connection. This means that what their activity constructs are outcomes that are revisable in the sense of always ongoing and social. Civic citizens do not command one another, but hold open what they say to criticism and regard their civic activities as calls for the response of others. Calling for a response from others is, as we also saw, an activity that must simultaneously accept their right to call for our response, whether directly when they criticize what we say, or indirectly, when they make claims that they hold open to criticism. This makes civic activity reciprocal in a different way than the mutual commanding of civil action. Finally, because the authority of connection that civic activity constructs is established in a forward-looking manner, the sense in which politics is a norm-governed activity must also shift. The model of democratic legislation imagines a set of authoritative norms that are established ahead of time, perhaps theoretically grounded, and which are not, at least in the normal course of legislation, up for grabs through the activity itself. This means that the activity of working out or establishing the norms is potentially of a different sort than the activity that the norms define. Constitution-writing and legislating are different activities, and their standards of excellence and the skills they require are also different. But if we are to picture political activity as establishing its authority in a forward-looking manner, then this also involves imagining that it establishes and authorizes the very norms that govern its activity. This means that the process of drawing out these civic norms and eliciting their authority is not different from the process of civic engagement itself, and thus that it cannot be done in a manner that is final, monological or decisive. Of course, this process of reciprocal and ongoing elucidation is precisely the method that Tully urges political philosophy to adopt (pp. 5–6). So it turns out that from the broadened field of authority I have invited you to adopt, we can appreciate not only the democratic content of Tully's essay, but the democratic nature of its method as well.

3

James Tully's Agonistic Realism

Bonnie Honig and Marc Stears

Political theory is often charged with being too ahistorical, abstract and removed from the political realities theory is supposed to illuminate or change. Caught up in canonical texts, gripped by ideal questions never asked by real politicians, like 'what is justice?' or 'which is the best regime?' or 'how are subjects formed?' political theory is said to list too far to one side, becoming all theory, no politics. On the other hand, when political theorists correct the imbalance and turn to complex historical case studies or the practicalities of daily life, they are accused of abandoning the big questions and grand narratives that dignify their mode of inquiry and distinguish it from mere journalism. Both timeless and timebound, it sometimes seems that political theory can do no right.

In the 1970s, Rawls's *A Theory of Justice* was welcomed because it made the case for systematic political theorizing after decades of political theory's confinement to canonical textual interpretation or the small, seemingly soluble questions of analytic philosophy. But to everything there is a season. Within ten years of the publication of *A Theory of Justice*, political theorists had already begun to worry about the cost of such systematic approaches, citing in particular their remove from the real world of actual politics.

Two of the most recent efforts to move towards a more real or realist political theory come from Raymond Geuss and James Tully.[1]

---

[1] Geuss develops his position on realism in a series of books. See R. Geuss, *History and Illusion in Politics*, Cambridge: Cambridge University Press, 1999; R. Geuss, *Outside Ethics*, Princeton: Princeton University Press, 2005; R. Geuss, *Philosophy and Real*

These two thinkers do not have a lot in common. Geuss endorses the inescapability of violence in politics while Tully deplores it, warning that violence only begets violence. Rather than accept realist claims about the obvious 'realities' of politics, Tully seeks to make real that which is often cast as utopian and ideal: pacifism. He lends pacifism a certain reality by citing instances of its practice and success, mining the empirical record for worldly events that realism too often effaces.

In this chapter, we look at Geuss's work, briefly, and then at Tully's in more detail, to outline what we take to be the politics of realism and the real. From the vantage point of that politics it becomes clear how these two thinkers, opposed in many ways, both deploy rhetorically a factical real – as uncontested – to support their claims of political possibility and actuality. We argue that contestations of the real are themselves part of the practice of realism understood as agonistic realism. These contestations are ever more pressing these days as the lines between truth and falsity, the real and the unreal, are blurred, and not only by media empires, corporations and governments for whom 'spin' is the stuff of daily life.

For Geuss, philosophy has drawn political theory into analytic and systematic approaches that operate at some remove from historically situated realities, deride the art of the possible and promote abstract unrealities of reason, consensus or right while abjuring the study of power and violence. By contrast with such abstract approaches, says Geuss, a realist will 'start from an account of our existing motivations and our political and social institutions (not from a set of abstract "rights" or from our intuitions)'.[2] Those actually existing motivations, as Guess sees them, are less than noble. Historical reflection on politics, he argues, demonstrates that people seek power and crave security. Power, decision, violence and the stabilizing influence of the state are

---

Politics, Princeton: Princeton University Press, 2008. Other examples of realist objections to ideal, abstract or systematic theory come from I. Shapiro, *The Flight From Reality in the Social Sciences*, Princeton: Princeton University Press, 2007; J. Issac, 'The Strange Silence of Political Theory', *Political Theory* 23 (4): 636–52, 1995.

[2] Geuss, *Philosophy and Real Politics*, p. 59.

key elements of political life. Guess's realism leads him to reject political theorists' longstanding quests for justice and to embrace in its place the less ambitious, supposedly more realistic end of modus vivendi arrangements, albeit dressed in the language of 'legitimacy'.

Having chastened the aspirations of political theory, Geuss endorses pessimism as a trait of historically informed realism: cooperation, solidarity, symbolization, hope and optimism are sidelined by Geuss, cast as 'unreal', 'ideal' or hopelessly 'optimistic'. But, contra Geuss, realism need not necessarily be pessimistic. In this chapter, we argue that a realist account of politics may find in the experience of political action inspiration to fight for noble ideals, rather than set them aside. Realists may also find in history and experience reason to press beyond modus vivendi arrangements to legitimacy and justice. Closer attention to history and to politics teaches us we may be more, not less, ambitious in our politics, and more idealistic than Geussian realism allows. These possibilities become clearer when we read Guess in connection with James Tully. Taken together, in contestatory context, Geuss and Tully inspire an alternative realism – a truly new realism we call 'agonistic' realism.[3]

Tully does not call himself a realist but he, no less than Geuss, also calls for political theory to begin with history and the realities of political life. He too rejects the ahistorical abstractions of philosophical approaches and the high normativity of much deliberative democratic theory. He faults them not just for abstraction, however, but also for the power they exercise. 'Elite political theory', as Tully calls the various rational, universalist or abstract approaches he criticizes, mistrusts the plural demoi of politics, seeks to constrain or inform or instruct popular will rather than attend to it and argues deductively in a way quite removed from the daily realities of lived experience, rather than

---

[3] In an earlier version of this chapter, which has since been much revised, we looked as well at the work of Bernard Williams, which Geuss appropriates for his realism but which we consider closer to Tully's position and which we dub agonistic realism. See B. Honig and M. Stears, 'The New Realism: From Modus Vivendi to Justice', in J. Floyd and M. Stears, eds, *Political Philosophy versus History?* Cambridge: Cambridge University Press, 2011.

inductively and in touch with political realities. Worse yet, abstractions like 'rights' and 'sovereignty' serve the interests of hegemony when they fold citizen-subjects into (post)colonial prioritizations of order over freedom, state institutional stability over self-governance.

For Tully, justice, freedom and self-governance are not abstractions and they are no mere ideals: that we may think they are is testimony to the sad success of elite political theory and of realists, who often cast freedom and true self-governance as chaotic and dangerous or unlikely and 'ideal'. In fact, Tully insists, practices of freedom and justice are a lived reality, often autonomous and stable. The realities of freedom are more visible when we build our theoretical positions inductively rather than deductively and attend to what Tully calls the 'rough ground' of politics, where we see not just violence, self-interest, political chicanery and instability but also action in concert, mutuality and non-violence. The latter are no less real than the so-called realities to which realists like Geuss seek to confine our attention. If realism means a commitment to describing what we see, then surely realists must concede that politics includes violence and consensus, agreement and strife, murderousness and reasonableness. Real politics shows we are incited by political engagement into rationality and violence, practicality and fantasy, war and solidarity. And if we attend to these realities, we may find ourselves inspired to strive for more than the modus vivendi style of politics that Geuss endorses. We may seek freedom and justice and insist that our actions in political life be oriented by fidelity to those ideals and illuminated by those aspirations. In short, Tully invites us to ask: why allow the so-called real to make us settle, when we instead we can unsettle the 'real'?

Tully does not call himself a realist but, once we see him as one, we can see that his work offers a way out of the paradox of politics, that difficult problem – so well articulated by Rousseau – of how to found anew given that we need good men to make good law but also need good law to make good men, as it were.[4] This problem of how to

---

[4] For analysis of the paradox, see B. Honig, *Emergency Politics: Paradox, Law, and Politics*, Princeton: Princeton University Press, 2009.

break the circle of chicken and egg is dismissed by realists like Geuss who claim that the goodness of law and men is simply of no particular interest in politics, except insofar as these get in the way of what needs to be done. Others, working in the area of normative theory, seek to solve the paradox by providing the norms whose absence they see as the cause of the problem: but normative theory's norms are often, as Geuss says, at quite a distance from the realities of political life and (at the same time even if paradoxically so) the unself-conscious carriers of some of those realities, as Tully argues, when he points to the uncomfortable continuities between their universalism and imperialism. A third way is offered by Tully, we argue. Tully sees in the elucidation and documentation of actually existing pacifism and freedom an important tactic whereby political theory can break the hold of realism's diminished expectations, while enlisting the traction of the real world of political experience. His examples provide orienting norms and ideals now harder to dismiss out of hand, because they are real and less violent than the norms of theorists whose universalism seems to him complicit with a history of first-world imposition.

Tully not only documents the realities of political idealism, seeking to infuse twenty-first-century politics with the hopes and aspirations of movements too long discounted as unserious, he also calls on political actors to act 'as if' they have already achieved the world that they seek to build together. With these two tactics, empirical documentation and imaginative leaping forward, with the 'here and now' and the 'as if', we conclude, Tully enters into the paradox of politics and breaks its spell. When he makes us alive to a possibility as an actuality, he incites us to actualize the possibility.

1. Raymond Geuss's realism

Politics, Raymond Geuss argues, is about power, 'its acquisition, distribution and use'.[5] Without direct attention to power and its

---

[5] Geuss, *Philosophy and Real Politics*, pp. 96–7, 25 and 90.

distribution – what Geuss describes as the Leninist question of 'who, whom?' – political theory can offer little guidance to those who need it. Geuss's essential objective is to restore the tradition of ideology critique in which the task is to use historical reflection to demonstrate how all political practices, including the practice of political philosophy itself, are always inherently in the service of power. To 'think politically' should always be 'to think about agency, power, and interests, and the relations among these' and 'a theoretical approach with no place for a theory of power is not merely deeply deficient but actively pernicious, because mystifying'.[6]

Thus, politics is not only violence. It involves 'attempts to provide legitimacy not simply for acts of violence, but for any kinds of collective action, such as deciding voluntarily to build a new road or change to a new unit of measurement (as was done during the French Revolution), or for that matter for any arrangements that could be seen as capable of being changed, controlled, modified or influenced by human action'.[7] All politics, in other words, requires its 'legitimatory mechanisms', which include 'mechanisms for changing beliefs, or generating new ones', for without those mechanisms, and without the stories of legitimation they convey, it would be impossible for political agents to act in concert let alone to sustain their achievements across time.[8]

Attempts to demonstrate the 'legitimacy' of particular courses of action are 'a part of real history, like most of the rest of life' and so stories of legitimacy, as Geuss calls them, necessarily differ radically across time and space depending on the contours of the precise struggle for power of which they are a part. Put another way, aspirations towards, or stories about, legitimacy, never solely assess or evaluate power, or seek its reform or restraint: they are always just another way to procure power.

The vast majority of political philosophers today miss this central point, Geuss contends, and as a result find themselves entangled in ever

---

[6] Ibid., 94.
[7] See R. Geuss, *Politics and the Imagination*, Princeton: Princeton University Press, 2010, pp. 31–42.
[8] Geuss, *Philosophy and Real Politics*, p. 35.

more abstract and idealistic discussions of the 'true' nature of legitimacy and how best to achieve it. This leads in part to a simple waste of time. Worse still, Geuss charges that in practice those who fail to see how legitimacy serves and does not check power enable the worst excesses of politics. Here Geuss connects together such otherwise dissimilar historical events as the French revolution, Soviet communism and Nazism.[9] Although Geuss was a critical theorist before he was a realist, here the echo is more to Popper than to Adorno.[10]

The only proper question for political theory then, is that of how human beings are capable of living together in a relatively orderly and peaceful way despite their instincts to control and dominate each other. Realists, he explains, should cleave to the 'basically Hobbesian insight' that 'political philosophy' is at its best when it concentrates on the 'variety of ways in which people can structure and organise their action so as to limit and control forms of disorder that they might find excessive or intolerable'.[11] Because conflict, disorder and competition for dominance are the essence of human interaction, political thinking should always focus on the avoidance of the dangers that follow from these features. There is, of course, a paradox here. For Geuss, politics is partly understood as simple competition for power, often in its crudest, most dominative form, but he prizes a particular kind of politics – state politics – as the means by which humans create order out of the most unlikely of material. This is the Hobbesian project, in other words, whereby the horrors of anarchy are avoided through a particularly limited kind of political aspiration focused largely on the controlling power of the modern state.

Thus it comes as no surprise to find Geuss enlisting the 'steely realism' of Thucydides. In *Outside Ethics*, Geuss argues that Thucydides showed us that 'hope' in politics is 'almost inevitably deluding and its power

---

[9]　Geuss, *Outside Ethics*, p. 13.

[10]　On the varieties of post-war realism, see M. Stears, *Demanding Democracy: American Radicals in Search of a New Politics*, Princeton: Princeton University Press, 2010, chapter 4.

[11]　Geuss, *Philosophy and Real Politics*, p. 22.

overwhelmingly destructive'.[12] Indeed, it is this very argument which Guess takes as evidence that Thucydides's history is 'realistic, values truthfulness, and is lacking the shallow optimism of later philosophy', notwithstanding other contending readings of Thucydides.[13] At other times, Geuss makes the argument in his own voice, as when he says 'Rites, rituals, and ceremonies', can be *mis*interpreted as being part of the very stuff of politics, their content revealing the intentions, aspirations, beliefs and commitments of those who practice them. Properly interpreted, however, they can be seen to be 'attempts to deal practically with phenomena that are the locus of extreme states of anxiety' about questions of power and powerlessness.[14] Religion too is firmly rejected as somehow 'unreal', belonging essentially to the past. It is true, Geuss admits, that some religious longing still finds political expression in even the most 'modern' of societies, but, he continues, 'there seems little to congratulate . . . on this'. 'Religious belief', he concludes, 'would have to be even more wilfully obscurantist [in 2005] than it was in 1805 because it requires active suppression of so much of humanity's active stock of knowledge'.[15]

Thus, Geuss's 'realism' is at some distance from the rich texture of the actual lived experience of real citizens and of the historical record of such experiences, both of which Geuss claims to wish to reconnect with political philosophy. Which is more 'real?' To treat aspirations towards legitimacy as mere mechanisms for domination? Or to see in them ongoing struggles for improvement within political life? Or both? If the last, we may grant that such struggles are always contingent, and contested, but still see in them evidence that the mere maintenance of peaceful order is not the only good to which politics is or should be directed. In sum, if Geuss usefully reorients political theory towards the practices of political life, his realism also leads us away from the accounts that practitioners of politics give of their own efforts and

---

[12] Geuss, *Outside Ethics*, pp. 221 and 224.
[13] Ibid., p. 225.
[14] Ibid., p. 138.
[15] Ibid., p. 152.

activities. The real it turns out, for Geuss, emerges only by abstracting rather severely from . . . the real.

The importance of this point can be underlined this way: what traits would a pacifist movement have to have for Geuss to accept it as un-illusory? Our sense is that no movement could clear this bar – all would be found illusory – and this suggests that for Geuss, realism and its commitments trump the real on which realism is supposedly based and from which its credibility is drawn. By contrast, James Tully seeks to elevate to the real those actions, movements and orientations that do exist but are rendered marginal, unreal or utopian by the now-entrenched demand that politics be realistic. In particular, Tully's commitment to pacifism in politics issues a precise challenge to Geussian realism and to political actors more generally. For Tully, political ideals are powerful and welcome elements of political life, not part of a threatening or foolishly unrealistic 'idealism' or utopianism in politics.[16] And there is nothing unreal nor unrealistic about pacifism in politics.[17]

2. James Tully's realism

As we have just seen, Geuss's realism is resolutely anti-utopian, measured rather than expansive or ambitious. The world of politics

---

[16] It should be noted, of course, that utopianism is properly a subject for realists as well. On the real impact of utopianism in politics see D. Leopold, 'Socialism and Utopia', *Journal of Political Ideologies* 12 (3): 219–37, 2007.

[17] On this, see S. Critchley, *The Faith of the Faithless: Experiments in Political Theology*, London: Verso, 2012, championing not just pacifism as realist but also small departures from it too: 'As is evidenced by Aeschylus's *Oresteia*, but also by the violence of colonization and decolonization and the multiple wars of the present and recent past, violence exerts a repetition effect from which subjects cannot seem to free themselves. We are caught ineluctably in a loop of violence and counter-violence, of justification and counterjustification. The world is cut in two by a violence that is in the very air we breathe and whose unforgiving political, mythic, and legal logic is cold, bloody, and irrefutable. In such a world, the platitudes of realpolitik will always appear reasonable. All that we have is the folly of a plumb line of nonviolence, a set of exceptional circumstances and a political struggle in which we wrestle with the infinite ethical demand. Such wrestling requires the virtues of tact, prudence, and a concrete understanding of the situation in which we find ourselves, combined with a stubborn – at times, indeed, belligerent – faith in what appears at each and every moment impossible: another, nonviolent way of conceiving the social relations amongst human beings', chapter 5.

is not the world of theory, he insists. Things go wrong, contingencies abound, practices are plural, fraught, contested. It is (sometimes) best to do least, or at least to do less than a theorist or idealist might advocate doing. For Geuss, any alternative approach to political life threatens to expand the ambit of politics dangerously and unreasonably; it invites the passion of the fanatic.

James Tully's perspective is almost entirely other. Unlike Geuss, Tully's historically grounded alternative does *not* see politics as the sole property of the state. As he contracts political theory's focus on the state's ambit, he makes room to attend to other scenes of politics, often squeezed out or marginalized as unimportant by political theorists on opposed sides of every other issue: liberals, deliberativist universalists and realists.

At first, Tully's approach as outlined in *Public Philosophy in a New Key* appears to place him not far from Geuss. Just as Geuss seeks to revive the tradition of ideology critique, revealing the power interests lurking behind high-sounding appeals to legitimacy, so *de*familiarization and expose are Tully's preferred approach. Tully sees power and inequality as intimately involved in the maintenance of the apparently safe, secure and familiar political institutional arrangements that other theorists simply assume are stable and well-ordered.

Like Geuss, Tully is particularly critical of putatively universal theories of legitimacy which, he argues, disguise particular, partisan projects. Since the Enlightenment, Tully insists, it has been 'assumed that there [is] some definitive ordering of legitimate political associations' and that, consequently, the 'role of political philosophy' is to work out the 'definitive theory of justice or the definitive democratic procedures of legitimation in which citizens themselves could reach final agreements on the just ordering of their associations'.[18] Such accounts, however, deny the inevitability of ongoing disagreement and dispute which are, in fact, constant and crucial elements of political life.[19] Nor is the

---

[18] J. Tully, *Public Philosophy in a New Key*, Two Volumes, Cambridge: Cambridge University Press, 2008, Volume II, p. 97.
[19] Tully, *Public Philosophy* II, p. 97.

denial without consequences: Claims to universality, certainty and immutability have been powerful weapons in the hands of some, and especially in the hands of the colonializing peoples and states who came to North American equipped with stories of the inevitability and universal desirability of a very particular kind of legitimate political life. Those stories helped to promote and legitimate brutal, exclusionary and dominating patterns of political rule and genocide.[20]

Despite these apparent similarities with Geuss's realism, however, the more optimistic nature of Tully's historically grounded realism emerges when Tully turns to offer potential solutions to the dangers that politics presents. Tully seeks to defamiliarize established habits of thought *not* in order to resist the siren call of aspiration – as with Geuss – but precisely in order to press upon us the need to find new and unsettling ways of thinking and acting. When Tully criticizes universalist aspirations to legitimacy, he does so to undo their depoliticizing effects and to motivate alternative practices of freedom that unsettle the normal order rather than guarantee its stability. For Tully, the focus on stability in political theory and practice displaces politics and serves to guard privilege and maintain injustice. By contrast with Geuss, who prizes stability as a bulwark against the harms of conflict, Tully is struck by the harms of stability itself. Tully does not allow the reality of conflict to force him to relinquish more aspirational aims. He seeks *more* than mere stability or even legitimation. He seeks 'just agreement'.[21] His aim is to promote an ongoing, transformative dialogue of equal parties in contention with each other. He wants those parties to recognize that they are bound by a sense of shared fate, mutual respect and common future and a shared past that is marred but not exhausted by relations of domination and acts of injustice.

Tully, too, turns to history to make his case. But whereas history offers constraint for Geuss, it offers promise to Tully. In the work on intercultural dialogue between Euro-Canadians and Canadian

---

[20] See ibid., pp. 16–42.
[21] Ibid., p. 238.

Aboriginals, for example, Tully sees not only genocide and domination but also a history of *mutuality* has been deliberately erased from Euro-Canadians' cultural memory as part of the colonial project. That mutuality, he argues, however, is no less real than the violence and domination on which we have since come to focus. For Tully, therefore, efforts to create intercultural dialogue today could learn from the first contact between Europeans and Aborigines. Lines of power and dependence were murkier then than in the later colonizing period – without the hospitality of the Aborigines the Europeans might not have survived – and the treaties that resulted promised a politics of almost unparalleled equality and common interest. Canada, he concludes, was founded on 'an act of sharing that is almost unimaginable in its generosity'.[22] Making the generosity unimaginable has been the task of decades of official history and elite political theory. Making it *reimaginable* is the task of Tully's new realism.

Tully's counternarration of Aboriginal and Canadian history is, therefore, descriptive – as always called for by realism – but Tully finds in the historical account an alternative to the domination and raw power politics that later intervened in the colonizing period and that realists tend to assume characterized the whole of the first people's/ settler relationship. Tully's nascent new realism is therefore committed to politics as the art of the possible but it is not degraded by that commitment because the possible is immense. That is why Tully can be both a realist and full of gratitude, optimistic and with a sense of possibility and renewal even though he is intent on identifying and responding to sedimented injustices that he knows can be only, at best, alleviated or recognized but never fully repaired.

A similar strategy was on display in *Strange Multiplicity* where what we might take to be instruments of domination – treaties – turn out in Tully's treatment, in a rather Hegelian way, to have an empowering dimension for those who were supposed to be subjugated by them.

---

[22] Tully, *Public Philosophy* I, pp. 244–5.

The reality of the treaty is said to be something other than subjugation (regardless of intent) and this attention to its performative power rather than, say, its illocutionary force, opens up an alternative that otherwise might not exist. The strategy is rather like perspectival seeing, as in Wittgenstein's example of the duck-rabbit. Once you see things otherwise, it is hard to go back. Wittgenstein calls this seeing as, and it is [arguably connected to – and may even be] the necessary condition of – Tully's recommendation to act as if the world we seek is already here, following Gandhi, that we should 'Be the change we want to see', to which we return shortly.

First, it is important to note that there remain grave difficulties here, however. Tully is persuasive when he portrays the practices of early Canadian treaty-making on which he pins so much hope, drawing our attention to their mutuality, generosity and creativity. But it remains arguable that such treaties were also instruments of domination, as Geuss would surely have it, even European lures into the colonizers' net. At the very least, there were surely elements of both power *and* mutuality, reciprocity *and* suspicion, pragmatism *and* domination at work in the actual practices that led up to the signing of treaties and then in the work those treaties did in solidifying intercultural relations into settled patterns of (in)equality.

Taiaiake Alfred argues the point in exactly this way, even casting the Nisga'as' Final Agreement of 1998 as 'a strategy of assimilation', as Tully himself points out.[23] But although Tully cites Alfred, he does not pursue the point further. When Tully focuses on the treaty and not the violence, on the mutuality and not the instrumentalization, he may inspire, he narrates and emplots in a certain partial and contestable way, no less than Geuss does. Tully draws our attention to some elements rather than others, seeking to avoid the pessimism to which realist political theory seems to gravitate almost inexorably. When Tully theorizes intercultural dialogue in Canadian politics, he

---

[23] Tully, *Public Philosophy* I, p. 275, citing T. Alfred, *Peace, Power, Righteousness: An Indigenous Manifesto*, Oxford: Oxford University Press, 1999.

may even direct our attention away from some of the actualities to which he says he is committed.[24]

Tully seems also to assume as a condition of negotiation the very thing we cannot assume in real politics: the mutual respect whose absence is the reason we need negotiation in the first place. Perhaps Tully's point is that if we adopt the manners specified by respect and recognition, we may come to experience more authentically the trust and civility whose absence the principles are designed to redress. This is the power of the 'as if'. However, when Tully says that, with recognition and then dialogue, 'consent can *replace* coercion and conflict', he seems to be a bit dazzled by his own ideal.[25] The risk here is that Tully ends up normativizing the real, presuming that the ideal standards to which he rightly aspires can be found and drawn upon in the 'real' world. In this, he mirrors Geuss's realism rather than interrupting it.

Tully addresses these very concerns at the conclusion of his *Public Philosophy in a New Key*, when he turns to what he believes history tells us of the possibility of citizen transformation even in the face of grave injustice and inequality. Through individual and collective effort, he insists, it is possible to glimpse a political life that might otherwise escape us.[26] Citizens should strive to model themselves on those who have best represented the ideals of dialogue and equal interaction with others in the past. If they do that, he implores, then history tells us that

---

[24] Notably, Tully does insist that intercultural dialogue is not an ideal speech situation (Tully, *Public Philosophy* I, p. 240), but he also develops his account of recognition obligations out of what he claims are implicit recognitions already granted (234) and in so doing seems to follow Habermas' strategy of identifying immanent norms from our communicative practice. Both of them are drawing on S. E. Toulmin, *The Uses of Argument*, Cambridge: Cambridge University Press, 1958 and noting that what you say involves commitments and entailments to which you can be held accountable – although it must be stressed that Tully rejects Habermas' strong quasi-transcendental thesis here, for a clear statement see the essay 'To Think and Act Otherwise', in *Public Philosophy* I.

[25] Tully, *Public Philosophy* I, p. 239. For the inspiration behind this idea, see L. Wittgenstein, *Philosophical Investigations*, Oxford: Blackwell, 1997, pp. 81 and 104.

[26] In this way, if not in others, Tully's work echoes Kant, who insisted that the gap between ideal and reality, or theory and practice, can best be rectified by better aligning practice – the real – with the demands of theory rather than by abandoning theoretically valid ideals. See I. Kant, *Kant: Political Writings*, H. S. Reiss, ed., Cambridge: Cambridge University Press, 1991.

they will – or at least might – succeed; they might recapture the spirit of inclusive dialogue, however elusive it may appear to be.

It is to Mahatma Gandhi that Tully turns to make this argument. Gandhi's politics, Tully argues, offered a form of 'civic organization and uncompromising non-violent confrontation and negotiation with those responsible for imperial relationships' and it did so not with the intention of securing a simply stable modus vivendi but rather 'with the aim of *converting* them to non-violent, democratic and peaceful relationships'. Gandhi and his followers did this by conducting themselves 'constructively'. They sought to live *as if* they already existed in the 'alternative world' that they wanted to 'bring about', eschewing violence, coercion, domination and power, and offering instead a 'singular style of civic life' in 'personal practices of self-awareness and self-formation'. This 'as if' solves the paradox of politics in which we can bring about change only by living as if we have already brought it about when we have not yet done so.[27] 'These are the daily practices of becoming an exemplary citizen', Tully concludes, 'and by focusing on their performance in real history we should learn to have optimism, even faith, in the possibilities of a new politics.[28] History's exemplarity is brought in to alleviate the paradox of the present moment.[29]

With this argument, Tully mobilizes a certain contestable account of Gandhi to inspire actors on the contemporary scene. But attention to other elements of Gandhi's politics presses us in a different direction, towards a more radical or more fully agonistic realism than that developed by Tully. Crucially, key elements of Gandhi's politics are missing in Tully's account. These concern most of all the nature of the opponent and of the circumstances in which the struggle for justice always – or at least often – takes place. Gandhi was well aware that particular kinds of action were more appropriate in the face of some

---

[27] For critical commentary on this move, see Stears, *Demanding Democracy*.

[28] Tully, *Public Philosophy* II, p. 308.

[29] For more on the idea of exemplars, see Melissa Lane: For example, M. Lane, 'Constraint, freedom, and exemplar', in J. Floyd and M. Stears, eds, *Political Philosophy versus History?* Cambridge: Cambridge University Press, 2011.

challenges rather than others, both in strategic and principled terms. Of the Palestinians, for example, he wrote in 1947/8: 'I wish they had chosen the way of non-violence in resisting what they rightly regarded an unwarrantable encroachment on their country' but 'nothing can be said against [their] resistance in the face of overwhelming odds'.[30] For Gandhi, it was necessary sometimes just to *oppose*, and not to seek to mend or convert. Sometimes, it is simply not appropriate to ask that we see the question from the other's point-of-view. Sometimes, non-violence is not apt. Simon Critchley provides a useful example here, that of Dietrich Bonhoeffer, who was 'eventually driven to drop the pacifism he adopted in the 1930s and participate in the attempted tyrannicide of Hitler and failed *coup d'état* against the National Socialist regime that led to his brutal execution in 1945, shortly before the end of the war. Bonhoeffer's ethics,' Critchley notes, 'does not rest on absolute, law-like principles, but on a freely assumed responsibility that, in extreme situations and as a last resort, is willing to act violently.' For Bonhoeffer, 'Responsible action involves . . . a "willingness to become guilty" (*Bereitschaft zur Schuldübernahme*): this is the price one pays for freedom'.[31]

Similarly, modes of personal transformation that were available to those engaged in the just struggle themselves were also always, in Gandhi's view, affected by the nature of the injustice to which they were addressed. The fight against colonialism, Gandhi thus believed, required not just training in openmindedness, generosity of spirit and a capacity for dialogue, it also demanded a relentless fearlessness and a sense of the profound dangers that politics presented. It was only by developing a deep-rooted *courage*, for example, that one could face-up to, and then begin to resist, the degradations and symbolic violence

---

[30] M. K. Gandhi, 'A Non-Violent Look at Conflict and Violence', *Harijan*, 26 November 1938.

[31] 'The extreme necessities of a critical situation, Bonhoeffer writes, "appeal directly to the free responsibility of the one who acts, a responsibility not bound by any law."' Critchley asks: 'Would such a strategy of resistance have been successful? In Bonhoeffer's case, we know that the attempted tyrannicide failed. But the point here is that I am not preaching nonviolence in all political cases, and no more am I arguing for some easy "clean hands" retreat from the state.' On the contrary.

constantly perpetuated by the false universalisms of the occupier.[32] Yet this courage is a crucially different – even contrasting – characteristic to those that might be demanded at another moment, a moment when the most horrific of political evils had been overcome and new political possibilities presented themselves.[33]

The picture Tully paints – a picture that prioritizes the possibilities of dialogue, of reason and of a coercion-free politics – may leave us unprepared for other dimensions of political struggles that Tully himself recognizes are ongoing. 'Be the change you want to be' is sometimes excellent political advice but, as Gandhi knew, a contextual political judgement may direct us to act otherwise. Tully's departure from other realists' faux minimalism (their assumptions about rationality, interest and conflict are, rather, maximal) essentially consists in dedicating himself to the preparation and training on which good democratic politics always depends, as when Tully notes, for example, that a certain 'kind of respect needs to be cultivated' among parties to the intercultural dialogue.[34] Such training may meet the needs of intercultural dialogue, in which the terrain of mutuality and respect is already mapped out, even if not fully actualized. But sometimes justice and equality must be fought for in ways for which Tully's respectful subjects of mutuality, trained for intercultural dialogue, may find themselves woefully unready.

---

[32] See M. K. Gandhi, *An Autobiography: The Story of My Experiments with Truth*, Boston: Beacon, 1957. We thank Brandon Terry for this point.

[33] Critchley cedes Gandhi to the other side too quickly but concludes rightly when he says: 'There are contexts where a tenacious politics of nonviolence, such as Gandhi's Kropotkinesque strategy of *Satyagraha*, can be highly effective. There are contexts where a *mimesis* of Gandhi's tactics might also prove successful, as was the case for several years in the civil rights movement in the United States in the 1960s and in the words and deeds of Martin Luther King. There are contexts where techniques of direct action that David Graeber calls "non-violent warfare" may prove effective and timely. There are contexts where a difficult pacifism that negotiates the limits of violence might be enough. But – and this is the point gleaned from our reading of Benjamin – there are also contexts, multiple contexts, too depressingly many to mention, where nonviolent resistance is simply crushed by the forces of the state, the police, and the military. In such contexts, the line separating nonviolent warfare and violent action has to be crossed. Politics is always a question of local conditions, of local struggles and local victories. To judge the multiplicity of such struggles on the basis of an abstract conception of nonviolence is to risk dogmatic blindness.' For example see, D. Graeber, 'The New Anarchists', *New Left Review* 13, January–February 2002.

[34] Tully, *Public Philosophy* I, p. 243.

There is no doubt that there is a risk in turning to violence and that is the risk that rightly worries Tully, as it did Hannah Arendt before him: 'violence begets violence.' But this worry too has a risk: that it establishes violence as brute facticity tethered to eternal returns of the same, rather than seeing it as a political vernacular itself subject to interruption, reinscription and contestation. The point is made by Robert Young when he says that violence is 'a phenomenon that has a history'. In Simon Critchley's parsing, violence 'is never a question of a single act, but of one's insertion into a historical process saturated by a cycle of violence and counter-violence. Violence is always a double-act "between human subjects, subjects whose experience of violence interpolates them in a repetition effect from which they cannot free themselves."'

3. Agonistic realism

Realists reject the ahistorical, abstract, false universalisms of most contemporary political philosophy. But many, like Geuss, talk about the hard realities of history while finding in it remarkably abstract and universal trends and traits – like power, conflict and the quest for stability. For James Tully, in contrast, the history of colonialism reveals that, often, this search for stability masks dangers and coercions. Instead, we should be attentive to historical moments such as the first contacts between Europeans and Aborigines which demonstrate that contrasting groupings are capable of finding, and often have found, mutually satisfactory arrangements capable of actions in concert that are not exhaustively marked by injustice, and coercion. We can experience something similar now and not have to settle for either oppression or perpetual unceasing antagonism if only we practice citizenship and exchange in the right spirit.

Each of these pictures of the historical realities of politics is, of course, partial. Pictures always are. But in this case there is an irony, for the partiality of the political picture presented by these realists would leave citizens crucially unprepared for the real challenges of political life. Geuss's citizens fail to aspire to (much less explore!) action in concert that might be transformative. Tully's citizens are more hopeful but possibly less prepared for some of the harsher realities that await them in political life. At times, Tully writes as if he envisions a more mutualist politics in which communities give up on state-centred actions and simply decide to live otherwise, starting new communities, enacting self-governance to the extent they can. There is no doubt that for many, such experiments in living can be transformative, though even they will have their remainders, as we know from the experiences of many utopian communities. Moreover, it is surely the case that simply being the change you want to see is not adequate for those committed to more direct confrontational forms of resistance to injustice. Those seeking mutual dialogue, freedom and justice will certainly sometimes find themselves facing violence, resistance and rejection. Tully's theory and his examples cast little light on the particular strategies they might have to deploy, or on the qualities of character they might need to develop in order occasionally to *overcome or overpower* rather than to convert or transform their rivals.[35] Second, Tully fails to explore how even when some in struggle do develop exemplary qualities of character such as those that Tully demands – qualities of openness, mutuality, generosity and consensual exchange – they might nonetheless be parasitic for their success on those who do not. Might it not be the case that every Gandhi needs a Bhagat Singh, every Martin Luther King Jr a Malcolm X?

The struggle to build a more just order requires attention *both* to the aspirational politics of many-sided exchange, to which Tully is so well attuned, and the harsher politics of 'who, whom?' to which Geuss draws our attention. Diminishing coercion on behalf of a more just, inclusive, consensual practice is, it seems to us, clearly desirable but a politics that thinks it is possible to *replace* coercion with consent leaves those who seek justice and equality ill-prepared for (some of) the battles ahead.

This is why we need an alternative realism. That realism, which we call agonistic realism, shares with other realists a sensitivity to the lived experience of historically located political actors, the denial of the

---

[35] Chantal Mouffe offers one sort of analysis in C. Mouffe, *On the Political*, London: Routledge, 2005, and Stears offers another in Stears, *Demanding Democracy*, especially chapter 5.

usefulness of the abstract universal, the alertness to the politics of power and exclusion. But an agonistic realism also crucially differs on some key points. Maintaining the spirit of optimism, of aspiration and of justice evident in Tully, agonistic realism seeks to prepare subjects more fully for the often violent contestations of political life. Indeed, an agonistic realism notes with some concern the *absence* of such contestation: It might be a sign that real recognition and mutuality have been actualized or it might be a sign of successful hegemony by a partial and oppressive or limiting regime. How would we know? Here the 'real' is undecidable.

And here we have the final element of an agonistic realism; it takes nothing for granted, not even the 'real'. In other words, agonistic realism is committed to the essentially contested character of even the 'real' itself. Agonistic realism assumes the critique of realism in art, developed by Jean-Francois Lyotard, is applicable as well to realism in politics: According to Lyotard, the problem with aesthetic realism is that it reaffirms the illusion that we can seize hold of the real, that photographs or television or other media can be windows to the REAL world. But, Lyotard insists, the truth is that the real is itself often an effect. And for this reason we need continuing, perpetual artistic dissent and the promulgation of ever newer forms of artistic endeavour to avoid complacency and even terror.[36] As Catherine Belsey explains in her gloss on Lyotard, the problem is not just that the picture we get from realists is inaccurate, as if a better description of the real would suffice and correct our vision. It is rather that realism protects us from doubt. It offers a picture of the world that we seem to know and in the process confirms our status as knowing subjects by reaffirming that picture as true. In sum, art here is confirmatory. Its message is that things are as we think they are. And we are who we think we are.

When Belsey explains that realist art generates a sense of security precisely by scaring us, she provides tremendous insight into Geuss's

---

[36] J. Lyotard, 'Answering the Question: What is Postmodernism?', in I. Hassan and S. Hassan, eds, *Innovation/Renovation: New Perspectives on the Humanities*, Madison: University of Wisconsin Press, 1983, pp. 329–41.

project, which seems so frightening but is nonetheless, attractive.[37] Such attraction, perversely, come from its capacity to frighten. What we fear feels more real than anything else and this, paradoxically, is reassuring, for in our fear we do not doubt, and this state of indubitability is reassuring even as what it portends is not.

Does this mean agonistic realism rejects the real it aims to encounter and mobilize, turning its back as it does so on the reassurances that others seem to crave? Not at all. It is not a question of being for or against the real. It is rather, as Jacques Derrida says, a matter of deconstructing the binary between artifice and actuality while nonetheless avoiding the fall into some sort of idealist rejection of the real. Such a rejection denies the actuality of 'violence and suffering, war and death' and casts these as 'constructed and fictive . . . so that nothing ever really happens, only images, simulacra and delusions'. Rather than partake in such denial, 'we must keep in mind,' said Derrida, 'that any coherent deconstruction is about singularity, about events and about what is ultimately irreducible in them.'[38] As we also know from Derrida, such singularity can be powerful in its impossible exemplarity for the future. As agonistic realists try to rebuild our futures together, we do well look to the events of history, and to the essentially contested realities of our own time in order to inaugurate or maintain futures worth having.

Doing so means taking up the storytelling imperative of past and future. That is to say, contra most realists, agonistic realists know the facts do not speak for themselves. They are disputed and framed and emplotted and sometimes hidden and disguised and obscured. They depend upon context which is always contestable, and upon practices of re-contextualization, which are always political. The real is not objective and it cannot stand on its own two feet. It needs care, nurturance, contestation and support. It is the public world on which politics depends and over which political battles occur. Although we have

---

[37] C. Belsey, *Poststructuralism: A Very Short Introduction*, Oxford: Oxford University Press, 2002, pp. 101–2.

[38] See J. Derrida, 'The Deconstruction of Actuality', 1993 interview quoted in C. Belsey, *Culture and the Real*, London: Routledge, 2005, p. 59.

criticized Tully for sometimes telling only half the story – presenting treaties as transformative instruments of mutuality and not as, also and undecidably, mechanism of domination – that criticism is part of a contretemps over what stories are most empowering for dissidents and for their shared futures of co-governance, imagination of which often animates dissidents to risk their lives and futures when they act.

When Tully tells the stories of great pacifists and collective experiments in living, he seeks to make real something whose reality we cannot take for granted. In this, he follows in the wake of Hannah Arendt who was committed to telling stories of exemplary actions partly because oppressive powers are committed to effacing them, and even more so because of the reason for that: such stories have the power to incite or redeem others who are otherwise isolated by their ignorance of the courage or imagination of their fellows. Arendt wished for more stories like's, the World War II German soldier who enlisted military vehicles to smuggle Jews to safety and facilitated the efforts of the Jewish underground in Vilna. Such stories showed, Arendt argued, that 'nothing can ever be "practically useless"', not as long as someone can tell its story (EIJ 233). Looking for heroic, courageous acts as a resource of political life may seem idealistic, but it is not so, Arendt insisted. She cited a Talmudic story – of the 'thirty-six unknown righteous men who always exist and without whom the world would go to pieces' – to justify the place of 'quixotic morality in [realist] politics'. Those 36 men, as it were, are always there, their stories waiting to be told and released into the in-between of human affairs.[39] But we now know that they come in many guises, ethnicities, genders and dimensions. If we are too often unaware of them that is surely because they are all too often invisible in the public sphere for reasons that Tully has detailed and with his work seeks to rectify.

---

[39] One of them was, in her view: 'Judah Magnes whose seemingly idealistic support for Jewish-Arab cooperation and federation in Palestine (JW 445) was for Arendt entirely realistic.' For more on this see J. Ackerman and B. Honig, 'Un-Chosen: Judith Butler's Jewish Modernity', in I. Zyrtal, J. Picard, J. Revel and M. Steinberg, eds, *Thinking Jewish Modernity: Thinkers, Writers, Artists, Shapers of Jewish Identity*, forthcoming.

4

Pictures of Democratic Engagement: Claim-Making, Citizenization and the Ethos of Democracy*

Aletta J. Norval

When thinking about practices of democratic engagement, it is useful to consider the circumstances under which questions concerning such practices arise. It is noteworthy, but not surprising, that contemporary political theorists consistently begin from some perplexing or dislocating moment, which then inspires the move to thinking of politics in terms of practices of democratic engagement.[1] This move can and does take many forms. Some political theorists seeks to eliminate traces of contingency from political life, while others take contingency to be the starting point, if not the spur for, thinking about politics in general and democratic politics specifically. In this chapter I focus on

* Acknowledgements: I first presented this paper at the 2011 APSA conference in Seattle. I would like to thank the participants in that session for useful comments and questions. In particular, my appreciation to Davide Panagia, Thomas Dumm and Robert Nichols for their incisive questions. In addition, thanks is due to Bonnie Honig who also provided me with written comments on an earlier version of this essay. Finally, thanks to David Howarth for always being available to discuss issues on short notice.

[1] Any account of democratic engagement should consider a range of questions, including (1) the articulation/expression of demands, addressing questions such as 'what are the political processes involved in the articulation of demands, and how do they relate to democracy?'; (2) the conditions of possibility of the staging of such demands, of making them visible; here the relevant questions to think about concern the circumstances under which novel demands appear on the political scene; as well as (3) a further set of questions concerning what we may expect of each other as democratic subjects, both in the process of this making visible of demands and in their further negotiation and contestation; the latter set of issues raise questions regarding what I would call 'democratic responsiveness'.

two theorists, both of whom start from the centrality of contestation (rather than a consideration of norms, rights and rules) in developing their respective accounts of democratic engagement. The pictures of democratic engagement that we find in the works of James Tully and Ernesto Laclau are distinctive, yet have enough in common to allow for useful insights to emerge from a reading that seeks to contrast these pictures without, however, assuming that they cannot be mutually supplementary.

As in Heidegger, for whom the character of equipment is revealed when it no longer functions as we expect, so for Cavell we elicit criteria in moments of crisis or perplexity. In this chapter, I will suggest that the views of Heidegger and Cavell in this respect correspond in an important sense to our political practices. It is when a practice is challenged, or is shown to be inadequate, that we are called upon to recount its criteria, to reconsider the point of the practices in which we engage.[2] I take the criteria so elicited to be functions of the judgements that we are prepared to make. They are not abstract norms set up over and above our practices, but the sedimented results of our practices, and they remain open to contestation and rearticulation.

Something like this view seems to me to inform the different conceptions of democratic engagement to be found in Tully's and Laclau's writings. Yet, while accepting this common ground, they articulate different ways of thinking about the ethos that would be commensurate with democratic forms of engagement. Importantly, they also relate differently to the range of activities and sites of engagement that would count as democratic. In this chapter I seek to flesh out these differences, while thinking about their intellectual roots in the two thinkers. I also reflect on the consequences of these differences for what we consider to be the democratic activities in which citizens and non-citizens alike engage.

[2] A. J. Norval, *Aversive Democracy*, Cambridge: Cambridge University Press, 2007, p. 63.

1. Contestation through the articulation of demands

Let me turn, first, to the articulation of demands and the concomitant construction of collective political identities that form the core of Laclau's writings. Sketching out an imaginary example, Laclau suggests that we think of politics in terms of the category of demands:

> Think of a large mass of agrarian migrants who settle in ... shantytowns on the outskirts of a developing industrial city. Problems of housing arise, and the group of people affected by them request some kind of solution from the local authorities. Here we have a *demand* which initially is perhaps only a *request*. If the demand is satisfied, that is the end of the matter, but if it is not, people can start to perceive that their neighbours have other, equally unsatisfied demands – problems with water, health, schooling and so on.[3]

Where does this emphasis on demands come from? For Laclau, it arises from the need to develop a non-substantive starting point for political analysis generally. As he puts it:

> If we want to gauge the specificity of a[n] ... articulatory practice, we have to isolate units smaller than the group ... The smallest unit ... corresponds to the category of 'social demand'.[4]

Regarding the nature of articulatory practices and their relation to agency, Laclau argues further that:

> Political practices do not *express* the nature of social agents but, instead, *constitute* the latter. In that case the political practice would have some kind of ontological priority over the agent – the latter would merely be the historical precipitate of the former. To put it in slightly different terms: practices would be more primary units of analysis than the group – that is, the group would only be the result of an articulation of social practices.[5]

---

[3] E. Laclau, *On Populist Reason*, London: Verso, 2005, p. 73.
[4] Ibid. In this, Laclau's analysis follows the move from Saussure to Hjelmslev in linguistics, shifting analysis from the level of the sign to that of the glosseme.
[5] E. Laclau, 'Populism: What's in a Name?', in F. Panizza, ed., *Populism and the Mirror of Democracy*, London: Verso, 2005, p. 33.

As is clear from the above, the key practice on which Laclau focuses is that of the articulation of demands. A social demand, he argues, has to be distinguished from a request. In each case it (the request or the demand) has to be 'addressed to an instance different from that within which the demand was originally formulated'.[6] A *request*, he argues, has the following structural features: it is addressed to an instance that has decision-making power; the authority of this body is not put into question by the request and finally, the request is punctual in character (it is not 'the tip of an iceberg or the symbol of a large variety of unformulated social demands').[7] That means that in contradistinction to demands, requests have as a non-verbalized assumption the legitimacy of each of the elements of the process: 'nobody puts into question either the right to present the request or the right of the decisory [sic] instance to take the decision.'[8] That is, requests function within institutionalized processes, and the assumption is that the request can be satisfied in a non-antagonistic, administrative manner.[9]

Demands, on the contrary, are requests that have not been satisfied. If a variety of demands remain unsatisfied, 'multiple frustrations' may trigger a process of equivalential reaggregation. In this case, each demand is/becomes the tip of an iceberg, such that each manifest claim is presented as one among a larger set of claims. Like requests, demands are also addressed to authorities (indicating the vertical character of demands: they are addressed by citizens to authorities), but there is no longer the expectation that institutions could or would satisfy the demands. In this case, the articulatory practice takes an anti-institutionalist form, yet one that is developed in the expectation that the existing institution be transformed in the process of struggle.

Laclau also distinguishes between different forms of collective identification on a similar basis. In the case of requests and isolated demands, the form of identification remains 'isolated'. He calls these

---

6   Ibid., p. 36.
7   Ibid.
8   Ibid.
9   Ibid.

democratic demands.[10] Where a plurality of demands remains unsatisfied we may find that through equivalential articulation, a broader social subjectivity is constituted. In this case, it is called a *popular* demand.[11] Laclau argues that the latter, at an incipient level, begins to constitute 'the people' as a historical actor.

From this, it is clear that there is an important relation for Laclau between equivalential articulations and democracy. Some form of this relation was already present in his early work with Chantal Mouffe, where they suggest that the subversive power of democracy (emerging from the French Revolution and in the Declaration of the Rights of Man) provides the discursive conditions that make it possible to propose different forms of inequality all as illegitimate and anti-natural, and thus equivalent to one another, allowing the spread of equality and liberty into increasingly wider domains.[12] In *On Populist Reason*, he argues that democracy is grounded on the existence of a democratic subject or 'a people', whose emergence depends precisely on the horizontal articulation between equivalential demands.[13] 'The people', as we have seen, he argues, does not refer to a pre-existing, substantive entity, such as a nation or ethnic group. Instead, it is a signifier for collective subjectivity per se, which emerges in and through the process of making demands.

A unifying signifier such as 'the people' play a dual role. On the one hand, it has an *active* role of representation as it *constitutes* the unity of a collectivity in the process of representing them; it does not simply reflect a pre-given totality. On the other, it *represents* a collectivity. Should the active or constitutive function of representation prevail without attention to the fact that a particular 'actor' is being represented, the link between the representative and the represented risks being broken. But if the representative simply reflects the represented, there is no possibility of drawing together a number of distinct demands into a

---

[10] This is a somewhat counter-intuitive way of thinking of democratic demands. I return to this issue later.

[11] Laclau, *On Populist Reason*, p. 74.

[12] E. Laclau and C. Mouffe, *Hegemony and Socialist Strategy*, London: Verso, 1985, pp. 154–5.

[13] Laclau, *On Populist Reason*, p. 171.

unity which exceeds the specificity of each of the demands. Hence, the *political* function of representation is of necessity one of maintaining the tension between the two extreme points of the continuum.

Notwithstanding these important points, Laclau does not elaborate what might make 'a people' or any other collectivity specifically *democratic*. Laclau also does not address a further crucial dimension of the relation between the articulation of demands and the constitution of a people, namely, the fact that a demand constitutes not only an oppositional relation *to* the state or to authority but also a relation *between* citizens of a democratic community. The assumption of an internal relation between the constitution of chains of equivalence among diverse demands and the possibility of the formation of a democratic community allows Laclau to posit democracy as an *imaginary horizon*, a space in which demands for equality and difference may be inscribed. Democracy from this perspective is more concerned with a certain mode of identification – and a particular way of life – than with formal political structures.[14] Yet what exactly this form of life might entail, and what more could be said about the mode of identification appropriate to democratic subjectivity, is left largely unaddressed. This is a lacuna to which James Tully's writings speak directly.

2. James Tully and practices of citizenization[15]

In *Public Philosophy in a New Key*,[16] as well as in a range of other publications, James Tully articulates a conception of political

---

[14] Ibid., p. 169.

[15] Tully argues that 'members of constitutional democracies become "citizens" not only in virtue of a . . . set of constitutionally guaranteed rights and duties enabling them to participate in the institutions of their association. They also acquire their identity *as* citizens – a form of both self-awareness and self-formation – in virtue of exercising these rights' (J. Tully, *Public Philosophy in a New Key*, Two Volumes, Cambridge: Cambridge University Press, 2008, p. 99). Furthermore, 'Citizenship is not a status given by the institutions of the modern constitutional state and international law, but negotiated practices in which one becomes a citizen through participation' (Tully, *Public Philosophy* II, p. 248).

[16] Henceforth in the text *Public Philosophy*.

contestation which, like Laclau, starts from a conception of contestability that runs all the way down. With regard to democratic practices, both Laclau and Tully suggest that their contestability is not something to be regretted and overcome.[17] Tully's position here is drawn from a Wittgensteinian account of use and meaning, as a 'negotiated practice' among participants in relations of practical interaction, in which 'the possibility of going on differently is always present', which in turn is situated clearly within an agonistic approach. As Tully argues:

> This pragmatic linguistic freedom of enunciation and initiation – of contestability and speaking otherwise – within the weighty constraints of the inherited relations of use and meaning is . . . internally related to a practical (extra-linguistic) freedom of enactment and improvisation within the inherited relations of power in which the vocabulary is used.[18]

Drawing on this account, in conjunction with insights from Arendt and Foucault, he further outlines a series of ways in which we (citizens) can engage in different forms of reasoning together (persuasion, dialogue, inquiry, negotiation, information-seeking, deliberation and eristic dialogue),[19] and can 'act otherwise' so as to contest the given norms and rules constraining our practices. These include,

1. Ways of acting otherwise within the rules of the game, modifying practices in often unnoticed, yet significant ways;
2. Raising problems about some aspect of a rule of the game, with the aim of modifying the practice;
3. Refuse to be governed by such practices by confrontation and struggle (including direct action, liberation, decolonization, revolt

---

[17] Tully, *Public Philosophy* II, p. 110. Tully argues that any practice of governance will be 'democratic' 'just in so far as the members of the organisation have some say and the opportunity to negotiate the way and by whom the power to govern their conduct is exercised in the organisation' (Tully, *Public Philosophy* I, p. 155).

[18] Tully, *Public Philosophy* II, p. 245.

[19] These forms of reasoning are practical, not theoretical, are agonistic in character and any agreements reached are always partial or conditional, 'open to reasonable redescription and challenge' (Tully, *Public Philosophy* I, p. 163).

and so on); where strategies of reform and problematization are unavailable, it is possible to[20]

4. Turn aside from governance relations and create alternative civic relationships.

Tully's account rests upon a prior shift in focus from the traditional emphasis in political theory on rights and duties, fundamental principles and constitutional essentials – what one may call the framework conditions – to 'being in dialogue over how and by whom power is exercised, which takes place both within and over the rules of the dialogues.[21] He argues in this respect, that:

> What shapes and holds individuals and groups together as 'citizens' and 'peoples' is not this or that agreement but the free agonistic activities of participation themselves.[22]

Hence, in line with his general approach, these are not abstract possibilities. Rather, they are situated and discussed within the context of what he calls a dilemma of democratic citizenship. This dilemma, he argues, consists in the fact that there are very different ways of being a citizen.[23] Broadly speaking, one can distinguish between modern and diverse or cooperative modes of citizenship, where a mode refers to an 'ensemble composed of a distinctive language of citizenship and its traditions of interpretation on the one hand, and the corresponding practices and institutions' on the other.[24] Tully puts it thus:

> The first way is to participate in the official institutions of representative democratic governments available to us at the local, national and global level. I call this *modern citizenship*. The other way is to participate outside or alongside these official institutions in a wide variety of

[20] Tully, *Public Philosophy* I, p. 24.
[21] Ibid., pp. 146–7.
[22] Note that Tully further argues that 'When these activities are unavailable or arbitrarily restricted, the members of a political association remain "subjects" rather than "citizens" because power is exercised over them without their say, non-democratically' (Tully, *Public Philosophy* I, p. 147).
[23] I return at the end of the chapter to a further specification Tully gives to this dilemma, namely, the structural constraints that modern forms of citizenship impose upon participants.
[24] Tully, *Public Philosophy* II, p. 246.

different ways. I call this cluster of alternative ways of being an active citizen *cooperative citizenship*. Both ways . . . involve citizens acting together in public and for the sake of public goods by exercising their civic response-abilities.[25]

In discussing the conception of contestation that informs Tully's arguments, I shall explore different aspects of the contrasting picture he paints between the different modes of being a citizen. Before doing so, it is useful to reflect somewhat further on these different possibilities of acting and being, and the ways in which they differ from and echo some aspects of the picture of democratic engagement outlined by Laclau. Once the distinction between modern and diverse modes of citizenship is introduced, the four options specified can be further divided into two groups, with the first two roughly corresponding to participating in the official institutions and sites of modern democratic governance, while options three and four correspond more closely to diverse citizenship in that they seek to capture ways of acting alongside or outside of existing institutions.

Attempting to map Laclau's account of democratic claim-making onto these four options has interesting results. At first sight, his account corresponds to the first two options: acting otherwise within the rules of the game so as to modify them resonates with his emphasis on the centrality of articulatory practices to politics; these precisely are hegemonic struggles. Laclau's intellectual debt here is clearly Gramsci's conception of war of position. Raising problems about some aspect of the rules of the game, with the aim of modifying the practices – the second option – comes closest to the practice of articulating political demands (rather than making requests, which take the terrain of engagement for granted). However, despite these similarities, Laclau's account here is one that is overwhelmingly vertical – demands are addressed to the state – while Tully's focus is on the horizontal relations between citizens. Option three, namely confrontation and struggle with a view to refuse to be governed, is a central part of Laclau's conception of politics as

---

[25] J. Tully, 'A Dilemma of Democratic Citizenship'. Paper delivered at the University of Victoria, 8 May 2010. Emphasis in original.

struggle for hegemony. But here once more there is a significant difference: for Laclau, politics is and remains informed by a struggle *for* hegemony; one could even argue that the telos of engagement in politics is hegemony, while Tully more clearly considers the possibility of withdrawing from the existing terrain of struggles, and setting up alternatives outside of state structures and institutions (option four).

Tully	Laclau
	Requests
	Engaging in existing institutions
	Adminstrative, non-political action
Acting otherwise within the rules of the game	Articulatory practices
Engaging in existing institutions	Engaging in existing institutions
Problematizing an aspect of the rule	Articulating demands
Engaging in existing institutions with a view to modify them	Engaging in existing institutions with a view to modify them
Refusal to be governed: strategies of resistance	Refusal to be governed: strategies of resistance
Anti-institutional	Anti-institutional, hegemonic struggles
Creating alternative spaces of existence	
Extra-institutional	

On this reading, Laclau is a theorist of political engagement and struggle, while Tully considers both engagement and disengagement as modes of operation.[26]

From modern to diverse/cooperative citizenship

First in *Public Philosophy*, and later in subsequent publications such as his lead essay for this volume, Tully sets out to provide an account

---

[26] It should be noted that the conception of populism outlined in Laclau's most recent work tends to emphasize confrontation and struggle – frontal opposition – as what is truly democratic, while engagement on the extant institutional terrain is sometimes treated as the mere administration of things, devoid of real politics.

of changes in the ways we conceive of citizenship. (This is not merely a descriptive account. Rather, it seeks to outline a particular *ethos* of citizenization.[27] I return to this issue at the end of the chapter.) This is done through providing a contrast between modern and diverse conceptions of citizenship, by drawing on conceptual developments, while situating these in the context of major historical processes (e.g. the development of the nation state, colonization, globalization). Tully's reading provides an account that is at once incisive, acute and historically sensitive, while not eschewing conceptual and normative issues and implications of the positions outlined.

The broad contrast looks something like this: the key features of modern citizenship, associated with modernization and colonization, includes the 'status an individual has relative to a set of institutions'[28] and the groundwork for this status is laid by the imposition of a formal structure of law such that 'outside the rule of law, there is no civilization and no citizenship'.[29] Hence, the focus is on citizenship as a 'universalizable legal status, underpinned by institutions'.[30] This conception of modern citizenship, 'with its membership codes, rights and duties', also characterizes 'all other practices of citizenship in relation to its unique form as the universal standard'.[31] It thus operates as the telos for societies on their way to full, modern citizenship and in the process it denigrates and rates as inferior any alternatives.[32] This is a familiar picture.

In contrast to this, diverse citizenship is associated with 'a *diversity* or multiplicity of different *practices* of citizenship in the West and the

---

[27] Tully argues that the distinction between 'democratic constitutional principles . . . and political ethos (modes of civic conduct) is analogous to the distinction between moral principles and ethics, or ethos' (Tully, *Public Philosophy* I, p. 145).

[28] This status is normally fleshed out in terms of four rights, with associated duties, including (1) civil liberties (liberties of the moderns, including the liberty to participate in the private economic sphere, to enter into contracts etc.); (2) participation rights (rights of the ancients); (3) social and economic rights; and (4) minority rights. Tully, *Public Philosophy* II, pp. 250–5.

[29] Tully, 'A Dilemma of Democratic Citizenship'.

[30] Tully, *Public Philosophy* II, p. 248.

[31] Ibid.

[32] Ibid., p. 268.

non-West'. Here the emphasis is on its diversity of forms, characterized not in terms of 'universal institutions and historical processes' but in terms of 'grass-roots democratic or civic *activities* of the "governed"',[33] so that citizenship is not a legal status, but a set of negotiated practices. As we have already noted, these negotiated practices go all the way down.[34] It is through participation in activities that one 'becomes a citizen'.[35] Citizenship is not simply assigned on the basis of a legal status.[36] Traditional political theory, Tully suggests, overlooks these activities of citizenization since they privilege rights, rules and institutions as what must be presupposed by these activities.[37] As a result, in contrast to civil citizenship that is institution-based, civic citizenship 'exists in relations',[38] where relations of governance are approached from a standpoint of citizen as agent (not as governed subject)[39] and where the freedom of the *Spielraum* is emphasized and practices of self-formation become central.[40] Law here is treated not as a set of institutionalized rules set over and against citizens, who must obey, but as a 'practical art'; 'the living rule of law is the pattern of interplay and interaction of the negotiated practices'.[41] Diverse citizens

---

[33] Ibid., p. 247. Emphasis in Original.

[34] As Tully puts it: 'It comprises civic activities and the ongoing contestation and negotiation over these practices by the participants and by those subject to and affected by yet excluded from them, and so on in turn. There is never the last voice or word' (*Public Philosophy* II, p. 270).

[35] Tully, *Public Philosophy* II, p. 248.

[36] Tully suggests that there are three ways in which the distinction between institutional status and practice is being made: (1) Civil/civic: civil citizens have legally guaranteed opportunities for participation; in the case of civic citizenship the emphasis is not on rights and duties, but on 'abilities, competences, character and conduct acquired in participation' (p. 271). The former marks a duty enforced by authorities, whereas the latter suggests creative engagement. (2) Libertas/freedom: liberty is a condition of being at liberty, thanks to the law; whereas freedom is not an opportunity but a manifestation: 'It is not a matter of official civil liberties and offices being open to participation . . . but of the citizenry *experiencing* a civic way of life that makes it a free city' (p. 272). (3) Use and practice (*usus*) brings into being a right (*ius*): 'Institutionalised rights come into being from the practice of corresponding activities and are . . . guaranteed by these activities' (p. 273).

[37] Tully, *Public Philosophy* II, p. 269.

[38] Ibid., p. 274.

[39] Ibid., p. 276.

[40] Tully draws on the work of Johan Huizinga, *Homo Ludens*, for the argument that game playing is freedom. See Tully, *Public Philosophy* I, p. 137.

[41] Tully, *Public Philosophy* II, p. 287.

employ 'contextual and comparative genres of reasoning', 'starting from the local languages and negotiated practices of citizens on location and compare and contrast their similarities and dissimilarities with each other from various standpoints, in contrast to the 'universalizing rationalities' of modern citizenship.[42]

Thus, we have an account of practices and modes of citizenship that divide into two clearly defined categories with sedimented, legal status and institutionalized forms of citizenship on the one hand, and more dispute-based, non-institutionalized, activity-based practices on the other. On the face of it, and despite differences in nuance and detail, this account is not far from that provided by Laclau, who also divides contestatory activities between institutionalized and non-institutional politics on the other. It is now necessary to turn to Tully's account of the subject formation associated with each mode of citizenship so as to see whether this contrast holds up when focussing on these aspects of the account.

Modes of citizenship and self-formation

One does not become a practitioner blindly. The requisite abilities are acquired in pre-linguistic interaction and by more or less elaborate and reflective practices of the self on the self in the course of learning one's way around in a specific relationship.[43]

Tully consistently emphasizes the critical activities and consequences associated with diverse citizenship. He argues, for instance, that a civic (in contrast to a civil) public sphere comes into being where 'those who are subject to a closed governance relation take it out of the darkness of the "private sphere" of being unquestioned. . . . subjecting it to the light and enlightenment of public scrutiny'.[44] One of the most important consequences of these critical activities is the fact that from the perspective of diverse citizenship, modern citizenship is disclosed

---

[42] Ibid., p. 270.
[43] Ibid., p. 278.
[44] Ibid., p. 284.

as but one historical form among others. Hence, the critical attitude associated with diverse modes of citizenship has the capacity to 'free us from the hold of the globally dominant language of modern citizenship' so as to de-subalternize other modes of citizenship.[45]

In contrast, modern citizenship is portrayed as uncritical and passive: a status is bestowed upon the citizen by law. Tully argues as much:

> A person has the status of citizenship in virtue of *being subject to* civil law in two senses: to an established and enforced system of law and to the 'civilising', pacifying or socialising force of the rule of law on the subjectivity (self-awareness and self-formation) of those who are constrained to obey over time.[46]

This status inculcates a modern or juridical conception of subjectivity, which is abstract and independent in character.[47] Insofar as participation is emphasized, it is limited to 'juridical citizens exercising democratic rights within modern institutions'.[48]

Struggles within and against these modern, 'civilizing' processes, such as struggles to be included in modern citizenship and to extend the use of political rights beyond the official public sphere – are described as 'struggles *for* new kinds of citizenship', that include acts of civil disobedience and rebellion. Importantly, Tully argues that these struggles *cannot* be called practices of citizenship in the modern tradition: 'what are seen as activities of citizenship by the civic tradition – struggles for new forms of recognition and extensions of citizenship – *fall outside* of modern citizenship with its institutional/status orientation'.[49]

The ethos of citizenization

This account of the different modes of citizenship-subjectivity is accompanied by an additional discussion of the ethos of each of the

[45] Ibid., p. 249.
[46] Ibid., p. 250.
[47] Ibid., p. 250.
[48] Ibid., p. 253.
[49] Ibid., p. 256. Emphasis added.

modes of citizenship. For instance, Tully argues that the questioning characteristic of diverse citizenship takes the form of what he calls 'civicization': that is a practice of 'non-violently negotiating and transforming the governance relationships' from the ground up. In *Public Philosophy*, Tully already suggests that non-violent action is the mode of activity that embodies the telos of practices of citizenization. Although Tully does not use this language, he argues that 'distrust and violence begets distrust and violence' and that this history of non-violence teaches us that 'there is another more powerful way that leads to peace'.[50] In 'A Dilemma of Democratic Citizenship', this argument is stated more forcefully. Here the argument is interweaved from the outset into both the pictures of citizenship that are presented.

In the case of modern citizenship, the violence structuring all relations is foregrounded: others are treated as things 'to be coerced, disciplined, reconstructed and socialised';[51] the violence of the modern history of colonialism is emphasized and the antisocial character of the modern citizen – as articulated in theorists such as Hobbes, Kant, Darwin, Marx, Mill and Freud – is emphasized. In this picture:

> Humans are basically antisocial, and antagonistic, and therefore untrustworthy outside of the coercive institutions of the modern state . . . Therefore, humanity needs a master to impose the basic institutions of social cooperation on these anti-social beings that will lead up through the stages of development and socialisation.[52]

By contrast, in the case of cooperative citizenship, non-violence and peaceable interactions are foregrounded (Ghandi, Martin Luther King, but not Mandela). Indeed, the ethos of cooperative citizenship is specified more closely now as one of non-violence and of cooperation:

---

[50] Ibid., p. 295. For an incisive discussion of the role of history in Tully's analysis, see, B. Honig and M. Stears, 'The New Realism: From Modus Vivendi to Justice', in J. Floyd and M. Stears, eds, *Political Philosophy versus History?* Cambridge: Cambridge University Press, 2011, pp. 177–205.
[51] Tully, 'A Dilemma of Democratic Citizenship', p. 28.
[52] Ibid., p. 12.

As we have seen, modern citizenship is founded on the premise that came into vogue in Europe in the 18th century: namely, that individuals, classes, races and civilizations are basically antisocial and antagonistic. This is the premise that underwrites the conclusion that institutions of modern democratic citizenship must be coercively imposed. For the cooperative tradition, this premise is another false dogma of modernisation.[53]

Cooperative citizenship emphasizes 'relationships of mutual cooperation and love among all forms of life on the planet' and these relationships, Tully suggests, 'are *more basic* than relationships of antagonism.'[54] This, he argues, is so in two senses. First, social relations of mutual aid actually are the most basic of social relationships and more competitive relations are parasitic on them. Second, these relations 'are themselves embedded in yet deeper ecological relationships of cooperation and mutual assistance among all the diverse forms of life on the planet.'[55] Hence, the differences between Tully and Laclau in this respect run deep, arising as they do from almost diametrically opposed conceptions of human subjectivity.

3. Further reflections

Let me now begin to reflect on what we can gain from Laclau and Tully's readings respectively, before posing some questions that stand in need of further reflection. In both cases, as I have argued, contestability is a central feature of the respective accounts, and in both cases, it goes 'all the way down', or so it seems at first blush. (There are, in each case as we have just seen, aspects of the account that do not seem to be open to contestation. These come into view more clearly when the accounts are contrasted with one another.)

[53] Ibid., p. 32.
[54] Ibid., Emphasis added.
[55] Ibid., pp. 32–3.

In both cases, although with different inflections, the authors posit something approaching a dichotomic division between, on the one hand, institutionalized and, on the other, anti- and extra-institutional modes of political engagement and action. There is a strong emphasis on and critical reading of the domain of sedimentation, institutionalization, the law and juridical subjectivity in both Laclau and Tully. This is contrasted to that of the diverse, action- and practice-oriented activities falling in the extra-institutional, issue-oriented domains. As noted, for Laclau the emphasis, nevertheless, remains on *hegemonic* practices, that is, on the principle possibility of change and rearticulation of existing institutions and relations.

In terms of subject formation, both authors emphasize the constitutive character of political action. Whereas Laclau's focus is on the constitution of collective agency, Tully's is on 'becoming a citizen'. However, it is also in this domain that the most important divergences appear. Laclau's account of subjectivity clearly falls within what Tully calls the modern citizenship, with its focus on antagonism and conflict. This, for Laclau, constitutes the heart of politics. As we have seen, Tully contrasts what he sees as the key features of this ethos of modern citizenship – violence, control, discipline and antagonism – to that of a peaceable, cooperative mode characteristic of diverse citizenship. The positing of these sharp divisions between modes of subjectivity corresponding to particular forms of political engagement and contestation, of course, reflects wider agreement in political theory on the institutional/extra-institutional divide and in some sense, does not come as a surprise. However, each of the authors *complicates* that picture by introducing further nuances: for Laclau, the institutional is both the crucial site of hegemonic struggle, and the site of non-political, administrative action. Tully, on the other hand, seeks to highlight the extra-institutional as a site of the development of alternative ways of living, which could act as invitations to a different way of doing things.[56] Even though this is not a point Tully develops, such invitations, no doubt, stand in need of

[56]　Tully, *Public Philosophy* II, p. 308.

generalization through a series of possible political practices, of which hegemonic struggles are one possibility. I would like now to reflect for a moment on whether these divisions necessarily follow from the theoretical presuppositions and conditions stipulated by each author.

I have dealt at length with this question in relation to Laclau's arguments elsewhere. So let me just summarize my argument here. His position changes over time with regard to the institutional/non-institutional division. In *On Populist Reason* it corresponds to the non-political, administrative/political divide. By contrast, in *Hegemony and Socialist Strategy* and elsewhere in earlier writings, Laclau emphasizes the centrality of a Gramscian strategy of 'war of position' to his account of hegemony, which must be exercised in the institutional as well as in the extra-institutional domain, the terrain of civil society. Political engagement and struggle, per definition, is not limited to one or the other. The struggle for hegemony includes the creation of new myths and their generalization into new political imaginaries that can inspire change and reorder existing relations.

On the question of the centrality of antagonism to subject formation there is complete consistency in Laclau's writings over time. From the start Laclau transforms the Saussurian distinction between syntagm and paradigm into an account of difference and equivalence where the drawing of political frontiers is given a privileged status. This results, ultimately, in his failure to distinguish between the individuation of identity on the one hand, and the formation of antagonisms on the other.[57] The consequence of this failure is the privileging of antagonism as a mode of subject formation. Indeed, it becomes the paradigmatic form of subject formation to the exclusion of (most) others. It also has serious consequences for his account of democracy. Earlier I have noted his distinction between democratic and popular subject positions, and the consequent emaciated account of democracy that follows from it. The failure to give sufficient attention to the specificity of a

---

[57] I discuss this further in A. J. Norval, 'Frontiers in question', *Acta Philosophica*, 2: 51–76, 1997.

democratic form of identification, I would argue, arises directly from this emphasis on frontier formation and the centrality of antagonism, as a paradigmatic form of political engagement.

If Laclau overemphasizes the antagonistic dimension, it is underplayed in Tully's work on diverse modes of citizenship. The reason for this, as we have seen, can once again be traced back to the way in which the division between modes of citizenship has been accounted for. There is no doubt that Tully characterizes the division between modern and diverse citizenship in a dichotomic fashion. As we have seen, this is the case both with respect to what is characterized as the ethos of each mode of citizenship, and with respect to the characteristic form of engagement and self-formation associated with each mode. Diverse citizenship is portrayed as sensitive to local languages and traditions, as multiple and nuanced, as open to diversity and plurality, as engaged in conversation, negotiation and contestation that takes a non-antagonistic form. The account of modern citizenship, by contrast, focuses more on its imposition on those not already included (the poor, women, minorities, indigenous populations and colonized nations, among others). In the face of standard accounts of modern citizenship, and of the continuing practices associated with it, this is no doubt a crucial and necessary corrective. Nevertheless, the account sits uneasily with some other dimensions of Tully's approach. Let me turn to those now.

4. Citizenship and agonism

Playing games is primordial and shared by every civilisation. It is the activity associated with and often equated with fun. Moreover, following Burkhardt and Nietzsche, game playing usually involves an 'agonal' or contestatory element.[58]

As I have indicated, Tully draws on Arendt, Foucault and Wittgenstein among others to develop an account of political engagement that is

---

[58] Tully, *Public Philosophy* I, p. 137.

serious about contestation, suggesting contestability goes all the way down. In this, Tully's work is truly exceptional and radical, attracting the ire of legal political theorists for whom the idea, for instance, of basic constitutional rules as contestable, is an anathema and who would reject the shift from constitutional democracy to democratic constitutionalism.[59]

In Volume I of *Public Philosophy* Tully outlines a general account of the agonistic freedom of citizens that has as its focus the playing of games. This account informs the shift from a focus on rights and abstract norms, to a form of reasoning in media res, as Owen puts it in his contribution to this volume. Instead of placing the theorist over and above the *demos*, the theorist is in the demos and every reflective citizen is treated as a public philosopher.[60] The resulting approach is a form of practical philosophy, oriented towards working on ourselves 'by working on the practices and problematisations in which we find ourselves.'[61] However, we should note that Tully does not seek merely to provide thick descriptions a la Geertz, but to provide a *critical* form of engagement with the conditions of possibility of those practices and forms of governance within which we find ourselves.[62] This is done through providing a critical survey 'of the languages and practices', supplemented by historical genealogies.[63] The primacy of practice is fleshed out in terms of the agonistic games of freedom we play.

Public Philosophy articulates one of the most radical responses available to the question: 'citizenship for whom?' On the first page of *Public Philosophy* he states that the term 'citizen' refers:

> to a person who is subject to a relationship of governance (that is to say, governed) and, simultaneously and primarily, is an active agent in the field of a governance relationship. While this includes the official sense of 'citizen' as a recognised member of a state, *it is*

[59]　Ibid., p. 4.
[60]　Ibid.
[61]　Ibid., p. 16.
[62]　Ibid.
[63]　Ibid., p. 17.

obviously broader and deeper, and more appropriate and effective for that reason.[64]

Here, citizen is a term that denotes *an active participant in the games of governance*, but is not restricted to citizenship in a narrower sense (a recognized member of a state). This is an extremely powerful conception for it allows us to characterize the activities of *all* those engaged in active contestation, regardless of their strict institutional status, as activities of citizens. This sense of citizenship also resonates with Tully's equally radical and powerful conception of democracy. Democracy, he argues, should also be understood in non-restrictive terms. That is, 'democratic games of modifying the rules of governance are not restricted to the formal institutions of constitutional democracy but can occur in *any* practice of governance'.[65] As Tully rightly argues:

> If the terms 'democracy' and 'participation' are used to refer only to the formal institutions of representative government, then . . . local and global struggles to democratise decision-making in dispersed practices of governance will not be seen as democratic practices.[66]

All the elements of the account here cohere together to draw a radical picture of democracy, citizenship and 'becoming a citizen' through participation in the multiplicity of relations of governance and games of politics shaping, informing and restricting our lives.[67] However, how precisely this account maps onto the division between modern and diverse citizenship stands in need of further clarification. I now turn to a closer consideration of this division.

---

[64] Ibid., p. 3. Emphasis added. This is echoed elsewhere in the text. For instance, Tully argues that 'Citizenship . . . is a form of identity that we come to acquire by being "free citizens", by engagement in the institutions of self-rule of a free people' (Tully, *Public Philosophy* I, p. 162).

[65] Tully, *Public Philosophy* I, p. 154.

[66] Ibid., p. 156.

[67] However, Tully also considers a more restrictive account of citizenship that foregrounds its insertion in a constitutional democracy. Here the domain of agonistic freedom is considerably narrower. This more restrictive account of citizenship also raises questions with regard to the division between modern and diverse modes of citizenship. I turn to a consideration of this issue in the concluding parts of this chapter.

5. Agonistic ethos?

There are two aspects of this division on which I would like to comment. One concerns the ethos associated with diverse citizenship, while the other concerns the characterization of the division between the two key modes of citizenship itself. Given the emphasis on game-playing as a feature of all civilizations, the characterization of agency as *homo ludens* and the centrality accorded to the playing of games as a contestatory activity, it is difficult to see how the sharp division between the two modes of citizenship can be maintained. If indeed, we are *homo ludens* then the game-playing will cut across the division. But so will the possibility of critical engagement, which as we have seen earlier, is primarily reserved for the account Tully provides of diverse citizenship. The concern here is whether Tully's account comes closer to and echoes the problems of a Habermas and a Rawls in this respect. This becomes very clear in their treatment of 'newly emergent democratic claims'[68] that are approached as if they always already could have been argued 'according to the protocols of public reason'.[69] Honig argues a similar point with respect to Habermas.[70] What is at stake here, as she points out, is how we *read* the past. In *Public Philosophy*, it seems that a reading of modern citizenship predominates that paradoxically underplays and even writes out the struggles constitutive of that tradition in favour of a focus on its sedimentation in law and institutions. This is what allows the sharp contrast with diverse citizenship to be set up, and what allows struggle and contestation to be reserved for the latter. To put it differently, the reading of the modern tradition of citizenship perhaps gives too much weight to the picture informing the self-constitution of that tradition, a picture that, as we know from Habermas and Rawls,

---

[68] As Jason Frank argues in his analysis of the staging of dissensus in Frederick Douglas's speeches, Rawls's account reads the arguments put forward by Douglas and Phillips suggesting that they '*could* have argued according to the protocols of public reason, and that had they had opportunities for proper reflection they *would* have argued in this way'. J. Frank, *Constituent Moments*, Durham: Duke University Press, 2010, p. 226.

[69] Frank, *Constituent Moments*, p. 226.

[70] B. Honig, 'Between Decision and Deliberation: Political Paradox in Democratic Theory', *American Political Science Review* 101 (1): 1–17, 2007.

privileges the working out of reason over time, rather than struggle and contestation as the basis of all discourses of right. In seeking to reserve contestation for the diverse tradition, Tully risks repeating that picture.

Part of the reason for this, is the argument put forward by Tully that despite advances made by reforms to the module of modern citizenship:

> these reforms have been *self-limiting* because they have taken place within and accepted the background institutions and processes that are claimed to be the basis of democratic citizenship. (A dilemma of democratic citizenship. They are *not open to democratic challenge* and negotiation by those who are subject to them and their effects worldwide.)[71]

Hence the focus on alternative forms of citizenship seeking to criticize 'the *enclosure* of citizens' response-abilities within official representative institutions'.[72] Although there is no doubt a significant measure of truth in this assessment, counter-examples abound, sufficiently so that we need to take heed of what they signify. This is the case both for struggles within and over one of the most sedimented institutional terrains, namely that of the law, as well as over the boundaries of citizenship. While there may well be as many setbacks and instances of misfires as there are of successful struggles, where these struggles succeed, on Tully's own account, we need to treat them as potentially exemplary cases. One case in point would be the contestation, waged under the Aliens Tort Claims Act, by Khulumani, a post-transitional social movement, campaigning to bring a number of large corporations to book over their aiding and abetting of the apartheid regime. Though

---

[71] Tully, 'A Dilemma of Democratic Citizenship', p. 15. Emphasis added. In *Public Philosophy* I, Tully argues that citizens frequently run up against unjustifiable limits: 'In any of these activities, there is always a vast ensemble of relationships that are not open to negotiation' and that '"structure" and limit the foreground field of possible actions' (p. 296). If citizens try to bring these structural relationships into the space of negotiation, 'they are met with refusal, often because the structural relationships are the very basis of the unequal power and universal claim to authority of the hegemonic partners' (p. 296).

[72] Tully, 'A Dilemma of Democratic Citizenship', p. 17.

the legal battle is not yet over, the movement has succeeded precisely in making visible an alternative way of conceiving of what is due to citizens in post-transitional contexts, such as the South African one, as well as putting corporations on notice, when operating in exploitative contexts.[73] Similarly, on the issue of the limits to citizenship, there are numerous struggles by illegal immigrants, *sans-papiers* and others that have managed to contest and challenge existing entitlements and the lack thereof.[74] Such struggles both make visible the extent to which all rights and entitlements finally rest on the taking of rights, as Honig suggests,[75] rather than the version of liberal rights discourse that writes struggle and contestation out of the self-understanding of modern liberal democracies. It also highlights the continuing importance of democratic engagement in institutional sites, where struggle for an alternative way of doing things remain of the greatest importance.

Let me now turn to the second question, namely that of ethos. In the earlier discussion of modes of citizenship and the question of ethos, I have noted a shift in terminology: Tully moves from using the term 'diverse citizenship' to that of 'cooperative citizenship'. This is obviously an important change, and it is so for two reasons. Let us look first at the shift in terminology. Characterizing the alternative tradition as 'diverse', Tully emphasizes the multiplicity, plurality and non-closure of this tradition, in terms of the range of activities it captures, the modes of subject formation and of reasoning. This characterization takes the form of what I would call, following Cavell, non-teleological perfectionism. It captures the sense in which the critical engagements and contestations call forth alternative possibilities of being and acting, but it does not – and I think this is important – prefigure the form those contestations may take. Once the term 'cooperative citizenship' is introduced, this situation changes. We no longer have a non-substantive, non-teleological

[73] See A. J. Norval, '"No Reconciliation without Redress": Articulating Political Demands in Post-transitional South Africa', *Critical Discourse Studies* 6 (4): 311–21, 2009.
[74] See, for instance, P. Nyers, 'Abject Cosmopolitanism: The Politics of Protection in the Anti-deportation Movement', *Third World Quarterly* 26 (6): 1069–93, 2003.
[75] B. Honig, *Democracy and the Foreigner*, Princeton: Princeton University Press, 2001, p. 99.

picture of contestation. Rather, this picture is replaced with a rather thicker, more substantive sense of the form and direction of contestatory practices. Notwithstanding the obvious historical importance of what is introduced as exemplary instances of the tradition – ranging from the activities of Ghandi and Martin Luther King to self-governing, democratic cooperatives – this shift in terminology quite drastically closes down the range of possible candidates for participation in the diverse tradition. There also seems to be a shift in terms of the range of possible contestatory activities in relation to existing institutions and traditions. Whereas in *Public Philosophy* Tully argues for a wide range of ways of acting differently, in 'A dilemma of democratic citizenship' there is a turn to a focus on ways of participating 'outside or alongside' official institutions.[76] Taken in conjunction with the emphasis on the structural limits posited by modern citizenship, there seems to be a move away from a 'war of position' in Gramscian terms, to an argument for engagement in activities of agonistic freedom that circumvents existing institutions, working alongside or outside them. Tully clearly seriously entertains the question of the difficult relation between cooperative citizens and modern reformers, arguing that it is a dilemma whether their activities will cancel one another out and work at cross purposes. Despite the fact that he suggests that cooperative citizens are 'happy to join modern "reform citizens" . . . if they are effective,'[77] the paradigm case of cooperative citizenship increasingly seems to be non-violent, citizenship-based movements re-appropriating democratically relevant capacities 'rather than seeking to reform modern citizenship from within or to overthrow the capitalist system from without.'[78] While this picture may be an attractive one, it is one that introduces important limitations and serious consequences for the way in which we think of democratic engagement. Although one has to lament the use of violence in politics, it is no doubt also true that violence not only begets violence as Tully suggests, it sometimes plays a part in allowing the fashioning

---

[76] Tully, 'A Dilemma of Democratic Citizenship', p. 1.
[77] Ibid., p. 23.
[78] Ibid., p. 25.

of less violent politics. As Honig and Stears put it, it may be the case that 'every Ghandi needs a Bhagat Singh, every Martin Luther King Jr a Malcolm X'.[79] Moreover, as they further point out, excluding these elements of democratic struggle from consideration may leave us ill-prepared for what may be required in the fight for justice and equality,[80] and certainly limits, with serious consequences, the range of activities that may legitimately be included under the category of democratic engagements. Beyond the difficult question of force and violence, the shift to alternative sites of self-governing risks shunning the more traditional, institutional sites of engagement, sidelining important struggles and the possibility of making a difference within such sites, for citizens and non-citizens alike.

6. Contestation, claim-making and a democratic ethos

Contest means play.[81]

At the start of this chapter, I argued that it is when a practice is challenged, or is seen to be inadequate or questionable for some reason, that we are called upon to recount the criteria of and to reconsider the point of the practices in which we engage, which we value and defend or criticize. It is precisely in this sense that the practices of citizenization described by Tully facilitate the making visible of aspects of the modern tradition that would otherwise remain hidden from view, thus continuing to underwrite practices of domination. The aspect-change brought about by such practices, in genealogical fashion, brings into view both the specificity of the modern mode of citizenship and highlights alternatives. If approached from the perspective of a

---

[79] Honig and Stears, *The New Realism*, p. 203.
[80] Ibid., p. 201.
[81] J. Huizinga, *Homo Ludens: A Study of the Play Element in Culture*, Boston: Beacon, 1955.

non-teleological perfectionist starting point, then both practices of citizenization and the articulation of demands may be viewed as forms of contestation that enact games of agonistic freedom. Taking a non-restrictive account of citizenization as exemplary of such games of contestation allows one to engage with challenges and modifications to existing regimes and practices of governance, without excluding, per definition, either a range of practices that do not conform to the model of either antagonistic forms of identification (Laclau) or an explicitly cooperative ethics (Tully). Each of them exemplifies a specific mode of citizen engagement, and neither should be taken as primary. Agonism – 'reciprocal incitation and struggle' – does not admit of these restrictions.

It is important that the range of possibilities of acting otherwise available to us is not restricted by premature exclusion, and that we also seek to develop practices of democratic engagement that reflect explicitly on the various possibilities, thinking about the circumstances under which we would engage in one rather than another form of action. What are the conditions that drive citizens to turn away from existing institutions? What are the consequences for democratic action of such a turning away from society? I have suggested that for Tully this possibility arises because of the inherent limitations he discerns in modern forms of citizenship. However, should we question this account of limitations, as I have suggested we do, the possibility of turning a move *away* from society into one that is simultaneously *towards* society, arises.[82] As Cavell puts it, such turning may surprise us. Thinking about a turning away from society as simultaneously opening up a turn towards it allows us to notice that the alternative ways of being and acting that are conceived of on the margins of society may become critical tools to re-engage society. Laclau's work on hegemonic struggle stands as a reminder that extra-institutional politics should

---

[82] I discuss the idea of such turning in more depth in 'Moral Perfectionism and Democratic Responsiveness: Reading Cavell with Foucault', *Ethics & Global Politics* 4 (1): 207–29, 2011.

not remain isolated; we should seek, through struggle, to re-establish articulations between the institutional and non-institutional domains. This, precisely, is the serious work done by such alternatives: democratic re-engagement through exemplary ways of living and acting is a well-spring of democratic imagination, and a source of critical change in society.

5

To Act Otherwise: Agonistic
Republicanism and Global Citizenship*

Duncan Bell

1. Introduction

James Tully's body of work constitutes one of the most innovative interventions in the current debates over global justice.[1] Combining erudite historical analysis with compelling political critique, he elucidates the diverse practices and complex legacies of European imperialism, connecting past and present in a manner unusual among contemporary political theorists. His historical scholarship, focusing above all on John Locke, helped place empire squarely on the agenda of historians of political thought.[2] It demonstrated, as much subsequent scholarship has confirmed, that questions of colonization and imperial governance were braided through the history of Euro-American political theory.[3] But Tully has moved beyond this historical genre

---

* Thanks to the following for offering comments and insights: Dan Matlin, Andrew Sartori, Sarah Fine, Bonnie Honig. All the usual disclaimers apply.

[1] For diverse variants, see T. Pogge, *World Poverty and Human Rights: Cosmopolitan Responsibilities and Reforms*, Cambridge: Polity, 2002; S. Caney, *Justice Beyond Borders: A Global Political Theory*, Oxford: Oxford University Press, 2005; S. Benhabib, *Another Cosmopolitanism*, Oxford: Oxford University Press, 2008; N. Fraser, *Scales of Justice: Reimagining Political Space in a Globalizing World*, New York: Columbia University Press, 2008; M. Hardt and A. Negri, *Empire*, Cambridge: Harvard University Press, 2000; D. Harvey, *Cosmopolitanism and the Geographies of Freedom*, New York: Columbia University Press, 2009.

[2] See especially J. Tully, *An Approach to Political Philosophy: Locke in Contexts*, Cambridge: Cambridge University Press, 1993.

[3] For recent overviews, see D. Bell, 'Ideologies of Empire', in M. Freeden, L. T. Sargent and M. Stears, eds, *The Oxford Handbook of Political Ideologies*, Oxford: Oxford University Press, 2013; J. Pitts, 'Political Theory and Empire', *Annual Review of Political Science* 13: 211–35, 2010; S. Muthu, ed., *Empire and Modern Political Thought*, Cambridge: Cambridge University Press, 2012.

to unpack the ways in which the imperial past haunts the present, a spectre not yet vanquished. Empire shapes the very categories in which we 'moderns' think about politics, as well as the institutions bequeathed to us by half a millennium of conquest and colonization. Tully's theoretical orientation – which I term 'agonistic republicanism' – was first systematically outlined in *Strange Multiplicity* and elaborated in the essays collected as *Public Philosophy in a New Key*.[4] He has now extended it further in his latest discussion of cooperative citizenship. The orientation is agonistic insofar as it stresses the irreducibility and inevitability of conflict and struggle in the negotiation of political life.[5] It is republican insofar as it seeks to harness the powers of active virtuous citizenship in enacting democratic freedom.[6] Drawing insights from a diverse array of thinkers, perhaps above all Quentin Skinner, Foucault and Wittgenstein, Tully outlines a form of radical republican theorizing sensitive to the rich tapestry of practices of governance and freedom found throughout the world.[7]

In the following pages I offer an assessment of Tully's ongoing project as a contribution to debates over global politics. The chapter is partly exegetical, partly critical, seeking both to outline some of the ways in which Tully frames the contemporary global condition while offering

---

[4] J. Tully, *Strange Multiplicity: Constitutionalism in the Age of Diversity*, Cambridge: Cambridge University Press, 1995; J. Tully, *Public Philosophy in a New Key*, Two Volumes, Cambridge: Cambridge University Press, 2008.

[5] For Tully, the benefits of an agonistic account of politics are manifold, for it emphasises the 'manifest reality of partisanship, dissent, disagreement, contestation and adversarial reasoning in the history and present of democratic societies and the positive role it plays in exposing and overcoming structures of inequality and injustice, fostering a critical democratic ethos and, *eo ipso*, creating autonomous citizens with bonds of solidarity across real differences.' Tully, *Public Philosophy* II, p. 110.

[6] For non-agonistic republican accounts of global politics, see the essays by C. Laborde, 'Republicanism and Global Justice: A Sketch', *European Journal of Political Theory* 9 (1): 48–69, 2010; P. Petit, 'A Republican Law of People', *European Journal of Political Theory* 9 (1): 48–69, 2010; D. Ivison, 'Republican Human Rights?', *European Journal of Political Theory* 9 (1): 31–47, 2010; L. Halldenius, 'Building Blocks of a Republican Cosmopolitanism: The Modality of Being Free', *European Journal of Political Theory* 9 (1): 12–30, 2010; J. Bohman, *Democracy across Borders: From Dêmos to Dêmoi*, Cambridge, MA: MIT Press, 2007.

[7] Tully's conception of theory as a critical mode of practical reasoning is outlined in the chapter by Anthony Laden, so I will not dwell on it here. Also see A. S. Laden, 'The Key to/of Public Philosophy', *Political Theory* 39 (1): 112–17, 2011.

some challenges along the way. I develop two related lines of argument, both of which flow from what I will call the 'asymmetry problem': the stark disjunction between his analysis of the pervasive impact of imperialism on the current global order and the critical resources that cooperative citizenship offers in response. Bonnie Honig hints at the problem when she writes that '[l]ike a realist, Tully sees the expansion of power, governance, and violence everywhere in the contemporary world, but, like a humanist, he insists nonetheless on hoping against hope for the human miracle against it.'[8] I question whether Tully's appealing humanism is sufficient to grapple with the depredations and power structures of the current imperial order. Section 2 outlines some salient features of Tully's conception of citizenship, while probing issues of subject formation, ethico-political education and the possibilities of mass civic mobilization. Section 3 challenges his argument about the primacy of non-violence, suggesting that it may be prohibitively self-limiting. In the spirit of dialogue which Tully's work so commendably embodies, I will pose these challenges as a series of questions, open to disputation and intended as an opening for further debate.

2. Global virtue ethics: Agonistic citizenship and the arts of the self

The current debates over global justice have been framed largely in terms of a prescriptive discourse of justice and human rights. Tully adopts a different theoretical stance. The aim of public philosophy, he argues, is

> . . . not to develop a normative theory as the solution to the problems
> of this way of being governed, such as a theory of justice, equality
> or democracy. Rather, it is to disclose the historically contingent

---

[8] B. Honig, '[Un]Dazzled by the Ideal: Tully's Politics and Humanism in Tragic Perspective', *Political Theory* 39 (1): 142, 2011. A potential tension in his account of empire is also picked up in D. Ivison, '"Another World is Actual": Between Imperialism and Freedom', *Political Theory* 39 (1): 131, 2011.

conditions of possibility of this historically singular set of practices of
governance and the range of characteristic problems and solutions to
which it gives rise.[9]

Political theory, then, should be seen as a mode of 'intersubjective and
open-ended practical reasoning' oriented 'to freedom before justice'.[10]
This represents a form of immanent theorizing, opposed to entering into
'dialogues with fellow citizens under the horizon of a political theory
that frames the exchanges and places the theorist above the *demos*'.[11]
On Tully's account, this latter conception of the role of the theorist is
paternalistic, demanding forms of coercion that replicate aspects of the
long history of imperialism. In contrast, adopting a democratic mode
of democratic theorizing leads, among other things, to scepticism about
the confident universalism of much Western political argument. For
Tully, purported universals are often false projections of local contingent
beliefs, though he insists that he is not opposed to universalism per se,
only to specific articulations of it. False universalism permeates both
liberal political philosophy (in the image of Rawls) and Critical Theory
(in the image of Habermas), and it served to justify imperialism in both
its historical and contemporary guises.[12] A further problem with much
existing political theory, according to Tully, is that it frequently fails as
a political enterprise, for its relentless abstraction and distance from
the lived experience of much of the world 'tends to promote a kind
of idle, talk-show chatter about public reason in some mythical public
sphere, overlooking the situated knowledge, local skills and passionate
partisanship of real democratic deliberation'.[13] Tully insists that
theorists need to focus their energies on elucidating and engaging the

---

[9] Tully, *Public Philosophy* I, p. 16.
[10] Tully, *Public Philosophy* II, p. 108. For Tully, political theorists are often too myopic: 'big
     abstract questions of normative legitimation' take up their attention, while 'practices of
     freedom on the rough ground of daily colonization usually fall beneath' their attention
     (*Public Philosophy* I, p. 288).
[11] Tully, *Public Philosophy* II, p. 4. Political philosophy, then, is the 'methodological
     extension and critical clarification of the already reflective and problematised character
     of historically situated practices of practical reasoning' (*Public Philosophy* I, pp. 28–9).
[12] See also the argument in P. B. Mehta, 'Cosmopolitanism and the Circle of Reason',
     Political Theory 28 (5): 619–39, 2000.
[13] Tully, *Public Philosophy* II, 111.

practices of quotidian politics. To the self-confident liberal cosmopolitan theorist, Tully's project might appear rather too conservative, incapable of prescribing the radical transformations required to address global inequalities and suffering, and held hostage to objectionable local practices and prejudices.[14] In turn, the Tullyian public philosopher will respond that the standard view of the role of political theory presents a deeply undemocratic account of the relationship between the theorist and the demos. This dispute enacts, in contemporary guise, the venerable tension between liberalism and democracy.

At the core of Tully's theory of radical democracy is an innovative, multi-faceted account of citizenship. A citizen, he argues, is any 'person who is subject to a relationship of governance (that is to say, governed) *and*, simultaneously and primarily, is an active agent in the field of a governance relationship.'[15] Citizenship comes in different forms, each comprising a bundle of practices, principles and institutions. The contemporary world is dominated by the regime of 'Modern Citizenship' – a modular assemblage of legitimating historical narrative, institutional architecture and a specified set of rights and duties embodied in law, that finds its ultimate realization in the capitalist representative democratic state. Citizenship, on this view, is a legal *status* granted to individuals within a complex array of governing institutions, and it is 'presented as a universal form of citizenship for all peoples.'[16] Yet it is an expression – perhaps the main expression – of a false and pernicious universal. Modern citizenship, Tully contends, is integrally related to both the past and present of Western imperialism. The model is embedded in, and is dependent

---

[14] For prominent variations on the cosmopolitan theme, see B. Barry, 'Statism and Nationalism: A Cosmopolitan Critique', in I. Shapiro and L. Brilmayer, eds, *Global Justice*, New York: New York University Press, 1999; C. Beitz, *Political Theory and International Relations*, 2nd edn, Princeton: Princeton University Press, 1999; M. Nussbaum, *Frontiers of Justice: Disability, Nationality, Species Membership*, Cambridge, MA: Harvard University Press, 2007; Pogge, *World Poverty and Human Rights*; J. Waldron, 'Minority Cultures and the Cosmopolitan Alternative', *University of Michigan Journal of Law Reform* 25: 751–93 1992.

[15] Tully, *Public Philosophy* II, 3. Emphasis in original.

[16] J. Tully, 'A Dilemma of Democratic Citizenship', Paper delivered at the University of Victoria, 8 May 2010, p. 5.

upon, a teleological theory of social development in which this particular conception of citizenship is figured as the end of history, even its consummation. This narrative has been emplotted in different ways during the previous five centuries, but the underlying structure of argument remains the same. During the nineteenth century, civilization was equated with progress and seen as the product – and the beneficent gift – of the Europeans. During the twentieth century this civilizational discourse was transfigured into the purportedly more palatable idioms of modernization, development and, finally, global governance. Imperialism casts a long shadow.

So much for the diagnosis, what of the medicine? Tully argues that it is necessary to supplant the hierarchical meta-narrative of imperial-globalization with an agonistic republican pluralism, embodied in a form of cooperative citizenship.[17] Citizenship in this sense is not a legal status but an ethos and a repertoire of practices adopted in relations of governance. 'The moment an individual or collective agent who is subject to or affected by any power relationship that governs their conduct no longer unreflectively obeys the rule, but turns and becomes an active agent in and of the relationship, that subject is on the road to becoming a citizen of the relationship.'[18] The cooperative species of citizenship, though, involves further elements, notably adherence to a set of agonistic dispositions and attitudes, including an openness to the other, sensitivity to difference, a commitment to self-criticism and dialogic engagement and awareness of the contingency of beliefs and norms. The agonistic ethos of democratic freedom constantly questions and challenges established institutions and governance relations. Nothing is foundational, nothing fixed; everything is open to debate and contestation.

One way of thinking about Tully's project – indeed arguably about all accounts of agonistic politics – is to see it is as an exercise in radical

---

[17] Tully has also called this 'plural', 'diverse' and global/local citizenship.
[18] Tully, 'A Dilemma of Democratic Citizenship', p. 20. For another imperial variant on the theme of citizenship, see D. Bell, 'Beyond the Sovereign State: Isopolitan Citizenship, Race, and Anglo-American Union,' *Political Studies* (2014, forthcoming).

virtue ethics.[19] Agonistic theorists stress, in one way or another, the absolute centrality of the character of the moral agent – of attitudes, dispositions and self-understandings – rather than focusing on rule-following or formal-legal status. William Connolly, for example, argues that his account of agonistic pluralism requires the development of two civic virtues – 'agonistic respect' and 'critical responsiveness'.[20] In order to fashion cooperative citizens it is essential to inculcate a minimal set of universal virtues – a *critical ethos* – to sustain the practices of agonistic politics. Subjects have to be (re)formed, oriented to a different kind of politics – to acting otherwise.

Tully seeks to overturn what he sees as a major intellectual obstacle to the realization of cooperative citizenship. A powerful tradition of thought, encompassing 'Hobbes, Kant, Darwin, Marx, Mill, Freud' and their heirs, insists on the inescapable but beneficial quality of *unsocial sociability*, the argument that in order to tame and productively direct the natural anti-social character of humans it is necessary first to socialize ('civilize') them through various kinds of institution-building.[21] On this modernist account, humans are basically 'antisocial, and antagonistic, and therefore untrustworthy outside of the coercive institutions of the modern state', and as a consequence, 'humanity needs a master to impose the basic institutions of social co-operation' on recalcitrant peoples.[22] Modern capitalist democracy, at the heart of which is modern citizenship, 'socializes asociality', channelling it into various competitive spheres, above all the market.[23] Modernity, then, is an institutional

[19] For Aristotelian reconstructions of virtue ethics, see J. Annas, *Intelligent Virtue*, Oxford: Oxford University Press, 2011, which identifies the acquisition and exercise of virtues with adopting and using practical skills, and R. Hursthouse, *On Virtue Ethics*, Oxford: Oxford University Press, 1999. It is in this quasi-Aristotelian moment, I would suggest, that Tully's work differs from the 'neo-republicans' such as Quentin Skinner and Philip Pettit, who offer a more instrumental account of the relationship between virtue and citizenship. For use of the term neo-republican, see Tully, *Public Philosophy* II, p. 111, n. 32.

[20] W. E. Connolly, *Pluralism*, Durham: Duke University Press, 2005, p. 126. As he argues elsewhere, 'we need periodically to work on ourselves to deuniversalize selective particularities that have become universalized by us'. W. E. Connolly, 'Speed, Concentric Cultures, and Cosmopolitanism', *Political Theory* 28 (5): 609, 2000.

[21] Tully, 'A Dilemma of Democratic Citizenship', p. 12.

[22] Ibid.

[23] Ibid., p. 13.

constellation that articulates a particular conception of human nature. Tully disputes the fundamental premise of the neo-Hobbesian tradition and offers an alternative picture in its place, although in 'The Dilemmas of Democratic Citizenship' he only hints at what this might look like. We might call this position *social unsociability* – a fundamental cooperative framework within which (agonistic) political contestation can take place. Cooperative citizens, he claims, 'argue that relationships of mutual cooperation and love among *all forms of life* on the planet are more basic than relationships of antagonism'.[24] This claim has two main dimensions. First, 'social relationships of mutual aid are much more fundamental than antagonism and struggle in human evolution'. And second, a holistic account of global social ecology, in which 'these social relationships of mutual aid are themselves embedded in yet deeper ecological relationships of cooperation and mutual assistance among all the diverse forms of life on the planet'.[25] Here he draws on the writings of Vandana Shiva, Albert Schweitzer and James Lovelock's Gaia hypothesis. This is a distinctly non-agonistic moment in the argument: contestation is characterized as a second-order phenomenon, taking place against a background of human harmony. This differentiates Tully from the harsher conflictual accounts of agonism offered, for example, by Chantal Mouffe and many realist writers, including Raymond Geuss.[26]

Here I want to raise some questions about the adequacy of Tully's account of citizenship.[27] One weakness in his project – or at least a subject which he needs to say more about – concerns the picture of social unsociability. It is currently underdeveloped, only hinting at the account of human nature invoked. Moreover, in its current formulation it seems to depend on some highly speculative and controversial claims

---

[24] Ibid., p. 32. Emphasis in original.
[25] Ibid., p. 33.
[26] C. Mouffe, *On the Political*, London: Routledge, 2005; R. Geuss, *Philosophy and Real Politics*, Princeton: Princeton University Press, 2008.
[27] I do not touch on any historical aspects. For questions about Tully's historical account of modern citizenship, see D. Armitage, 'Probing the Foundations of Tully's Public Philosophy', *Political Theory* 39 (1): 124–30, 2011.

about human evolution, though it seems clear that Tully could make the argument for cooperative citizenship without invoking the Gaia hypothesis of Kropotkinian visions of mutual aid. A further question concerns the way in which agonistic republican citizens are to be brought into being, especially on a global scale. How can we move from a world shaped by neo-liberal subjectivation and the deformation of ethico-political life under the forces of capitalism, racism and militarism, to one in which cooperative citizenship is the norm not the admirable exception. This is a profoundly difficult transition problem. It can also be seen as a species of the 'paradox of politics': Tully's account of the proper functioning of an agonistic democratic politics presupposes the existence of a body of cooperative citizens, but this citizenry can only fully be brought about, and allowed to function properly, in an agonistic republican polity.[28]

If I am right about this, it follows that subject (re)formation and ethico-political education are prerequisites of the project of cooperative citizenship. What kind of education, and how is it to be secured? There are two different issues here. First, within democratic constitutional states, does the government – or some other governing institution – have an obligation to provide a form of education that trains individuals in the arts of cooperative citizenship?[29] Without a fundamental shift in educational norms it seems unrealistic to wait for a diverse range of existing practices to converge on a cooperative ethos capable of undergirding an agonistic politics to challenge both contemporary imperialism and the 'deeply sedimented' regime of modern citizenship. It is hard to see how the project can get off the ground in anything other than a limited, localized sense. But creating such an education system presents a further paradox, for it would

---

[28] The paradox of politics is, of course, derived from Rousseau's account of founding in Book II of the *Social Contract*. See especially B. Honig, 'Between Decision and Deliberation: Political Paradox in Democratic Theory', *American Political Science Review* 101 (1): 1–17, 2007.

[29] For different perspectives, see D. Bell, 'Agonistic Democracy and the Politics of Memory', *Constellations* 15 (1): 148–66, 2008; and M. Nussbaum, 'Cosmopolitanism and Patriotism' in J. Cohen, ed., *For Love of Country: Debating the Limits of Patriotism*, Boston: Beacon, 1996.

mean that it is necessary to inoculate aspects of that system from practices of democratic contestation, because (the right kind of) education serves as the precondition for it. The second issue concerns the widespread realization of cooperative citizenship outside the boundaries of democratic constitutional states. On the modernist model, the pedagogical strategy is clear: the spread (through direct coercion or informal imperialism) of a form of legal and political architecture which trains peoples in the arts of modern citizenship. Imperial powers assume the role of Solonic law-giver, short-circuiting the problem of founding. This is empire figured as educative technology. But what are the pedagogical strategies of cooperative citizenship?

In a recent talk, Tully responded to a question about the education of citizens by pointing to schools on the Eastern seaboard of the United States and in Central America that taught forms of agonistic respect.[30] This is admirable but surely exceptional: for every progressive school teaching the arts of cooperative citizenship, there are dozens of others teaching a variety of attitudes antithetical to the ethos cooperative citizenship requires. Think only of the power of conservative faith schools in many countries or the common insistence that school history curricula teach celebratory accounts of national pasts. Another possibility, in tune with Tully's own line of argument, is that political activity and engagement themselves serve, in a Millian sense, as a school of democracy. There is something to this, though the results are likely to be very uneven and there is no guarantee that they will necessarily produce the particular kind of ethos that agonistic democracy requires. At the least, then, Tully needs to further develop an account of ethico-political pedagogy, of the ways in which it is possible to inculcate the critical ethos that is presupposed by his picture of politics.

Here it is worth drawing a distinction between two modes of citizenship which, though related, differ in key respects. *Active citizens*

---

[30] J. Tully, 'The Crisis of Global Citizenship', Seminar in Political Thought and Intellectual History, University of Cambridge, 8 February 2010.

engage in practices of cooperation and contestation, mobilizing to challenge existing norms and values. *Cooperative citizens* likewise engage in social cooperation and contestation, but they do so in the name of a politics defined by openness to difference, to practices of self-criticism and with a recognition that politics is a field in which nothing is ever fixed. While there are plenty of examples of the former that Tully can point to, I would submit that cooperative citizens are much rarer on the ground than he allows. Active citizenship can be witnessed in the growing influence of conservative religious groups in the United States and throughout the Middle East and South Asia, where people are mobilizing to impose a particular moralized view of politics on their compatriots (and maybe the world as a whole). Similar dynamics can be seen in the resurgence of Far Right political parties in Europe. These are exemplary active citizens, cooperating with each other to 'be the change' (in Tully's and Obama's terms) and to confront existing power structures. But they are certainly not cooperative citizens, for they believe in the fixity of forms of life, the absolute, non-negotiable, often God-given, nature of various principles and commands that (among other things) deny forms of human equality and freedom.

Tully would presumably be wary of a Solonic norm-giver – Rousseau's solution to the paradox of politics – but absent this, and absent a state-enforced educational program, it is not clear how a regime of cooperative citizenship could begin to seriously challenge modern citizenship. Relying on the bottom-up, self-organizing powers of citizens is certainly not fruitless; there are successful examples to which he can point. But here the asymmetry between diagnosis and prescription leads to problems. In a global landscape dominated by vast concentrations of capital and military power, how can this vanguard have any systematic or transformative effect? Is it a recipe for permanent subalternization, doomed to remain forever interstitial, an illuminating example of how life might be lived otherwise? Or is that enough?

This leads to a related worry: perhaps cooperative citizenship is least effective where it is most urgently required. Tully concentrates his energies on intra-democratic debate, noting that the 'the orientation of practical philosophy should not be to reaching final agreements on universal principles or procedures, but to *ensuring that constitutional democracies are always open* to the democratic freedom of calling into question and presenting reasons for the renegotiation of the prevailing rules of law, principles of justice and practices of deliberation.'[31] But what of people(s) throughout the world struggling for change outside the norms and institutions of the modern regime of citizenship? Tully is right that modern citizenship was globalized through the agency of European and later American imperialism, and that this process has continued in various iterations. But this globalization was and is highly uneven: in many states which profess modernist citizenship its norms are more often breached than upheld. It is far more common to pay lip service to democracy and constitutionalism that it is to live within their embrace. In much of the world, regimes of modern citizenship would surely be better than what people actually have, however preferable agonistic forms may ultimately be. Cooperative citizenship seems best suited to challenging the failures of existing forms of citizenship, chiefly by drawing on some of its own resources. It seeks to overcome the failures of that which produced it. As such, it acts as a powerful mode of immanent critique. Is it, then, most effective when it is parasitic on modernist citizenship?

3. Political violence, empire and the limits of global justice

When applied to the global level, Tully's public philosophy 'consists of historical and critical studies of global relationships of horrendous inequality, dependency, exploitation and environmental damage, and of corresponding practices of civic freedom of global and local citizens to transform them into democratic relationships.'[32] Imperialism forms the

---

[31] Tully, *Public Philosophy* II, p. 110. Emphasis added.
[32] Ibid., p. 6.

core of his 'historical and critical studies'. This distinguishes Tully from most contemporary political theorists who either ignore imperialism altogether or think of it in the past tense, as a state of affairs that once produced injustices that may (or may not) be the subject of legitimate claims for rectification. For Tully, imperialism never went away.

He identifies four main 'discourses' and three main forms of Western imperial governance.[33] The discourses are interlocking justificatory arguments that have been utilized to legitimate Western conquest and rule. First, Europeans have often claimed a *ius commercium*, a right for Western states and corporations to enter into relations with other peoples. Most commonly, the *ius* has been interpreted as encompassing distinct rights to trade and to convert peoples to Western forms of life. The second discourse is the corresponding duty of hospitality that peoples throughout the world are supposed to owe to imperial powers. Failure to uphold this duty leads to the third discourse, which is the right of the imperial powers to use force to 'open' societies which refuse to engage in commerce with them. Finally, there is a right (even duty) of purportedly 'civilized' states to transform the world in their own image, to drag it from backwardness into the bright light of modernity. This has been justified in a variety of ways: 'to improve, to civilize, develop, modernize, constitutionalize, democratize, and bring good governance and freedom.'[34] All are expressions of a powerful imperialist imaginary.

Empire has also assumed diverse institutional forms. *Settler colonialism* saw the creation of 'new Europes' throughout the world, leading either to the extermination or assimilation of indigenous populations. The legacies of this mode of governance can be seen most clearly in North America and the Pacific. *Indirect colonial rule* involved the creation of small administrative cadres – either acting on behalf of the imperial state or through private corporations – to govern local populations through political technologies including divide-and-rule,

---

[33] J. Tully, 'Lineages of Contemporary Imperialism', in D. Kelly, ed., *Lineages of Empire: The Historical Roots of British Imperial Thought*, Oxford: Oxford University Press, 2009, pp. 11–12.

[34] Tully, 'Lineages of Contemporary Imperialism', p. 11.

co-opting local elites, establishing capitalist labour markets and legal regimes and so forth. Like the first, this modality of empire helped to globalize modern citizenship. It was prevalent in India and much of the Middle East and Africa. Both kinds of imperialism have created toxic legacies, but neither finds widespread support today. Instead, a third modality, with its roots in the nineteenth century, structures the current international system: *informal imperialism*.[35] Under conditions of informal imperialism, there is no need to govern populations and territories through formal-legal means because the most powerful states 'induce local rulers to keep their resources, labour, and markets open to free trade dominated by western corporations and global markets, thereby combining "empire and liberty"'.[36] In the nineteenth century, free trade imperialism was one of the main instruments through which Britain integrated much of Latin America into the imperial capitalist system. During the twentieth century, and especially following the catastrophic failure of alternative models of Nazi and Soviet imperialism, it emerged as the preferred mode of domination by the leading imperial powers, chiefly the United States. This is the contemporary expression of liberal civilizing imperialism; modern citizenship stands at its ideological core. Along the way it has been (mis)labelled modernization and development, and it now functions under the rubric of globalization, 'the continuation of Western imperialism by informal means and through institutions of global governance'.[37]

This analysis represents a standing reproach to much of the liberal normative debate over global justice. Despite their good intentions, liberal theorists (and politicians) are frequently stuck in an historical loop, unreflectively reproducing a mode of benevolent civilizing imperialism. As Tully notes, many purportedly anti-imperial languages and practices 'are neither outside of contemporary imperialism nor the means of

---

[35] Tully also refers to this (following Robinson and Gallagher) as 'free trade imperialism', and as 'interactive' or 'infrastructural' imperialism.

[36] Tully, 'Lineages of Contemporary Imperialism'.

[37] Tully, *Public Philosophy* II, p. 7. For a parallel critique (albeit one with a different conclusion), see T. McCarthy, *Race, Empire and the Idea of Human Development*, Cambridge: Cambridge University Press, 2009.

liberating us from imperialism'.[38] For example, 'the dominant forms
of representative democracy, self-determination and democratisation
promoted through international law are not alternatives to imperialism,
but, rather, the means through which informal imperialism operates
against the wishes of the majority of the population of the post-colonial
world.'[39] Liberal theorists are thus, according to Tully, often unwitting
heirs of the long history of European imperial dominance.

> The protection of self-determination and democratic government under
> international law and the exercise of powers of self-determination and
> democratic self-rule are internal to informal post-colonial imperialism,
> at least in their present form. They are literally the two main ways by
> which the conduct of subaltern states is governed by informal imperial
> rule: that is, through supporting, channelling and constraining their
> self-determining democratic freedoms.[40]

Tully offers a brilliant conspectus of the ways in which the history
of Western political thought, even in its most apparently progressive
manifestations, has been implicated in the justification of oppression,
occupation, displacement, even extermination. He is particularly
good at moving beyond textual criticism and conceptual analysis to
uncover the institutional preconditions that have proved necessary for
the enactment of many of the policies put forward by defenders of the
modern regime of citizenship. But while I am very sympathetic to his
diagnosis of the pathologies of the current international system, and
to the connections he traces between imperialism past and present,
I want to raise some questions about the lessons he draws from this
analysis. In particular, there is a disconnect between his account of the

---

[38] Tully, *Public Philosophy* II, p. 130. See also the discussion in Ivison, 'Another World is
Actual', pp. 133–4, 135. On Kantian imperialism, see Tully, *Public Philosophy* II, chapter 1.
For a different view, see S. Muthu, *Enlightenment Against Empire*, Princeton: Princeton
University Press, 2003.

[39] Tully, *Public Philosophy* II, p. 158.

[40] Ibid., p. 53. 'Cosmopolitan theorists work out, by a process of solitary reflection on
the European history of representative government and democracy, and then project
globally, prior to any exercise of representative popular sovereignty in forums of
democratic dialogue, a cosmopolitan public law that lays down the preconditions of
global practices of democracy' (*Public Philosophy* II, p. 63).

sheer historical *weight* of imperialism – the way in which it continues
to fundamentally shape many of the dominant practices, norms and
structures in the international system – and his prescribed cooperative
remedies.

Before doing so, however, it is important to note that Tully offers a
partial response to this line of argument. He does so by differentiating
his account of empire from the influential critique of Hardt and Negri,
as well as many post-colonial critics. Imperialism, he writes, is not as
'global and total as it appears, and alternative, non-imperial ways of
living in the present are not only *possible*, but *actual* to some degree
in the lived experience of millions of people'.[41] There are two main
reasons for this. First, imperialism is only a 'feature' of the dominant
languages and practices; it does not exhaust them. Moreover, such
features are contingent aspects of those languages and practices, and
they are therefore capable of being transcended or eliminated, at least
in principle. This opens up the space for subaltern agency and for
exercising the arts of agonistic citizenship. The second point is that
under informal imperialism there is more space for working against
the hegemonic powers than under direct imperial governance. I concur
with both of these points. Despite these qualifications, though, Tully
presents imperialism as a pervasive and profound influence on the
contemporary world, one that shapes many of the institutions, laws
and norms that govern us, and which is upheld in the interests of the
dominant actors – those who have very few incentives to democratize
the distribution of power in the system. His analysis, he admits, is
'gloomy'.[42] Imperialism is 'deeply sedimented'.[43]

What, then, can be done to confront this vast system of oppression
and injustice? Or as Tully himself phrases the question, 'what can
citizens who are subject to these imperial relationships (in both the

---

[41] Tully, *Public Philosophy* II, p. 130, n. 8, discussing Hardt and Negri, *Empire*. 'Imperialism
       has not made the world over to the extent the promoters and critics presuppose' (Tully,
       Public Philosophy II, p. 164).
[42] Tully, *Public Philosophy* II, p. 164.
[43] Ibid., p. 67.

North and the global South) do to transform them into non-imperial, democratic relationships by bringing them under their shared authority?'[44] It is here that I think Tully's answer is incomplete, or at least underdeveloped. One of the main reasons for this is that he does not view the use of force as a legitimate element of the arts of cooperative citizenship. Proclaiming an Arendtian aversion to violence, Tully sees force as the antithesis of politics rather than a constitutive dimension of it. When violence breaks out (agonistic) politics has failed.[45] But he goes further than Arendt, valorizing the benefits of non-violence, which he construes as an ethical injunction: 'it is necessary to turn the other cheek and try gradually to bring [others] into a relationship of conversation, negotiation and conversion to non-violence.'[46] This is not pacifism as 'passive resistance', but rather, following in the footsteps of Mahatma Gandhi and Martin Luther King Jr, it is the operation of 'very active non-violent arts of government and citizenship.'[47] Violence, Tully concludes, '*begets* violence and anti-democratic politics. Non-violence and democracy *begets* non-violence and democracy'. The only way to break out of spirals of bloodshed is to approach the 'other' non-violently, 'with an open hand rather than a closed fist'.[48]

Advocacy of non-violence can be read in several different ways, and Tully is not always clear about where he draws the lines. It could be interpreted in a strong pacifist sense: non-violence as an absolute prohibition on the use of force, whatever the circumstances. A slightly weaker claim would permit the use of violence in situations of personal self-defence, in which an immediate and overriding threat to bodily integrity is met with force. A yet weaker claim is the imperative to deploy non-violent strategies against repression *in the first instance*, an argument that allows for the use of violence after some yet-to-be-specified threshold has been crossed. At times Tully gestures in this

---

[44] Tully, *Public Philosophy* I, p. 7.
[45] H. Arendt, *On Violence*, New York: Harcourt Brace and Company, 1970.
[46] Tully, 'A Dilemma of Democratic Citizenship', p. 29.
[47] Ibid., pp. 30 and 31. Tully also lists Abdul Ghaffar Khan, Gene Sharp, Petra Kelly and Vandana Shiva as inspirations.
[48] Tully, 'A Dilemma of Democratic Citizenship', p. 30.

direction, noting for example that 'direct confrontation' and 'rebellion and revolution' are an integral albeit extreme practice of civic freedom.[49] However, he does not explore the conditions in which they are justified, and elsewhere he defines the arts of cooperative citizenship in strictly non-violent terms. Do people stop being (cooperative) citizens when they move from non-violent agonism to violent resistance, or is violence recognized as a legitimate part of the arts of citizenship? It is not clear. Tully does not appear to be an absolutist pacifist, but the position that he argues for allows very little room for the use of force. However, I would argue that a comprehensive conception of agonistic citizenship requires a normative account of the conditions in which the use of organized violence against oppression is legitimate.

Tully's argument for non-violence also adduces some empirical claims. The empirical argument aims to demonstrate that non-violence can be a very effective force for change – maybe even *the* most effective form. 'It is the great changes in the ethical behaviour of citizens that move governments to end slavery, enfranchise women, enact climate change legislation, end unjust wars, recognize indigenous peoples or adopt effects human rights; not the other way around.'[50] Cooperative citizens, he insists, have many options available to them to challenge existing power structures. They 'use non-violent networks of persuasion and pressure to bring the powers-that-be to the negotiating table, whether this is an official or an ad hoc table. These activities comprise the great local and global arts of *non-violent citizen-based negotiation*.'[51] The arts include 'protests, petitions, boycotts, non-co-operation, arguing and bargaining, alternative dispute resolution, and transformative justice'.[52] Tully invests great hope in such non-violent practices, suggesting that their cumulative power 'can move and transform the mode of being (hearts and minds) of unjust and

---

[49] See, for example, his claim about 'at the extreme, the Lockean activity of overthrowing an unjust government and setting up a new one' (*Public Philosophy* II, p. 99).
[50] Tully, 'A Dilemma of Democratic Citizenship'.
[51] Ibid., p. 28.
[52] Ibid., p. 24.

free-riding parties, bring unjust power relationships under democratic authority or all those subject to or affected by them, and thus change the world from the ground up.'[53] What, though, if it turned out that the empirical argument for the effectiveness of non-violence is weak, or at least weaker than Tully allows? Would the ethical imperative to do no harm still hold, even if it unintentionally helped to maintain the status quo?

When pushed by Bonnie Honig on the role of reason and violence, Tully responded by clarifying the relationship between the two. However, he does so by deflecting the question. He suggests that one of the purposes of his work has been to highlight the prevalence of a false argument that snakes through the Western tradition of political thought.

> This is the assumption that certain conditions must be in place and humans must be subject to them before it is possible to engage in non-violent reasoning altogether (cooperating and contesting forms of cooperation). Accordingly it is irrational to try to reason with another person or people prior to imposing coercively over them a secure structure of law, for only once they have been pacified, civilized or modernised by forceful subjection to a structure of cooperation of some kind or another (military rule, Western law, primitive accumulation, labour discipline, markets, state structures, restructuring policies) is it then reasonable to reason non-violently with them. Thus violence is both reasonable and necessary to establish democracy and peace.[54]

Such a view, he argues, has been central to the justification of imperialism and it remains a core component of its contemporary 'informal' expressions. But the assumption is false: there is no necessary connection between violence, reason and peace. This is highlighted above all by the successful evolution of the tradition of non-violence over the last century.

---

[53] Tully, 'Lineages of Contemporary Imperialism', p. 150.
[54] J. Tully, 'Dialogue', *Political Theory* 39 (1): 157, 2011.

I want to push Tully on this point, because it seems to me that there are a number of problems to be confronted with this strict adherence to practices of non-violence. We need not accept the argument about pre-conditionality, or the claim about a necessary internal relation between reason and violence, to recognize that sometimes, just sometimes, force may be the best or only option available. While there are plenty of inspirational examples of peaceful cooperative life, it remains the case, as Tully himself recognizes, that the global field of action is itself fundamentally structured by hegemonic institutions and practices, with violence a routinized strategy deployed to maintain the existing system. While there is some room for agency, it is highly restricted. It seems, then, this argument involves form of idealization that, unlike the diagnosis, does not really grapple adequately with the power relations that uphold the global order.

Non-violence is, all things being equal, preferable to violence as a means to resolve conflicts and bring about sociopolitical change. Moreover, practices of non-violent resistance did help to bring about some social change during the last century and a half.[55] But things are rarely equal, and the feasibility of non-violence is the exception not the rule. The actions of Martin Luther King Jr and Gandhi are worthy of great respect and sometimes emulation, at least where possible, but the efficacy of non-violence as a strategy is largely dependent on the institutional and normative context in which it is utilized. Sometimes the circumstances open a space in which power can be countered or derailed by non-violent forms of action. This was the case with Indian resistance to British rule and the American civil rights struggle, Tully's key examples. But even in these cases, non-violence was typically shadowed by violence, or the threat of it. In India, Gandhian non-violence was accompanied by other, violent resistance movements, and British rule was ultimately brought to an end by Japanese imperialism and its subsequent weakening through a

---

[55] For a valuable survey, see D. Cortright, *Peace: A History of Movements and Ideas*, Cambridge: Cambridge University Press, 2008.

prolonged global conflict.[56] The (partial) success of the US civil rights movement was a product of various interlocking factors and cannot be reduced to the efficacy of heroic non-violence. The dynamics of the Cold War, changes in the structure of the American political economy and the shifting balance of power in Washington, were all important variables. So too was the fear of black violence – symbolized above all by Malcolm X – which King and his followers successfully played on in formulating their strategies.[57] Another feature unites both cases: they occurred within the framework of the modern regime of citizenship. They were fights over the interpretation and application of extant rules and conventions: it was possible to appeal to existing laws, principles or norms – of equality, liberty, citizenship or rights of national self-determination – that were not being properly enacted. At times, then, it is arguable that Tully falls foul of romanticized view of the power of non-violence, one which is then generalized beyond the specific conditions which facilitate it as a modality of politics into situations where it is almost invariably bound to fail.

Alternatives to the absolutist non-violent stance were outlined by Frantz Fanon and Nelson Mandela. Fanon justified the use of violence against the French colonial regime in Algeria, arguing in *The Wretched of the Earth* that it was both a necessary military response and (perhaps less plausibly) that it performed a range of cathartic psychological tasks.[58]

---

[56] Note, for example, that armed resistance against Britain, notably the Indian National Army under Subhash Chandra Bose, had a significant impact on British thinking about the future viability of the empire. P. W. Fay, *The Forgotten Army: India's Armed Struggle for Independence 1942-1945*, Ann Arbor: University of Michigan Press, 1994.

[57] S. Tuck, *We Ain't What We Ought to Be: The Black Freedom Struggle from Emancipation to Obama*, Cambridge, MA: Harvard University Press, 2010, p. 322. On this account, Malcolm X played bad cop to King's good cop. Note too that non-violent protests were often protected by armed activists: L. Hill, *The Deacons for Defense: Armed Resistance and the Civil Rights Movement*, Chapel Hill: University of North Carolina Press, 2006; T. Tyson, 'Robert F. Williams, "Black Power," and the Roots of the Black Freedom Struggle', *Journal of American History* 85 (2): 540-70, 1998. ('Our vision of the African American freedom movement between 1945 and 1965 as characterized solely and inevitably by nonviolent civil rights protest obscures the full complexity of racial politics', p. 570). See also the interesting analysis in M. Stears, *Demanding Democracy: American Radicals in Search of a New Politics*, Princeton: Princeton University Press, 2010, chapter 5.

[58] F. Fanon, *The Wretched of the Earth*, London: Penguin, 2001. See also the famous 'Preface' by Jean-Paul Sartre. For discussions of his justification of violence, see N. C. Gibson, *Fanon: The Postcolonial Imagination*, Cambridge: Polity, 2003, chapter 5.

He was an inspiration for many anti-colonial resistance movements. For Mandela, non-violence was part of a repertoire of resistance to the brutal apartheid regime, but one that ran its course and failed. As he wrote,

> ... the hard facts were that fifty years of nonviolence had brought the African people nothing but more and more repressive legislation, and fewer and fewer rights ... [I]n May and June of 1961, it could not be denied that our policy to achieve a nonracial state by nonviolence had achieved nothing and that our followers were beginning to lose confidence in this policy ... Each disturbance pointed clearly to the inevitable growth among Africans of the belief that violence was the only way out – it showed that a government which uses force to maintain its rule teaches the oppressed to use force to oppose it.[59]

Both the Algerian and South African cases were arguably legitimate examples of violent resistance to oppression, violence to counter violence. Tully may concur that both were extreme but defensible instances of civic freedom. My suspicion, though, is that these kinds of situations are far more common than those in which non-violence can secure victory over oppressive regimes. Think, for example, of the 'Arab Spring', in which a combination of violent and non-violent strategies were employed (in different combinations) across Libya, Syria, Egypt, Bahrain, Yemen and others. In Libya, rebellion turned into violent revolution. In Iran, the non-violent 'Green Revolution' of 2009 was crushed by state power. In Syria, non-violent protests morphed into armed rebellion after the Assad regime met banners with machine gun fire and tanks. Tully's optimism about the arts of non-violent citizenship needs qualifying. None of this guarantees that violence will work of course. Sometimes it appears to; often it does not.

But there are other circumstances which are perhaps slightly less clear-cut, but in which we might also ask about the limits of non-violence.

---

[59] S. Johns and R. H. Davis, eds, *Mandela, Tambo, and the African National Congress: The Struggle Against Apartheid 1948–1990: A Documentary Survey*, Oxford: Oxford University Press, 1991, pp. 119–20.

What about resistance to the structural violence of global poverty and immiseration? The current debates over global justice remain largely silent on the issue. Thomas Pogge provides a bracing example.[60] In *World Poverty and Human Rights* he makes three interlocking empirical claims. First, that the extant global economic system is the product of a long history of European imperialism. Second, it is structured in such a way that it benefits the Global North at the expense of the Global South, impoverishing hundreds of millions throughout the world (it is this argument which motivates his influential account of negative duties). And third, the current global conjuncture, in which millions die of remediable starvation and preventable diseases every year, constitutes a 'full size crime against humanity', indeed a crime that has killed far more people that the Holocaust.[61] This catastrophe, he continues, is traceable to a set of identifiable practices and institutions – namely, the policies of the dominant powers in the capitalist world system. It represents 'the imposition, by our governments, in our name, of a coercive global order that perpetuates severe poverty for many who cannot resist this imposition.'[62]

I imagine that Tully would agree with this analysis, if not with other aspects of Pogge's neo-Kantian cosmopolitan project. Yet this argument raises an important question: what are the rights of (violent) resistance against such oppression? Or, in Tullyian language, when (if at all) can cooperative citizens utilize violence as part of a repertoire of practices of

---

[60] In a number of places, Tully identifies Pogge as a fellow-travelling critical scholar concerned with challenging global structures of oppression. For example, see Tully, *Public Philosophy* II, p. 221. On resistance and Pogge's account of global justice, see also G. D. Blunt, 'Transnational Socio-Economic Justice and the Right of Resistance', *Politics* 31 (1): 1–8, 2011.

[61] Pogge, *World Poverty and Human Rights*, p. 25.

[62] Pogge, *World Poverty and Human Rights*, p. 23. Here lies one of the main differences between Pogge's account and that of many other global justice theorists. Pogge's argument about the negative duties owed by the global rich to the global poor depends on the adequacy of his empirical account of the structure of the international system. If the empirical argument does not hold, he cannot motivate the negative duties argument (though a positive duties argument would then kick in). This difference would, presumably, have significant consequences for how we might think about resistance. For challenges to Pogge's account, see, for example, J. Cohen, 'Philosophy, Social Science, and Global Poverty', in A. M. Jaggar, ed., *Thomas Pogge and His Critics*, Cambridge: Polity, 2010; M. Risse, 'How Does the Global Order Harm the Poor?', *Philosophy and Public Affairs* 33 (4): 349–76, 2005.

civic freedom? Nowhere in Pogge's or Tully's texts is there any sustained answer. Instead, we are presented with a range of ways in which the problem can be ameliorated – how the system can be changed so that it no longer arises. For Tully, the answer lies in inculcating the non-violent arts of cooperative citizenship and allowing people to self-govern in democratic constitutional regimes. For Pogge (and many other cosmopolitan theorists) the answer lies in a radical transformation of the principles and practices of global resource redistribution (in his case, through the creation of a 'Global Resources Dividend'). However, all of these proposals are dependent on very major shifts in the existing global order, requiring that those who benefit most from the current system give up many of the instruments of their power. Perhaps in the long run such plans will come to fruition. But what about now? If a crime against humanity is being committed, if millions of people are dying or suffering *today*, then why is it not legitimate to use force in response? It seems counter-intuitive, at the very least, to insist on the primacy of non-violent action – of Gandhi over Fanon – or to wait until improbable changes to the global economic and political architecture can be brought about at some indefinite point in the future.

In summary, then, I think we need to revisit the two mantras that Tully sets himself firmly against: 'democracy cannot be brought about by democratic means' and 'peace cannot be brought about by peaceful means'.[63] We do not need to accept these rigid formulations to recognize that peaceful citizen action cannot always bring about peaceful transformation and that democracy is not always brought about by democratic means.

4. Conclusion

For Tully, no political argument, no perspective, no norm, is ever final or fixed. Conclusions are only tentative opportunities for further

---

[63] Tully, 'A Dilemma of Democratic Citizenship', p. 13.

reflection, for raising other questions. In this chapter I have sought to take up this challenge by pressing him on aspects of his argument about cooperative citizenship. I have suggested that there is a tension running through his powerful and provocative writing on global politics. While he offers a compelling 'gloomy' account of the ongoing and deeply sedimented practices of imperial domination that continue to shape the lives of millions, cooperative citizenship fails to offer sufficient resources to resist the imperial order.

6

Civil Disobedience as a Practice of Civic Freedom

Robin Celikates

1. Introduction

The novel approach to the study of politics that James Tully has developed in recent years under the programmatic title of 'Public Philosophy' seeks to escape certain forms of narrowmindedness that have led the mainstream of political philosophy to pay insufficient attention to the perspectives of other disciplines as well as alternative approaches, new kinds of problems and the concerns of 'ordinary' agents.[1] To avoid these shortcomings, Tully's aim is 'not to provide foundations for, but to reflect critically *on* our well-trodden ways of thought and action, rendering them less indubitably foundational, and thereby disclosing possibilities of thinking and acting differently'.[2] This leads him to favour a dialogical and conflict-oriented approach over the dominant monological and consensus-oriented one. More specifically, his approach centres on the complex, contested and open-ended nature of struggles for recognition and self-determination and the temporary character of the institutional arrangements that aim at resolving these struggles and at creating stability. This methodological

---

[1] See J. Tully, *Public Philosophy in a New Key*, Two Volumes, Cambridge: Cambridge University Press, 2008. This section incorporates material from my review of these two volumes: R. Celikates, '*Public Philosophy in a New Key: Volume I: Democracy and Civic Freedom/Volume II: Imperialism and Civic Freedom* by James Tully', *Constellations* 18 (2): 264–66, 2011.

[2] Tully, *Public Philosophy* I, p. 70.

shift has normative consequences as well: Since political theory cannot provide the normative foundations for the organization of political life and only citizens who can regard themselves as free are able to decide how to organize their lives together, freedom, not justice or equality, is the only candidate for the central value of democratically conceived political theory and practice.[3]

As Tully shows in 'The Agonistic Freedom of Citizens', what it means to be a citizen, and not a mere subject, under the conditions of political and cultural plurality can only be determined in the course of a dialogue – a conflictual exchange – that allows for those who are affected to actually have a say. Such a dialogue is at the same time an expression of and a struggle for political freedom. This dialogical orientation forbids any recourse to the 'legislative stance' and commits the theorist to being open to the experiences people make in the practices in which they engage, to listening to them and to learning from them, that is, entering into 'pedagogical relationships of reciprocal elucidation between academic research and the civic activities of fellow citizens'.[4] The assumption, constitutive of the dominant paradigms of social and political theory, that the theorist's task is to construct and spell out universal norms and principles or to analyse causal processes operating behind the backs of ordinary agents, which elevates him or her above the *demos*, turns out to be deeply mistaken. Of course, political discourses and practices are governed by norms, but these norms and the (e.g. constitutional) framework they establish cannot be removed from political struggle and negotiation: 'Politics is the type of game in which the framework – the rules of the game – can come up for deliberation and amendment in the course of the game.'[5] Tully calls the practices of resistance and transformation that citizens engage in by following the norms governing their practices in a variety of ways, by questioning and renegotiating them, and by challenging the

---

[3] On the theoretical and normative implications of this 'exemplary' way of theorizing, see D. Owen, 'Political Philosophy in a Post-Imperial Voice: James Tully and the Politics of Cultural Recognition', *Economy and Society* 28 (4): 520–49, 1999.

[4] Tully, *Public Philosophy* I, p. 3.

[5] Ibid., p. 146.

existing forms of domination, exclusion and assimilation 'practices of civic freedom'. Crucially, these struggles for more civic and democratic forms of governance go beyond the established and hegemonic forms of representative government and the corresponding 'official' understandings and practices of citizenship.

Existing notions of citizenship tend to conceive of the citizen as a private person equipped by the state with certain rights that protect his or her autonomy as, primarily, an economic actor. Tully sketches a different account of citizenship that defines citizens by referring not chiefly to their legal status or to their subjection to practices of governance but to their political agency and their effective participation in the practices of collective self-determination. Only such an active, even activist, conception of citizenship can do justice to the constitutive link between democracy and freedom.

As Tully insists in 'The Unfreedom of the Moderns in Comparison to Their Ideals of Constitutional Democracy', the incompatibility of the ideals underlying democratic constitutionalism with the current form of globalization triggers 'struggles *of* and *for* democratic freedom, practices of freedom in which democratic actors seek, by means of traditional and new forms of deliberation and negotiation, to challenge and modify the non-democratic ways they are governed.'[6] In order to adequately understand these practices, a distinction has to be made between what Tully calls 'modern' citizenship, which is an institutional status inherently tied to the Western nation state and its 'liberal' self-understanding, and 'diverse' and 'cooperative' citizenship, which is conceived of as a set of negotiated and internally complex practices in which agents express and cultivate their 'freedom *of* and *in* participation, and *with* fellow citizens'.[7] By 'exercising power *together as* citizens', they are 'doing democracy'.[8]

More recently, Tully has elaborated on this distinction between these two opposed modes of citizenship. For the purposes of this essay, the most important feature of modern citizenship is that it conceives

---

[6] Tully, *Public Philosophy* II, p. 113.
[7] Ibid., p. 272.
[8] Ibid., p. 291.

of citizenship in terms of a status defined by the rights and duties of individuals, with negative liberties taking pride of place. As Tully points out, this 'right not to be interfered with in these [private economic] activities by the *demos*' corresponds almost exactly to what Benjamin Constant called 'the liberty of the moderns'. As Constant insists against what he seems to regard as a utopian longing for a return to the Greek *polis* and 'the liberty of the ancients', 'the aim of the moderns is the enjoyment of security in private pleasures; and they call liberty the guarantees accorded by institutions to these pleasures'.[9]

This essentially liberal framework also has consequences for how the right to political participation is understood: It is limited to participation in elections, the official channels of the public sphere and the institutions of civil society, which are seen as instrumentally necessary to establish and maintain the 'security' Constant identifies as the core of the modern citizen's concern. Other forms and practices of citizenship that do not fit this dominant framework are removed or marginalized. Despite attempts at reform, for example, from the proponents of deliberative democracy, this results in a 'self-limiting' or 'low intensity form of democratic citizenship that reproduces a structural democratic deficit';[10] 'If they wish to act as citizens and exercise their participatory freedom, they are constrained to do so only in the public sphere, only through the exercise of communicative capacities, only through official channels, and only in relation to representative parties and ministries.'[11] In addition, these institutions and channels are not only limited but often prove to be so in ways that make it impossible or at least difficult for citizens to address these limits – they themselves become obstacles to democratic action.

To address 'structural democratic deficits' of this kind, citizens therefore turn to a counter-model of cooperative citizenship, which is

---

[9] B. Constant, 'The Liberty of the Ancients Compared with that of the Moderns', in *Political Writings*, Cambridge: Cambridge University Press, 1988, p. 317; J. Tully, 'A Dilemma of Democratic Citizenship', Paper delivered at the University of Victoria, 8 May 2010, p. 7.

[10] Tully, 'A Dilemma of Democratic Citizenship', p. 15.

[11] J. Tully, 'The Crisis of Global Citizenship', Seminar in Political Thought and Intellectual History, University of Cambridge, 8 February 2010, p. 11. See also the exchange between Rainer Forst and James Tully in *Political Theory* 39 (1), 2011, pp. 118–23, 145–60.

already manifested in their multiple practices. Cooperative citizenship is not a status that citizens are granted by official institutions but a form of democratic agency that 'comes into being when citizens *call into question* some aspect of a relationship that they bear (as subjects)'.[12] This questioning takes place when citizens employ 'arts of citizenship' that include 'protests, petitions, boycotts, non-cooperation, arguing and bargaining, alternative dispute resolution, and transformative justice'.[13]

In what follows I will examine the meaning, justification and role of civil disobedience as a related but distinctive 'art of citizenship', an 'unofficial' yet historically and politically prominent form of citizen participation that implicitly forms part of Tully's arsenal of democratic practices. By showing how the most influential discussion of civil disobedience in contemporary political philosophy – the one offered by John Rawls – fails to take into account crucial features of this genuinely democratic form of political practice, I want not only to complement Tully's inventory of the practices of cooperative citizenship but also to supplement his critique of the liberal mainstream of political philosophy with a prominent and striking example.[14] My aim is to show how Rawls's specific approach to the questions of political philosophy under the label 'ideal theory', while not strictly speaking irrelevant, can have a distorting and potentially even ideological effect on the discussion of what are from his perspective questions of non-ideal theory, such as, crucially, the definition, justification and role of civil disobedience.

2. Rethinking civil disobedience

As is well-known, Rawls took the principles established by an ideal theory of justice not only to define 'a perfectly just society' but also to tell us how, that is, according to which principles, we ought to act here

---

[12] Tully, 'A Dilemma of Democratic Citizenship', p. 20.
[13] Ibid., p. 24.
[14] Tully at times seems to offer a less 'liberal' and more 'democratic' reading of Rawls, based on *Political Liberalism*, see Tully, *Public Philosophy* I, pp. 110–12.

and now, that is, 'under less than favorable conditions' and confronted with 'instances of injustice'.[15] In his view, 'nonideal theory presupposes that ideal theory is already on hand. For until the ideal is identified, at least in outline – and that is all we should expect – nonideal theory lacks an objective, an aim, by reference to which its queries can be answered.'[16] Rawls's discussion of civil disobedience can be seen as a touchstone both for the critics and for the defenders of ideal theory. This is no gratuitous choice. Rawls himself singles it out as the only case of non-ideal theory which he discusses at some length in *A Theory of Justice* – a discussion that has proved to be highly influential. Furthermore, at least on a broadly Rawlsian understanding of the limits of the duty to obey the law, a theoretical account of civil disobedience is a necessary complement to any non-ideal theory which addresses forms of institutional injustice that are in principle avoidable.

According to Rawls, ideal theory is 'the only basis for the systematic grasp of [the] more pressing problems' of non-ideal theory: 'The discussion of civil disobedience [. . .] depends upon it [. . .] a deeper understanding can be gained in no other way.'[17] As I will try to show in expanding on Tully's critique of constructivist theorizing, however, the opposite is the case: ideal theory, far from being the only available route to a deeper understanding, *undermines* the very attempt. Although Rawls gives us an illuminating account of the meaning, justification and role of civil disobedience, his account, in all of these three dimensions, is inherently limited and one-sided.[18] My critique will focus on the definition and the justification, but it will also have implications for an adequate understanding of the political and social role of civil disobedience.

---

[15] J. Rawls, *A Theory of Justice*, Cambridge, MA: Harvard University Press, 1971, pp. 351, 245. It is worth noting that Rawls does not return to the topic in *Political Liberalism*.

[16] Rawls, *A Theory of Justice*, pp. 89–90.

[17] Ibid., p. 9.

[18] Although my critical remarks will be limited to Rawls's discussion of civil disobedience, they can be generalized and, with some adjustments, directed against other discussions of civil disobedience that also proceed from the starting point of ideal theory, like the ones put forth by Ronald Dworkin and, to a lesser extent, Jürgen Habermas. See R. Celikates, 'Ziviler Ungehorsam und radikale Demokratie – konstituierende vs. konstituierte Macht?', in T. Bedorf and K. Röttgers, eds, *Das Politische und die Politik*, Berlin: Suhrkamp, 2010, pp. 274–300.

The definition of civil disobedience

Rawls begins his discussion by defining civil disobedience as 'a public, nonviolent, conscientious yet political act contrary to law usually done with the aim of bringing about a change in the law or policies of the government [by which] one addresses the sense of justice of the majority of the community', all 'within the limits of fidelity to law', that is while recognizing the fundamental legitimacy of the existing system.[19] Given the ideal-theoretical framework of his theory of justice, this definition has some intuitive plausibility, although it is unclear in what exact relation it is supposed to stand to that framework. It does, however, run into serious problems.

Consider the first three elements of the definition to which counter-examples from what are usually considered paradigmatic cases of civil disobedience are easily found. The first element is that civil disobedience according to Rawls is a *public* act. As is well-known, Henry David Thoreau – who is usually credited with inventing the very expression – protested against slavery and the Mexican War by withholding his taxes, a decision he made public only several years later. To this example Rawls could respond – in my view correctly – that it is closer to conscientious refusal than to civil disobedience proper. It is, however, a further question of what 'public' is supposed to mean here. A second look shows that for Rawls civil disobedience is public insofar as 'it is engaged in openly with fair notice; it is not covert or secretive'.[20] The exercise of some well-established forms of civil disobedience – blocking an intersection, occupying a port or obstructing the deportation of so-called illegal immigrants, to give just a few examples – depends on *not* giving the authorities fair notice in advance. It would be strange to exclude these forms of protest by definition, whatever else one may think of them.

According to the second element of the definition, civil disobedience is *non-violent*. The plausibility of this requirement – which is broadly

---

[19] Rawls, *A Theory of Justice*, pp. 364 and 366.
[20] Ibid., p. 366.

accepted, also, it seems, by Tully himself – obviously depends on how broad or narrow the concept of violence is taken to be. Does violence include only serious violations of the physical integrity of others? What about violence against property, violence against oneself or minimal violence in self-defence, and what about exerting psychological pressure? In a notorious series of cases, German courts have in the past ruled that it constitutes an act of violent coercion incompatible with peaceful protest to exert psychological pressure on others, for example, by blocking the road and thus forcing them to stop their cars in order to avoid an accident. Equally, the American Civil Rights Movement has often been criticized as violent on account of the violence its 'non-violent' protests have (intentionally and for strategic reasons) provoked on the part of the state's security apparatus.[21] Rawls does not take up these questions, and they are also sidestepped in Tully's insistence on the non-violent character of democratic civic action.[22] In the absence of further elaboration, making non-violence part of the definition of civil disobedience raises both theoretical and political worries. Furthermore we can ask whether defining civil disobedience as non-violent does not foreclose important normative and strategic questions about weighing the costs of different forms of disobedience (and of remaining inactive), especially in the face of severe (but still local) injustice.[23]

According to the third element of Rawls's definition, civil disobedience is a *conscientious* act. But why should only disobedience out of reasons of conscience count as civil disobedience? Putting the need to draw some distinction between civil disobedience and conscientious objection to one side, we may wonder whether one could not disobey for all sorts of at least *prima facie* legitimate reasons, for example, reasons of self-respect or political responsibility, that are not conscientious *at least* in a

[21] See J. A. Colaiaco, 'Martin Luther King, Jr. and the Paradox of Nonviolent Direct Action', *Phylon* 47 (1): 16–28, 1986.

[22] Tully, *Public Philosophy* II, pp. 294–5.

[23] See J. Raz, *The Authority of Law*, Oxford: Clarendon, 1979, pp. 262–75, where he argues (p. 267): 'The evil the disobedience is designed to rectify may be so great, that it may be right to use violence to bring it to an end. [. . .] some lawful acts, may well have much more severe consequences than many an act of violence: consider the possible effects of a strike by ambulance drivers.'

narrow sense. There is, I would argue, something like advocatory civil disobedience (e.g. in the animal rights movement and, more broadly, in response to the pressing questions of ecological ethics focused on by Tully),[24] which is not necessarily conscience-based and could indeed be undertaken with a more or less strategic attitude.[25] Rawls seems to focus on conscientious civil disobedience in order to cope with what in the discussion about the allocation of social bads has come to be called the 'NIMBY' problem: the empirically widespread 'not in my backyard' variety of civil disobedience where people protest, for example, against a new highway or toxic waste dump being built in their quiet and peaceful neighbourhood.[26] But again Rawls's focus turns out to be too narrow in excluding these forms of civil disobedience – however difficult their justification might turn out to be – from the very definition.

The remaining two elements of Rawls's definition suffer from underdetermination. First, consider the *appeal to the majority's sense of justice*. In many cases, civil disobedience seems at odds with and indeed directed against the majority's moral sentiments; it is often failures of this sense of justice that make civil disobedience necessary in the first place. In fact it is difficult to see why one should appeal to it at all when the majority's sense of justice is taken to be systematically distorted or biased and has shown itself to be largely immune to critical challenges.[27] Of course, one could further qualify the sense of justice in a way that removes it from what people in a society take to be just and unjust as a matter of contingent fact. But turning it into a non-empirical court of appeal in this way raises the problem of relating the actual,

[24] Tully, *Public Philosophy* II, chapter 3.
[25] Gandhi speaks of 'vicarious' civil disobedience (which is, in his view, of course still conscientious in some broad sense), see M. K. Gandhi, *Non-Violent Resistance and Social Transformation. Moral and Political Writings*, Volume 3, Oxford: Clarendon, 1987, p. 93.
[26] See A. Sabl, 'Looking Forward to Justice. Rawlsian Civil Disobedience and its Non-Rawlsian Lessons', *The Journal of Political Philosophy* 9 (3): 328, 2001.
[27] Tully (*Public Philosophy* I, p. 315) notes 'the multiplicity of ways in which individuals and groups are excluded from calling into question the imposed norms through which they are recognised, governed and blocked from entering into a dialogue over their legitimacy, thereby rendering assimilation, silent oppression or the recourse to non-violent and violent resistance the only alternatives.'

radically deficient sense of justice to its idealized counterpart, which the practitioners of civil disobedience are supposed to ascribe to their fellow citizens in spite of their actual convictions and behaviour. Even on this understanding, it is unclear to whose sense of justice Martin Luther King Jr, for example, appealed – in cases such as this one, the determination of the addressee, the relevant majority, will not be an obvious matter.[28] Furthermore, there are cases of civil disobedience which cannot be construed as appealing to anyone's sense of justice but aim at increasing the political and economic costs for a certain political option (animal rights activists may again serve as an example, having often lost any hope that the majority can really be brought to care about the fate of animals[29]).

The final element of Rawls's definition – that civil disobedience takes place within the limits of *fidelity to law* – is supposed to distinguish it from more radical and revolutionary forms of protest and resistance that put into question the political system itself. The line between these different forms of illegal protest, however, apart from being politically contested and subject to reasonable disagreement in practice, may be more difficult to draw in theory than Rawls's definition suggests. As Tully insists again and again, in law and elsewhere, the alternative is not between obeying a rule and breaking it or being loyal to the legal system and rejecting it.[30] Consider again the case of King and other participants in the US Civil Rights Movement. It is not clear that they were only aiming at more or less local corrections within the existing system or that their disobedience was an expression of their recognition of the system's general legitimacy. Again, this seems to depend on how 'the system' is defined here. Rawls's restriction stands in some tension with a much more radical attitude that is characteristically expressed

---

[28] Rawls discusses King in J. Rawls, *Political Liberalism*, New York: Columbia University Press, 1996, pp. 250–1, in a somewhat laboured way, trying to make sense of the fact that King justified his actions not only by reasons that are, according to Rawls's standards, 'public' but also by reference to comprehensive moral and religious doctrines.

[29] For some of the problems involved see M. Humphrey and M. Stears, '*Animal Rights Protest and the Challenge to Deliberative* Democracy', *Economy and Society* 35 (3): 400–22 2006.

[30] Especially Tully, *Public Philosophy* I, chapter 2.

in King's statement that 'The thing to do is get rid of the system'.[31] Although the distinction between civil disobedience and more radical forms of dissent is not useless, the way Rawls builds it into his definition certainly obscures its gradual and politically contested character. As David Lyons points out with reference to Thoreau, Gandhi and King, 'none of these three regarded the prevailing system as "reasonably just" or accepted a moral presumption favoring obedience to law'.[32] Under these circumstances, the condition that civil disobedience has to stay 'within the limits of fidelity to law' in order to count as civil disobedience at all ceases to be plausible.

These shortcomings of Rawls's definition of civil disobedience are no accident. They rather seem to follow, at least in part, from treating ideal theory as an independent starting point and working towards a definition of this decidedly non-ideal political practice from there. Taking this perspective obscures the fact, easily observable in recent political history, that civil disobedience can be, at least to a certain degree, non-public, violent, based on motives other than conscientious considerations, that it can forgo or refuse appealing to the majority's sense of justice and that it can be revolutionary in scope without ceasing to be civil disobedience. These features would have been revealed by any contemporary and historical survey of that practice, as Tully's approach recommends it as a starting point.[33] A more encompassing and pluralistic view of civil disobedience was of course already available in Rawls's day: During the time he was working on *A Theory of Justice*, which significantly overlaps with the Vietnam War (1959–75) and the protest against it, he must have had occasion to observe the so-called draft card burnings (which took place from 1965 onwards, provoking the government to quickly pass a law in the same year making the burning of draft cards a crime). This protest was justified by a mix of reasons

---

[31] M. L. King, *A Testament of Hope: The Essential Writings and Speeches*, New York: Harper Collins, 1991, p. 47.

[32] D. Lyons, 'Moral Judgment, Historical Reality, and Civil Disobedience', *Philosophy and Public Affairs* 27 (1): 1 and 33, 1998.

[33] Tully, *Public Philosophy* I, chapter 1.

that eludes the clear separation into civil disobedience, conscientious objection and selective refusal that Rawls was developing at that very moment in dissociating himself from available alternative accounts.[34]

In the face of these problems and in order not to preclude effectively the practical deliberations of citizens themselves, it seems appropriate to define civil disobedience in a way that is less normatively demanding and therefore less restrictive, as an intentionally unlawful and principled collective act of protest (in contrast to both legal protest and 'ordinary' criminal offenses or 'unmotivated' rioting) that has the political aim of changing specific laws, policies or institutions (in contrast to conscientious objection, which is protected in some states as a fundamental right). This somewhat minimalist definition deliberately leaves open whether civil disobedience always has to be public, non-violent, only directed at state institutions, limited in its goals and restricted to transforming the system within its existing limits, as well as whether accepting punishment is a necessary criterion. Although civil disobedience has to be distinguished from both legal opposition and revolutionary revolt and other forms of resistance, as we saw, these boundaries are politically contested in practice and cannot be drawn as easily as Rawls's theory suggests. Not least for this reason, the question of definition should not be mixed up with the question of justification (and perhaps that of strategy as well).

The justification of civil disobedience

The limitations of the ideal-theory perspective on civil disobedience and the need for a more practice-based and pluralist perspective are even more evident when we turn to the second part of Rawls's discussion of

---

[34] These cases entered the discussion about civil disobedience via the writings of Howard Zinn; see especially H. Zinn, *Disobedience and Democracy. Nine Fallacies on Law and Order*, Cambridge, MA: South End, 2002, pp. 77–82. It is remarkable that Rawls even cites this work, which was first published in 1968, in TJ, p. 364, n. 19 and refers to Zinn as someone who 'defined civil disobedience more broadly' – without really addressing the problems this raises for his own approach. It bears mentioning that Rawls first published his thoughts on the topic in an article titled 'The Justification of Civil Disobedience' in 1969, a revised version of which then came to make up part of chapter 6 of *A Theory of Justice*.

civil disobedience, which focuses on its conditions of justification. In a nutshell, my argument will be that Rawls's conception imposes too many constraints on the justifiability of this kind of political practice, again foreclosing meaningful practical deliberation by the agents themselves.

According to Rawls, an act of civil disobedience (understood according to the definition just discussed) is justified when it opposes 'serious infringements of the first principle of justice, the principle of equal liberty, and [. . .] blatant violations of the second part of the second principle, the principle of fair equality of opportunity', when it is used as a 'last resort', and when it is coordinated with other protesting groups in order to avoid 'serious disorder'.[35] We can first note the striking fact that violations of the difference principle are explicitly excluded from the potential grounds of justification of civil disobedience. The reason for this is that according to Rawls civil disobedience should be restricted to easily detectable violations of clear demands of justice. Dworkin seems to have a similar point in mind in distinguishing between 'matters of principle' and 'matters of policy' and arguing that civil disobedience should be restricted to the former (thus, protesting against the infringement of civil liberties may count as justified civil disobedience while protesting against nuclear weapons may not – obviously this distinction is itself politically contested in a way that Dworkin's ideal theory is insufficiently attentive to).[36] In any case, there is a further condition which has to be in place for the question of the justification of civil disobedience to get off the ground: We have to be dealing with what Rawls calls a 'nearly just society',[37] or a 'state of near justice',[38] where 'this implies that it has some form of democratic government, although serious injustices may nevertheless exist'.[39]

---

[35] Rawls, *A Theory of Justice*, pp. 372–4.
[36] See R. Dworkin, *A Matter of Principle*, Cambridge, MA: Harvard University Press, 1985, chapter 4. For a critical discussion, see R. E. Goodin, 'Civil Disobedience and Nuclear Protest', *Political Studies* 35 (3): 461–6, 1987.
[37] Rawls, *A Theory of Justice*, p. 363.
[38] Ibid., p. 371.
[39] Ibid., p. 382.

Rawls's discussion of the justification of civil disobedience also runs into several problems. Let me just point out two of them. First, Rawls's requirements of justification (although they do not seem to be intended as requirements in the strict sense[40]) are *too narrow*. Some of the violations of the difference principle will be no less clear than violations of the other two principles, the principle of equal liberty and the principle of fair equality of opportunity (and obviously some violations of the principle of equal liberty might also turn out to be rather difficult to detect). Furthermore, violations of the difference principle will, if they exceed a certain measure, affect the fair value of the basic liberties (especially of political freedom) emphasized by Rawls himself, who acknowledges that 'the duty to comply is problematic for permanent minorities that have suffered from injustice for many years'.[41] On this basis, Tommie Shelby has convincingly argued that the lack of justice in a basic structure and the legitimate need to uphold one's self-respect may alter the set of obligations, and thus the potential grounds for resistance, we may legitimately ascribe to those who are systematically disadvantaged.[42] There are thus reasons for doubting that these grounds for resistance can all be reduced to 'serious infringements of [. . .] the principle of equal liberty, and [. . .] the principle of fair equality of opportunity'.[43]

Perhaps more importantly, another justification of civil disobedience that has arguably become more and more important since the time of Rawls's writing and turns out to be a focus of Tully's concern is also excluded by the narrowness of Rawls's analysis. Protesters often claim that their civil disobedience is justified on account of procedural and

[40] See ibid., p. 371: 'Of course, the conditions enumerated should be taken as presumptions; no doubt there will be situations when they do not hold, and other arguments could be given for civil disobedience.' Fair enough – but it remains somewhat obscure what follows from this caveat for the rest of his discussion.

[41] Ibid., p. 355.

[42] See T. Shelby, 'Justice, Deviance, and the Dark Ghetto', *Philosophy and Public Affairs* 35 (2): 2, 126–60, 2007, especially p. 160: 'It is crucial, given the duty of justice and on grounds of self-respect, that the ghetto poor make manifest their principled dissatisfaction with the existing social order, either through politically motivated modes of deviance or in some other recognizable way.'

[43] Rawls, *A Theory of Justice*, p. 372.

institutional democratic deficits that may leave the principle of equal liberty intact while restricting the effective participation of citizens in democratic self-government (the development of semi-oligarchic party structures, the problem of agenda-setting and the pushing through of foreign policy decisions against public opinion may come to mind).[44] Similarly, the justifications provided by animal rights activists for their acts of civil disobedience cannot be justice-based in Rawls's sense.[45] In line with Tully's theoretical ethos, I see no reason why these justifications should be dismissed out of hand – indeed, I take it to be a serious deficit (with politically problematic effects) if a theory of civil disobedience does not account for them because it has ex ante limited the range of permissible justifications on the basis of ideal theory without any concern for the social and political reality of protest that a contemporary and historical survey would have uncovered.

Second, Rawls's analysis of the justification of civil disobedience seems to lead him into the following *dilemma* since he leaves it almost entirely open under which conditions a society should be regarded as 'nearly just' or 'reasonably just'[46] while at the same time exhibiting 'serious infringements' and 'blatant violations'[47] of the principles of justice: If, on the one hand, the society in question is 'nearly just', as Rawls presumes, one may well wonder why it is impossible to reach by legal means the transformations aimed at by the necessarily illegal means of civil disobedience; if, on the other hand, the society in question is marked by injustices of such a magnitude that the legal channels of political action are effectively blocked we seem to be faced with a systematic violation of equal political rights that makes it difficult to stick to the label of a 'nearly just' society and that according to Rawls

---

[44] See D. Markovits, 'Democratic Disobedience', *Yale Law Journal* 114: 1897–952, 2005. For a more global perspective see Tully, 'The Crisis of Global Citizenship'.

[45] See P. Singer, *Democracy and Disobedience*, Oxford: Clarendon, 1973, p. 90: 'It is, he [Rawls] says, wrong to be cruel to animals, although we do not owe them justice. If we combine this view with the idea that the justification of civil disobedience must be in terms of justice, we can see that Rawls is committed to holding that no amount of cruelty to animals can justify disobedience.'

[46] Rawls, *A Theory of Justice*, p. 365.

[47] Ibid., p. 372.

himself might thus warrant more militant forms of resistance that cross the line to what Joseph Raz has called 'revolutionary disobedience'. Indeed, as I already pointed out, it seems something of a stretch to claim that what are usually considered to be paradigm cases of civil disobedience – Thoreau, Gandhi and King – took place in societies that should be regarded as 'reasonably' or 'nearly just' (at least one of these cases, King and the Civil Rights Movement, is regarded as a paradigm case by Rawls himself; indeed his discussion in *A Theory of Justice* seems largely motivated by a desire to account for the legitimacy of this movement and its strategy of civil disobedience).[48]

The focus on fundamental rights that is characteristic for the discussion of civil disobedience within the liberal tradition of political philosophy tends to exclude from view certain forms of socio-economic inequality, as well as procedural and institutional democratic deficits that systematically prevent citizens from effectively engaging in collective self-determination and that will in many cases also qualify as potential grounds of justification.[49] As we will see, this goes hand in hand with underestimating the transformative potential of civil disobedience.

The role of civil disobedience

The third part of Rawls's discussion concerns the political and social role of civil disobedience. Here I will limit myself to pointing out a very general problem, namely the conservative tendency or status quo bias that seems inherent in the way Rawls understands civil disobedience, namely as a sort of warning signal to existing institutions and political leaders which they can then use to increase the stability of the existing

[48] See Sabl, *Looking Forward to Justice*, p. 311, for the interesting suggestion to understand the 'nearly just' society as 'a piecewise just society': 'one in which justice is prevalent [...] within a powerful "in group"' while being withheld from members of excluded groups. While this reinterpretation may cover the societies which Thoreau, Gandhi and King opposed, it is unclear to me whether it can preserve the normative force that Rawls intended his formulation to have.

[49] For a more general statement of this problem, see J. Tully, *An Approach to Political Philosophy: Locke in Contexts*, Cambridge: Cambridge University Press, 1993, chapter 7.

order. According to Rawls, 'A general disposition to engage in justified civil disobedience introduces stability into a well-ordered society, or one that is nearly just.'[50] This seems to underestimate the transformative quality civil disobedience has as a specifically extra-institutional form of political practice the democratic and democratizing potential of which has been stressed by theorists from Arendt to Tully. From such a more radically democratic perspective we can also describe the role of civil disobedience in more general terms as the illegal but 'legitimate dramatizing of the tension between the poles of positive law and existing democratic processes and institutions on the one hand, and the idea of democracy as self-government on the other, which is not exhausted by established law and the institutional status quo'[51] – or, in a formulation also taken up by Tully, of the tension between 'constituent power' and 'constitutional form'.[52]

While from a liberal perspective, civil disobedience mainly appears as a form of protest of individual rights bearers against governments and political majorities that transgress the limits established by constitutionally guaranteed moral principles and values, a radical democratic perspective does not view civil disobedience primarily in terms of limitation. It views it rather as the expression of a democratic practice of collective self-determination, as a dynamizing counterweight to the rigidifying tendencies of state institutions. From this viewpoint, this episodic, informal and extra- or anti-institutional form of political action also allows citizens to protest and participate, when – as is often the case in representative democracies – the official and regular institutional channels of action and communication are closed to them or are ineffective in getting their objections across. Rather than being viewed as the actions of individual rights bearers, civil disobedience thus emerges as an essentially collective and political practice of contestation – as one form the 'struggles *of* and *for* democratic

---

[50] Rawls, *A Theory of Justice*, p. 383.
[51] U. Rödel, G. Frankenberg and H. Dubiel, *Die demokratische Frage*, Frankfurt am Main: Suhrkamp, 1989, p. 46.
[52] Tully, *Public Philosophy* II, pp. 197–202.

freedom [. . .] to challenge and modify the non-democratic ways they are governed'[53] takes – in which the vertical form of state authority is confronted with the horizontal power of the association of citizens or the governed, the 'low-intensity representative democratic institutions and modern constitutional formations' with the 'participatory or high-intensity democratic forms of democracy and self-determination'.[54]

Focusing on the role of civil disobedience also, once more, raises the question about the nature of 'nearly just' societies and the possible merit the stabilization of these societies (as opposed to their transformation into 'fully' or 'even more' just societies) might have. Throughout my discussion there has been a certain tension between Rawls's insistence on the 'nearly just' character of the society he assumes for the discussion of his most prominent example from non-ideal theory and the real-world counterexamples I have referred to. Maybe Rawls would not consider our societies to be 'nearly just' societies. However, his specification that 'nearly just' societies are characterized by 'some form of democratic government, although serious injustices may nevertheless exist' does not seem to be too distant from actually existing liberal democracies. More importantly, such a defence would raise the question of what use a *non-ideal* theory could possibly be if it did not apply to the circumstances of our non-ideal reality (but only to some sort of intermediate reality that is significantly more ideal than ours while at the same time being significantly less ideal than the ideal). As we have seen, the whole point of non-ideal theory is supposedly to address 'the pressing and urgent matters [. . .] we [and not some idealized distant relatives] are faced with in everyday life'.[55]

As I hope my discussion has shown, starting from the perspective of ideal theory can be seen as having a seriously distorting effect on the non-ideal discussion of the question of civil disobedience. The distortions I

---

[53] Ibid., p. 113.
[54] Ibid., pp. 206 and 158: Also see H. Arendt, 'Civil Disobedience', in *Crises of the Republic*, New York: Harcourt, Brace and Company, 1972; E. Balibar, 'Sur la désobéissance civique', in *Droit de cité*, Paris: PUF, 2002; and for a more detailed discussion: Celikates, *Ziviler Ungehorsam*.
[55] Rawls, *A Theory of Justice*, p. 9.

have pointed out are not due to the fact that Rawls subscribed to the wrong ideal theory, so we should not try to avoid them by looking for a better ideal theory. Only a decidedly non-ideal (and, at the same time, more political) approach will lead to a more convincing analysis of the meaning, justification and role of civil disobedience (within this analysis elements of ideal theory may well play a certain role) and avoid what Elizabeth Anderson calls 'the epistemic infirmity of ideal theory'.[56]

3. Conclusion

Let me close with two final quotes from Rawls and some remarks on the merits of the alternative and resolutely non-ideal – 'practical, critical and historical'[57] – approach that we find in the work of James Tully, as well as on two further challenges.

Here is the first quote:

Precise principles that straightway decide actual cases are clearly out of the question. Instead, a useful theory defines a perspective within which the problem of civil disobedience can be approached; it identifies the relevant considerations and helps us to assign them their correct weights in the more important instances. If a theory about these matters appears to us, on reflection, to have cleared our vision and to have made our considered judgments more coherent, then it has been worthwhile.[58]

I hope to have shown that Rawls's discussion of civil disobedience fails to meet these standards he himself sets for it. Here is the second quote: 'political philosophy is always in danger of being used corruptly as a defense of an unjust and unworthy status quo, and thus of being ideological'.[59] I hope to have shown that Rawls's discussion of civil

---

[56] E. Anderson, 'Toward a Non-Ideal, Relational Methodology for Political Philosophy: Comments on Schwartzman's *Challenging Liberalism*', *Hypatia* 24 (4): 135, 2009.
[57] Tully, *Public Philosophy* I, p. 16.
[58] Rawls, *A Theory of Justice*, p. 364.
[59] J. Rawls, *Justice as Fairness*, Cambridge, MA: Harvard University Press, 2001, p. 4, n. 4.

disobedience by offering an overly restrictive account of the definition, justification and role of disobedience fails to take the necessary precautions in order to avoid this danger.

In order to avoid the methodological and epistemological deficits of ideal theory, and the potentially ideological effects that result from them, we should follow Tully's advice and start from a critical analysis of current political practices and struggles, the injustices and social pathologies they address, and the expectations and hopes they express, for example, from the different forms of actually existing civil disobedience and the different modes of its conceptualization and justification. This seems to be the best way to avoid the narrowness of Rawls's definition of civil disobedience, of his inventory of legitimate justifications and of the role he has scripted for it – a narrowness we can also describe as yet another effect in theory of the modern 'official' notion of citizenship as it has informed the political reality of liberal democracy:

> Since these types of struggles are *for* new kinds of citizenship and by means of people who are not official citizens, or official citizens who often act beyond the official limits of citizenship of their generation, they cannot be called practices of citizenship in the modern tradition. They are classified as acts of civil disobedience or rebellion. If these illegal struggles are successful and the extensions institutionalised, then the extensions are redescribed retrospectively as stages in the development of modern citizenship and incorporated within its framework, as in the cases of working-class struggles giving rise to social and economic rights, women gaining recognition as citizens, civil rights movements and recognition of cultural minorities. Thus, what are seen as activities of citizenship by the civic tradition – struggles for new forms of recognition and extensions of citizenship – fall outside of modern citizenship with its institutional/status orientation.[60]

Furthermore, and in the dialogical spirit Tully not only ethically advocates but methodologically justifies, it would also allow us to take

---

[60] Tully, *Public Philosophy* II, p. 256.

more seriously what those actually struggling understand themselves to be struggling for, which can be different from what philosophers – in a potentially paternalizing and anti-democratic attitude – think they are or should be struggling for from an ideal point of view. As the non-ideal theorizing in the tradition of critical theory, feminism and pragmatism that is also exemplified in Tully's work attests, this does not mean that one has to uncritically take as the last word the views of those involved. There still is a normative and critical role for theory to play. This role, however, is not a function of the purity of normative theory, it is not detached from political and social practice and it cannot be performed in isolation from more descriptive and explanatory forms of theorizing.

Apart from the theoretical and normative problems individual cases will raise, there are, however, two remaining challenges of a more fundamental nature for an approach that avoids the pitfalls of ideal theory. These challenges are raised both by Tully's recurrent reference to local struggles and forms of resistance and cooperative action in general and the preceding discussion of civil disobedience in particular. It is true that the emphasis on these alternative practices of civic freedom can save us from the twin danger of resigned adaptation to the status quo and its apocalyptic condemnation, from reformism as well as from a romantic longing for a total revolution that links its heroic politics to putting 'the system' as such into question. However, the question of how the diverse socio-economic and political conditions and the forms of structural violence to which people are differentially subjected on a global scale affect their political agency, their capacity to seize the always-existing possibility of transformation and resistance, still remains. Certainly, civil disobedience can be one way of making oneself heard: 'If the duty to listen and respond is ignored and dialogue suppressed, then civic freedom takes the many forms of civic dissent and disobedience to bring the powerful to the table.'[61] However, *who* exactly is able to engage in effective practices

---

[61] Tully, *Public Philosophy* I, p. 130.

of this kind under conditions of exclusion and marginalization and to what effect is a further question.

Moreover, it is unclear whether these largely local practices of resistance to global relations of economic and political domination really pose a challenge to the 'informal imperialism' of the global capitalist order that Tully so brilliantly analyses. Do these more or less local forms of cooperative citizenship really amount to alternative ways of living together, albeit in the interstices of the existing order, or are they merely defensive and ultimately necessarily local and limited forms of withdrawing as far as possible from the global market and its supporting structure of governance? The fact that the practices of civic freedom seem open mainly to what can be regarded as already recognized and thus to a certain extent privileged groups of citizens and the fact that the social and political conditions under which cooperative citizenship can be effectively exercised, for example, in the form of civil disobedience, do not always seem to obtain, pose a double challenge – the challenge of accessibility and of transformative efficacy, as we might call them – to political and social theory in the democratic spirit epitomized in Tully's writings. The gap between theory and practice thus might turn out to be a limit even for a theory that, as far as possible, conceives of itself as practice.

7

Modern versus Diverse Citizenship:
Historical and Ideal Theory Perspectives

Andrew Mason

James Tully's recent work has provided us with new and illuminating ways of thinking about citizenship that mark a refreshing change from the familiar contrast between liberal and republican approaches.[1] Tully's main distinction is between what he calls modern and diverse (or cooperative) traditions. In relation to the nation state, the modern tradition conceives of citizenship in terms of the possession of a particular set of rights and duties and their corresponding institutional preconditions. These rights are regarded as providing universal standards which can be used to assess the imperfect institutional forms that citizenship takes in practice. In contrast, the diverse tradition recognizes a multiplicity of different practices rather than a single set of standards. It conceives of citizenship as a cooperative relationship that does not require any particular institutional setting, and which may cross territorial boundaries, but which takes place in the context of relations of governance. It obtains primarily between equals exercising power together and it is oriented towards securing the enjoyment of public or civic goods, whether through (creative) use of the options available to them, or by employing strategies of negotiation or non-violent confrontation in order to expand that range of options.[2]

---

[1] See J. Tully, *Public Philosophy in a New Key*, Two Volumes, Cambridge: Cambridge University Press, 2008, especially chapter 9; J. Tully, 'A Dilemma of Democratic Citizenship'. Paper delivered at the University of Victoria, 8 May 2010.

[2] Influenced by Wittgenstein, Tully rejects the idea that citizenship in general, or indeed any particular tradition of thinking about citizenship, can be captured in terms of some rule that governs the proper use of that term, so he might resist my general characterization of 'diverse civic citizenship'. See Tully, *Public Philosophy* II, pp. 244, 270–1, 279. But even

Although Tully is drawing an important distinction between two different modes of thought and practice, there is a bias in his characterization that in my view needs attention before we can properly address the issue of the relationship between them. The modern or 'civil' tradition is characterized warts and all, so much so that it looks as if citizenship in this tradition is inseparable, both in principle and in practice, from tyranny. It is wedded to a robust right to private property, of a sort that is bound to generate serious inequalities, and it is imperialist in its ambitions, seeking to export its ideals and practices to other peoples.[3] In contrast, Tully portrays the diverse or 'civic' tradition in a positive and appealing light: people act as citizens when they work together as equals and employ non-violent strategies in order to secure various common goods. As a result, it is hard, perhaps even conceptually impossible, to find examples where the practice of citizenship in the civic tradition is bad or undesirable. But we should worry about these characterizations to the extent that they make it appear as if 'civil citizenship' is inherently bad and 'civic citizenship' inherently good.[4]

Indeed it is unclear why we should suppose that civil citizenship, either in theory or in practice, is as flawed as Tully makes it out to be. Although he would no doubt regard this observation as beside the point, we can certainly imagine a set of institutions and practices that would bear some continuity with that tradition, but which had no imperialistic ambitions, were more inclusive and which stood firmly opposed to tyranny and exploitation. Whether civic citizenship is as flawless as Tully seems to suggest is also open to question. There are practices with family resemblances to his exemplars of civic citizenship that should make us wonder about his rationale for what is included

---

if my characterization leaves out, or marginalizes, some strands of that tradition, it picks out a central way in which citizenship is understood within it.

[3] Tully, 'A Dilemma of Democratic Citizenship', p. 5.

[4] Tully does begin *Dilemma of Democratic Citizenship* by saying that civil citizenship is seemingly an equally democratic and praiseworthy form of citizenship (ibid., p. 2), but it is clear that he does not think that this appearance survives sustained reflection upon it.

and what gets excluded. For example, community action groups which pursue campaigns against the settlement of asylum seekers in the local area[5] would apparently be excluded by it, as would 'vigilante' groups which seek to drive out suspected paedophiles from a neighbourhood.[6] Potentially at least, these are cooperative practices in which the participants relate to each other as equals, even if they are not oriented towards genuine civic goods. There are also cooperative activities that aim to secure genuine civic goods but which involve hierarchical relationships rather than relationships between equals because they are structured by inequalities of power based on race, class or sex. Each of these types of activity have similarities with the practice of civic citizenship but on Tully's scheme they would not count as such, either because they do not aim at genuine civic goods or because the relationships are not of the right kind since they are not between equals. But we might ask, given the similarities, why not regard them as examples of civic citizenship, albeit less (than) appealing illustrations of it? Indeed we might think that, unless Tully is prepared to regard them in this way, he will be hard pressed to find very many real historical examples of civic citizenship at all, and that he is much too optimistic about the widespread existence of cooperative relationships between equals in which genuine civic goods are pursued non-violently.

1. Methodological issues

The asymmetry in Tully's characterization of the civil and civic traditions seems to emerge from his different ways of approaching them. Although he approaches civic citizenship in the spirit of what

---

[5] Consider the opposition of local groups in the United Kingdom to various plans to build accommodation centres for asylum seekers in their areas: www.telegraph.co.uk/news/uknews/1421759/Uproar-over-asylum-centre-plan.html (Accessed 18 March 2011).

[6] Of course, this will involve cases of mistaken identity. In an infamous case in the United Kingdom a hospital paediatrician was driven out of her house in a village in South Wales after vigilantes confused her job title with 'paedophile': see www.guardian.co.uk/uk/2000/aug/30/childprotection.society (Accessed 16 March 2011).

might loosely be called 'ideal theory', his account of civil citizenship is almost entirely historically situated. As a result, the former needs to be tempered by more attention to some less desirable activities with family resemblances to those that he regards as exemplifying the tradition, while the latter would benefit from some 'ideal theorizing' that situates it in the context of what I call a justice account of citizenship, and which would enable us to see it as a highly imperfect realization of something that is much better.

This unavoidably raises major questions about method. Let me develop my implied contrast between two different ways of studying civil citizenship: an approach that begins from ideal theory and a historically situated approach. According to the former, we start by asking what rights and duties the members of a state would possess in a perfectly just society, that is, a society in which basic institutions were organized in accordance with the correct or most defensible principles of justice, and each person acts from the principles of justice that govern their individual behaviour. An approach such as this one might bracket feasibility constraints altogether,[7] or it might adopt only a relatively weak constraint of this kind, for example, the Rawlsian requirement that the principles selected should be realizable in the best of foreseeable worlds.[8] This approach need not remain at the level of ideal theory, however. After arriving at a set of principles for determining the rights and duties of citizens in a perfectly just society, a theorist could then move from these principles to the non-ideal circumstances of the society in question, raising queries about the ways in which actual institutions fall short when judged from the perspective of the ideal, and devising rather different principles to apply to these circumstances – principles that depart from the ideal because they address the question of how best to approximate it in a particular historical context, involving a complex set of institutions, practices, power relations and individual

---

[7] G. A. Cohen, *Rescuing Justice and Equality*, Cambridge, MA: Harvard University Press, 2008, pp. 250–4.

[8] J. Rawls, *Justice as Fairness*, Cambridge, MA: Harvard University Press, 2001, p. 13; J. Rawls, *Political Liberalism*, New York: Columbia University Press, 1996, p. xix.

motivations, while taking into account other values apart from justice, and the costs associated with reforms, both moral and non-moral.

Contrast this approach that begins from ideal theory with an historically situated one that starts from an analysis of our actual practices, including how they have emerged, how they differ from what we once had, the power relations they involve, the motivations of the flesh and blood actors who participate in them, the incentives and disincentives that are created by the institutions within which these practices operate and the traditions of thought embodied in them. This approach looks at the historical processes that have led to changes in the rights accorded to citizens, and which have influenced (or even driven) the behaviour of individual states within the state system, and examines the forces which have transformed that system. It then extracts the normative presuppositions of these practices, that is, the actual norms and principles that inform them. Once these norms and principles have been identified, they can be subjected to critique. But according to this approach, well-grounded critique must start from an account which is possible in the light of our best analysis of historical context, even though it may also apply (whether implicitly or explicitly) norms that transcend the practices, such as norms of non-domination or non-exploitation.

My purpose in distinguishing these different approaches is not to argue that there is one right way to proceed. It seems to me that they have different strengths, and the decision about which to adopt depends at least in part upon the purposes of one's investigation and the issues that are being addressed. In practice I suspect that the approaches will converge to a considerable extent when each is fully developed. Even if ideal theory aims to provide us with an abstract understanding of what justice is, if we want to know what justice requires of us here and now, we will need a detailed analysis of our current historical circumstances and the possibilities they contain. A historically situated approach may be able to extract the norms that govern our current practices and institutions, but if we are to reflect upon those norms in a fully adequate way, we will need to draw upon resources that, at least to some extent, transcend these practices and institutions. Insofar as the approaches I have distinguished nevertheless diverge in the way they are employed, they need not be regarded as mutually exclusive. Furthermore, each carries with it various dangers when it is pursued in the absence of the other.[9] Ideal theory may be so far removed from our non-ideal circumstances that the gap between them is unbridgeable, especially when unhelpful idealizations are involved[10] or when issues of what is feasible are bracketed entirely. Ideal theory may also be guilty of wishful thinking if it supposes that something is genuinely empirically possible simply because it can be imagined.[11] Historically situated approaches face a different set of dangers. They may lack a worked out set of norms with which to assess practices: conceptions of non-domination and non-exploitation may be invoked as if they were self-evident without acknowledging that they are subject to deep contestation. These approaches will also suffer from 'sour grapes reasoning' or adaptive preference formation if they in effect deny that something is

---

[9] See A. Mason, 'Just Constraints', *British Journal of Political Science* 34 (2): 251–68, 2004; For recent discussion of ideal theory and its strengths and weaknesses, see C. Farrelly, 'Justice in Ideal Theory: A Refutation', *Political Studies* 55 (4): 844–64, 2007; A. Sen, 'What Do We Want from a Theory of Justice?', *Journal of Philosophy* 103 (5): 215–38, 2006; I. Robeyns, 'Ideal Theory in Theory and Practice', *Social Theory and Practice* 34 (3): 341–62, 2008; A. Swift, 'The Value of Philosophy in Nonideal Circumstances', *Social Theory and Practice* 34 (3): 363–87, 2008; L. Valentini, 'On the Apparent Paradox of Ideal Theory', *Journal of Political Philosophy* 17 (3): 332–55, 2009; A. J. Simmons, 'Ideal and Nonideal Theory', *Philosophy and Public Affairs* 38 (1): 5–36, 2010; A. Mason, 'Rawlsian Theory and the Circumstances of Politics', *Political Theory* 38 (5): 658–83, 2010.

[10] Onora O'Neill expresses concerns about idealization, distinguishing it from abstraction. Abstraction 'is a matter of bracketing, but not of *denying*, predicates that are true of the matter under discussion' (O. O'Neill, *Towards Justice and Virtue: A Constructive Account of Practical Reasoning*, Cambridge: Cambridge University Press, 1996, p. 40. Emphasis in original). Idealization, in contrast, involves making claims that are, strictly speaking, false, as a way of simplifying an argument. For example, Rawls's assumption that everyone is 'rational and able to manage their own affairs' and that the subject matter of a theory of justice is the basic structure of society conceived 'as a closed system isolated from other societies' are idealizations. See J. Rawls, *A Theory of Justice*, Cambridge, MA: Harvard University Press, 1971, pp. 248 and 8.

[11] John Dunn argues that forcing political theorists 'to locate the levels of moral ambition they espouse within their best causal understanding of the human world as this is . . . precludes them in consequence from subordinating their understanding of how it really is to the importunities of their own projective desires' (J. Dunn, *Interpreting Political Responsibility*, Cambridge: Cambridge University Press, 1990, p. 196).

valuable simply because it cannot be achieved.[12] Fusing conceptual and historical analysis may obscure the way in which existing institutions and practices can properly be regarded as a departure from a genuine ideal rather than as merely oppressive.

In relation to the civil tradition, at least, Tully seems to employ a historically situated method, and to my mind he does fall into the trap of perceiving it in a one-sided way. He tends to see it in a manner that he concedes is encouraged by the perspective of diverse citizenship, that is, as neither the exemplification of 'freedom nor democracy but the culmination of five hundred years of relentless 'tyranny' against local citizenship and self-reliance'.[13] I do not deny that by using a historically situated method Tully has gained insight into the practice of civil citizenship, but I also believe that an approach that begins from ideal theory could act as a corrective to the biases involved in his portrayal of it compared to civic citizenship. (Indeed it seems to me that his study of civic citizenship combines elements of both approaches in a way that, though fruitful, is also partly responsible for creating the asymmetry I have identified.)

2. An ideal theory approach

If we begin with ideal theory, we will in effect be treating citizenship as fundamentally a moral rather than a legal concept. A purely legal

---

[12] G. A. Cohen makes this point in the context of discussing the ways in which socialists have come to terms with the thought that in the present circumstances the best that is possible is some form of capitalism, rather than true socialism which requires equality of a kind that is unachievable in a capitalist system. Socialists who accept this analysis do not have reason to be fully satisfied with the best possible form of capitalism. If they were fully satisfied with it, their reasoning would involve adaptive preference formation. They would in effect be deciding that there is no reason to want 'true socialism' because it is impossible to achieve here and now: perhaps they change their evaluative criteria or perhaps they change their view of how well true socialism measures up to those criteria, but they do so merely because of its unavailability: G. A. Cohen, *Self-Ownership, Freedom, and Equality*, Cambridge: Cambridge University Press, 1995, pp. 254–7.

[13] Tully, *Public Philosophy* II, p. 267.

concept of citizenship equates it with membership in a polity, and sees it as consisting in whatever legal rights and entitlements are enjoyed in virtue of that membership and in whatever legal duties, obligations or responsibilities are attributed on the basis of it. These will differ from one state to another and hence, from the perspective of the legal concept, what is involved in being a citizen of a state may vary.[14] The moral concept, in contrast, specifies an ideal: it spells out the moral rights or entitlements that ought to underpin legal rights and entitlements – and that have to be enjoyed in order for a relationship to count as one of full citizenship – and the moral obligations, duties or responsibilities which are necessarily incurred in that relationship. The moral concept may nevertheless allow that the moral rights and entitlements of citizens, and the moral duties and responsibilities of citizenship, may legitimately vary from one state to another, for it can maintain that these are context-sensitive. It can also allow that the legal rights and entitlements of citizens may legitimately vary from one state to another even when moral rights and entitlements remain the same, for there may be different ways in which the same moral rights and entitlements can be secured by a legal system.

What I have elsewhere called the justice account of citizenship,[15] provides us with one obvious way of unpacking the moral notion of citizenship. Although a justice account of citizenship need not be anchored in ideal theory, one that is can (in my view) illuminate some of the terrain that Tully is charting, especially that part of it which pertains to civil citizenship.[16] Justice accounts maintain that the moral rights, duties and virtues of citizenship are ultimately derived in some

---

[14] However, insofar as the legal concept of citizenship allows us to draw a distinction between being a mere subject and being a citizen, it cannot entirely bracket normative issues concerning the content of these rights, entitlements and obligations.

[15] See A. Mason, 'Citizenship and Justice', *Politics, Philosophy and Economics* 10 (3): 263–81, 2011; A. Mason, *Living Together as Equals: The Demands of Citizenship*, Oxford: Oxford University Press, 2012.

[16] Strictly speaking, what I am calling the justice account of citizenship need not start from ideal theory, that is, from a theory which attempts to characterize a perfectly just society. Instead it could start from a theory of what justice requires in a particular society at a given time, given its traditions and what is feasible – but this is not the form that the justice account has normally taken.

way from considerations of justice. The moral rights of citizenship are understood as requirements of justice and the duties of citizenship are understood primarily as the means through which a citizen promotes the conditions required to create or sustain justice in her society or discharges the duties of justice that she owes to her fellow citizens. As a result, according to this account, a normative theory of citizenship is parasitic upon a logically prior theory of justice.[17] The justice account of citizenship need not suppose that the moral rights of citizenship are everywhere the same. The principles of justice which these rights express, or from which they are derived, may permit both moral and legal rights to vary depending upon particular features of the polity in question and particular features of the relationships between citizens. Justice requires government and institutions to treat those subject to them as equals, but what that involves may depend upon the differences between them.

The justice account is really a family of views because different theories of justice generate different versions of it. Some versions take the view that all fundamental principles of justice apply independently of how individuals are related to each other, and assign moral rights and entitlements with no regard to citizenship, but argue that the institutions of particular states should be designed with a view to protecting the rights of their own citizens, and to forcing or enabling fellow citizens to discharge their duties of justice specifically in relation to each other, on the grounds that this constitutes the best way of realizing these fundamental principles. (Justice accounts of this kind may nevertheless be critical of the existing state system, on the grounds that a system of independent sovereign states is not the best way of realizing fundamental principles of justice. They may, as a result, favour dispersing the political authority that is concentrated in the traditional nation state, perhaps in the manner recommended by some theories of cosmopolitan democracy.) Other versions maintain that fellow citizens

---

[17] For this reason John Tomasi refers to the justice account as the derivative interpretation of citizenship: J. Tomasi, *Liberalism Beyond Justice: Citizens, Society, and the Boundaries of Political Theory*, Princeton, NJ: Princeton University Press, 2001, pp. 57–61.

are related to each other in a way that means that some fundamental principles of justice apply to them that do not necessarily apply to others (e.g. fellow citizens might be regarded as part of a cooperative scheme for mutual advantage, and this might be thought to license the application of egalitarian principles to them but not to outsiders), while allowing that there are other principles, such as those that concern human rights, which apply equally to everyone.[18]

According to the justice account, to act as a citizen is to act out of a concern for what justice requires in relation to one's fellow citizens. Citizenship is not merely understood as a status. Citizens are conceived as being under special duties towards one another to sustain and promote the institutions that secure their rights and entitlements. The justice account supposes that when citizens live under just, or reasonably just, institutions, then they have a duty to support these institutions that they owe to their fellow citizens. Versions of the justice account may also hold that the maintenance of reasonably just institutions requires citizens to keep a watchful eye on government, and for this reason they may suppose that the fulfilment of the duties of citizenship requires extensive public engagement of a kind that is often associated with the republican tradition.[19] In a society where institutions and policies are significantly unjust, the justice account may argue that the duties of citizenship are even more demanding and that they require citizens to devote a considerable portion of their energies to seeking the reform of institutions and policy.

---

[18] See, for example, T. Nagel, 'The Problem of Global Justice', *Philosophy and Public Affairs* 33 (2): 113–47, 2005; A. Sangiovanni, 'Global Justice, Reciprocity, and the State', *Philosophy and Public Affairs* 35 (1): 3–39, 2007; For relevant discussion also see M. Blake, 'Distributive Justice, Coercion, and Autonomy', *Philosophy and Public Affairs* 30 (3): 257–96, 2001; M. Risse, 'What to Say About the State', *Social Theory and Practice* 32 (4): 671–98, 2006; C. Armstrong, 'Coercion, Reciprocity, and Equality Beyond the State', *Journal of Social Philosophy* 40 (3): 297–316, 2009.

[19] Elsewhere I argue that the justice account has both liberal and republican variants. See A. Mason, 'Citizenship and Justice', *Politics, Philosophy and Economics* 10 (3): 263–81, 2011 and A. Mason, *Living Together as Equals: The Demands of Citizenship*, Oxford: Oxford University Press, 2012, chapter 1. Tully tends to regard both liberal and republican views of citizenship as variants within the civil or modern tradition. See Tully, *Public Philosophy* II, p. 273.

Nor need the justice account restrict the duties of citizenship to a duty to create or to support just institutions. Such a view of the limits of these duties might seem to go naturally with the idea that principles of justice apply only to the basic structure of society, but that restriction is hard to sustain. Indeed there is a general argument for applying principles of justice widely, including to personal behaviour that takes place within, or in the shadow of, the basic structure. If the reason for applying principles of justice to the basic structure of society is that this structure has profound effects on the life chances of individuals, then this provides grounds for applying principles of justice (though not necessarily the same ones) to any practices or patterns of behaviour which also have such effects, including practices and patterns of behaviour that are part of civil society.[20] If this argument can be sustained, acting on duties of justice and the corresponding duties of citizenship may require considerable self-sacrifice – even if there are personal prerogatives which permit citizens to depart from these duties when compliance with them would be particularly burdensome.[21] Indeed we might think that there is a duty of citizenship to act justly towards one's fellow citizens and to ensure that one does not seek or gain unfair advantages in relation to them.[22] In this way, justice accounts of citizenship can occupy some of the space that Tully retains for the civic view, for they can acknowledge the way in which people may act together as citizens to fulfil such duties.

---

[20] On the basis of a nuanced form of this argument, Cohen has argued that Rawls cannot consistently deny that the difference principle should apply to personal economic choices, such as an individual's decisions about what career to pursue, what wages to negotiate and how hard to work, as well as to the basic structure of society. See G. A. Cohen, *Rescuing Justice and Equality*, Cambridge, MA: Harvard University Press, 2008, part I; for relevant discussion, see also L. Murphy, 'Institutions and the Demands of Justice', *Philosophy and Public Affairs* 27 (4): 251–91, 1998; T. Pogge, 'On the Site of Distributive Justice: Reflections on Cohen and Murphy', *Philosophy and Public Affairs* 29 (2): 137–69, 2000; A. Williams, 'Incentives, Inequality, and Publicity', *Philosophy and Public Affairs* 27 (3): 225–47, 1998; D. Estlund, 'Liberalism, Equality, and Fraternity in Cohen's Critique of Rawls', *Journal of Political Philosophy* 6 (1): 99–112, 1998.

[21] See Cohen, *Rescuing Justice and Equality*, pp. 10–11, 61–2, 71–2.

[22] See Mason, *Living Together as Equals*, chapter 5.

3. Adjusting Tully's analysis

How does Tully's analysis of civil citizenship look from the perspective
of a justice account that starts from ideal theory? As I have noted, there
are different versions of such a justice account, distinguished in part
by their different views of the moral rights of citizens. Justice accounts
are not necessarily wedded to an unlimited right of private property in
the means of production of the kind presupposed in a purely capitalist
market, and which Tully regards as central to the modern tradition
and to an adequate diagnosis of the causes of global inequality,
environmental degradation and the expansionist tendencies of states.
Justice accounts can – and, in my view, should – reject the idea that
there is such a right, and they can be critical of the imperatives in the
existing state system which contribute to militarism, and which make
imperialism a permanent threat. They can also be critical of the idea
that states are under a duty to open their doors to free commerce[23]
and that they are under a duty of civilization.[24] They need not regard
civil citizenship as undemanding or suppose that the exercise of the
political rights it involves is optional in the sense that there is no
duty to exercise those rights;[25] they can suppose that citizens have an
imperfect (or even a perfect) duty to do so. They need not take the
view that citizenship has a bearing only in the public not the private
sphere;[26] they can, for example, suppose that there are obligations of
citizenship that extend into the personal sphere, to take a fair share of
domestic burdens[27] or to do one's bit for the environment. Nor need
they presuppose a 'one size fits all' conception of institutions,[28] for they
can allow that different institutions and policies will best realize the
abstract principles of justice in different societies, given their different
histories and cultures.

---

[23] Tully, *Public Philosophy* II, p. 258.
[24] Tully, 'A Dilemma of Democratic Citizenship', p. 11; Tully, *Public Philosophy* II, pp. 261–2.
[25] Tully, 'A Dilemma of Democratic Citizenship', p. 9.
[26] Ibid.
[27] See Mason, *Living Together as Equals*, chapter 4.
[28] Tully, 'A Dilemma of Democratic Citizenship', p. 16.

To Tully, this will seem beside the point. Even if civil citizenship *can* be conceived in these terms, this is not the form in which it has been manifest historically. But a historical perspective here is not the only one that is relevant. The civil tradition looks rather different when it is seen through the lens of the justice account. Of course, Tully is aware of the possibility of adopting this rather different perspective. Why then does he refuse to take it up, and indeed why does he give a characterization of civil citizenship which makes it almost impossible to do so? I think he has a combination of different reasons. From a normative perspective, he thinks that whatever its promise, civil citizenship has failed to deliver in terms of justice or indeed democracy: the rights it protects have been exercised in the service of tyranny and oppression, and any attempt to rethink civil citizenship will have to face the enormous democratic deficit that its institutions involve. That may all be true, but it simply poses a challenge for any approach that starts from ideal theory, including justice accounts that do so – a challenge that, for example, theorists of cosmopolitan democracy, who advocate the dispersal of the political authority that is currently concentrated in the nation state, have attempted to meet. As Tully argues, models of cosmopolitan democracy may have their own inadequacies[29] – they often fail to expose the limitations of representative forms of democracy, or to recognize that different models of government may better realize democracy and indeed justice in different cultural contexts, and they often leave non-democratic forms of governance unchallenged. But they nevertheless overcome some problematic aspects of the civil tradition, and pave the way for the development of new models of democracy that address the deficiencies of representative forms of government and that seek to democratize non-democratic forms of governance.

From a historical perspective, Tully has worries about any account of the development of civil citizenship that might make it seem that it has a *telos* towards which it is inexorably moving, or indeed that it has gradually moved towards that telos because of some collective

---

[29] Tully, *Public Philosophy* II, pp. 63–4.

appreciation of an ideal of full inclusion. It would surely be a mistake to think that historical change that better realizes an ideal is necessarily motivated by a widespread commitment to it – or even to see such change as evidencing an 'underlying' common commitment to the ideal[30] – as opposed to regarding it in general as a concession extracted at great cost through a struggle against oppression.[31] But surely we gain at least some understanding of the (admittedly, partial) value of actually existing liberal-democratic institutions by seeing them as an imperfect realization of rights and entitlements that are grounded in genuine considerations of justice.

This response might seem to ignore deeper problems with approaches that begin from ideal theory and which may lie behind Tully's refusal to take up the perspective that is afforded by any justice account of citizenship that is grounded in ideal theory. (Indeed Tully might allow that justice accounts of citizenship can illuminate civil citizenship and the relationship between it and civic citizenship, but argue that if they are to do so, then they must eschew ideal theory.) What, then, are the potential pitfalls of ideal theory in this context? First, it might be argued that we simply do not need an ideal theory in order to be able to understand the potential value of the institutions and practices that are constitutive of civil citizenship. And, as Amartya Sen has argued, we can make comparative judgements about what institutions and policies would be *more* just without knowing what would be required for *perfect* justice:[32] we can know, for example, that a state of affairs in which states settle conflicts between them peacefully and do not use violence simply to further their own ends is better than one in which they resort early to the use of military force, and employ violence to further their own economic interests. Second, it might be argued that ideal theory is a 'top down' approach which neglects the point that notions of justice are disputed, so there will be no justice account of citizenship that can

[30] Ibid., p. 266.
[31] Ibid., p. 256.
[32] Sen, *What Do We Want*, especially pp. 216, 221–2, 237; A. Sen, *The Idea of Justice*, London: Penguin Books, 2009, pp. 12–18. For a response, see Simmons, *Ideal and Nonideal Theory*, pp. 34–6.

command universal assent. There is nothing to be gained politically or even normatively from an approach that starts from ideal theory, even if it is informed by the best available theory of justice, because that theory will inevitably be a matter of contest and its implementation will fail to give due weight to democracy itself, since any genuine commitment to democracy would require institutional arrangements to be the object of democratic discussion and decision-making.

Both of these responses have force, but in my view they do not defeat a justice account of citizenship that starts from ideal theory, as long as its role and point is properly understood. It is true that we can often evaluate institutions and practices without the benefit of an ideal theory, and indeed that we can also make comparative judgements about whether one state of affairs is better or worse than another without being in possession of such a theory. But I think Rawls was nevertheless right when he claimed that a *systematic* grasp of the issues involved is possible only with the aid of ideal theory.[33] This might be regarded as question-begging on the grounds that a systematic grasp of this kind is impossible anyway; for example, it might be argued that no such grasp is available because there is no theory – no set of principles – which we can use to specify what would count as a perfectly just society. While I accept (on broadly Wittgensteinian grounds that Tully himself would probably find congenial) that the very possibility of moral and political thought does not depend on their being such principles, whether or not they are available can only be determined by trying to provide them.[34]

In response to the second objection, it should be conceded that any justice account will be disputed, drawing as it must on some controversial conception of justice. But this does not mean that an approach that

---

[33] J. Rawls, *A Theory of Justice*, Cambridge, MA: Harvard University Press, 1971, p. 9.

[34] If moral particularism is true, then it follows that there is no reason to think that there must be a set of principles of justice which determine what a perfectly just society would look like, but it does not follow that there cannot be a set of principles of this sort (see A. Mason, 'Justice, Holism and Principles', *Res Publica* 25: 179–94, 2009; for the Wittgensteinian argument, see J. McDowell, 'Virtue and Reason', *The Monist* 62 (3): 331–50, 1979; for other relevant discussion, see J. Dancy, *Ethics Without Principles*, Oxford: Oxford University Press, 2004; S. Mckeever and M. Ridge, *Principled Ethics: Generalism as a Regulative Ideal*, Oxford: Oxford University Press, 2006).

starts from ideal theory is necessarily top down in a problematic way. Those who develop an ideal theory are not committed to a conception of themselves as philosopher kings or to thinking of themselves as law-givers in Rousseau's sense. They can recognize that they are presenting one vision of the justice account among several that are reasonable, and that the *legitimate authority* to enforce the rights and entitlements presupposed in it can only derive from a democratic political process of some kind. Nor need justice accounts that start from ideal theory deny the general truth that in practice the recognition of these rights and entitlements will come about only as a result of political struggle on the part of marginalized or oppressed groups.

How then does an approach that begins from ideal theory help us to understand better the relationship between modern and diverse citizenship? My view is that once we perceive actually existing civil citizenship through the lens of ideal theory, as a highly imperfect realization of a defensible justice account anchored in ideal theory, and we think of the actual practice of civic citizenship as involving a wider range of cases, some of which at best imperfectly realize the ideal of people working together as equals in pursuit of civic goods, then we can see that modern and diverse citizenship are potentially complementary: they provide a conceptualization of two different kinds of imperfect practice, each of which needs the other. Civil citizenship, as we experience it here and now, is defective, because, first, its institutional forms protect various legal rights, such as a right to private property in the means of production, that at the very least need to be limited and their exercise regulated in various ways, to ensure that they serve justice rather than injustice, and second, the political authority that continues to be concentrated in these institutions needs to be reconfigured so that it relies less on representative forms of government and is dispersed in part to new democratic bodies above and below the level of existing nation states. Furthermore, non-democratic forms of governance, including bureaucratic, authoritarian or systemic forms,[35] need to

---

[35] See Tully, *Public Philosophy* II, p. 50.

be brought under democratic control, insofar as that is feasible and beneficial. As Tully argues, practices of diverse or civic citizenship have a crucial role to play in bringing to light these injustices and democratic deficits and in struggling to overcome them. But civic citizenship, as we experience it, is also defective in various ways, and its practice needs to be regulated and constrained by institutions of civil citizenship that are informed by principles of justice and democracy: first, the goods that are pursued within practices of civic citizenship are often misunderstood or corrupted, with the result that participants in these practices act unjustly or badly (e.g. they seek to protect their way of life against the influx of asylum seekers or economic migrants, when in fact they owe duties of justice to them – and indeed where their own way of life would be enhanced by the presence of these immigrant groups); second, genuine goods are pursued in ways that are unjust (e.g. action-groups target suspected paedophiles, violating their rights in an attempt to drive them out of local communities); third, the relations within civic-minded groups are often not among equals because they involve unacknowledged hierarchies of various kinds.

4. Conclusion

I have not tried to defend a specific version of the ideal of civil citizenship. But I have argued that we should not suppose that civil citizenship can be understood fully by reference to its current institutional forms and the practices that support (and are supported by) these forms, and I have gestured towards some ways in which it might plausibly be held that there is a gap between the ideal of civil citizenship and the institutions and practices that claim to embody it. Tully seems to be torn between (on the one hand) the view that the civil tradition is fundamentally flawed not only in practice but also in theory, and that we should abandon it in favour of the civic or cooperative tradition, and (on the other hand) the view that, suitably reconfigured, the civil tradition can be viewed as an attempt to develop and realize something that is genuinely worthwhile. I would urge him to adopt the second view in a less ambiguous manner, to adjust his conception of both of these traditions, and to acknowledge the ways in which, appropriately reconfigured, they can be mutually supportive. Grounded in a more adequate theory of justice, ideals of civil citizenship can help to identify institutional structures that define the space within which citizens can act, whether as individuals or together, to fulfil their citizenly duties to secure various common goods and to counter injustice, in practices that the civic tradition is sometimes better equipped to understand and to appreciate. Democracy itself, at least when it is of a more full-blooded kind, would then have a further role to pay in legitimizing these institutional structures in the face of disagreement between advocates of different conceptions of justice concerning what form these structures should take. As it stands, Tully's rather bleak picture of civil citizenship sits uneasily with his too rosy view of civic citizenship. The rosy view of civic citizenship is achieved by excluding potentially problematic cases by definitional fiat, while the bleak picture of civil citizenship arises from a refusal to see it as an imperfect realization of something that might be better. But that should not detract from the fact that Tully has provided us with an important distinction between these two different traditions that enables us to ask questions that would otherwise be hard to raise.[36]

---

[36] For helpful comments on an earlier draft of this chapter, I would like to thank David Owen.

8

Instituting Civic Citizenship

Adam Dunn and David Owen

. . . if men wish to be free, it is precisely sovereignty they must renounce.

Hannah Arendt

What we need however is a political philosophy that isn't erected around the problem of sovereignty . . . We need to cut off the King's head: in political theory that has still to be done.

Michel Foucault

In his essay, and recent work more generally, James Tully sets up a contrast between two 'modes of citizenship', where this phrase refers to both 'a distinctive language of citizenship and its traditions of interpretation' and 'the corresponding practices and institutions to which it refers and in which it used'.[1] The basic contrast between these two modes – modern civil citizenship and diverse civic citizenship – is sketched thus:

> Whereas modern citizenship focuses on citizenship as a universalisable legal status underpinned by institutions and processes of rationalisation that enable and constrain the possibility of civil activity (an institutionalised/universal orientation), diverse citizenship focuses on the singular civic activities and diverse way that these are more

---

[1] J. Tully, 'On Local *and* Global Citizenship: An Apprenticeship Manual', in *Public Philosophy in a New Key: Volume II, Imperialism and Civic Citizenship*, Cambridge; Cambridge University Press, 2008, p. 246.

or less institutionalised or blocked in different contexts (a civic activity/contextual orientation). Citizenship is not a status given by the institutions of the modern constitutional state and international law, but negotiated practices in which one becomes a citizen through participation.[2]

Our concern in this chapter is the question of how, from the standpoint of diverse or civic citizenship, we are to understand the relationship of citizenship (as 'negotiated practices in which one becomes a citizen through participation') to the status of citizenship, to civic right and to civic institutions. Elucidating these two modes will put us in a better position to understand this relationship and the implications of Tully's argument for contemporary political struggles and transformations. We will begin by drawing attention to the contrast between the basic *orientations* of diverse-civic and modern-civil modes of citizenship and the ways in which these distinct orientations manifest themselves in order to draw out both Tully's critique of sovereignty and the sense in which diverse citizenship is a non-sovereign citizenship.

1. Orientations

Tully's analysis adopts an approach to subjectivity (common to Nietzsche, Heidegger, Wittgenstein and Foucault) in which, as Menke notes of Foucault, 'the praxis of practice . . . is the medium of constitution of subjectivity'.[3] Through the praxis of practice, we acquire the abilities that are, at once, the ability to perform actions that realize the goods of the practices in which we are engaged and the ability to direct our own activity; thus 'subjectivity is the practical self-relation of self-direction that is located in being able to carry

---

[2] Tully, 'Local and Global Citizenship', p. 248.
[3] C. Menke, 'Two Kinds of Practice: On the Relation between Social Discipline and the Aesthetics of Existence', *Constellations* 10 (2): 200, 2003.

something out'.[4] What distinguishes the two modes of citizenship is not necessarily the practices in which they are engaged but the orientation or, more precisely, *practical attitude* with which they engage in the activity, that is, their practical attitude as participants in a practice, where such attitudes cannot simply be chosen (acquired or secured by decisions)[5] but must be acquired through practice, especially practices of 'citizenization'. This 'practice'-based approach to subjectivity explains two fundamental features of Tully's reflections on citizenship. It explains, first, why he focuses on 'modes of citizenship' as both marking out distinctive practical attitudes to the practice of citizenship and specifying the practices of citizenization through which these practical attitudes are acquired or inculcated.[6] It also explains, second, why he can claim that diverse or civic citizens can act as such even when participating within 'the same institutions' as modern citizens, including, for example, institutions such as the modern state.[7] Seeing that the contrast between these orientations is the difference between the practical attitudes towards the governance of self and others practised by participants in these practices is fundamental to any consideration of the two practical attitudes that Tully identifies. (Note that this fundamental feature also explains why Tully engages in a form of genealogical analysis in which philosophical enquiry is necessarily also historical enquiry; the two attitudes that he addresses are not separable from their historical manifestations even if it is also the case that they are not reducible to their historical forms.)

In general terms, 'modern citizenship' as a mode of citizenship/ citizenization stands towards citizenship 'as a [legal] status within an institutional framework', whereas 'diverse citizenship' is oriented to citizenship 'as *negotiated practices*, as praxis – as actors and activities

---

[4] Ibid., p. 201.
[5] Ibid., p. 209.
[6] It is hard to overestimate the significance of this point for understanding Tully's argument and the way in which it is conducted. Thus, for example, it would be a mistake to interpret him as simply sketching two 'conceptions' of citizenship which could either be specified by ideal theory or fleshed out through historical examples because such an approach to his argument would miss what was central to it.
[7] Tully, 'Local and Global Citizenship', p. 269.

in contexts'.[8] On the former view, civil action necessarily presupposes an institutional structure of legal rules; on the latter view, primacy is accorded to 'the concrete games of citizenship and the ways that they are played'.[9] Thus, in relation to diverse citizenship, Tully stresses: 'Civic activities – what citizens do and the ways they do them – can be more or less institutionalised and rationalised (in countless forms), but this is secondary'.[10] Notice that this general contrast already constructs a fundamental difference in the mode of self-relation of individuals to themselves as citizens. The mode of citizenship-formation characteristic of the modern civil stance is of the individual standing to him- or herself as occupant of an 'office' specified by a range of rights and duties, whereas that of the diverse civic stance is of the individual standing to him- or herself as an agent with a (non-fixed) range of powers. One way in which this contrast discloses itself is in the contrast between these practical attitudes as attitudes towards autonomy. As Tully notes, the contrast can be cast in terms of the grammatical distinction between liberty and freedom in which the latter but not the former can be predicated of actions.[11] Civil citizens stand towards themselves as persons who are *at liberty* (i.e. free from subjection to the will of another) in virtue of their enjoyment of the civil rights and duties that compose the office of citizenship under law to take up opportunities to participate as political equals in determining the law to which they are subject as subjects of a given political institution of governance. By contrast, civic citizens 'manifest the freedom *of* participation':

> Civic freedom is not an opportunity [to participate] but a manifestation: neither freedom *from* nor freedom *to* . . ., but freedoms *of* and *in* participation, and *with* fellow citizens. The civic citizen is not the citizen of an institution (a nation-state or an international law) but the free citizen of the 'free city': that is, *any* kind of civic world or democratic 'sphere' that comes into being and is reciprocally held aloft by the civic

---

[8]   Ibid. Emphasis added.
[9]   Ibid., p. 269.
[10] Ibid.
[11] Ibid., p. 272.

freedom of its citizens, from the smallest *deme* or commune to glocal federations.[12]

This contrast has significant implications for how we understand rights in citizenship contexts. On the modern view, civil rights[13] are necessary institutional preconditions of citizenship in that they comprise the entitlements, liberties, immunities and powers which secure the liberty of the citizen, that compose the condition of being *at liberty*. On the civic view, rights are neither necessary nor sufficient conditions of civic freedom. Rather, Tully argues, rights are products of civic activity and are secured by such activity.[14] But what is the value of rights on this view? This is left somewhat vague in Tully's account but if we focus on his understanding of freedom and the citizen/governor relationship, we can develop an account of the value of rights from a civic perspective.

Tully's understanding of civic freedom is predicated on the basic claim that human beings in relationship are characterized by 'field freedom':

> The freedom of *Spielraum* (free play) in the field of any relationship is both the existential field – the room or space of manoeuvrability (the range of possible moves) – and the experiential ways in which partners can and do disclose and act on their possibilities – the games (*Spiel*) they play *in* the relationship or in the confrontation of its limits. . . . Humans are always unavoidably *homo ludens*, creative game players and prototypical civic citizens before and *as* they take on any other identities.[15]

The fact that power can only be exercised over people insofar as they are free in this sense implies that the relationship of governor and citizen can never be one in which the citizen's subjectivity is *determined* by the governor. The governor 'cannot eliminate completely the interactive and open-ended freedom *of* and *in* the relationship or the room to appear

---

12 Ibid.
13 'Civil rights' here refers to what are more usually called civil, political, socio-economic and cultural rights: see Tully, 'Local and Global Citizenship', pp. 250–6.
14 Tully, 'Local and Global Citizenship', p. 273.
15 Ibid., p. 277.

to conform to the public script while thinking and acting otherwise, without reducing the relationship to one of complete immobilisation.'[16] But while this point is fundamental for Tully in making clear that, for example, the freedom exhibited in the struggles of indigenous peoples is 'in the sparsely, limited *Spielraum* open to them,'[17] he also effectively acknowledges through this example that the exercise of civic freedom by indigenous peoples is quite compatible with their being subject to political domination.

To clarify this point, consider the contrast between 'civil' and 'civic' attitudes towards the citizen/governor relationship. From a civil stance, the citizen/governor relationship is an hierarchical institutional relationship which specifies, in broadly contractual fashion, a set of rights and obligations between the parties to the relationship (as well as procedures for adjudicating disputes between them) and is structured in terms of the authority of command. Governors who meet the relevant legitimacy conditions are entitled, within a contractually specified range of rule, to issue imperatives (in the form of law) which citizens are obliged to obey. By contrast, the civic standpoint sees the citizen/governor relationship is a scene of agonistic interaction in which governors seek to structure the field of possible action of citizens, to govern civic activity – and citizens, as free agents, reciprocally seek to structure the field of possible actions of governors, to 'civicize' governance. Both partners, ideally, 'enter into and subject themselves to the give and take of negotiation in and over the relationship they share':[18]

> A citizen/governance relationship is an interdependent, interactive and open-ended partnership of mutual enabling, nurturing and reciprocal learning. . . . If the governed fail to exercise their freedom of having a say in and over the governance relationships they bear and speak truth to power, they never become citizens. They remain

---

[16] Ibid., p. 278; although Arendt's reflections on the concentration camp point to a limit in respect of this claim.

[17] Tully, 'Local and Global Citizenship', p. 278.

[18] Ibid., p. 281.

unfree and servile 'slaves': that is, subjects of monological or 'despotic' relationships of command and obedience. . . . Reciprocally, if the governors refuse to listen and enter into negotiations, and either silence citizens or treat their demands as free speech to which they have no obligation to respond, they never become good governors. They remain unaccountable 'tyrants'. . . .[19]

In contexts of domination, citizens can exercise civic freedom but only in a limited way which is not capable of transforming the context of governance, of 'civicizing' the relationship between governors and governed. But it is at just this point that we may think that reflection of the value of rights becomes significant, for while rights are not necessary or sufficient conditions of civic freedom, they are (or can be) *enabling* conditions of civic freedom and, in particular, of the *effective* exercise of civic freedom in ways that matter for governor-citizen relations. Rights can play a variety of roles here; reducing the costs of political participation, distributing powers to citizens and stabilizing forms of respect-recognition. Our point is simply that civic citizens have compelling reasons to struggle – as, of course, historically they have – for those rights which are sufficient to make the exercise of civic freedom effective even in the face of the limitations and dangers of identifying political freedom with a set of rights.

Acknowledging this point potentially recasts the significance of citizenship-as-a-legal-status for the civic point of view in that, at least in its rights dimension, citizenship as a legal status may be construed as a general right that enables civic agents to engage in effective negotiation with their governors. That citizenship-as-a-legal-status has this enabling function is sharply demonstrated by considering the position of those excluded from it. Citizenship is not, however, simply a matter of rights but also duties and virtues. The salience of these from a civic stance emerges when we recall Tully's claim that if 'the governed fail to exercise their freedom of having a say in and over the governance relationships

---

[19] Ibid., p. 282. One might say that if governors do not enter the relationship, they do not actually become governors at all but rather commanders.

they bear and speak truth to power, they never become citizens'. By construing participation as a duty and good participation as a virtue in the way that the republican tradition does, citizenship-as-a-legal-status can function as an enabling device for converting the governed into civic citizens. None of this entails that citizenship-as-a-legal-status is prior to civic citizenship, on the contrary; what it does demonstrate is that there are reasons internal to the civic stance for constructing the legal status of citizenship. There are also, as we will argue shortly, reasons internal to this view for constructing institutions to facilitate the effective exercise of civic freedom.

Drawing out this point helps explain how a 'civil' view of citizenship can emerge as a stance that 'forgets' the civic freedom which both grounds and is served by citizenship-as-a-legal-status. On the basis of this 'forgetting', it comes to identify political freedom with a rationally justifiable civil status and set of civil institutions; this 'forgetting' thus finds intellectual expression in a re-conceptualization of political authority 'as an authority that was independent of relationships of interdependency and called "sovereignty"'.[20] The intellectual sources of this 'forgetfulness' are various; Tully's claim is that the hinge around which the transition from civic to civil stances was accomplished was the 'civil thesis of the superiority of institutional rule' that was developed in the aftermath of the Thirty Years War (and which provided ideological support to the imperialist projects of European states in the non-European world). The development of the institutionalization thesis, on Tully's account, is accomplished in the early modern period:

> The civil theorists argued that the existing practices of governance and citizenship constituted an informal, haphazard, conflict-ridden, uncertain and insecure crazy quilt of overlapping jurisdictions that gave rise to the Thirty Years War. Civil philosophers, lawyers and administrators explained that only centralisation and institutionalisation would resolve these problems of informal (under-

[20] Tully, 'Local and Global Citizenship', p. 289.

institutionalised and under-rationalised) practices of law, governance and citizenship.[21]

The important point here is that one can be sceptical of the civil stance but still hold that they had a legitimate point concerning the institutional character of early modern Europe – and if we acknowledge this, it raises a fundamental question for the civic stance concerning the relations between civic citizenship and political institutions. The question can be put thus: if the modern sovereign state is the institutional expression of modern civil citizenship, what kind of institution can give expression to diverse civic citizenship? Since institutions are secondary from a civic point of view, they can take diverse forms but we may reasonably ask whether there are kinds of institutions whose 'inner logic' aligns with the practices of citizenship and citizenization characteristic of civic citizenship? This issue appears to be somewhat underexplored in Tully's argument and yet if he is to have a cogent response to the concerns reasonably raised by civil theorists, it is a pivotal issue. It is thus to this topic that we now turn.

2. Institutions

The first step to answering the question of how to institutionalize civic citizenship is to set out what qualities would make an institution count as aligning with civic citizenship, or what it would take for it to be conducive to the same. An institution conducive to civic citizenship goes beyond serving as a mere repository for past civic victories; it would also support and mirror the practices of civic citizenship. This support can come in various forms, but most obviously consists of providing civil rights and recognized forms of interaction that facilitate engagement by reducing, and equalizing, the costs of participation. The more the political institutions work to expand the *Spielraum* of

---

[21]   Ibid., p. 288.

political actors, the easier effective engagement will be. And, to the degree an institution enables civic practices, it also mirrors them. Civic citizenship is a free relationship between fellow civic actors; at the limit, the institution too can take on this form, erasing the distinction between citizen and governor. This is the aspect under which its inner logic most closely matches civic citizenship; the target here is Tully's 'citizens acting together', in which institutions do feature as targets of civic action.[22]

This discussion of the inner logic of institutions draws on two sources: first, the relatively few positive mentions of institutions in Tully's work; second, Arendt's 'council system' of government, which she offered as an alternative to party politics. The former focuses on Tully's discussion of the 'cooperative' as the civic equivalent to a corporation; the similarities between cooperative and council will set the stage for establishing the latter's fitness of match with civic citizenship as Tully describes it.

To begin, then: Tully's positive account of institutions. The ambivalence in Tully's approach to institutions is best revealed in his taxonomy of 'citizen partnerships', one species of which is citizenized cooperation outside of government: 'citizens organise and run an entire activity on the basis of citizen partnership, not in relation to a government, but to citizenise the activity for its own sake (rather than submit to institutionalisation or governance).'[23] There are two implicit claims this contrast relies on: first, that what takes place within institutions is necessarily governance rather than citizenship; second, that the non-governmental partnership these citizens create somehow evades taking on institutional form. Tully appears at times (such as the preceding quotation) to be drawing on a distinction between organization and institutionalization which aligns the cooperative activities of civic citizenship with non-institutionalized forms of organization in contrast to the institutionalized forms of organization

---

[22] Ibid., pp. 302–3.
[23] Ibid., p. 291.

characteristic of civil citizenship. But while such a distinction can certainly be drawn, it stands in tension with Tully's acknowledgement that civic activities 'can be more or less institutionalised and rationalised (in countless forms)'.[24] Indeed, he gives examples of this kind of citizen activity which undermine any putative difference between civil and civic citizenship in terms of a contrast between institutionalized and non-institutionalized forms of organization. Thus, he appeals to 'classic examples of citizen partnerships' such as 'the celebrated practices of direct democracy, village commons and urban communes . . . such as Porte Allegre . . . and the Zapatistas'.[25] These examples are not treated in any detail but all have an institutional form – and, indeed, Tully takes the institution of the 'cooperative' as the exemplary form of this kind of citizenly activity (which has the side-effect of bypassing the forms of cooperation which more closely resemble governmental forms).[26] Tully may, of course, be tempted into formulations such as that we are criticizing by his identification of 'institutionalization' with the institutional thesis of the civil theorists but he should resist this temptation since, as we have argued on grounds internal to Tully's analysis of the two modes of citizenship, it is not institutions as such but the practical attitudes that we take to them and that they evince which is critical.

Let us then focus on the cooperative as the exemplary institutional mode of civic organization:

> If the private corporation is both the basis and flagship of modern citizenship . . . then the commonplace cooperative is the comparative organisation of the civic tradition. Here, citizens ignore the civil division between (non-democratic) private and (representative) public spheres . . . [t]hey participate as democratic citizens governing themselves directly in the economic sphere (and other spheres),

---

[24] Ibid., p. 269.
[25] Ibid., p. 291.
[26] That Tully presents the cooperative as 'good twin' to the corporation complicates this somewhat; although this moves the discussion from politics-direct to economic control, it does so by insisting on the cooperatives' thoroughly *public* quality.

citizenising the same kinds of activity that corporations privatize . . .
many cooperatives are not for profit but for living democracy and
mutual aid.[27]

Any organization which can be compared to a corporation – even a small
one – cannot be entirely ad hoc. The same is true of any organization able
to meaningfully act towards the two goals Tully lists in this quotation;
it is very likely to need a sophisticated structure. This is more true if the
cooperative is seen as an equal to larger private corporations, as it may
have to be if it is to effectively contest the privatization of the economic
sphere, or if it is to really stand as the opposing 'flagship' organization.

But there is also the question of what the cooperative does *differently*
from the corporation when acting in the same sphere, which difference
manifests in the kinds of relationship that the organization is built
on. The corporation, like the sovereign state, rests on the kind of
'centralization and institutionalization' favoured by the civil theorists.
The cooperative's citizenization efforts overturn this, making the
relationships between the citizens themselves central by investing in
them the motive force of the system; this is what it would mean to
make public the matters that an organization deals in. (One obvious
corollary to this: to the degree that the state's functions are made subject
to sovereignty relations, it becomes a private matter.)

It is unclear whether this quite matches Tully's actual presentation of
the differences between the political realm and the economic domain.
At one point, he presents the two kinds of struggle that characterize
these arenas as if their outcomes are fundamentally different: 'When
citizens overthrow a local structural relationship or convert it into a
citizen/governance relationship (or a citizen relationship in the cases
of cooperatising private corporations).'[28] This seems to suggest that, for
Tully, the manager is dispensable in a way the governor is not. And if so,
the indispensability of the governor's position suggests the inevitable

---

[27] Tully, 'Local and Global Citizenship', pp. 291–2.
[28] Ibid., pp. 298–9.

presence of a distinction between governor and governed and, hence, under contemporary conditions, the persistence of sovereignty structures.

Is there good reason to be this pessimistic, even after conceding that the private corporation – Tully's 'flagship' civil institution – can be fundamentally reformed? That rather depends on how we read what is done when civic citizens transform a private corporation into a cooperative; at least some of the powers and responsibilities of management are required parts of a company of whatever shape and the civic citizens must, for their own case, work out how best to citizenize these indispensables. Each must be distributed in an approximation of direct democracy, or else left in place but subjected to democratic oversight. The latter option leaves a manager-type figure (and the concomitant sovereignty-system) in place; the former does not. To say that the former is not a live option for the political sphere would be de facto to accept the institutionalization thesis proposed by the civil theorists (which Tully clearly does not). It seems then that Tully must accept that the governor/governed relationship can, like the manager/managed relationship, be reconfigured in a way that erases the distinction and with it the hierarchical command relationship that it manifests. However, whereas Tully deploys the cooperative as the civic institution that can replace the private corporation in economic life, he does not articulate a clear alternative in relation to the political field. This lack of a suitably scalable and flexible alternative is liable to lead to political pessimism.

Such a pessimistic outlook may also arise from Tully's analysis of the glocalization efforts of civic citizenship, in spite of one of the goals Tully ascribes to citizenization efforts: the aim of 'democratizing democracy'.[29] This is a transformative process, to be sure, but one that is (in this description) limited to working within existing forms (alongside civil citizens) without addressing the underlying logics of those

---

[29] Ibid., p. 302.

systems.[30] This is especially troubling in light of Tully's recognition of the difficulties of continued civic struggles; he recognizes that another 'dominating layer of structural relationships' lies waiting behind every local victory of civic citizenship.[31] If local systems of governance can only be made into ameliorated forms of civil governance, then the playing field between citizen and global system can never be made level – and Tully's argument begins to support a rather gloomy outlook.[32] The playing field-levelling efforts at the glocal level are instead limited to the creation of 'glocal negotiating networks', which networks make easier the process of combating iniquities by combining disparate civic organizations.[33]

Yet this work would be made easier by entrenching rights of participation, by reducing and equalizing the costs of civic participation. And this would in turn make it easier for the privileged civic citizens to meet their obligations to the non-privileged; 'It should not be the burden of the wretched of the earth to refuse to submit and act otherwise . . . but of the most powerful and privileged.'[34] It is perhaps obvious that helping others is easier when one's own participatory rights do not need to be continually reasserted on a case-by-case basis. But Tully's obligation-claims for the civic citizen go beyond this, to include a responsibility to steer 'negotiations into . . . institutions of the most effective nation-state or . . . negotiate directly in civic society'.[35] How much easier this would be if the civic citizens in those 'most effective' states have entrenched rights of participation and concomitant duties of assistance, creating recognized conduits for expressing both civic engagement and solidarity.

---

[30] Cf. ibid., pp. 302–3.
[31] Ibid., pp. 298–9.
[32] Note that this is not an argument that civic citizenship could (or should) ever come to a rest. Instead, the claim is merely that civic activities are well-served by entrenching advances, by ensuring the game is as close to fair as possible.
[33] Tully, 'Local and Global Citizenship', p. 305.
[34] Ibid.
[35] Ibid.

3. Non-sovereign institutions

In *Strange Multiplicity*, his earlier work addressing the struggles of cultural minorities, Tully advocated 'compact' or 'diverse' federalism as a mode of institutional response to 'modern constitutionalism' (i.e. the mode of constitutionalism that is aligned with modern civil citizenship). The key component of this response was that the self-governing states (or provinces, or cities) that formed a confederation retained their autonomy, with the federal government's powers limited to those explicitly granted by the sub-federal polities, who retained sovereignty in the sense of being entitled to withdraw these powers from the federal government.[36] This response is likely to look somewhat too 'modern' from the standpoint of Tully's more recent reflections but it indicates the importance for the articulation of an alternative to the logic of sovereignty of a form of bottom-up authorization in which civic freedom is given institutional expression. Such a form of institutionalization is proposed by Arendt. Our turn to Arendt's loosely sketched 'council system' of government need only show that not all political institutions need be, at base, institutions of sovereignty, while the parallel between Arendt's councils and Tully's cooperatives shows that the former is not alien to Tully's conception of civic citizenship, but a companion to it.

Arendt's description of the council system is far from systematic enough to be taken as a blueprint. Rather, what we find in Arendt's work is a set of historical examples, in which citizens have worked together to manage public goods in scenarios where the regular mechanisms of governance and power have broken down. Intermingled with these post-crisis examples of citizens making do is Thomas Jefferson's late-in-life enthusiasm for a ward system of government, a kind of very fine-grained federalism.[37] It is the use of Jefferson that suggests Arendt thinks

---

[36] J. Tully, *Strange Multiplicity: Constitutionalism in an Age of Diversity*, Cambridge: Cambridge University Press, 1995, pp. 140–5.

[37] J. Medearis, 'Lost or Obscured? How V.I. Lenin, Joseph Schumpeter, and Hannah Arendt Misunderstood the Council Movement', *Polity* 36 (3): 447–76, 2004, gives a detailed view of how the historical examples differ from Arendt's account of them.

the councils can have more longevity than the citizens' organizations which 'had sprung up everywhere, completely independent of one another' and 'turned an almost accidental proximity into a political institution'.[38] In the absence of state power, these councils necessarily were non-state groupings of citizens, organized for various purposes (the list of which purposes takes in both geography- and occupation-based interests[39]).

In two of her historical examples,[40] Arendt finds evidence that the councils could be something more than a stop-gap measure for coping with political calamity; they 'lasted just long enough to show in bare outlines what a government would look like ... founded on the principles of the council system'.[41] She draws selectively on Jefferson to augment this view, while silently omitting those parts of Jefferson's work which suggest the initiative power within the ward system remains centralized.[42] Thus, her account of the historical councils credits them with federating in such a way that each council did not lose its own 'power to constitute', retaining control of their 'capacity to act and to form opinions'[43] even as they banded together into federated units. In retaining this power, each council remains, to return to Tully's phrasing, a site of civic engagement. There is, of course, always the risk that this site could itself either become inequitably organized to the benefit of some individual participants or degenerate into mere lip service. The first is a permanent risk of any organization; the second is less a problem for this kind of organization since it is far easier, in the usual course of things, to deactivate a dormant right to meaningful participation than it is to create one anew.

One important virtue of the council system, as Havercroft notes, 'is its scalability and flexibility':

---

[38] H. Arendt, *On Revolution*, London; Penguin, 1965, pp. 266–7.

[39] Ibid., p. 267.

[40] These are the Russian Revolution of February 1917 and the Hungarian Revolution of 1956.

[41] Arendt, *On Revolution*, p. 266.

[42] For example, T. Jefferson, *Jefferson: Political Writings*, Cambridge: Cambridge University Press, 1999, p. 183.

[43] Arendt, *On Revolution*, p. 267.

One could imagine a whole system of councils growing upwards from local neighbourhood councils all the way to a global council. Such a council system would not . . . have to govern all human affairs. Council systems could be set up to govern different issue areas. Council systems do not necessarily have to be bound to particular territories. They could be formed to govern issues of transnational concern, such as the environment or human rights. Finally, councils do not necessarily have to extend all the way up to the global level or all the way down to the neighbourhood level. They can be adapted to govern the scope and scale of the problem for which they were formed.[44]

But with Jefferson's centralizing rejected, what mechanism (or mechanisms) will play the role of coordinating and organizing distinct councils? This is less than clear, beyond the specification that each council retains its own prerogative (which specification makes them suitable as exemplars of civic citizenship). To default to a model of priority in which the rule is that councils *must* defer to the more-general bodies would obviously undo the distinctive quality of the council system. To have the more-general councils directed by the 'base-level' councils would be less objectionable, but would make the members of the former into mere instruments of the latter. It would return sovereignty and command to the system, something which is to be avoided for the sake of keeping it from transforming into something which will rob one or other set of participants of civic engagement.

To gain some sense of how the system can operate without resorting to a command-hierarchy, we turn to Sitton's commentary on the councils. He recognizes the lack of formal coercive apparatus in Arendt's councils and offers the following (brief) account of their working without it:

it would appear that the councils would be related through mutual respect, coupled with the practical recognition that coordinated action is necessary. No single council would have to be persuaded that the course of action upon which the others had decided was the correct

---

[44] J. Havercroft, *Captives of Sovereignty*, Cambridge: Cambridge University Press, 2011, p. 240.

one. Rather, each council would have respect for the opinions of the others and realize that certain things must be done, whether that particular council agreed or not . . . The very phrase 'higher council' would therefore not refer to any coercive power but to [being concerned with a larger area].[45]

This is not much to go on as a guide to resolving these kinds of disputes in practice; all it really does is assert the primacy of discussion among citizens as the source of any such accommodation. Yet this is a vast improvement, in terms of the opportunities for meaningful engagement, in a system in which the 'height' of a body signifies the range of its command. While a council system may need some mechanism for breaking deadlocks, there is no reason in principle for thinking that such mechanisms cannot take civically acceptable forms.

What advantages does a citizenry organized along roughly these lines possess? Two advantages are primary. First, this form augments the powers of citizens by stabilizing a mode of acting-in-concert. Second, it greatly multiplies the opportunities for engaging in civic citizenship. One way it does this is by lowering the barriers to participation, providing a recognized regular opportunity which, in its various institutions, clearly invites citizens to participate. This would have the further effect of enhancing the practice itself; regular participation leads to *better* participation through sheer force of habituation. It also thereby improves the speed and responsiveness of civic citizens by reducing the need to either create ad hoc organizations anew or struggle to coopt existing ones. Efforts can be directed to whichever issue is at hand, rather than legitimating the citizens' rights to raise an issue at all. A permanent home for activities of this kind, one seen to be legitimate, is more robust and hence more able to resist systemic pressures; if regarded as legitimate, a council cannot simply be dismissed or made silent by state force. In this way too, the power of the citizenry is augmented. Barriers are also lowered with respect to the

---

45 J. F. Sitton, 'Hannah Arendt's Argument for Council Democracy', in L. P. Hinchman and S. K. Hinchman, eds, *Hannah Arendt: Critical Essays*, Albany: State University of New York Press, 1994, p. 314.

results of civic citizenship once institutional forms are both thoroughly infused with civic values and regarded as the legitimate expressions of democratic voice (this would be a considerable advantage since one problem civic citizenship necessarily faces without it is the problem of competing interests and sources of legitimacy). Most fundamentally, however, the council system presents an arena in which civic citizens can practise civic citizenship and hence acquire, sustain and reproduce that practical attitude towards the government of self and others in which their freedom consists.

In sum, Arendt's council system provides Tully's account with an exemplary mode of instituting civic citizenship which it is currently lacking and thereby enables him to begin to offer a cogent rejoinder to civil devotees of the institutional thesis. It is of course true that the practice of the council system would need to be worked out more fully in the course of instituting it, but the fundamental point is that it provides a non-sovereign logic of institutionalization and a frame within which to reflect on, and develop, existing organizations of civic citizens.

4. Conclusion

Our concern in this chapter has been to focus on Tully's account of diverse-civic citizenship in terms of the issues that are, in our view, under-elaborated in Tully's own reflections. Starting from the recognition that the crucial difference between modern-civil and diverse-civic citizenship is a difference in practical attitude, we have been concerned to show that civic citizenship can accommodate concerns related to civil rights, citizenship-as-a-legal-status and political institutions. It has compelling internal reasons to do so: these three are ways of reducing and equalizing the costs of exercises of civic freedom and of augmenting the powers of citizens. But it also has such reasons because these elements can support those practices of citizenization that allow civic citizens to practise civic citizenship, to develop and sustain this practical attitude, and hence to become what politically they are.

Part Three

Reply

9

On Global Citizenship:
Replies to Interlocutors

James Tully

1. Introduction

I am humbled and grateful beyond words to the authors of this edited volume for their outstanding chapters on various aspects of local and global citizenship.[1] Each contribution raises issues that advance our understanding of this immensely complex and important field of practice and research on which living democracy, peace, social justice and ecological well-being depend here and now and in the future. It is a great privilege to be asked to respond and a daunting task to do so. I cannot hope to reply to all the rich insights the authors bring to light from different perspectives. Rather, I would like to comment on the challenging arguments that have enabled me to see the mistakes and limits of the tentative sketch I offered in *On Global Citizenship* and the *Afterword*. In my responses I have tried to show how mistakes can be corrected, questions addressed, limits overcome and how we might work together in moving forward. Echoing the spirit of Duncan Bell's concluding paragraph, I hope this dialogue becomes part of an ongoing reciprocal elucidation of practices of local and global citizenship among scholars and active citizens around the world: that is, an engaged public philosophy for our times.

---

[1] For the sake of simplicity I will refer to 'local and global citizenship' as 'global' citizenship hereafter.

Public philosophy

I would like to begin with a short note on the type of public philosophy I employ in the study of global citizenship. The contributors bring out several features of it with great clarity by contrasting it with other better-known approaches. Laden, Celikates and Mason contrast it with civil philosophy and ideal theory; Honig and Stears with Raymond Geuss's realism and their own agonistic realism; Norval with Ernesto Laclau's method; Bell with republican and other historical-critical approaches; and Dunn and Owen with institution-based theory. To expand just slightly, public philosophy as I practice it is a type of academic research that aims to enter into interdisciplinary dialogues of mutual learning not only with other academics but also with citizens of the world, in the broadest sense of this polysemic term, who are engaged in the problems and struggles we are trying to understand. Researchers listen to and learn from the often marginalized or silenced ways that those suffering from injustices experience and articulate them and the practices of reasoning and acting together they develop in response. Reciprocally, researchers bring to the discussion academic research that throws critical light on the problematic situation by explicating its history and contemporary configuration, and which helps to disclose and clarify the range of possible ways of thinking and acting in relation to it. As Michael Temelini puts it, rather than 'talking about' what citizens can or should do, this approach consists in 'talking with' citizens in dialogues of reciprocal enlightenment.[2]

Civil and civic citizenship

In addition to the exploration of a multiplicity of local and global practices of citizenship in the introductory essay, I also attempt to

---

[2] M. Temelini, 'Dialogical Approaches to Political Struggles over Recognition and Distribution', *Critical Review of Social and Political Philosophy*, 13 April 2013. For a more detailed explanation see J. Tully, *Public Philosophy in a New Key, Two Volumes*, Cambridge: Cambridge University Press, 2008, Volume I, chapters 1–3.

explicate two very general action-guiding modes of disclosure of the field or 'world' of citizenship under which these practices are experienced by citizens and studied by researchers.[3] For historical and philological reasons I call these civil and civic modes of citizenship, but also representative and cooperative (direct), modern and diverse, institutional and activity-based and so on when I draw attention to their specific features. I would like to present a brief synopsis of my lengthy account of civil and civic citizenship in *On Global Citizenship* before responding to the questions about them.

Civil citizenship discloses the field of global citizenship as constituted by the legal, political and economic rights and duties, institutions and processes of historical development of modern states with representative governments, the international system of states under international law, the institutions of global governance and the traditions of democratic theory that have developed forms of critical reflection on these rights, institutions and processes. Civil citizenship exists within these rights, institutions and processes. Civil citizens participate by exercising their communicative powers in elections, political parties, deliberation in official public spheres and civil disobedience with the hopes of exercising influence on elected representatives who exercise governmental power through legislative deliberation and law-making. The laws are seen as imperatives enforced by coercion that can be justified to citizens or challenged by them in the courts and public spheres. This model is standardly seen as a universal model of citizenship and democracy in the civil tradition.

Civic citizenship discloses the field in a much broader and pluralistic manner, even taking the self-organization of the ecosphere as the commonwealth of all forms of life in which human citizenship has its home. The institutional form of modern representative civil

---

[3] I refer to these two modes of citizenship here as action-guiding modes of disclosure of a field of practice and study. Depending on the context, I also often use Wittgenstein's term 'picture' and Foucault's term 'form of problematization' to refer to both the languages of disclosure of a field of human experience and the activities and institutions in which it is woven. I take these three terms of art to be complementary tools of analysis of the same phenomena.

citizenship appears as one type of governor-citizen relationship among many types and even the representation of it in civil theories is seen as misrepresenting its history and the activities of citizens within it. From the civic perspective, citizenship comes into being whenever and wherever people who are subject to or affected by practices of governance become active co-agents within them; exercising the powers of having a say (negotiating) and having a hand (powers of self-organization and self-government) in and over the relationships that govern their interaction. 'Civic freedom' is the situated, relational freedom manifest in the countless activities of bringing the relationships of disputation and resolution, recognition and distribution, and action-coordination that comprise practices of governance in this broad sense under the shared democratic agency and authority of those subject to or affected by them.

The primary examples of civic citizenship are everyday practices of grass-roots political, social, economic and ecological democracy where the members discuss and exercise powers of self-organization and self-government themselves (citizen-citizen relationships) prior to any separation of ruler and ruled or governor and citizen in representative practices of government. They become citizens by democratizing or 'cooperating' their relationships of living and working together. These activities of reasoning and acting together provide the ground for civic relationships of representative government in which citizens conditionally delegate some of their powers of self-government to representatives (citizen-governor relationships). These dialogical relationships of representation extend civic practices of democratic governance from the local to the state-centred and the global. The relationships within institutions of modern representative government are acceptable insofar as they enable the exercise of civic freedom within and on them. Civic citizenship practices of these two broad types are the means by which cooperative practices of self-government can be brought into being and the means by which unjust practices of governance can be challenged, reformed and transformed by those who suffer under them, becoming co-agents of them (practices of negotiation).

2. Anthony Simon Laden

Civil and civic authority and reasoning

Beginning with a quotation of one of my comparative synopses of these two pictures of citizenship, Laden presents a comparative explication of the different types of authority relations characteristic of civil and civic citizenship: command and connection respectively. He brings to light and analyses in detail five differentiating features of authority, as well as their contrasting features of public reasoning, in civil and civic ways of disclosing, enacting, institutionalizing and governing the world of citizenship. His explication deepens and broadens our understanding of these crucial dimensions of civil and civic citizenship beyond my analysis. I would like to discuss it first because it brings out features of civic and civil citizenship that are helpful in my responses to some of the other contributions.

As Laden notes, the authority of command of civil citizenship is the standard model of authority in general, whereas the authority of connection of civic citizenship is barely recognized, and when it is, it is not even seen as a relation of authority. Yet the authority of connection is the conversational ground of more formal types of authority. It takes a concerted effort to bracket the authority of command and bring the underlying phenomena of civic authority to reflective awareness. Laden is able to engage in this kind of phenomenology of authorizing and reasoning together because he focuses on citizenship as *activities* of citizens-being-in-the-world with each other, conversing, dissenting, challenging, reasoning and acting together for the sake of common or public good in everyday practices, and thus the corresponding relationships of authority they bring into being and sustain, or fail to do so, come into view.

He investigates authoritative relationships of connection in examples of self-government (citizen-citizen relationships) and representative government (citizen-governor relationships).[4]

This important work on authority is part of Laden's broader project of approaching practical reason, not as a faculty that constructs universally binding imperatives or discovers strategically rational means to defeat opponents, but as the underlying informal and embedded activities and interactive norms of reasoning-in-practice-with-others. Unlike civil philosophers, he also takes practical reasoning to encompass the embodied afflictive and positive emotions (such as empathy and compassion) and the human senses that connect and attune humans to each other and social and ecological lifeworlds.[5] On this civic view, the shared authority of connection arises within everyday non-coercive and non-imperative ways of conversing and reasoning by means of open-ended proposals and responses, and acting-with others. These ways of 'working and living together' make up a complex form of life out of which more specialized forms of reasoning and authority arise and on which they depend. If, in contrast, one begins from a disembedded and formalized civil perspective, the inter-subjective world of civic citizenship inside and outside institutions of civil citizenship – 'the *praxis* of practice' – disappears from view.[6] In taking this turn, Laden follows Hannah Arendt and others who, since the early twentieth century, have sought to recover the lifeworld of conversing, reasoning, authorizing and exercising power in concert that often goes without saying in standard accounts.[7]

One striking feature of Laden's chapter is the extent to which the authority of command pervades the relations of modern representative democracy and civil citizenship. In the transition from dictatorship to representative democracy the model of a ruler unilaterally commanding

---

[4] As he points out, the seeds of representation are already present in the exchange of opinions between citizens.

[5] Laden sets out this philosophical approach in A. S. Laden, *Reasoning: A Social Picture*, Oxford: Oxford University Press, 2012.

[6] As Adam Dunn and David Owen mention in their chapter.

[7] For a recent survey of this field of research from Edmund Husserl to the present see E. Thompson, *Mind in Life: Biology, Phenomenology and the Sciences of Mind*, Cambridge, MA: Harvard University Press, 2007.

the ruled was (and is) roundly criticized and partially abandoned. Notwithstanding, the command-obedience model of authority and the force of reason decreeing unconditionally binding imperatives (civil principles and laws) continue to inform the three elements that distinguish representative democracy from dictatorship and the five axes of authority within them that Laden explicates. These continuities of unilateral and hierarchical ruler-ruled relations are legitimated by the fiction that the people under modern representative democracy are simultaneously ruler and ruled – sovereign and subject – and thus 'self-governing'. They impose the fundamental principles of justice and constitutional laws on themselves, and representatives legislate in accord with these principles and fundamental laws. This modern picture of civil democratic authority comes in two immensely influential forms. The people actually engage in 'general will' formation and obey the basic imperative laws of which they are the authors (Rousseau) or the hypothetical idea of the possibility of the 'omnilateral' construction and coercive imposition of the basic private and public laws on each other guides elected representatives in making laws, influenced by, but not obligated to, public sphere deliberation of civil citizens (Kant).

Laden's chapter unsettles this standard model of representative democracy by presenting another way of thinking about the freedom and authority of citizens and governments that abjures the sovereign-subject model and the non-democratic relations it legitimates. He brings to light five features of relationships of civic freedom that render them authoritative and are genuinely reciprocal, mutual, forward-looking, distributive of authority among participants and ongoing. The resulting authoritative yet non-imperative and non-coercive relationships of mutual connection are manifestly more democratic and egalitarian than the contrasting authoritative relationships of command along all five axes. It is not too much to say that the series of contrasts in itself calls into question, and perhaps undermines, the authoritativeness of command relationships and presents a democratic alternative to them; one that is not only possible but actual, if we would only look and see. This is an important contribution to the civic tradition of Arendt and

Foucault, who, for different reasons, argued that we should reject the sovereign-subject model of citizenship if we wish to be free; and of the millions of civic citizens who have done this in practice.[8]

Moreover, Laden, like Arendt, argues that this civic way of reasoning, authorizing and exercising power together in addressing local and global injustices is not based on command or consensus, but on cooperation and contestation. Ongoing practices of agreement and disagreement, contestation and conflict, reform and transformation, take place within its shared way of life: that is, its members' commitment to challenge and to transform injustices and resolve disputes by the arts of civic engagement he describes. This shared authoritative way of life is sustained, as Wittgenstein puts it, by the creative agonistics of reciprocal disagreement and agreement both within and over its shared norms and objectives of cooperation.[9] It is worth noting that perhaps the most successful social movement of the last 100 years, the feminist movement, brought into being and continues to sustain this tricky civic mode of ongoing cooperation, contestation and non-consensus. Feminists enact in their own self-organizations the civic freedom they seek to bring about in the hierarchical gender relationships they confront and work to transform.[10]

Two transformation questions

Of course, one has to bring out and analyse other types of power relations and dynamics that are present in the civic forms of reasoning and acting together Laden discusses, especially, but not only, the governmentality or protocolic power relations in communication mediated by technologies and networks.[11] Furthermore, two central

---

[8] On Arendt and Foucault on sovereignty, see J. Havercroft, *Captives of Sovereignty*, Cambridge: Cambridge University Press, 2011.

[9] See Tully, *Public Philosophy* II, chapter 2.

[10] See J. Tully, 'Thinking along with Feminism and the Abyss of Freedom', unpublished presentation at the American Political Science Association Annual Meeting, 30 August 2008.

[11] See Tully, *Public Philosophy* II, chapters 3, 4 and 6, and A. Galloway, *Protocol: How Control Exists after Decentralization*, Cambridge, MA: MIT Press, 2004.

questions need to be addressed. First, why and how should the most vulnerable subalterns take the risk of speaking and acting and inviting a response in the radically unequal and uncivic relationships in which they find themselves when they try to do so? Second, how is it possible to move the commanders and third-party beneficiaries of the non-democratic and unjust relationships of command that structure the world of informal imperialism in which we live, and which are backed up by vast means of legitimation, manipulation and violence, to listen and respond truthfully? That is, how can they possibly be moved to enter into relationships of connection with those they exploit and oppress and to treat these negotiations as authoritative, rather than as opportunities for dissimulation, manipulation, inclusion and assimilation or marginalization?

These two 'transformation questions' are raised by Bonnie Honig and Mark Stears, Robin Celikates, Aletta Norval and Duncan Bell. They are, in many respects, the classic questions of democratic citizenship. Michel Foucault, for example, found them to be at the centre of the reflection on Athenian democracy in the classical period and suggested that they have been central to the civic tradition of democracy ever since.[12]*Public Philosophy in a New Key* is a series of attempts at responses to them in different contexts and forms in which they arise. Before I respond to the contributors' formulations of them, I will point out how Laden's analysis of civic and civil authority complements Hannah Arendt's analysis of civic and civil power, for my response turns in part on this important distinction.

Arendt on civil and civic power

If, as Laden argues, the standard picture of authority is the command model, then, from Arendt's perspective, this would be because power is standardly misconstrued in terms of command in the first place. In

---

[12] M. Foucault, *The Government of Self and Others: Lectures at the Collège de France*, F. Gros, ed., New York: Palgrave Macmillan, 2010; and M. Foucault, *The Courage of Truth*, F. Gros, ed., New York: Palgrave Macmillan, 2012.

On Violence she argues that almost all theories and models of power are based on the command-obedience model of one individual or collective agent exercising control, directly or indirectly, over another agent.[13] The exercise of power through the law in representative government replicates this model by construing laws as commands (imperatives) and the practical reason that discovers them and their background universal principles of justice is said to exercise the analogous unconditionally binding force of reason on the subject. This, she argues, is not a type of power at all, but rather, the confusion of power with monological relations of violence, domination and force. Power as 'power-over' self and others is modelled after the violent act by which one agent imposes its will over another and the other submits, which thereby lays the foundation for civil order, as, for example, in the influential theories of Hobbes and Kant. Prior to this violent act there is a war of all against all or antagonistic relationships. As Kant succinctly summarizes this violent and anti-democratic presupposition, man 'thus requires a master to break his self-will and force him to obey a universally valid will under which everyone can be free'.[14] This then provides the prototype for the model of law as command. Modern theorists try to demarcate a difference in kind between control by violence and institutional rule by command by calling the latter 'coercion', but it remains a difference in degree, not in kind. This is why the command relationships in civil law and governance are often seen as not much more than the 'velvet glove' of force with a patina of legitimation. Thus, Arendt argues, it should not be called power at all, but force of various kinds.

This whole way of thinking about power as power-over presupposes and builds on the prior separation of ruler and ruled. In the West it has its historical origins in Plato's separation of ruler and ruled. Once this picture is accepted, it obscures and eclipses the type of power

[13] H. Arendt, *On Violence*, New York: Harcourt Brace & Company, 1970. For my interpretation of Arendt on power and on violence and non-violence in this classic text, see J. Tully, 'Hannah Arendt on Violence and Nonviolence', President's lecture Series, University of Oklahoma, 25 April 2011.

[14] I. Kant, 'Idea for a Universal History with a Cosmopolitan Purpose', in H. S. Reiss, ed., *Political Writings*, Cambridge: Cambridge University Press, 2001, pp. 41–53, and 46.

constitutive of government and citizenship in the sense of participatory democratic self-organization and self-government, since its initial conditions render non-violent and democratic self-organization and self-government impossible. The power of people to organize, reason, act and improvise together 'in concert' (i.e. without violence or a master) is what she calls 'power' in the proper sense and I call 'power-with'.

The power-with constitutive of democratic self-government is different in kind from power-over. It is the inter-subjective power people with an irreducible yet negotiable plurality of reasonable opinions of the public good bring into being and carry on non-violently by speaking and reasoning non-imperatively (exchanging persuasive stories, opinions, arguments, proposals and counter-proposals, compromises and so on) *and* by exercising powers of self-organization and self-government together in direct and representative forms of government.[15] Power-with is not only different from but also incompatible with violence and the power of command. It *is* the power of non-violence and connection. This civic form of power and freedom is the living basis of government and citizenship. Violence, power-over and the authority of command can exact compliance and often control dissent, but they cannot bring into being the underlying cooperative and connective relationships of citizenship and governance on which power-over relations of governance depend and simultaneously occlude and devour. This complex phenomenon, Arendt argues, is illustrated in revolutions where the people withdraw their coerced cooperation in the operation of an unjust regime – in campaigns of boycott, strike, non-cooperation and acting otherwise – and the authority of the regime collapses (as in the non-violent Egyptian Spring).

Arendt's analysis of civil power-over and civic power-with seems to me to be the complement to Laden's analysis of civil and civic authority and reasoning. They both argue that power-with and authority relationships of civic freedom are the basis of the mutual understanding, trust and fraternity necessary to respond effectively to the injustices we

---

[15] H. Arendt, 'Socrates', in J. Kohn, ed., *The Promise of Politics*, New York: Schocken, 2005.

face. And they both argue that we cannot even begin to imagine *how* to respond justly to concrete instances of injustice without entering into these dialogical relationships of mutual learning with those who suffer the injustices.[16]

The crisis of global citizenship

If Laden and Arendt are correct, civil and civic relationships are co-present in the institutions of modern citizenship. Civic activities are occluded and limited by the institutionalized and enframing command relationships of the civil citizenship, the separation of public reasoning from the exercise of powers of self-government and the protection of monumental concentrations of power from democratization by placing them in the private sphere, under the protection of the primary right of non-interference by the demos. These limits of the official institutions of citizen participation give rise to what I call the crisis of global citizenship. In *On Global Citizenship* and *Afterword* I show how both civil and civic citizens respond to the crisis and how the civic responses seek to address the two transformation questions.

In her response, Norval sets out a chart of these experiments in civic citizenship and critically assesses them in her chapter. Honig and Stears argue that, to be effective, civic citizens need to abandon their commitment to non-violence and be prepared to use violent means when necessary. Celikates explores civic practices of negotiation as alternatives to the limits of civil disobedience and raises the first transformation question. Bell scrutinizes all of the civic practices of negotiation and cooperation, finds them inadequate to the task of the second transformation question and recommends the use of violence. Mason probes the various ways in which civic and civil citizens can join hands and support each other. Dunn and Owen analyse the role of

---

[16] For a complementary argument from another tradition, see M. Johnson, *Moral Imagination: Implications of Cognitive Science for Ethics*, Chicago: University of Chicago Press, 1993.

three types of institutions in enabling civic participation. To these we now turn.

3. Bonnie Honig and Mark Stears

Agonistic realism

I am grateful to Bonnie Honig and Marc Stears for comparing my practice-based and dialogical approach to politics with the realism of Raymond Geuss and their own agonistic realism. I have learned a great deal from their chapter, their other works and an earlier exchange with Honig on violence and non-violence.[17] I particularly appreciate the careful work of comparing and contrasting these three approaches because I am constantly testing the perspectival hypothesis of Nietzsche and Wittgenstein: that is, there is a plurality of approaches to the study of politics, each of which has its own disclosive insights and limitations and, consequently, humans learn about politics by comparing and contrasting a variety of perspectives on the aspectival world of politics.[18]

The main difference between Geuss's realism and my approach, according to Honig and Stears, is that I include in the 'real' not only violence, self-interest, political chicanery and instability, as do realists, but also non-violence, action in concert, mutuality in practice and justice and freedom, which realists tend to construe as always empty and dangerous 'legitimatory mechanisms' that cloak self-interested motives and actions. And, they continue, 'if realism means a commitment to describing what we see, then surely realists must concede that politics includes violence and non-violence, strife and agreement, murderousness and reasonableness'. Since I agree with this and also with the role of agonistics in politics, my approach overlaps

---

[17] B. Honig, '[Un]Dazzled by the Ideal: Tully's Politics and Humanism in Tragic Perspective', *Political Theory* 39 (1): 131–44, 2011; J. Tully, 'Dialogue', *Political Theory* 39 (1): 145–60, 2011.

[18] Tully, *Public Philosophy* I, chapter 1.

with the category they use to describe their own approach – agonistic realism – in these two respects. However, this is where the similarities end. They draw attention to a number of dissimilarities between our two approaches that set them apart.

First, Honig and Stears assert that my approach rests on a language of disclosure of the 'factical real' that is uncontested, whereas they argue that contestations of the real are part of politics and so of their approach. I do not see how they draw this conclusion from my work or from their own careful description of it.

My approach begins with listening carefully to those suffering the lived experience of injustices in their own ways of knowing and articulating them. This application of the norm of always listening to the other side helps to free us from our own sedimented descriptions of the real and disclose new possibilities, as they note. It brings these perspectives into dialogue and negotiation in an open-ended variety of sites with defenders of the status-quo and the best available academic research; it presents a wide variety of formal and informal democratic ways these conflicts can be provisionally resolved locally and globally, yet always open to dissent, review and renegotiation in the future.[19] In this ongoing cycle of always beginning again, there is no proposition, discourse or practice that is not open to be tested by the best available testing practices, and these too are open to challenge. However, the testing of aspects of the given itself always takes place against a whole background network of presuppositions and ways of acting that cannot be called into question at the same time, since they provide the shared ground against which the norm, practice or mode of disclosure is tested. We can always turn and call into question some aspect of the ground of our testing practices, but this requires in turn some shared background practice of testing that is not in question, as a condition of intelligibility of the test or contestation, and so on, no matter how radical the challenge to the rules of the prevailing norms of contestation is, such as overthrowing them, refusing to play, and inventing a

---

[19] Ibid., chapter 9.

new game (i.e. acting otherwise). Contestation and cooperation are equiprimordial in this interdependent sense.[20] Thus, the civic approach to the contestability of what is given to us as the real (or the ideal) is different from Honig and Stears's poststructural view that contestation goes all the way down.[21]

Violence and non-violence

The second difference is not in method but a fundamental difference regarding the role of violence in politics. I suggest that one defining feature of contemporary civic citizens is that they 'are learning to be non-violent game players, and one of their most important civic activities today is the teaching and practice of non-violent dispute resolution and disarmament'.[22] In my writing and lectures since 2009 I have put forward for debate the best arguments and evidence for a politics of non-violence and against the violent power politics of modern states and revolutionary movements that have been advanced over the last century by the civic non-violent peace and justice movements. The preparation for and use of violence is one of the greatest injustices on the planet today. It leads to the slaughter of hundreds of millions of humans and massive destruction of the environment. Its logic is self-perpetuating and self-escalating; it is employed to protect other global social, economic, ecological and political injustices from democratic change; it draws science, technology, social science, education, funding and human cooperation away from addressing these other problems; it generates fear and hatred of others; it undermines non-violent diplomacy and dispute resolution; it requires command relationships and it has many other blowback effects on everyday life. In *On Violence* Arendt presents four good arguments that the cumulative effects of violence

---

[20] Ibid., chapter 2, and see J. Tully, 'Testing Freedom Clarified: Reply to Daniel Weinstock', *Literary Review of Canada*, February 2010.

[21] Celikates and Bell make a similar point about the situated approach to contestation of the civic tradition. See my response to Norval for more on cooperation in this volume.

[22] Tully, *On Global Citizenship*.

in the twentieth century render the further use of violence irrational and calls for fundamental change.[23] The only reason it continues to be used, she argues, is that no substitute has been found. The argument of non-violent civic theorists and practitioners from the same decade onwards is that the substitute for violence and power politics was found in the early twentieth century and has been undergoing testing and development in theory and practice ever since. It is the politics of non-violence and it has the capacity to bring about the fundamental change that is called for. My aim is to bring these case studies and arguments back into mainstream political theory and to have them tested in critical dialogues with the defenders of violence.

Honig and Stears acknowledge that traditions of non-violence exist. Within the dominant world of violent power politics, non-violent, self-organized communities exist; they have invented hundreds of techniques of non-violent agonistics for negotiating with and transforming of violent actors and regimes and bringing into being power-with relationships. Some of these have been successful and significant. This is all part of the real for them. However, they assert that violence not only exists all around us, which no one denies, but that violence must be seen as a normatively acceptable means of politics in certain circumstances, alongside non-violence, and thus a necessary feature of agonistic realism and of the realist mode of agonistic citizenship they endorse.

The view that it is normatively acceptable and strategically effective to use both violent and non-violent means to struggle for freedom, justice and peace is a distinct third mode of citizenship, different from both civic and civil citizenship. It is endorsed by Celikates, Norval and Bell as well. Agonistic realists share the acceptability of violence with both the realist and civil traditions; yet, whereas the latter restrict violence to an instrument of states, agonistic realists endorse the use of violence by agonistic citizens. I would say that these three traditions are dominant in contemporary political theory. Non-violence is rarely discussed in

---

[23] Arendt, *On Violence*, pp. 4–9.

mainstream political theory and the study of examples of non-violent practice is equally marginal in empirical political science.

Honig and Stears state their thesis of violence as a sometimes legitimate and effective means of political action in two different ways. First, they say that 'sometimes, non-violence is not apt' in reference to Gandhi's comment on the Palestinians use of violence in resisting overwhelming odds. However, I think this is a misinterpretation of the point Gandhi is making. Gandhi always argued that if one does not have the training, organization and courage to resist non-violently, then it is better, in terms of the virtue of courage, to resist with violence than to engage in passive non-resistance, which is cowardly. He is not saying that non-violence is not 'apt' in this case. Rather he is repeating what he says many times elsewhere. Non-violence is the tool of the strong, not of the weak, and if you do not have the courageous strength and training to overcome violent opponents with non-violent means – 'to be prepared to die, but never to kill' – then it is better (i.e. more courageous) to stand up and use violence in response to violence in some specific cases, than to be cowardly and not resist at all.[24]

The second and seemingly most important argument for Honig and Stears is a quotation from Simon Critchley:

> Violence 'is never a question of a single act, but of one's insertion into a historical process saturated by a cycle of violence and counter-violence.' Violence is always a double act 'between human subjects, subjects whose experience of violence interpolates them in a repetition effect from which they cannot free themselves.'

I do not see how this justification of the use of violence differs at all from the realist tradition of violence of Geuss and others. The standard justification of violence in modern power politics is that it is an unavoidable response to the violence of others or the preparation for violence of others, and it is undertaken only for the sake of self-defence. On this view, one must use non-violence as much as possible,

---

[24] For instance, T. Merton, ed., *Gandhi on Nonviolence*, New York, New Directions, 1964, pp. 46–7.

but nevertheless prepare for and use violence if the other prepares for violence or attacks. In times of peace, prepare for war. Yet, the reciprocal preparation for violence undercuts the mutual trust on which peaceful relations depend and generates the security dilemma, which leads to mutual distrust, fear and hatred, war preparation, arms races and indebtedness, pre-emptive or responsive violence and counter-violence, victory of one side, war preparation to defend the new regime and so on. This is precisely the logic that Critchley and other realists describe. The quotation concedes and endorses interpolation into the security dilemma logic of the 'repetition effect' of the preparation for and use of violence.[25]

Honig and Stears put this assertion forward as if it were an uncontestable truth about the real. This not only goes against the grain of their commitment to the contestation of any aspect of the real, but the civic tradition of non-violence has contested this reigning dogma for over a century. Why can people not free themselves from subjection to this repetition effect by ethical practices of the self, non-cooperating with violence, living non-violently in their own community-based organizations and engaging in non-violent agonistics against violent opponents, when we now have examples, research and theories that show that humans can and do exercise this kind of civic freedom and change their world?

For example, Gene Sharp has shown that non-violent movements around the world have developed hundreds of techniques of non-violent agonistics that are capable of converting violent adversaries

---

[25] This security dilemma lies at the centre of the modern system of armed states and state-seeking revolutionary movements and terrorist networks and at the centre of security studies. One of the first and most incisive diagnosis of its repetitious effect and call for complete unilateral disarmament by the strongest is F. Nietzsche, 'The Means to Real Peace', in *Human, All too Human: A Book for Free Spirits*, Cambridge: Cambridge University Press, 1986. Like Gandhi, he concludes: 'To disarm while being the best armed, out of an elevation of sensibility – that is the means to real peace, which must always rest on a disposition for peace: whereas the so-called armed peace such as now parades about in every country is a disposition to fractiousness which trusts neither itself not its neighbor and fails to lay down its arms half out of hatred, half out of fear. Better to perish than to hate and fear, and twofold better to perish than to make oneself hated and feared – this must one day become the supreme maxim of every individual state.'

into actors willing to negotiate their differences non-violently. He has also shown that techniques of non-violent civic defence can replace armed forces. Erica Chenoweth and Maria Stephan have shown that these non-violent negotiation techniques, backed by broad-based participation, can be effective in transforming small and large unjust regimes, backed by violence, by examining over 300 cases in the last 100 years.[26] The power of non-violence, they argue, is more powerful than violence. Richard Gregg, H. J. N. Horsburgh, Joan Bondurant and Jonathan Schell – four theorists of non-violence – have explained in detail the unique transformative power of non-violent agonistics and shown how it can be used to replace violence across the board. The Dalai Lama and ThichNhat Hahn have explicated the practices of a global ethics of negative and positive non-violence (non-harm and active compassion) as a comprehensive way of life. The non-violent movements in the Middle East and Aung San Suu Kyi in Myanmar have furnished yet more examples. These are authors and actors who are scarcely unfamiliar with the reality of violence and counter-violence. Yet, contra Critchley, they are able to free themselves from it in practice and theory, to put non-violence into practice and theory and to test continuously non-violent ways of being in the world.[27]

Moreover, one of the key lessons of a century of non-violent civic agonistics is that even occasional recourse to violence has the effect of undermining the higher ethical and transformative plane that

---

[26] E. Chenoweth and M. J. Stephan, *Why Civil Resistance Works: The Strategic Logic of Nonviolent Conflict*, New York: Columbia University Press, 2011. They examine 323 violent and non-violent cases. More than 100 cases are non-violent and roughly three-quarters of these (83 or so) are ranked as partial successes or successes (pp. 9–11).

[27] G. Sharp, *The Politics of Nonviolent Action*, Boston: Porter Sargent, 1973; G. Sharp, *Waging Nonviolent Struggle*, Boston: Porter Sargent, 2005; G. Sharp, *From Dictatorship to Democracy*, 4th edn, Boston: Albert Einstein Institute, 2010; R. Gregg, *The Power of Nonviolence*, New York: Schocken, 1966; H. J. N. Horsburgh, *Non-Violence and Aggression: A Study of Gandhi's Moral Equivalent of War*, Oxford: Oxford University Press, 1968; J. V. Bondurant, *Conquest of Violence: The Gandhian Philosophy of Conflict*, Princeton: Princeton University Press, 1989; J. Schell, *The Unconquerable World: Power, Nonviolence and the Will of the People*, New York: Henry Holt and Company, 2003; Dalai Lama, *Beyond Religion: Ethics for a Whole World*, Toronto: McClelland and Stewart, 2011; T. Nhat Hahn, *Peace Is Every Step: The Path of Mindfulness in Everyday Life*, New York: Bantam, 1992; M. J. Stephan, ed., *Civilian Jihad: Nonviolent Struggle, Democratization and Governance in the Middle East*, New York: Palgrave Macmillan, 2005.

non-violent actors bring into being through their non-violent interaction with violent opponents, discrediting them in the eyes of potential third-party supporters and legitimating the further use of violence by the powers-that-be. This is why violent defenders of unjust power structures routinely plant *agents provocateurs* in non-violent organizations. This first effect then tends to lead either to submission or set in motion the 'repetition effect', and the violent means then 'overwhelm the ends' as Arendt puts it.[28]

Despite this evidence, Honig and Stears, as well as Norval and Bell, ask without further ado if Malcolm X's advocacy of violence helped, rather than harmed, the non-violent civil rights movement of Martin Luther King Jr and the supportive non-violent students' movement. Yet, Malcolm X himself said that he was a 'zombie' when he advocated violence as a member of the Nation of Islam. After his returned from Mecca in March 1964, he advocated an alliance with non-racist whites and said he was for violence only if non-violence means postponing addressing the 'American black man's problem' just to avoid violence or if it means delaying the solution.[29] According to the non-violent movement neither of these were the case in 1964 and violence would only delay the solution. This speech was then followed by his astonishing 'Bloodless Revolution' speech. Here he argued that all previous and contemporary revolutions have been violent, but the United States is in a unique position of being 'the first country . . . that can actually have a bloodless revolution'. The reason for this is the destructive impotence of American military power in response to popular revolts throughout the world. It is able to deliver horrendous destructiveness from the air, yet it is powerless to stop popular revolution in hearts and minds of the people, and, if necessary, in hand-to-hand combat on the ground. As Americans come to realize the futility of counter-revolutionary violence, non-violent revolution will become possible. He then went on to outline

---

[28]   See the analysis in Gregg, *Nonviolence*, pp. 87–9.
[29]   See Malcolm X: Biography, note 9, at www.spartacus.schoolnet.co.uk/USAmalcolmX. htm.

his new strategy: black community empowerment, voter registration and education, economic self-sufficiency, independent politics and international support networks (a constructive programme).[30] He was brutally assassinated shortly after.

Thus, from the perspective of the civic traditions of non-violent agonistics, Honig and Stears's realist agonistics that includes both violence and non-violence appears to remain uncritically within the dominant realist tradition and to interpolate us into its cycles of violence and counter-violence. It is by disclosing the world of politics from other languages and epistemologies of the lived experience of non-violence and entering into them by imaginative empathy that we can free ourselves from the seeming inescapability of violence and disclose the possibilities and actualities of a world of non-violence. Yet, the language of agonistic realism, as it is presented in this chapter, forecloses this possibility.[31]

Civic ethics and constitutive means

Honig and Stears also suggest that I portray the civic practitioners of non-violence as acting 'as if' they have already achieved the world that they seek to build together in order to bring it about in reality. This may be an accurate description of the self-understanding of some non-violent activists, especially those who take a more instrumental attitude to non-violent means. However, I do not think it captures the phenomenology of non-violence as an ethical and political way of life as a whole – as a different mode of being-in-the-world with others. Let me try to sketch this out briefly or we are going to miss the revolutionary

---

[30] The 'Bloodless Revolution' speech is readily available on YouTube. For the new strategy see 'The African Sojourner', The Life of Malcolm X, The Malcolm X Project at Columbia University, www.columbia.edu/cu/ccbh/mxp/africa.html. For the revolutionary power of constructive programmes see my response to Bell in this volume.

[31] For another formulation of agonistic realism that is closer to civic citizenship, see M. Stears and M. Humphrey, 'Public Reason and Political Action: Justifying Citizen Behavior in Actually Existing Democracies', *The Review of Politics* 74 (2): 285–306, 2012. I address some of their concerns about the civil tradition of public reasoning in my response to Masonin this volume.

character of non-violent politics and the challenge it poses to some fundamental assumptions of modern politics.[32]

Non-violent civic citizens strive to organize, interact, exercise power together and resolve their disputes non-violently in the communities in which they live and in agonistic negotiations with violent defenders of the injustices of the world. And these two types of non-violent civic freedom are grounded in more personal practices of non-violent relations to themselves: curbing afflictive emotions, cultivating empathy and compassion, non-harm of other living beings in one's diet and relation to the living earth and so on. Of course, these three general types of non-violent practice prefigure a larger world if their activities have transformative effects beyond the small-scale practices in which they are enacted.[33] However, I do not think it is correct to say that their 'attitude' is to act 'as if' the larger non-violent world 'to come' is already actual. Rather, their ethical orientation is focused on bringing into being and carrying on a non-violent world here and now: that is, the 'world' they are actualizing in every breath and step they take.[34] This non-modernist mode of being and temporality is expressed in the ethical norm of 'non-attachment to ends'.

Participants do not see non-violence as a means instrumental to some future end. There is no separation of means and ends and no modernist temporality of some good 'to come' that goes along with this separation. Once these two assumptions are accepted, it is possible to think of the means as instrumentally related to an end that is different in kind from the means, and thus to argue that either non-violent or violent means can lead to a non-violent and democratic future, as in the dominant theories of global peace and justice by means of violence of Hobbes and Kant on one side and Franz Fanon and Che Guevara on the other hand. In contrast, the ethos of non-violence is that the means are everything, as the seed is to the full grown plant. Peace is

---

[32] See Bondurant, *Conquest of Violence.*
[33] For more on these types of non-violent practice see my response to Bell in this volume.
[34] Nhat Hahn, *Keeping the Peace.*

not an end. Peace is the way. On this view, means are 'constitutive' rather than instrumental. Non-violent civic freedom is the only way to a non-violent and democratic future. Accordingly, practitioners are not oriented to some future to come as if it were actual. They are oriented to the present. To care for the future is to care for what one is saying and doing here and now.

To put this in the language of civic citizenship, civic citizens are committed ethically to always interacting with others as free in the civic sense: that is, as capable of entering into relationships in which they work out their differences and forms of cooperation through non-violent negotiations and contestation, even if the other initially tries to use violence to settle differences and impose cooperation. This mode of being in the world with others rules out seeking to master others. It also rules out treating others violently, since violence involves treating oneself and others as things to be manipulated and killed, no matter what end one invokes to justify this dehumanization. A defender of violent-non-violent agonistics might respond that war is a contest, so violence is nevertheless consistent with a commitment to contestation all the way down. But, this is not so. To kill the other is not to respect contestation but to end it.[35]

On preparation

Another objection Honig and Stears, Norval and Bell raise to non-violent politics is that those who engage in it would be 'unprepared' if they trained only for the various types of non-violent dialogue. This is true. However, education in the wide variety of types of dialogue is only one important part of the world of non-violent negotiation. Non-violent civic activists prepare for agonistics with violent opponents in five main ways that I discuss in my response to Bell. Moreover, they

---

[35] And, the objective of modern violence is to avoid any actual contest of combat by technological means as much as possible. As Norval notes, this was one of Johan Huizinga's main criticisms of modern warfare in *Homo Ludens*. It is no longer a game.

prepare from an early age and in all sorts of contexts. They do this by rejecting 'Rousseau's paradox' that Honig and Stears and Norval raise.

Like many modern political theorists Rousseau assumes that humans step from a pre-civil state of nature into the general will and political society, and thus have no experience of reasoning together to form a general will or to act as good citizens. Hence the paradox.[36] But the picture is false. Children begin to question the rules, goals and effects of the games in which they find themselves and to negotiate their change as early as five years old. These are activities of proto-civic citizenship. Moreover, as Foucault disclosed in his historical studies of governmentality, the world is composed of practices of governance and governmentality in which humans exercise their civic freedoms to various degrees. The formal institutions of centralized states that are standardly treated as the sole realm of government and citizenship in modern political theory and practice are one small subset of these practices of governance within and beyond states. Acting for public good in building or reforming the formal institutions of states is a continuation of modes of thought and action already acquired elsewhere, either in everyday practices of governance in which proto-civic activities are encouraged or in resistances to practices where they are discouraged.[37]

I take up further questions of violence and non-violence in the responses to follow. For all the reasons I give in these responses, I believe that the use of violence is incompatible with civic freedom and thus with civic citizenship. Although Honig and Stears's agonistic realism shares many features with the tradition of civic citizenship, the acceptance of violence makes it a distinct tradition of active citizenship, more strategic and militant and less ethical than civic. These two traditions overlap throughout the twentieth century in complex ways, but, for the reasons I give in this section and in response to Norval and

---

[36] Rousseau states the paradox in book 2, section 7 of J. Rousseau, *The Social Contract: Or Principles of Political Right*, London: Wordsworth Editions, 1998.

[37] Tully, *On Global Citizenship*.

Bell, it is important to distinguish them.[38] I am grateful to Honig and Stears for provoking me to realize this.

Treaty negotiations

In conclusion, Honig and Stears and Bell criticize me for 'sometimes presenting treaties as transformative instruments of mutuality and not as, also and undecidably, mechanisms of domination'. I would like comment on this because my treatment of treaties is illustrative of my practice-based and dialogical approach to the study of politics and I believe that practices of treaty negotiations are one of the most important non-violent practices for resolving disputes and coordinating the interaction of the diverse peoples of the world.

In *Strange Multiplicity* and 'Struggles of Indigenous Peoples for and of Freedom' I present the many ways that treaty negotiations have been abused to dispossess indigenous peoples of their traditional territories, relocate on reserve the tiny minority who survived dispossession, war and disease, and subject them to the laws of settler societies and capitalist economic development.[39] Perpetrators and defenders of these abuses have tried to justify them on the grounds that these 'processes' subdue, cultivate and improve the wild earth, by turning it into private property, and civilize pre-civil peoples, by assimilating them into civilization and modernization. These developmental stories and the impositional theories of justice that accompany them continue to be widely accepted today. It is difficult for settlers to see their basic injustice unless they can move around and see them from an indigenous perspective. Along with Taiaiake Alfred (Haudenosaunee) and Dale Turner (Anishnaabek) I spent three years at the Royal Commission on Aboriginal Peoples listening to indigenous people tell their stories about treaties. Although

---

[38] In D. Cortright, *Peace: A History of Movements and Ideas*, Cambridge: Cambridge University Press, 2008, David Cortright argues that it is one of the central tensions within European peace movements throughout the twentieth century.

[39] J. Tully, *Strange Multiplicity: Constitutionalism in an Age of Diversity*, Cambridge: Cambridge University Press, 1995; Tully, *Public Philosophy* I, chapter 7.

they are perfectly aware of how the treaties have been abused and surrounded by violence, they argue that these were violations of the spirit and intent of the treaties. Treaties were used in the early 'peace and friendship' period and should be used today to settle disputes and work out non-violently forms of shared rule and separate rule over their respective territories between equal, self-governing and co-existing native and non-native peoples or nations (as in the Two Row Wampum treaty relationship). Moreover, when they criticize modern treaty processes, they do so on the grounds that these pseudo-treaty processes fail to live up to the immanent norms of practices of treaty negotiations. Once treaties are seen from both the norms immanent in treaty negotiations and indigenous understandings of the place of humans in the world, the injustice of the grand legitimations of dispossession and imposition of 'primitive accumulation' become obvious.

In contrast to the anthropocentric and impositional view of justice of the settler side, many indigenous people hold the view that justice is attunement to the normative and reciprocal gift relationships among all living beings. Humans take care of all their non-human relations and they reciprocate. These interdependent relationships of mutual care sustain life on earth: hence 'mother earth'. Justice consists in the continuous attunement of human relationships and practices to the more-than-human biological and ecological relationships in which they already participate. This is the way of life indigenous to Great Turtle Island, the 'profound America'. In contrast, relating to the living earth as private property is the fundamental injustice from which all others follow; akin to treating your mother as a thing to be owned and exploited.[40]

It is difficult to imagine two more different civilizations trying to live together on one continent. How do indigenous peoples imagine that

---

[40] A. J. Hall, *Earth into Property: Colonization, Decolonization and Capitalism*, Montreal: McGill-Queens University Press, 2010; J. Borrows, 'Landed Citizenship: An Indigenous Declaration of Interdependence', in *Recovering Canada: The Resurgence of Indigenous Law*, Toronto: University of Toronto Press, 2002; T. Alfred, 'Acknowledgements', in *Wasase: Indigenous Pathways of Action and Freedom*, Toronto: University of Toronto Press, 2009.

treaty negotiations can conciliate them? The answer many give is not only that treaty negotiations enable justice as imposition-modernization on settler territory and justice as attunement to continue on indigenous earth, it is also that indigenous ways of continuously trying to live in better attunement with the biotic relationships on which we depend will provide an example that settlers will come to see as less destructive than the one they brought with them. Just as importantly, indigenous people argue that participation in the non-violent relationships of treaty negotiations are themselves transformative.[41] Participation in reciprocal relationships of cooperation, ceremonies, contestation, conciliation and repolishing constitutive of treaty negotiations gives participants the potentially transformative experience of interacting in civic practices that are a micro-polis of the macro-polis they inhabit as earthlings.[42] These are non-violent ways indigenous peoples resist assimilation and try to indigenize settlers.

I wrote up this vision of treaties and showed how it could be reciprocally endorsed by non-indigenous peoples from within their Western traditions of justice, including justice as attunement, and thus provide the basis for redress of past violations and norms for future treaty negotiations.[43] A version of this is published in *Public Philosophy*.[44] Taiaiake and I have gone on to criticize modern treaty processes that fail to live up to the immanent standards in our writing, public speaking and lectures.[45] Thanks to centuries of contestation by indigenous peoples, the Royal Commission and many other activists and scholars, indigenous and non-indigenous, common law courts and the United Nations Declaration on the Rights of Indigenous Peoples

---

[41] For the transformative power of non-violence, see my response to Bell below.
[42] R. A. Williams, *Linking Arms Together: American Indian Treaty Visions of Law and Peace 1600–1800*, Oxford: Oxford University Press, 1997.
[43] For Western traditions of justice as receptivity and attunement, see R. Dawson, *Justice as Attunement: Transforming Constitutions in Law, Literature, Philosophy and the Rest of Life*, Oxford: Routledge, 2013.
[44] Tully, *Public Philosophy* I, chapter 8.
[45] For example, J. Tully, 'Reconsidering the BC Treaty Process', *Speaking Truth to Power: A Treaty Forum*, Ottawa: Law Commission of Canada and BC Treaty Commission, 2001, pp. 3–19.

(2007) have begun to see treaties in this way to some extent and to strike down dispossession and extinguishment treaties as invalid. Those involved in treaty negotiations, networks of civic citizens in local communities and ecologists have formed alliances with indigenous peoples in these struggles for justice with respect to land claims, self-government and the environment.[46] Many of the leading environmental and earth scientists and activists now see their new Gaia hypothesis as similar to the much older mother earth working hypothesis of indigenous peoples. These practices of decolonization face continuous resistance and require continuous civic practices of freedom within and alongside treaty negotiations to keep them going. Nevertheless, despite all the centuries of force and fraud that surround treaty negotiations and undermine indigenous ways of life, both survive and appear to be gaining strength.[47]

These are the reasons I 'sometimes' mention the transformative power of non-violent treaty negotiations more than the abuses of them. I agree with Robert Williams and John Borrows that looking at treaty negotiation from this perspective brings to light the empowering history of civic agency of indigenous peoples for over 500 years, in contrast to the victimization picture of the 'mechanisms of domination' perspective.[48] Moreover, Williams argues that the non-violent practices of treaty negotiations provide a way of resolving disputes and coordinating the interaction among peoples and their diverse ways of life throughout the world that could replace the recourse to violence. In favouring this perspective, I share with Honig and Stears their admirable 'partiality' for stories that 'are most empowering for dissidents and for their shared futures of co-governance'.

---

[46] For examples see L. Davis, ed., *Alliances: Re/envisioning Indigenous-non-Indigenous Relationships*, Toronto: University of Toronto Press, 2010.

[47] For this qualified hypothesis, see J. Tully, 'Consent, Hegemony, and Dissent in Treaty Negotiations', in J. Webber, and C. M. Macleod, eds, *Between Consenting Peoples*, Vancouver: University of British Columbia Press, 2010.

[48] Williams, *Linking Arms Together*, and J. Borrows, *Drawing out Law: A Spirit Guide*, Toronto: University of Toronto Press, 2011.

4. Aletta J. Norval

The critical and collaborative dimensions of civil and civic citizenship

Aletta Norval presents a characteristically incisive and insightful comparison of my work on global citizenship with the exciting work of Ernesto Laclau. I have learned from Laclau and Chantal Mouffe for many years and Norval's comparison enables us to see clearly the similarities and dissimilarities. Moreover, I have learned and borrowed from Norval's groundbreaking work on aversive democracy. Her summary of civic citizenship and of the specific sense of 'democracy' that I associate with it are excellent. She also raises some characteristically insightful questions that I will try to address. However, before I do so, I would like to clarify one misunderstanding concerning civil citizenship and its interrelationships to civic citizenship.

Norval claims, first, that I portray civil citizenship as uncritical and passive and, second, as dichotomous to civic citizenship. Civil citizens are neither uncritical nor passive and their participation overlaps and joins hands with civic citizenship in complex ways. Civil theorists, especially in the Critical Theory tradition, are critical of institutions and agents that fail to live up to the universal ideals of justice immanent within the institutions and processes of modernization of the modern module of citizenship. They present and debate theories of justice and their justifications and proposals for reform of the civil institutions and processes. Their critiques have been central to progressive politics in Europe for over 200 years.[49] The objection civic citizens raise is that the tradition is often not critical of basic assumptions and features of the civil institutions, such as those that shield the causes of global injustices from civic democratization by placing them in the private sphere, the presumption that the ideal is already immanent within modern

---

[49] For this estimation, see J. Tully, 'The Crisis of Global Citizenship', *Radical Politics Today*, July 2009.

institutions and their theoretical representations of them renders critique self-limiting and these limits constrain them to treat any other global tradition of political thought or organization as on the path to this institutional form or as being illegitimate.[50]

In practice, reform-minded civil citizens are active. They work within the institutions of modern institutions, almost always in alliances with civic citizens, to reform these institutions: to enfranchise the excluded, to extend rights of participation in official public spheres, social and economic rights and rights of participation domestically and internationally, and to bring these institutions to those that do not have them by policies of transitional justice. As unquestionably important as these great civil reform movements are, the objection civic citizens raise is that working within the official institutions runs up against unjustifiable limits to democratic participation. It tends to channel and appropriate all kinds of creative civic practices of grass roots democracy in what the civil tradition calls 'civil society' into the restrictive and often incapacitating procedures of the official public spheres and thus into mere influence power. When the limits to reform within are reached, civil citizens carry on within as best they can and civic citizens carry on by going beyond these limits and engaging in the negotiation and cooperation activities Norval summarizes, which they continue to see as citizenship practices.

I am not sure how Norval came to her disjuncture assumption that civic citizens do not also participate within the official institutions of participation, but *solely* alongside or outside and I apologize if it was an infelicitous phrase on my part. It is definitely not the case. Civil and civic citizens work together in these institutions until they run up against their limits, as I show in the *Afterword*.[51] For instance, she mentions

---

[50] For this objection in more detail than Tully, *On Global Citizenship*, see Tully, *Public Philosophy* II, chapters 4, 5 and 8. For limitations of civil theories of the public sphere, see J. Tully, 'On the Multiplicity of Global Public Spheres', in C. Emden and D. Midgley, eds, *Beyond Habermas: Democracy, Knowledge and the Public Sphere*, New York: Berghahn, 2012.

[51] See also my response to Mason in this volume.

a number of examples of citizens working within the institutions of modern states to reform them as if these are solely examples of civil citizenship, whereas they are good examples of civic and civil citizens working together. They are working for reform of the legal and political institutions by legal and political means *and* by actors (illegal immigrants) and by diverse means that are not recognized as legal, which are, by definition, practices of civic engagement.[52] As Howard Zinn has shown, the traditions of civic citizenship have their own histories of the struggles that built and continue to reform the institutions of modern citizenship. They do not see them as preconditions and containers of citizenship, the outcome of inevitable processes, Rousseaian founding moments or top-down processes of transitional justice. As Dunn and Owen note, they see them as the ongoing creation of civic citizens struggling for participatory, social, economic and minority rights before they have these rights to do so, and, so, eo ipso, by civic means. I do not think that Norval would disagree with this once the misunderstanding is clarified.

Cooperation and contestation

Norval argues that civic agonistics should not be constrained by an orientation to cooperation with those who are or will be subject to or affected by the contestation and by the change the contesters are arguing for. She finds this too prescriptive. I disagree. A condition of civic agonistics being the exercise of civic freedom is that the others affected are treated as partners with the capacity of civic freedom, of having a voice and being co-negotiators with the contesters. This entails treating them, and not others in the agonistic struggles, in certain ways; showing them how the proposed reform or revolution of the current system of unjust action-coordination will affect them and be willing to

---

[52] Many of the examples in Tully, *Public Philosophy* I, chapters 4–8 and Tully, *Public Philosophy* II, chapters 3, 4 and 8 are of this general type.

listen and respond to their reply. If this condition is bypassed and some of those affected are ignored or treated as things to be manipulated, mastered or treated violently, or if contestation is seen as good and an end in itself, then these forms of agonistics fall outside what I consider to be the field of civic agonistics. Far from being incompatible with diversity, as Norval suggests, this commitment to taking into account the views of those you disagree with is the only way to recognize and work out acceptable modes of cooperative federalism and other types of recognition and accommodation among the diverse forms of human organization on the planet.[53]

I realize how challenging this responsibility is in practice and how often it is ignored on the grounds that the others affected are somehow less than worthy of consideration, the contesters know what is good for them, the contesters are just and the others unjust so there is no reason to listen any further, there is not enough time to consult, or that the 'all affected' principle is utopian and contradictory. In addition, these sorts of arguments against listening to the other often rest on the dubious presumption that such non-democratic means will somehow lead to democratic outcomes. Like Arendt, I believe we should reject these specious arguments if we are to free ourselves from the destruction of human and non-human life that has been unleashed under their authority.[54]

For these reasons of non-violent and cooperatively oriented contestation I would say that the kind of agonistic citizenship Norval presents is different in kind from civic citizenship and similar to Honig and Stears's agonistic realism. Nevertheless, I would also say that civic citizenship belongs to a larger family of what Norval calls 'aversive citizenship', albeit a gentler and more conciliatory member.

---

[53] See also my response to Honig and Stears on cooperation and contestation in this volume.

[54] For an acute analysis of the 'all affected' principle to which I am indebted, see D. Owen, 'Constituting the Polity, Constituting the Demos: On the Place of the All Affected Interests Principle in Democratic Theory and in Resolving the Democratic Boundary Problem', *Ethics and Global Politics* 5 (3): 129–52, 2012.

5. Duncan Bell

Civic citizenship, sociality and informal imperialism

Duncan Bell and I come from the same historically oriented school of political thought. I have learned an enormous amount from his groundbreaking scholarship in the history of European political thought and of the history of Western imperialism in particular. Perhaps because we share so much he has done a masterful job of summarizing my work on the history of globalization: that is, the rise and triumph of informal imperialism over colonial imperialism after decolonization. I am relieved to read that he too thinks this way of disclosing the present state of globalization helps us to see some of the limits and possibilities of theories and practices of global citizenship more clearly than other representations and theories, or so I argue. I am also grateful to him for his elucidation of the working hypothesis of civic citizenship and giving it the name 'social unsociability' in contrast with the Hobbes-Kant premise of unsocial sociability all the way down. Social unsociability is the social, ecological and spiritual working hypothesis of autopoiesis or Gaia: that the ground of our being is interdependent relationships of mutual aid or compassionate cooperation: of cooperating through exercising civic freedom in and on the imperfect practices of cooperation (in the sense of compliance) in which we find ourselves and act. This is of course a much older working hypothesis than the modern antagonistic premise that marginalized it in the West, yet it has its own tradition in the modern period as well.[55]

Bell suggests that my approach to citizenship is republican, and he is not alone in this. It is certainly true that the republican tradition has civil and civic wings, the former associated with Philip Pettit and the latter with Hannah Arendt in our time. However, I hope that both modes disclose a field of histories, institutions and practices of citizenship that is much broader and diverse than this important tradition. Moreover,

---

[55] See *Afterword* and references.

while the participatory wing of republicanism shares some of the 15 features of civic citizenship, it tends to be exclusively state-centred, to accept violence and coercively imposed duties and to share many of the institutional conditions of the civil tradition.[56]

The civic tradition includes the diversity of practices of citizenship in practices of governance throughout the world, whether state or non-state. Many of its contemporary features have developed over the last 200 years out of worldwide traditions of grass-roots, community-based and cooperative economic and social democracies, innovations in party politics, participatory budgeting, union movements, economic, social and ecological movements, anti-war movements, decolonization, revolution, non-governmental organizations, networking and practices of governance and citizenship of indigenous peoples. Moreover, civic citizens reflect on and test in practice not only their understanding of violence and non-violence, as above, but also, and equally fundamentally, their practices and provisional theories and representations of their practices of 'doing democracy' as they go along. These reflective practices of subjecting their practices and representations of them to negotiation en passant constitute the signature characteristic of civic citizenship in contrast to the civil understanding of the role of theoretical frameworks above the demoi.[57] For this reason the global phenomena of civic citizenship cannot be represented and studied accurately under a republican framework or any other framework, for any framework is brought into the practices of reciprocal elucidation as a condition of the civic freedom of those working with it, as Laden, Celikates, Dunn and Owen and Bell note. This condition holds as well for using and testing the family resemblance features of the concept of civic citizenship I propose; some of which will no doubt not survive the testing. To quote Nietzsche: 'all concepts in which an entire process is semiotically concentrated elude definition: only that which has no history is definable.'[58]

---

[56] See Tully, *On Global Citizenship*.

[57] See Mason and my response. For how this works in practice, see Tully, *Multiplicity of Global Public Spheres*.

[58] F. Nietzsche, *On the Genealogy of Morals*, K. Ansell-Pearson, ed., Cambridge: Cambridge University Press, 1996.

Bell's central objection to my analysis of the arts of civic citizenship is that it is an inadequate remedy to my diagnosis of informal imperialism. He presents such a careful interpretation of my work and such well-argued objections to it that I was swept away by his persuasiveness. Nevertheless, now that I have had time to reflect, I would like to try to persuade him to reconsider his conclusion, as he points out I am constrained to do by my own method. A full response is given in the non-violent and democratic literature I have referred to. I will try to briefly summarize some main themes.

The transformative power of non-violence

The initial step is, as Bell suggests, to say something about non-violent civic education. This is a well-developed field of counter-mainstream civics in communities, social movements, schools and engaged teaching and research universities throughout the world. There are five areas of civic education in the five main, interdependent and mutually supportive types of practices of civic citizenship. These five types of practices of acting in concert and the corresponding types of education embody five modalities of the transformative power of non-violence.

The first area of civic education comprises meditative and group practices of care of the self. These educate children and adults to deal with their harmful emotions, habits and reactions; to cultivate the four stages of empathy that enable them to attend to and understand the suffering of oneself and others and to cultivate compassion that moves them to act to alleviate that suffering. This is the first axis of the transformative power of non-violence: non-violent relations of the self on the self (self-compassion). Education and exercise in the transformative, non-violent practices of the ethics of the self is the ground of all other non-violent practices: being peace. This is not only the ethical teaching of the great practitioners of non-violence such as Gandhi, ThichNhat Hahn, Dalai Lama, Martin Luther King Jr and Thomas Merton. The same fundamental point concerning the primacy of ethics of the self in relation to practices of freedom in the world of power relations is also made by Michel Foucault:

> If we take the question of power, of political power, situating it in the more general question of governmentality understood as a strategic field of power relations in the broadest and not merely political sense of the term, if we understand by governmentality a strategic field of power relations in their mobility, transformability, and reversibility, then I do not think that reflection on this notion of governmentality can avoid passing through, theoretically and practically, the element of a subject defined by the relationship of self to self . . . an ethics of the subject.[59]

The second area of education is civic engagement in self-organizing and self-governing practices of bringing about common goods. These begin in looking after the classroom or hood, growing vegetables, making and cleaning up after meals, making utensils, studying where food, clothing, shelter and funding come from and under what conditions and how other humans and the environment are affected by what they are doing. These civic communities are extended out to larger constructive programmes through networking with others schools, cooperatives and community-based organizations.[60] This axis is pertains to the transformative power of non-violence: engagement in power-with practices.

The third area of civic education is in the arts of cooperation and non-violent contestation in dialogue. This begins with non-violent techniques of classroom communication and civic dialogues between teachers and students: questioning what is being taught, how it is being taught and non-violent practices of disputation and resolution. These civic practices of contestation do not necessarily transform all

---

[59] M. Foucault, *Hermeneutics of the Subject: Lectures at the Collège de France, 1981–1982*, New York: Palgrave, 2005, p. 252. For more detail see, M. Foucault, 'The Ethics of the Concern for Self as a Practice of Freedom', in P. Rabinow, ed., *Ethics, Subjectivity and Truth*, New York: New Press, 1997. In a manner somewhat similar to Arendt, Foucault came to conceptualize power independent of and in contrast to violence and force from 1979 to his death in 1984 (see M. Foucault, 'The Subject and Power', in J. B. Faubion, ed., *Power: Essential Works of Foucault*, New York: New Press, 2000).

[60] For one approach to this, see B. Moyer, *Doing Democracy: The MAP Model for Organising Social Movements*, Gabriola Island: New Society, 2001.

master-pupil relationships, but they teach students and teachers how to enter into various types of dialogues and to challenge command authority relationships and demand justifications that they can test and accept or reject. This area comprises education in the wide variety of verbal and non-verbal (performative) types of dialogue available in Western and non-Western cultures. Moreover, as we have seen, these include the varieties of dialogical relationships among humans and non-human beings as fellow citizens of an ecological commonwealth of all forms of life.[61] This is the most familiar axis of the transformative power of non-violence: the power of receptive, reciprocal and critical dialogues.

The fourth and most difficult area of education is in the types of civic negotiations that involve non-violent agonistics with violent others. These are oriented to moving violent actors around by non-violent ways to see the superiority of non-violent, cooperative and contestatory ways of settling disputes through negotiation and dialogue. That is, these are negotiations with actors who have not had the advantage of a civic education. There are over 200 techniques for different situations. One of the most basic in my opinion is an education in the non-violent martial arts that enable an individual or collective agent: (1) to discourage a potential attacker from attacking just in the way they comport themselves; (2) to disarm and overthrow violent opponents by using their aggressive behaviour to throw them off balance, into dis-equilibrium and undermine their confidence in the efficacy of violence; (3) to be able to withstand blows and continue to uphold the stance of concern and readiness to settle things by negotiation and compromise; (4) to be willing to die for a negotiable just cause but never to kill (self-suffering) and (5) thereby to implant the suggestion in others that there is a superior, ethical and

---

[61] See A. S. Laden, 'Learning to be Equal: Just Schools and Schools of Justice', in D. Allen and R. Reich, eds, *Democracy, Education and Justice*, Chicago: University of Chicago Press, 2012. For this broad and deep sense of dialogical human relationships, see J. Stout, *Democracy and Tradition*, Princeton: Princeton University Press, 2004. For my capacious conception of verbal and non-verbal practices of dialogue, see J. Tully, 'Deparochializing Political Theory: The Dialogue and Interbeing Approach', *The Conference on Deparochializing Political Theory*, University of Victoria, 2–4 August 2012.

reasonable way to resolve the dispute – by being moved and moving to non-violent agonistics of types three, two and one above. In all five dimensions, the power of non-violence is acting on both opponents and bystanders by the experience and sight of an entirely different and ethically superior way of interacting and resolving differences.

This complex logic of non-violent interaction with violence is the fourth axis of the transformative power of non-violence. It is often considered the fundamental transformative power of non-violence since it transforms the opponents and the relationship between them from one mode of being to another. Along with constructive programmes it is at the core of Gandhi's Satyagraha. It is called the jiu-jitsu logic of non-violence because it uses the movements and dis-equilibrium of the opponent to bring about the transformation. The non-violent actors are not only offering and suggesting a non-violent alternative in which they can combine their energy and work together rather than wasting it in futile conflict, they also manifest this alternative in their interaction *and* envelope the violent others in these non-violent and potentially transformative relationships. They are being peace and making peace at one and the same time. Most of the more complex and mediated techniques and strategies of non-violent agonistics are derived from and extend the bodily logic of interaction and transformation of this famous phenomenological prototype.[62] It is the non-violent tradition's alternative to the violent tradition's prototype of the 'repetition effect' of violence and counter-violence: the means of freeing ourselves from this allegedly inescapable effect and weaving ourselves into non-violent relationships at the same time.[63]

The other technique that is equally important is non-cooperation. As we have seen, the civic tradition claims that unjust regimes rest

---

[62] See Gregg, *The Power of Nonviolence*, for the classic presentation of the phenomenological analysis of the transformative jiujitsu logic on non-violence. Gregg studied with Gandhi and then brought this analysis to North America and it was adopted by Martin Luther King Jr. For an excellent example of training in martial arts as a preparation for and manifestation of peaceful social relationships, see *Thousand Waves Martial Arts and Self-Defense Center*, Chicago, IL, www.thousandwaves.org.

[63] For the 'repetition effect' of violence, see my response to Honig and Stears in this volume.

not on violence or manufactured consensus but on cooperation in the sense of compliance. Therefore, the basic technique of dealing with an unjust regime from Étienne de la Boétie to the Egyptian Spring and non-violent Intifada is to withdraw cooperation in the everyday reproduction of the unjust system of cooperation.[64] Non-cooperation includes techniques of slowdowns, work-to-rule, absenteeism, strikes, boycotts, complete withdrawal of support, encouraging others to join the campaign (especially the military), civic disobedience practices and so on; as long as these evince concern for the opponents and the readiness to negotiate. That is, non-cooperation campaigns are organized cooperatively in accord with the demands of civic freedom and this spectacle of the high moral ground also helps to undermine the authority and power, and so the support, of the violent regime in contrast.

Research shows that non-cooperation requires the reciprocal support of the other types of civic practice: practices of the self, constructive programmes of community-based organizations and unions that provide the food, shelter and so on that the unjust regime formerly provided, and the negotiation practices towards which non-cooperation aims to move the contest. Community-based organizations provide a non-violent way of life for supporters and safe haven to which the campaigners can return during the long spells between campaigns and jail terms. They regain their strength, engage in constructive work and discuss strategy.[65] The failure to coordinate all types of non-violent practice is what Gandhi called his Himalayan blunder.[66] Cooperative non-cooperation is fairly easy to teach in practice and there are

---

[64] For Étienne de la Boétie, see E. La Boétie, *Discourse on Voluntary Servitude*, Cambridge: Hackett Publishing Company, 2012.
[65] For an excellent analysis of the synergy of non-violent agonistics and community-based organizations, see M. E. King, *A Quiet Revolution: The Palestinian Intifada and Nonviolent Resistance*, New York: Nation Books, 2007, and M. E. King, 'Palestinian Civil Resistance against Israeli Military Occupation', in Stephan, *Civilian Jihad*, pp. 131–56. For similar findings in the non-violent Egyptian revolution, see J. Tully, 'Middle East Legal and Governmental Pluralism: A View of the Field from the Demos', *Middle East Law and Governance*, 4: 1–39, 2012.
[66] Merton, *Gandhi on Non-violence*, p. 90.

hundreds of examples to learn from since the great anti-war movements after World War I.[67] If they are organized at the neighbourhood, city, national, regional and international level through the United Nations, such non-violent networks have the capacity to remove unjust rulers and to deter their rise to power in the first place – as peaceniks from Albert Einstein, Aldous Huxley, Bertrand Russell and Gene Sharp to the millions who research and practice it today have argued as against the proponents of war and the means to peace and justice.

The fifth area of non-violent education is in anti-war research on the global problem of war. This consists in the history and present of the escalating global system of war, war preparation and arms trading among the states and state-seeking revolutionary and terrorist movements, and the limits of official disarmament talks. As I mentioned in response to Honig and Stears, it brings into relief the diabolical global complex of war and militarization and how it is mobilized to protect the structural causes of other global problems – of poverty, exploitation, environmental destruction and climate change – from being brought under the democratic authority of the billions who suffer and die under them. This is the fifth axis of the transformative power of non-violence. This kind of critical education has the capacity to free students from taking the modern political system of violence and counter-violence for granted and being interpolated into it. And it enables them to see the other four transformative practices of a non-violent way of life as both the replacement for this life-destroying system and the means of replacing its root and branch.

This is a very crude sketch of a vast literature. However, I hope it begins to address Bell's question concerning education by bringing to light the contours of the field of non-violent civic education and practice and its transformative potential.

Of course this counter-mainstream civic education is up against the hegemonic education in command relationships, consumerism

---

[67] See P. Ackerman and J. Duvall, *A Force More Powerful: A Century of Non-Violent Conflict*, New York: St Martin's, 2000; Chenoweth and Stephan, *Why Civil Resistance Works*; and Sharp, *Politics of Nonviolent Action*.

and violence in mainstream institutions and media. Children are bombarded by images of violence and consumption from an early age. They also grow up with video games in which they kill thousands of people yet remain untouched by it, mirroring operators of unmanned drones. This constant experience can generate a form of subjectivity that turns adversaries into non-human enemies easily, sees killing as ordinary and has few if any moral qualms about it; a pathological form of subjectivity that used to take years of military training and indoctrination to instil. The powerful and privileged tell them that violence and collateral damage are necessary to protect their negative freedom to consume and they employ the poor to do the killing for them. In university, students are mostly taught that violence is necessary either to uphold their free way of life or to contest it, and non-violence is effective only within and between Western-style democracies (the democratic peace thesis). In these ways they are almost interpolated into the repetition-effect picture of the real shared by the right and left, and, eo ipso, into inadvertently reproducing the global injustices that the logic of violence and counter-violence holds in place. Unfortunately for the status quo and fortunately for life on earth, even this military-industrial-university-media complex is unable to interpolate us all the way down. Inquisitive students begin to ask questions, not only within this captivating picture of the real, but about the picture itself (even in Cambridge). This initial exercise of civic freedom leads them to explore non-violent alternatives, to experiment with them in practice and so to create the non-violent counter-world of practices and education I have just sketched.

Violence and non-violence

Bell claims that the examples I give of non-violent practices of civic citizenship and education are inadequate, ineffective and insufficient in addressing the global injustices I diagnose. They 'barely ruffle the hegemonic forms of politics'. It appears to me that Bell sees the non-violent practices of civic citizenship in this dismal light because he discloses them from within some of the unquestioned institutional assumptions of civil citizenship and instrumental assumptions of Geussian and agonistic realism. This framework occludes their presence and transformative possibilities. In response, I would like to try to bring these incapacitating background assumptions into the space of questions and, in so doing, bring into a better light the transformative possibilities inhabiting the real.

For example, Bell asserts that practices of non-violent civic citizenship take place only within certain institutional and normative preconditions of modern states.[68] This is one of the basic assumptions of the civil tradition: violence outside modern states and non-violence within and between states. Yet, this classic binary of modern politics has been called into question and rendered dubious by critical international relations theorists over the last 20 years. Moreover, there is ample evidence from the empirical social sciences that there is more violence within and by modern states, state-seekers and the global institutions of the system of states than there is outside of them or their reach. He also claims that civic citizenship is only possible as an 'internal modification of existing, partially realised democratic norms'.[69] Why is this and how was the pre-existing democratic norm brought into practice in the first place? It seems to rest on the civil and realist assumption that humans are incapable of self-organization and thus require a master to impose the institutional conditions. But, again, this is surely a questionable assumption – challenged by countless examples of self-organizing democratic communities in the worst of contexts.

He cites Mandela in support of the use of violence. Yet, recent research suggests that the failure of non-violence in this case was due to the five practices of non-violent civic citizenship and education not being sufficiently established.[70] The politics of non-violence is less than 100 years old, whereas the politics of violence is over 2,000 years old. Non-violence should not be rejected on the basis of one failure in

---

[68] Bell, in this volume.
[69] Ibid.
[70] For example, Ackerman and DuVall, *A Force More Powerful*, pp. 335–68.

its early years, but, rather the failure should be learned from and the lessons applied in the future (as the Palestinian non-violent movement is now doing).[71] Reciprocally, Bell does not reject violence even though he points out that it fails many times. He also cites Fanon as giving him another reason to embrace violence. Yet, he does not ask if the violent struggle created the 'new man' in Algeria that Fanon theorized it would, or if it created an armed state and a male elite dependent on external financial and military support and at odds with the majority of its own citizens, as Fanon feared it would?[72]

Instrumental and constitutive means

The largest assumption that appears to underlie Bell's analysis of examples of regime change is that violence and non-violence are taken to be instrumental and non-constitutive means to an end, and thus they can be judged solely by their effectiveness in seizing power. In his analysis of examples of the relative effectiveness of violence and non-violence he does not ask the following questions of violent regime change. What is the relative destructiveness of human life (combatants and civilians, directly and indirectly), infrastructure and the environment of violent versus non-violent regime change? What does it do to the psyches of humans to teach them to hate, fear and dehumanize each other to such an extent that the mass killing of combatants and innocent civilians of modern warfare are seen as acceptable means and victory as the justifiable ends?[73] What is the effect of the use of violence, military command-obedience relations and external support required to seize power on the leaders of the new regime and the institutional structures

---

[71] For the experience of non-violence in the First Intifada, see M. E. King, *A Quiet Revolution: The Palestinian Intifada and Nonviolent Resistance,* New York: Nation, 2007.

[72] For the definitive non-violent agonistic response to Fanon, see B. Deming, 'Revolution and Equilibrium', in *Revolution and Equilibrium,* New York: Grossman, 1971.

[73] See D. Grossman, *On Killing: The Psychological Cost of Learning to Kill in War and Society,* New York: Little Brown and Company, 1995. In contrast, according to Nietzsche (and Gandhi and King) one of the most important ethical norms of non-violence is that it is 'better to perish than to hate and fear, and twofold better to perish than to make oneself hated and feared' (note 25 supra).

they put in place, or which continue through from the old regime (the Lenin effect)? How democratic and just is the new regime? None of these standard criteria of comparison are employed, leaving the sole criterion of effectiveness as the de facto seizure of power. Yet, it surely is impossible to compare violence and non-violence without addressing these questions.

In addition, Bell does not mention the tragedy of decolonization that is the central theme of postcolonial studies.[74] All the 'effective' violence of decolonization and the combined efforts of the non-aligned movement were unable to create states that are significantly less violent, or more democratic and egalitarian than any other modern state. Violence may put new rulers in place, modify the structures of inequality to some extent in changes and even change the ordering of hegemonic and subaltern states in the global system, but in effectively addressing any of the global problems that are the concern of progressive civil and civic citizens and agonistic realists, the results are not too promising. And where there are significant improvements, are these the results of violence or are they results of civic movements, community-based organizations and power-with relationships that derive from other sources? Whether one considers the evidence of decolonization or the current wars in the Middle East, Iraq and Afghanistan in light of these questions, the evidence seems to suggest that 'violent regime change doesn't work'.[75]

More fundamentally, non-violent movements have a completely different view of victory. They do not see victory as defeating an opponent and taking power. Their aim is the transformation of

[74] For the tragedy of decolonization, see D. Scott, *Conscripts of Modernity: The Tragedy of Colonial Enlightenment*, Chapel Hill: Duke University Press, 2004; V. Prashad, *The Darker Nations: A People's History of the Third World*, New York: New Press, 2007. For a Gandhian responses to it, see D. Jefferess, *Postcolonial Resistance: Culture, Liberation and Transformation*, Toronto: University of Toronto Press, 2008; R. J. Young, *Postcolonialism: A Very Short Introduction*, Oxford: Oxford University Press, 2003; and J. Singh, *Beyond Free and Equal: Subalternity and the Limits of Liberal Democracy*, Department of Political Science, University of Toronto PhD Dissertation, 2012.

[75] See A. B. Downes, G. Grandin, J. S. Nye, N. C. Crawford, J. D. Fearon, M. Kaldor, J. Tirman, T. Lindberg and J. Landy, 'Regime Change Doesn't Work', *Boston Review* 36 (5): 16–34, October 2011.

the world system of violence and power-over that holds inequality, exploitation and environmental injustice in place. They work to convert unjust and violent adversaries to non-violent dispute resolution and to transform the unjust power relationship between them into one that is open to negotiation by its partners. This movement transforms, rather than seizes, power-over into power-with. Non-violent actors *require* this active participation of their opponent in order to test the validity of their claim of justice, which, prior to the negotiations is one-sided and monological. In the course of transforming power-over to power-with and reasoning-over to reasoning-with, the partners come to combine their creative energy in the construction of a new relationship of shared authority of connection. This is 'another realism'.[76]

I would propose therefore, that, contrary to Bell, the overwhelming evidence suggests that it is not non-violence but violence that cannot be the answer to the transformation question. It can make only minor modifications to the existing national and global systems of power. What continues to make war and command relations appear to be the means to peace and democracy, despite the evidence, is the unexamined assumption that they are instrumental means to these ends. Once the assumption is examined it becomes evident that they cannot be the transformative means for the simple reason that they are the constitutive means of the present system.[77] Once we realize that means are pre-figurative it also becomes evident that non-violent practices of civic citizenship are the constitutive means to peace and democracy. Peace and power-with democracy do not grow out of the barrel of a gun or the binding force of an imposed system of imperatives, but in and out of the 'grass-roots' of everyday practices of civic freedom.[78]

Bell and many others argue that the non-violent and democratic step-by-step approach to change is too little too late. It merely ruffles the

---

[76] For this analysis, see H. J. N. Horsburgh, 'The Distinctiveness of Satyagraha', *Philosophy East and West* 19 (2): 171–80, 1969; Gregg, *Power of Nonviolence*, pp. 52–66, K. Mantena, '"Another Realism" The Politics of Gandhian Nonviolence', *American Political Science Review* 106 (2): 455–70, 2012; and Gandhi, *Non-violent Resistance*.

[77] See *Afterword* and my response to Honig and Stears in this volume.

[78] This is also Arendt's view in Arendt, *On Violence*.

feathers of the hegemons. The big problems we face need big solutions. From the perspective of cooperative citizenship this response is just more of the same thinking that has given rise to the problems we face.[79] Vandana Shiva, drawing on her experience in the Chipko movement, puts the cooperative reply in the following way:

> As Gandhi showed in his life, and as we experience in earth democracy, small scale responses become necessary in times of dictatorship and totalitarian rule because large scale structures and processes are controlled by the dominant power. The small becomes powerful in rebuilding living cultures and living democracies because small victories can be claimed by millions. The large is small in terms of the range of people's alternatives. The small is large where unleashing people's energies are concerned.[80]

Finally, it is worth mentioning that none of the pro-violence contributors discuss the central question of the anti-war movement. Like the critics of non-violence, and often in response to them, anti-war authors and activists discuss the extraordinary circumstances in which individual acts of violence in self-defence might or might not be acceptable if and only if they do not initiate a slippery slope to more violence. Although, as we have seen, for most this consideration takes second place to the fundamental ethical, moral and spiritual teaching that you should not kill another human being.[81] However, focusing exclusively on these individual or small-scale cases overlooks a much larger global problem of which individual cases are constituent elements. This central question is how to disarm the violent and destructive system of states and state-seekers and put in place a substitute before it destroys life on earth. This has been the central question since World War I.[82] A non-violent substitute and means of substitution have been slowly

---

[79] Tully, *On Global Citizenship*.

[80] V. Shiva, *Earth Democracy: Justice, Sustainability and Peace*, Cambridge: South End, 2005, p. 183.

[81] Although none of the defenders of violence saw this moral issue as a question they needed to address in their contributions, Bell discusses it from a realist perspective in D. Bell, ed., *Ethics and World Politics*, Oxford: Oxford University Press, 2010, pp. 93–110.

[82] See the articles in H. Zinn, ed., *The Power of Nonviolence*, Boston: Beacon, 2002, for the persistence of this central question.

brought into being and experimented with ever since. And, as we have seen throughout, the role of individual conduct is central to this transformative solution. Yet this central issue is neither mentioned or examined by the contributors, as if violence and counter-violence can either go on forever as a basic feature of the real or guarantee perpetual peace by the 'mechanical process of nature'.[83] This shows how people like me have failed to carry on the academic non-violent tradition and how much work we need to do to bring this central global problem and the non-violent response back into mainstream discussions and subject it to reciprocal elucidation. I hope this exchange with the trenchant questions posed by Bell helps to move one small step in this direction.

6. Robin Celikates

Civil disobedience and civic agonistics

I am most grateful for this exceptionally careful interpretation and interrogation of my work on global citizenship. He shows with a striking example how ideal theory can undermine democratic action unless a theory is dethroned and seen as democratic advice offered by a fellow citizen to other citizens engaged in democratic action and subject to reciprocal elucidation.[84] I agree with the analysis of the limits of civil disobedience and the strengths of his alternative way of thinking about resistance to unjust laws.[85] I also agree with his emphasis on the collective character of many practices of freedom that are characterized as civil disobedience. I wonder if we could describe his alternative as civic agonistics in relation to civic law. By 'civic law' I mean the view of law not as a formal or autonomous system of imperatives that subjects

---

[83] The latter is Kant's view in the guarantee section of 'Perpetual Peace: A Philosophical Sketch', Kant, *Political Writings*, 108.

[84] See Tully, *Public Philosophy* I, chapter 9 and my response to Mason below for this civic role of ideal theory.

[85] Celikates does not take up the question of whether Rawls can be interpreted as closer to his own civic perspective, even in the quotations he cites, as, for example, Laden interprets Rawls.

simply obey, but as a negotiated system of norms (of various kinds) with which all the different actors who are subject to the laws interact as active agents of the law's unfolding in practice. The law in the first instance is not a written document but the interaction that takes place under the written law as signpost. This interactional or manifestation view of the nature of law seems a more accurate representation of the real world of law than the imperative theory.[86] It also seems more appropriate to Celikates's interpretation of the kinds of civic negotiation that the ideal theory of civil disobedience both conceals and pre-emptively designates as illegal. Many of these practices may well show up as not only ethical in the civic sense but also as legal under the interactional representation of law.

What are violence and non-violence?

Celikates says I sidestepped the question of the definition of violence and non-violence. This is correct. It is an important question with a long-contested history in philosophy and practice, as with all important concepts, and I am working on a critical and genealogical response to it. In the meantime, let me provide an initial response. In my provisional opinion, non-violent movements do not see themselves as working under a general theory that gives definitive definitions to their key concepts and definitive answers to all question that arise. They reject this approach for the same reasons as Celikates does in his chapter. Rather, they see themselves as a self-critical movement that is trying to bring into being and carrying on a mode of being in the world (of non-violence) and, as such, that mode of being is always self-critically in question in everything they say and do. The priority of conduct to theory and the testing relationship internal to conduct is what Gandhi called Satyagraha and 'experiments in truth' and Foucault called 'the courage of truth'.[87]

---

[86] Tully, *On Global Citizenship*; Tully, *Public Philosophy* II, chapter 7; and see J. Brunee, and S. J. Toope, *Legitimacy and Legality in International Law: An Interactional Account*, Cambridge: Cambridge University Press, 2010.

[87] See my response to Honig and Stears in this volume.

At the centre of this ethos is the constant questioning of the distinction between violence and non-violence within the non-violent movements and along a spectrum of ways people inhabit non-violence as a way of life. At one end of the spectrum are the great non-violent movements such as Jainism, engaged Buddhism, Quakers, the followers of Jesus in the beatitudes, deep ecologists, vegetarians and Gandhians who strive to hold to the truth of their being that non-harm and compassion (the two main axes of non-violence) must be evinced in all one's relationship to oneself and to all other living beings. At the other end of the spectrum are the strategic non-violent movements that exercise non-harm and compassion exclusively in relation to human beings and as a mode of action exercised primarily in the political realm to overthrow unjust regimes and disarm states.[88] There is also, as Celikates mentions, the axis of analysis of structural forms of violence and non-violent responses to them.[89] Despite the differences and disagreements, I would say that there is general agreement on the negative or non-harm norm that you should not kill any human being and on the positive or compassionate norm that you should always do unto others as you would have them do unto you in similar circumstances.

These two norms demarcate the basic distinction between violence and non-violence. They are also two of the most enduring, tried and true ethical maxims in the world and they appear in most ethical and spiritual traditions. The difference is that the non-violent movements strive to realize them in every step they take. The more specific questions Celikates raises are taken up within these two norms and in relation to the way one inhabits the spectrum within them. They are then debated, tested in practice, reformulated and debated again, generation after generation, in an ongoing learning process.[90] This is no different

---

[88] Gene Sharp, Erica Chenoweth and Maria J. Stephan are good examples of this wing of peace studies.

[89] The leading non-violent theorist of structural violence is Johan Galtung: see J. Galtung, *Peace by Peaceful Means: Power and Conflict, Development and Civilization*, London: Sage, 1996, and www.transcend.org.

[90] For example, some argue there are exceptions to not using violence against humans in exceptional and containable circumstances, either by individuals or states. For an introduction to these questions within non-violent traditions, see K. R. Christensen, *Nonviolence, Peace, and Justice*, Toronto: Broadview, 2010.

than any other self-critical praxis-based movement that subjects its ways of being to continuous questioning and reciprocal elucidation. The feminist movement is another good example of a movement of this civic approach; an approach that Celikates endorses and employs superbly himself.[91]

The first transformation question

Celikates asks *who* is able to engage in acts of dissent and disobedience to bring the powerful to the negotiation table or to reclaim the commons and exercise their powers of self-organization. My answer is that many more people are able than the already recognized and privileged groups of citizens he mentions. When, where, by whom and how civic freedom emerges into the light of day is unpredictable and its effects are also unpredictable. The reason why it is possible is the 'Achilles' heel' of relations of power: the fact that they are exercised over agents who have a constrained room to manoeuver to some extent and the exercise of civic freedom within them can effect not only the power relations but also the background structures of domination that hold them in place.[92] I have drawn attention to hundreds of examples that surprise theorists and social scientists. They can emerge in what appear to be the most impossible conditions (the phenomenon of 'paradise in hell') or the most privileged.[93] Who predicted Gandhi, King, micro-credit, the global renaissance of local social and economic cooperatives, reclaiming the commons, the Egyptian non-violent spring, the occupy movements, the Italian 'benicomuni' movement or countless other less visible examples? We do not need yet another theory that purports to tell us beforehand the necessary and sufficient conditions of the

---

[91] Celikates seems at times to be asking for my own opinion on his specific questions. I have opinions but what I am trying to do is to describe a whole field of non-violent citizenship, not my opinions within its shared yet questionable and questioned norms.

[92] Tully, *On Global Citizenship*.

[93] For an exemplary anti-Hobbes and pro-Kropotkin argument that people in the worst of situations can be self-organizing and self-governing, see R. Solnit, *A Paradise Built in Hell: The Extraordinary Communities that Arise in Disasters*, New York: Penguin, 2009.

emergence of the legitimate and effective agent of change. We need instead humbler forms of engaged academic research that are attentive to what people are trying to say and do in such practices of freedom, how they do it and the ways they are marginalized and misrepresented. This is precisely the kind of research Celikates presents so well in his chapter.[94]

7. Andrew Mason

Civil and civic philosophy

Andrew Mason's contribution is the finest example of the openness of the tradition of civil philosophy to enter into a critical dialogue with the tradition of civic or public philosophy. The aim of the dialogue is not to win out over the other but to learn the strengths and weaknesses of each. They are, as he says, 'complementary'. I would like to explore how these two approaches can join hands just as civil and civic citizens join hands in practice.

Mason defines the central difference clearly. It is the role of civil philosophers to set out the general theory of justice that provides a normative framework for democracy and citizenship independent of the demos: that is, of those who are subject to this general framework. Citizenship is 'derivate' of justice. Civil philosophers are 'experts' in this epistemic sense. Civil philosophy can allow for a robust degree of democratic participation within this framework and for legal and political pluralism. Mason goes further in this democratic and pluralist direction than any other contemporary civil philosopher. His willingness to put into the space of questions many enduring features of the civil tradition, including private property, and to learn from criticisms of the history and imperialism of the civil tradition, bring immensely important reforms to the civil tradition and, if accepted, would reform

---

[94] I respond to his question of the effectiveness of such practices in my response to Bell in this volume.

civil institutions from the inside in a formidable way. The five revisions of the civil tradition he suggests complement similar revisions that civic philosophers have recommended and thus provide an example of how the two approaches can be complementary.

The central difference between the two remains. In the civic tradition, philosophers do not have the status of an expert. Their formulation of a general theory of justice is treated as a proposal or clarification by one citizen to fellow citizens, to be discussed, tried out in practice, revised or rejected, just like any other proposal, as Laden explains. The modes of practical reasoning in philosophy departments are not of a higher order and authoritative over the modes of practical reasoning in practices of democratic self-government. Through reciprocal elucidation they work together to take advantage of the best of each. The basis of justice is democracy: a people subject to a system of rules have a say on them and a hand in cooperating and changing them (including their philosophers). Of course there are rules that make the exchange of reasons among citizens over rival theories of justice themselves just, but these too are questionable in the course of the discussions en passant, in the way I mentioned in response to Honig and Stears, or the citizens would be unfree, and this would be unjust. Since there is always 'reasonable disagreement' over theories of justice in theory and concrete practice, for the reasons Rawls gave, this doubly reflexive feature of civic deliberation is a necessary condition of both freedom and justice.[95] This is a non-derivative or equiprimordial approach to justice and democracy. Justice is dialogical all the way down, whereas for Mason, dialogue is absent from his principle of what justice requires (p. 9). Mason recognizes this central difference between the two traditions and responds that the two traditions can work together and be mutually corrective. I agree with him. In the final section of the *Afterword* I set out a number of ways in which civil and civic citizens can join hands and work together.

---

[95] Tully, *Public Philosophy* II, chapter 4.

Mason gives some examples of unjust civic citizenship practices to show that I have an uncritical bias towards the civic tradition. Yet, all the examples fall foul of the audialteramparterm, or 'all subject to and all affected', feature of civic citizenship. Those 'excluded' are not only affected by being subject to the exercise of power, and the power in the examples is power-over, not power-with. He is correct to say that civic and civil citizenship are family resemblance concepts and thus not all instances have the same features. However, the 'having a say' norm in civic citizenship is so basic to the civic freedom family that its absence is sufficient grounds for criticizing and transforming the practices by means of critical and practical civic freedom. The family resemblance with respect to this feature is the diversity of ways of having a say in democratic practices versus the tendency of the civil tradition to make one small institutional set of ways essential. There are certainly less and more appealing examples of civic citizenship.

Conversely, Mason suggests that I characterize the civil tradition historically and emphasize its bad features in practice. This is partially correct. I have tried to write a genealogy of the module of civil institutions and the tradition of theoretical reflection on them and the roles they have played and continue to play in Western imperialism. I make no apology for that. I have also tried to show how critical theorists within the tradition have criticized and tried to reform some of the imperial and exploitive features of civil institutions and theories from Locke to Habermas. However, I have also tried to show that reforms of the institutions and criticisms of the theories have been self-limiting: specific institutions and theoretical presuppositions have remained as necessary pre-conditions and presuppositions beyond question. I have discussed several of these in my response to other contributors. I am not the first to point out these limits. The motley crew I call civic citizens and civic philosophers have pointed these limits out before me and shown how to go beyond them in practice and theory far better than I have done myself. I have tried to carry out this critical project in two ways: first by starting within the conventions of the civil tradition and showing how a radical immanent critique can bring the pre-conditions and presuppositions into question and go beyond them; and, second, by showing how an external critique from the civic tradition can expose the same limits and alternatives to them.[96] I find the critical work of Mason to be complementary to this project I am engaged in. His five revisions of the civil tradition, for example, constitute an immanent critique that is more radical than any other contemporary civil philosopher I have come across. I do not think that these revisions are 'beside the point' (p. 11). They are the beginning of a dialogue.

Joining hands and working together to change the world

Finally, Mason suggests that civil and civic citizens can join hands and work together. I agree. When I wrote 'A Dilemma of Global Citizenship', I did not see how they could work together. This is the article that Mason read and commented on. However, I came to see afterwards various ways in which they can work together in practice and in academic research. I included these ways in the final section of the *Afterword*. They seem to me to be complementary to Mason's suggestion. I hope that this too is the beginning of a dialogue among civil and civic researchers and in which Mason's work plays a major role.

8. Adam Dunn and David Owen

Civic and civil understandings of institutions, rights and representation

I appreciate the exceptionally careful explication and exploration of civic freedom carried out by Adam Dunn and David Owen in their contribution. They show how civic citizenship is enhanced by three types of political institution: rights, citizenship as a legal status and participatory democratic councils and representative democratic federations. This

---

[96] Ibid., chapter 5.

continues the exploration of the ways in which civil and civic citizens can join hands and change the world in the *Afterword*, Mason's chapter and my response. Dunn and Owen make the crucial qualification that such institutional forms of governor-citizen relationships are not necessary or sufficient conditions of civic citizenship, since, as they point out, citizens historically and presently struggle by civic means for such institutions (and others) before they have them. They are rather 'enabling conditions' in many circumstances. Let us examine this more closely.

In response to their question of what institutions are appropriate to civic citizenship, especially governor-citizen relationships, I would like to make a distinction between two ways of inhabiting institutions by drawing on Laden's chapter. Civil and civic citizens inhabit the same institutions of the modern module, yet in different ways. Civil citizens tend to make a categorical distinction between the institutions and the activities that take place within them: the structure-agency distinction. The background relationship constitutive of the institutions can often be command relationships and members often interact informally in everyday relations of connection within them (in ministries, private corporations, constitutional orders and so on). It they wish to challenge the command-obedience relationships, they standardly have recourse to courts and legislatures in hopes of regulating them from the outside. This accords with the civil understanding of law and of rule-following more generally.

Civic citizens inhabit the same institutions in a different way. They attempt to exercise their civic freedom not only in everyday informal connection relations with their co-workers but also in having a say and a hand in the background institutional and command relationships as well. They make attempts to democratize or civicize the institutions from the inside and they see the institutions as legitimate just insofar as the powers-that-be within them are responsive to their attempts.[97] That is, institutional structures are internally related to the activities that take

---

[97] Of course, a democratic test of a command relationship may provide good reasons to leave it in place under certain conditions, but this is to place it under the authority of those subject to it in an indirect or trustee way.

place within them.[98] This thesis accords with the civic understanding of law and rule-following, as Dunn and Owen point out. This is what I call democratic constitutionalism in contrast to the constitutional democracy of the civil tradition.[99]

Democratically minded civil participants join democratizing co-workers insofar as legal means to do so are in place. Civic citizens go further and engage in extra-legal civic activities to win these kinds of legal means, as Celikates illustrates in his chapter. The classic contemporary example of working together in this regard is the spread of the legal 'duty to consult' the members of a governmental or private institution. This is a revolutionary extension of participatory duties and rights into institutions formerly protected from democratization. Its reach also spreads beyond the members of an institution to the local communities and stakeholders affected by its policies.

Thus, civil and civic citizens have these two different yet overlapping and often complementary ways of disclosing and acting within the three types of institutions Dunn and Owen mention. The civic tradition has a more demanding account of the representative relationship than the standard civil one of elections and public deliberation. The relationship between citizens and governors itself is a cooperative and parrhesiastic relationship, as I illustrate with the dialogue between Polyneices and Jocasta.[100] The civic account of federal relationships also enables the reciprocal civic freedom of the individual and group members of the federation.[101] I also think that these traditions provide two different ways of thinking about rights and that the civic way has not received the attention it merits.[102]

The civil tradition standardly claims that human rights are something that can be unilaterally declared by an authority because they are self-evident or universal. These human rights presuppose and are exercised

---

[98] See Tully, *On Global Citizenship*; Tully, *Public Philosophy* I, introduction.
[99] Tully, *Public Philosophy* II, chapter 4.
[100] Tully, *On Global Citizenship*.
[101] Tully, *Public Philosophy* I, chapter 5.
[102] See J. Tully, 'Human Rights and Enlightenment: A View from the Twenty-First Century', in K. E. Tunstall, ed., *Self-Evident Truths? Human Rights and the Enlightenment: The Oxford Amnesty Lectures*, New York: Bloomsbury, 2012.

in a canonical set of modern legal, political and economic institutions. These institutions have to be coercively imposed prior to the exercise of human rights since they are the pre-condition of the exercise of human rights. Among these institutions is the modern state, which establishes the basis for human rights and coercively remedies their violations. To declare, project and then spread these institutions around the world, to be socialized into them and to exercise human rights within them is to be on the path of development. This tradition became dominant in the nineteenth century and it remains paramount today. It is the view of human rights from the perspective of a legislator who has the power to project rights and institutions over the world. It is the Enlightenment project.

The civic tradition treats human rights as proposals. They need to be proposed to fellow citizens by fellow citizens, rather than declared by an authority. The reason for this is that human rights are not self-evident, but, rather, they are always open to question and critical examination by the humans who are subject to them. They gain their normative force by being exercised, reflexively tested, interpreted and negotiated en passant. Moreover, there is not one universal set of institutions in which human rights can be exercised. There is a plurality of political, economic and legal institutions in which human rights can be realized and these too gain their legitimacy from being open to the contestation of self-determining persons and peoples who are subject to them. Human rights and their institutions are not prior to democratic participation, but, rather, human rights and democracy go together, hand in hand. It follows that human rights and their institutions cannot be coercively imposed. They have to be both spread and enforced by democratic and non-violent means, or else they have to be retrospectively democratized and transformed by those subject to them if they are initially imposed unilaterally. Enlightenment does not consist in a developmental and institutional endpoint, but rather in the continuous deepening of the co-articulation of human rights and democratic participation in exercising and improving them, world without end. This is a civic tradition of rights.

I suggest that this way of thinking about rights should be studied, not because it has all the answers, but because it has responses to many of the current objections to the dominant way of thinking about rights and alternatives to them. As with the other two types of institution Dunn and Owen discuss, these two traditions of rights overlap to some extent. Many rights theorists and activists within the civil tradition work to make the articulation, application and exercise of rights regimes more participatory. There is no reason why they cannot listen to and learn from civic citizens exercising a say and a hand in transforming the narrow neoliberal rights regimes imposed on them around the world and especially in the Third World. And, if they are serious about reform, they can also learn from civic activists how to exercise their correlative responsibility to walk the talk and help to bring them about: by, for example, joining global boycotts of and non-cooperation with violators of the rights they profess in the civil sphere. These mutually supportive alliances between civil reformers and civic activists have been indispensable in advancing human rights in conjunction with democratic participation – the only way they have democratic legitimacy – over the last 200 years.

9. Conclusion

Between thoroughly self-organizing and self-governing cooperatives and Weberian institutions that function as sedimented structures of domination lies a vast field of intermediate cases that exhibit degrees of institutionalization. Dunn and Owen are correct in arguing that the three types of institution, each with degrees of institutionalization, can help to enable civic and civil citizens to engage in activities for public good in the relationships of the institutions. Civil theorists are correct to emphasize that such institutions provide stability for these activities. However, it remains important not to reify institutions as 'preconditions' of the activities: that is, as institutions that are prior to and independent containers of them. The activities that take place within the relationships of these types of institution cannot be explained entirely from this institutional perspective. Activities within institutions interact not only within, but also *with* the institutional conditions. Institutional conditions and activities are internally related.

The civic perspective brings this interaction to light. Institutions are negotiated practices to varying degrees and their history is accordingly unpredictable. This is important for global citizens for the following reason. Institutions always enable certain forms of activity and disable others. The questions for citizens are: what kinds of activity do they enable and disable, for whom, for what goods and to what effects? For example, institutionalized neoliberal rights enable individual and corporate market freedoms (for some) while disabling social and economic rights, collective cooperation and self-determination and democratic diversity. For citizens to be free and institutions just, those who are subject to them and their effects have to be able to test these institutions in the course of their activities within them: to raise these questions, reason together about them and be able to modify or transform them. When these interactions between institutional conditions and civic freedom are in operation the institutions are stable 'for the right reasons'. They are degrees of democratization that civic citizens bring to institutionalization. I thank Dunn and Owen for enabling us to see this crucial connection clearly.[103]

I would like to thank the contributors once more for their outstanding contributions and the four series editors, especially David Owen, for bringing together such a rich and challenging collection.

---

[103] For their helpful comments I am grateful to Michael Carpenter, Karuna Mantena, Anthony Laden, David Owen and Timothy Smith.

Bibliography

Abernathy, D. B., *The Dynamics of Global Dominance: European Overseas Empires, 1415–1980*, Yale: Yale University Press, 2000.

Ackerman, P. and Duvall, J., *A Force More Powerful: A Century of Non-Violent Conflict*, New York: St Martin's, 2000.

Ackerman, J. and Honig, B., 'Un-Chosen: Judith Butler's Jewish Modernity', in I. Zyrtal, J. Picard, J. Revel and M. Steinberg, eds, *Thinking Jewish Modernity: Thinkers, Writers, Artists, Shapers of Jewish Identity*, forthcoming.

Alfred, T., *Peace, Power, Righteousness: An Indigenous Manifesto*, Oxford: Oxford University Press, 1999.

—, *Wasase: Indigenous Pathways of Action and Freedom*, Toronto: University of Toronto Press, 2009.

Allen, D., 'Law's Necessary Forcefulness', in A. S. Laden and D. Owen, eds, *Multiculturalism and Political Theory*, Cambridge: Cambridge University Press, 2007.

Amoore, L., eds, *The Global Resistance Reader*, London: Routledge, 2005.

Anderson, E., 'Toward a Non-Ideal, Relational Methodology for Political Philosophy: Comments on Schwartzman's *Challenging Liberalism*', *Hypatia* 24 (4): 130–45, 2009.

Anderson, K., *A Recognition of Being: Reconstructing Native Womanhood*, Toronto: Sumach, 2000.

Anghie, A., *Imperialism, Sovereignty and the Making of International Law*, Cambridge: Cambridge University Press, 2007.

Anheier, H., Glasius, M., Kaldor, M. and Holland, F., eds, *Global Civil Society 2004–2005*, London: Sage, 2004.

Annas, J., *Intelligent Virtue*, Oxford: Oxford University Press, 2011.

Archibugi, D., Held, D. and Köhler, M., eds, *Re-imagining Political Community: Studies in Contemporary Democracy*, Cambridge: Polity, 1998.

Arendt, H., *The Human Condition*, Chicago: University of Chicacgo Press, 1958.

—, *On Revolution*, London: Penguin, 1965.

—, *On Violence*, New York: Harcourt, Brace and Company, 1970.

—, *Crises of the Republic*, New York: Harcourt, Brace and Company, 1972.

—, *Between Past and Future: Eight Exercises in Political Thought*, Harmondsworth: Penguin, 1977.

—, *The Promise of Politics*, J. Kohn, ed., New York: Schocken, 2005.

Armitage, D., 'Probing the Foundations of Tully's Public Philosophy', *Political Theory* 39 (1): 124–30, 2011.

Armstrong, C., 'Coercion, Reciprocity, and Equality Beyond the State', *Journal of Social Philosophy* 40 (3): 297–316, 2009.

Ayers, A., 'Demystifying Democratization: The Global Constitution of (Neo) Liberal Polities in Africa', *Third World Quarterly* 27 (2): 312–38, 2006.

Bacevich, A., *American Empire: The Realities and Consequences of U.S. Diplomacy*, Cambridge, MA: Harvard University Press, 2002.

Bacher, J., *Petrotyranny*, Toronto: Dundurn, 2000.

Bakan, J., *The Corporation: The Pathological Pursuit of Profit and Power*, London: Penguin, 2004.

Baker, G. P., 'Following Wittgenstein: Some Signposts for Philosophical Investigations', in S. Holtzman and C. Leich, eds, *Wittgenstein: To Follow a Rule*, London: Routledge, 1981, pp. 143–242.

Balibar, E., 'Sur la désobéissance civique', in *Droit de cité*, Paris: PUF, 2002.

Barber, B., *Consumed: How Markets Corrupt Children, Infantilize Adults, and Swallow Citizens Whole*, New York: Norton, 2007.

Barlow, C., *Blue Covenant: The Global Water Crisis and the Coming Battle for the Right to Water*, Toronto: McClelland and Stewart, 2007.

Barry, B., 'Statism and Nationalism: A Cosmopolitan Critique', in I. Shapiro and L. Brilmayer, eds, *Global Justice*, New York: New York University Press, 1999.

Beitz, C., *Political Theory and International Relations*, 2nd edn, Princeton: Princeton University Press, 1999.

Bell, D., 'Agonistic Democracy and the Politics of Memory', *Constellations* 15 (1): 148–66, 2008.

—, 'Citizenship, Race and Empire: Isopolitanism and the Anglo-World, 1900', unpublished manuscript, University of Cambridge, October 2011.

—, 'Ideologies of Empire', in M. Freeden, L. T. Sargent and M. Stears, eds, *The Oxford Handbook of Political Ideologies*, Oxford: Oxford University Press, 2012.

Bell, D., ed., *Ethics and World Politics*, Oxford: Oxford University Press, 2010.

Belsey, C., *Poststructuralism: A Very Short Introduction*, Oxford: Oxford University Press, 2002.

—, *Culture and the Real*, London: Routledge, 2005.

Benhabib, S., *Another Cosmopolitanism*, Oxford: Oxford University Press, 2008.

Benton, L., *Law and Colonial Cultures: Legal Regimes in World History, 1400–1990*, Cambridge: Cambridge University Press, 2002.

Bergmann, F., *On Being Free*, Notre Dame: University of Notre Dame, 1977.

bin Laden, O., *Messages to the World: The Statements of Osama bin Laden*, London: Verso, 2005.

Blake, M., 'Distributive Justice, Coercion, and Autonomy', *Philosophy and Public Affairs* 30 (3): 257–96, 2001.

Blunt, G. D., 'Transnational Socio-Economic Justice and the Right of Resistance', *Politics* 31 (1): 1–8, 2011.

Bohman, J., *Democracy across Borders: From Dêmos to Dêmoi*, Cambridge, MA: MIT Press, 2007.

Bondurant, J. V., *Conquest of Violence: The Gandhian Philosophy of Conflict*, Princeton: Princeton University Press, 1989.

Boot, M., *Savage Wars of Peace*, New York: Basic, 2003.

Borrows, J., *Recovering Canada: The Resurgence of Indigenous Law*, Toronto: University of Toronto Press, 2002.

—, *Drawing Out Law: A Spirit Guide*, Toronto: University of Toronto Press, 2011.

Bowden, P., *Caring: Gender-Sensitive Ethics*, London: Routledge, 1997.

Brandom, R. B., *Making it Explicit: Reasoning, Representing, and Discursive Commitment*, Cambridge, MA: Harvard University Press, 1998.

—, *Reason in Philosophy: Animating Ideas*, Cambridge: Harvard University Press, 2009.

Brett, A. and Tully, J., eds, *Rethinking the Foundations of Modern Political Thought*, Cambridge: Cambridge University Press, 2006.

Brewer, T., *The Retrieval of Ethics*, Oxford: Oxford University Press, 2009.

Brodie, J., 'Introduction: Globalization and Citizenship beyond the Nation State', *Citizenship Studies* 8 (4): 323–32, 2004.

Brown, J. M. and Parel, A., eds, *The Cambridge Companion to Gandhi*, Cambridge: Cambridge University Press, 2011.

Brunee, J. and Toope, S. J., *Legitimacy and Legality in International Law: An Interactional Account*, Cambridge: Cambridge University Press, 2010.

Buber, M., *I and Thou*, New York: Scribner, 1970.

—, *Between Man and Man*, London: Routledge, 2002.

Caney, S., *Justice Beyond Borders: A Global Political Theory*, Oxford: Oxford University Press, 2005.

Capra, F., *The Web of Life: A New Synthesis of Mind and Matter*, New York: Anchor, 1996.

Carroll, J., *House of War: The Pentagon and the Disastrous Rise of American Power*, New York: Houghton Mifflin, 2006.

Carse, J., *Finite and Infinite Games: A Vision of Life as Play and Possibility*, New York: Ballantine, 1986.

Celikates, R., 'Ziviler Ungehorsam und radikale Demokratie – konstituierende vs. konstituierte Macht?' in T. Bedorf and K. Röttgers, eds, *Die Politik und das Politische*, Berlin: Suhrkamp, 2010.

—, '*Public Philosophy in a New Key: Volume I: Democracy and Civic Freedom/ Volume II: Imperialism and Civic Freedom* by James Tully', *Constellations* 18 (2): 264–66, 2011.

Chakrabarty, D., *Provincializing Europe: Postcolonial Thought and Historical Difference*, Princeton: Princeton University Press, 2000.

—, *Habitations of Modernity: Essays in the Wake of Subaltern Studies*, Chicago: University of Chicago Press, 2002.

Chenoweth, E. and Stephan, M. J., *Why Civil Resistance Works: The Strategic Logic of Nonviolent Conflict*, New York: Columbia University Press, 2011.

Chopra, D., *Peace is the Way: Bringing War and Violence to an End*, New York: Three Rivers, 2005.

Christensen, K. R., *Nonviolence, Peace, and Justice*, Toronto: Broadview, 2010.

Cohen, G. A., *Self-Ownership, Freedom, and Equality*, Cambridge: Cambridge University Press, 1995.

—, *Rescuing Justice and Equality*, Cambridge, MA: Harvard University Press, 2008.

Cohen, J., 'Philosophy, Social Science, and Global Poverty', in A. M. Jaggar, ed., *Thomas Pogge and His Critics*, Cambridge: Polity, 2010.

Colaiaco, J. A., 'Martin Luther King, Jr. and the Paradox of Nonviolent Direct Action', *Phylon* 47 (1): 16–28, 1986.

Coles, R., *Beyond Gated Politics: Reflections for the Possibility of Democracy*, Minneapolis: University of Minnesota Press, 2005.

Connolly, W. E., 'Speed, Concentric Cultures, and Cosmopolitanism', *Political Theory* 28 (5): 596–618, 2000.

—, *Pluralism*, Durham: Duke University Press, 2005.

Constant, B., *The Liberty of Ancients Compared with that of Moderns*, Cambridge: Cambridge University Press, 1988.

Conway, J., 'Citizenship in a Time of Empire: The World Social Forum as a New Public Space', *Citizenship Studies* 8 (4): 367–81, 2004.

Cortright, D., *Peace: A History of Movements and Ideas*, Cambridge: Cambridge University Press, 2008.

Critchley, S., *The Faith of the Faithless: Experiments in Political Theology*, London: Verso, 2012.

Curry, P., *Ecological Ethics: An Introduction*, Cambridge: Polity, 2011.

Dalai Lama, *Beyond Religion: Ethics for a Whole World*, Toronto: McClelland and Stewart, 2011.

Daly, H. and Cobb, J., *For the Common Good: Redirecting the Economy Community, the Environment, and a Sustainable Future*, Boston: Beacon, 1994.

Dancy, J., *Ethics Without Principles*, Oxford: Oxford University Press, 2004.

Davis, L., ed., *Alliances: Re/envisioning Indigenous-non-Indigenous Relationships*, Toronto: University of Toronto Press, 2010.

Davis, M., *A Planet of Slums*, London: Verso, 2005.

Dawson, R., *Justice as Attunement: Transforming Constitutions in Law, Literature, Philosophy and the Rest of Life*, Oxford: Routledge, 2013.

Deming, B., *Revolution and Equilibrium*, New York: Grossman, 1971.

de Sousa Santos, B., *The Rise of the Global Left: The World Social Forum and Beyond*, London: Zed Books, 2006.

de Sousa Santos, B., ed., *Democratizing Democracy: Beyond the Liberal Democratic Cannon*, London: Verso, 2005.

Dobson, A., 'States, Citizens and the Environment', in Q. Skinner and B. Stråth, eds, *States and Citizens: History, Theory, Prospects*, Cambridge: Cambridge University Press, 2003.

Dower, N., *An Introduction to Global Citizenship*, Edinburgh: Edinburgh University Press, 2003.

Dower, N. and Williams, J., eds, *Global Citizenship: A Critical Introduction*, New York: Routledge, 2002.

Downes, A. B., Grandin, G., Nye, J. S., Crawford, N. C., Fearon, J. D., Kaldor, M., Tirman, J., Lindberg, T. and Landy, J., 'Regime Change Doesn't Work', *Boston Review* 36 (5): 16–34, October 2011.

Dunkley, G., *Free Trade: Myth, Reality and Alternatives*, London: Zed Books, 2003.

Dunn, J., *Interpreting Political Responsibility*, Cambridge: Cambridge University Press, 1990.

—, *Democracy: A History*, Toronto: Penguin, 2005.

Dworkin, R., *A Matter of Principle*, Cambridge, MA: Harvard University Press, 1985.

Escobar, A., 'Latin America at a Crossroads', *Cultural Studies* 24 (1): 1–65, 2010.

Estlund, D., 'Liberalism, Equality, and Fraternity in Cohen's Critique of Rawls', *Journal of Political Philosophy* 6 (1): 99–112, 1998.

Euripides, *The Phoenician Women*, New York: Penguin, 1983.

Evans, P., 'Is an Alternative Globalization Possible?' *Politics and Society* 36 (2): 271–305, 2008.

Evans, T. and Ayers, A., 'In the Service of Power: The Global Political Economy of Citizenship and Human Rights', *Citizenship Studies* 10 (3): 289–308, 2006.

Fanon, F., *The Wretched of the Earth*, London: Penguin, 2001.

Farrelly, C., 'Justice in Ideal Theory: A Refutation', *Political Studies* 55 (4): 844–64, 2007.

Fay, P. W., *The Forgotten Army: India's Armed Struggle for Independence 1942–1945*, Ann Arbor: University of Michigan Press, 1994.

Finley, M. I., *Democracy Ancient and Modern*, London: Hogarth, 1985.

Flannery, T., *Here on Earth: A Natural History of the Planet*, New York: Atlantic Monthly, 2010.

Fontana, D., *The Meditator's Handbook: A Complete Guide to Eastern and Western Meditation Techniques*, London: Thorsons, 1992.

Foucault, M., *Ethics, Subjectivity and Truth*, P. Rabinow, ed., New York: New Press, 1997.

—, 'Confronting Governments: Human Rights', in J. B. Faubion, ed., *The Essential Works, Volume III*, New York: New Press, 2000.

—, 'The Subject and Power', in J. B. Faubion, ed., *Power: Essential Works of Foucault*, New York: New Press, 2000.

—, *Fearless Speech*, J. Pearson, ed., Los Angeles: Semiotexte(e), 2001.

—, *Hermeneutics of the Subject: Lectures at the Collège de France, 1981–1982*, New York: Palgrave, 2005.

—, *The Government of Self and Others: Lectures at the Collège de France*, F. Gros, ed., New York: Palgrave Macmillan, 2010.

—, *The Courage of Truth*, F. Gros, ed., New York: Palgrave Macmillan, 2012.

Frank, J., *Constituent Moments*, Durham: Duke University Press, 2010.

Fraser, N., 'Rethinking the Public Sphere: A Contribution to the Critique of Actually Existing Democracy', in C. Calhoun, ed., *Habermas and the Public Sphere*, Cambridge, MA: MIT Press, 1992.

—, *Scales of Justice: Reimagining Political Space in a Globalizing World*, New York: Columbia University Press, 2008.

Friedman, T., *The Lexus and the Olive Tree*, New York: Farrar, Strauss, Giroux, 1999.

Furlough, E. and Strikwerda, C., eds, *Consumers against Capitalism? Consumer Cooperation in Europe, North America, and Japan 1840–1990*, Lanham: Rowman and Littlefield, 1999.

Galeano, E., *Open Veins of Latin America: Five Centuries of the Pillage of a Continent*, New York: Monthly Review, 1997.

Gallagher, S., *How the Body Shapes the Mind*, Oxford: Clarendon, 2005.

Galloway, A., *Protocol: How Control Exists after Decentralization*, Cambridge, MA: MIT Press, 2004.

Galtung, J., *Peace by Peaceful Means: Power and Conflict, Development and Civilization*, London: Sage, 1996.

Gandhi, M. K., 'A Non-Violent Look at Conflict and Violence', *Harijan*, 26 November 1938.

—, *An Autobiography: The Story of My Experiments with Truth*, Boston: Beacon, 1957.

—, *Nonviolent Resistance* (Satyagraha), Boston: Schocken, 1961.

—, *Non-Violent Resistance and Social Transformation. Moral and Political Writings, Volume 3*, Oxford: Clarendon, 1987.

—, *All Men are Brothers: Autobiographical Reflections*, New York: Continuum, 2005.

—, *Gandhi: Hind Swaraj and Other Writings*, A. Parel, ed., Cambridge: Cambridge University Press, 2007.

—, *The Essential Writings*, J. Brown, ed., Oxford: Oxford University Press, 2008

Geuss, R., *History and Illusion in Politics*, Cambridge: Cambridge University Press, 1999.

—, *Outside Ethics*, Princeton: Princeton University Press, 2005.

—, *Philosophy and Real Politics*, Princeton: Princeton University Press, 2008.

—, *Politics and the Imagination*, Princeton: Princeton University Press, 2010.

Gibson, N. C., *Fanon: The Postcolonial Imagination*, Cambridge: Polity, 2003.

Goodin, R. E., 'Civil Disobedience and Nuclear Protest', *Political Studies* 35 (3): 461–6, 1987.

Graeber, D., 'The New Anarchists', *New Left Review* 13, January–February 2002.

Grandin, G., *Empire's Workshop: Latin America, the United States and the Rise of the New Imperialism*, New York: Metropolitan, 2007.

Gregg, R., *The Power of Nonviolence*, New York: Schocken, 1966.

Grimes, K. M. and Milgram, L., eds, *Artisans and Cooperatives: Developing Alternative Trade for the Global Economy*, Tucson: University of Arizona Press, 2000.

Grossman, D., *On Killing: The Psychological Cost of Learning to Kill in War and Society*, New York: Little Brown and Company, 1995.

Hall, A. J., *Earth into Property: Colonization, Decolonization and Capitalism*, Montreal: McGill-Queens University Press, 2010.

Halldenius, L., 'Building Blocks of a Republican Cosmopolitanism: The Modality of Being Free', *European Journal of Political Theory* 9 (1): 12–30, 2010.

Halperin, S., *War and Social Change in Modern Europe: The Great Transformation Revisited*, Cambridge: Cambridge University Press, 2004.

Hanh, T., *Keeping the Peace*, Berkely: Parallax, 2005.

Harding, S., *Animate Earth: Science, Intuition and Gaia*, White River Junction Vermont: Chelsea Green, 2006.

Hardt, M. and Negri, A., *Empire*, Cambridge: Harvard University Press, 2000.

Harvey, D., *Cosmopolitanism and the Geographies of Freedom*, New York: Columbia University Press, 2009.

Havercroft, J., *Captives of Sovereignty*, Cambridge: Cambridge University Press, 2011.

Hawken, P., *Blessed Unrest: How the Largest Movement in the World Came into Being and Why No One Saw it Coming*, New York: Viking, 2007.

Heidegger, M., *Being and Time*, New York: Harper and Row, 1962.

Held, D., *Models of Democracy*, Cambridge: Polity, 1996.

Held, D. and McGrew, A., eds, *The Global Transformations Reader: An Introduction to the Globalization Debate*, 2nd edn, Cambridge: Polity, 2003.

Heyes, C., *Line Drawings: Defining Women Through Feminist Practice*, Ithaca: Cornell University Press, 2000.

Hill, L., *The Deacons for Defense: Armed Resistance and the Civil Rights Movement*, Chapel Hill: University of North Carolina Press, 2006.

Hines, C., *Localization: A Global Manifesto*, London: Earthscan, 2000.

Honig, B., *Democracy and the Foreigner*, Princeton: Princeton University Press, 2001.

—, 'Between Decision and Deliberation: Political Paradox in Democratic Theory', *American Political Science Review* 101 (1): 1–17, 2007.

—, *Emergency Politics: Paradox, Law, and Politics*, Princeton: Princeton University Press, 2009.

—, '[Un]Dazzled by the Ideal: Tully's Politics and Humanism in Tragic Perspective', *Political Theory* 39 (1): 131–44, 2011.

Honig, B. and Stears, M., 'The New Realism: From Modus Vivendi to Justice', in J. Floyd and M. Stears, eds, *Political Philosophy versus History?* Cambridge: Cambridge University Press, 2011.

Honneth, A., *The Struggle for Recognition*, J. Anderson, trans., Cambridge, MA: MIT Press, 1996.

Horsburgh, H. J. N., *Non-Violence and Aggression: A Study of Gandhi's Moral Equivalent of War*, Oxford: Oxford University Press, 1968.

Hoy, D., *Critical Resistance: From Poststructuralism to Post-Critique*, Cambridge, MA: MIT Press, 2004.

Huizinga, J., *Homo Ludens: A Study of the Play Element in Culture*, Boston: Beacon, 1955.

Humphrey, M. and Stears, M., 'Animal Rights Protest and the Challenge to Deliberative Democracy', *Economy and Society* 35 (3): 400–22, 2006.

Hunter, I., *Rival Enlightenments: Civil and Metaphysical Philosophy in Early Modern Germany*, Cambridge: Cambridge University Press, 2001.

Hursthouse, R., *On Virtue Ethics*, Oxford: Oxford University Press, 1999.

Ikenberry, J. G. and Slaughter, A., *Forging a World of Liberty under Law: US National Security in the 21st Century*, The Princeton Project on National Security, The Woodrow Wilson School of Public and International Affairs: Princeton University, 2006.

Ishay, M. R., *The History of Human Rights: From Ancient Times to the Globalization Era*, Berkeley: University of California Press, 2004.

Issac, J., 'The Strange Silence of Political Theory', *Political Theory* 23 (4): 636–52, 1995.

Ivison, D., 'Republican Human Rights?' *European Journal of Political Theory* 9 (1): 31–47, 2010.

—, '"Another World is Actual": Between Imperialism and Freedom', *Political Theory* 39 (1): 131–7, 2011.

James, W., 'The Moral Equivalent of War', *McClure's Magazine* 35: 463–68, 1910.

Jefferess, D., *Postcolonial Resistance: Culture, Liberation and Transformation*, Toronto: University of Toronto Press, 2008.

Jefferson, T., *Jefferson: Political Writings*, Cambridge: Cambridge University Press, 1999.

Johns, S. and Davis, R. H., eds, *Mandela, Tambo, and the African National Congress: The Struggle Against Apartheid 1948–1990: A Documentary Survey*, Oxford: Oxford University Press, 1991.

Johnson, C., *Nemesis: The Last Days of the American Republic*, New York: Metropolitan, 2006.

Johnson, M., *Moral Imagination: Implications of Cognitive Science for Ethics*, Chicago: University of Chicago Press, 1993.

Kagan, R., *Dangerous Nation: America's Foreign Policy from its Earliest Days to the Dawn of the Twentieth Century*, New York: Vintage, 2007.

Kahn, I., *The Unheard Truth: Poverty and Human Rights*, New York: W.W. Norton and Company, 2010.

—, *Kant: Political Writings*, H. S. Reiss, ed., Cambridge: Cambridge University Press, 1991.

Kaplan, R. D., *Imperial Grunts: The American Military on the Ground*, New York: Random House, 2002.

Katsiaficas, G., *The Subversion of Politics: European Autonomous Movements and the Decolonization of Everyday Life*, New York: Humanities, 2007.

Khalidi, R., *Resurrecting Empire: Western Footprints and America's Perilous Path in the Middle East*, Boston: Beacon, 2004.

King, M. E., *A Quiet Revolution: The Palestinian Intifada and Nonviolent Resistance*, New York: Nation, 2007.

—, 'Palestinian Civil Resistance against Israeli Military Occupation', in M. J. Stephan, ed., *Civilian Jihad: Nonviolent Struggle, Democratization and Governance in the Middle East*, New York: Palgrave Macmillan, 2005.

—, *A Quiet Revolution: The Palestinian Intifada and Nonviolent Resistance*, New York: Nation, 2007.

King, M. L., *A Testament of Hope: The Essential Writings and Speeches*, New York: Harper Collins, 1991.

Kinzer, S., *Overthrow: America's Century of Regime Change from Hawaii to Iraq*, New York: Henry Holt, 2006.

Kompridis, N., *Critique and Disclosure: Critical Theory between Past and Future*, Cambridge, MA: MIT Press, 2006.

Kurlansky, M., *Nonviolence: Twenty-Five Lessons from the History of a Dangerous Idea*, New York: Modern Library, 2006.

La Boétie, E., *Discourse on Voluntary Servitude*, Cambridge: Hackett, 2012.

Laborde, C., 'Republicanism and Global Justice: A Sketch', *European Journal of Political Theory* 9 (1): 48–69, 2010.

Laclau, E., *On Populist Reason*, London: Verso, 2005.

—, 'Populism: What's in a Name?' in F. Panizza, ed., *Populism and the Mirror of Democracy*, London: Verso, 2005.

Laclau, E. and Mouffe, C., *Hegemony and Socialist Strategy*, London: Verso, 1985.

Laden, A. S., 'Democratic Legitimacy and the 2000 Election', *Law and Philosophy* 21: 197–220, 2002.

—, *Reasoning: A Social Picture*, Oxford: Oxford University Press, 2012.

—, 'Learning to be Equal: Just Schools and Schools of Justice', in D. Allen and R. Reich, eds, *Democracy, Education and Justice*, Chicago: University of Chicago Press, 2012.

—, 'The Key to/of Public Philosophy', *Political Theory* 39 (1): 112–17, 2011.

Lane, M., 'Constraint, Freedom, and Exemplar', in J. Floyd and M. Stears, eds, *Political Philosophy versus History?* Cambridge: Cambridge University Press, 2011.

Leopold, D., 'Socialism and Utopia', *Journal of Political Ideologies* 12 (3): 219–37, 2007.

Loader, I. and Walker, N., *Civilizing Security*, Cambridge: Cambridge University Press, 2007.

Lovelock, J., *Gaia and the Theory of the Living Planet*, London: Gaia, 2005.

—, *The Revenge of Gaia: Why the Earth is Fighting Back – and How We Can Still Save Humanity*, London: Penguin, 2007.

Lyons, D., 'Moral Judgment, Historical Reality, and Civil Disobedience', *Philosophy and Public Affairs* 27 (1): 31–49, 1998.

Lyotard, J., 'Answering the Question: What is Postmodernism?' in I. Hassan and S. Hassan, eds, *Innovation/Renovation: New Perspectives on the Humanities*, Madison: University of Wisconsin Press, 1983.

Malinowski, B., *Freedom and Civilization*, Bloomington: Indiana University Press, 1944.

Mamdani, M., *Citizen and Subject: Contemporary Africa and the Legacy of Late Colonialism*, Princeton: Princeton University Press, 1995.

—, 'Beyond Settler and Natives as Political Identities: Overcoming the Legacy of Colonialism', *Comparative Studies in Society and History* 43 (4): 651–64, 2001.

Mander, J. and Tauli-Corpuz, V., eds, *Paradigm Wars: Indigenous Peoples' Resistance to Economic Globalization*, San Francisco: International Forum on Globalization, 2005.

Markell, P., 'The Rule of the People: Arendt, Archê, and Democracy', *American Political Science Review* 100 (1): 1–14, 2006.

Markovits, D., 'Democratic Disobedience', *Yale Law Journal* 114: 1897–952, 2005.

Marx, K., *Capital: A Critique of Political Economy, Volume I*, London: Penguin Classics, 1990.

Mason, A., 'Just Constraints', *British Journal of Political Science* 34 (2): 251–68, 2004.

—, 'Justice, Holism and Principles', *Res Publica* 25: 179–94, 2009.

—, 'Rawlsian Theory and the Circumstances of Politics', *Political Theory* 38 (5): 658–83, 2010.

—, 'Citizenship and Justice', *Politics, Philosophy and Economics* 10 (3): 263–81, 2011.

—, *Living Together as Equals: The Demands of Citizenship*, Oxford: Oxford University Press, 2012.

McCarthy, T., *Race, Empire and the Idea of Human Development*, Cambridge: Cambridge University Press, 2009.

McDowell, J., 'Virtue and Reason', *The Monist* 62 (3): 331–50, 1979.

Mckeever, S. and Ridge, M., *Principled Ethics: Generalism as a Regulative Ideal*, Oxford: Oxford University Press, 2006.

McKinnon, C. and Hampsher-Monk, I., eds, *The Demands of Citizenship*, London: Continuum, 2000.

McNally, D., *Another World is Possible: Globalization and Anti-Capitalism*, Winnipeg: Arbeiter Ring, 2006.

Medearis, J., 'Lost or Obscured? How V. I. Lenin, Joseph Schumpeter, and Hannah Arendt Misunderstood the Council Movement', *Polity* 36 (3): 447–76, 2004.

Medina, J., *The Unity of Wittgenstein's Philosophy: Necessity, Intelligibility, and Normativity*, Albany: SUNY Press, 2002.

—, *Language*, London: Continuum, 2005.

Mehta, P. B., 'Cosmopolitanism and the Circle of Reason', *Political Theory* 28 (5): 619–39, 2000.

Menke, C., 'Two Kinds of Practice: On the Relation between Social Discipline and the Aesthetics of Existence', *Constellations* 10 (2): 199–210, 2003.

Merton, T., ed., *Gandhi on Non-violence*, New York: New Directions, 2007.

M'Gonigle, M. R. and Stark, J., *Planet U: Sustaining the World, Reinventing the University*, Gabriola Island: New Society, 2006.

M'Gonigle, M. R. and Takeda, L., 'The Liberal Limits of Environmental Law: A Green Legal Critique', *Pace Environmental Law Review*, 30, 2013: 1005–115.

Mignolo, W. D., *Local Histories/Global Designs: Coloniality, Subaltern Knowledges and Border Thinking*, Princeton: Princeton University Press, 2000.

Milanovic, B., *Worlds Apart: Measuring International and Global Inequality*, Princeton: Princeton University Press, 2005.

Moran, E. F., *People and Nature: An Introduction to Human Ecological Relations*, Oxford: Blackwell, 2006.

Mouffe, C., *On the Political*, London: Routledge, 2005.

Moyer, B., *Doing Democracy: The MAP Model for Organising Social Movements*, Gabriola Island: New Society, 2001.

Murphy, L., 'Institutions and the Demands of Justice', *Philosophy and Public Affairs* 27 (4): 251–91, 1998.

Muthu, S., *Enlightenment Against Empire*, Princeton: Princeton University Press, 2003.

Muthu, S., ed., *Empire and Modern Political Thought*, Cambridge: Cambridge University Press, 2012.

Nagel, T., 'The Problem of Global Justice', *Philosophy and Public Affairs* 33 (2): 113–47, 2005.

Nhat Hahn, T., *Peace is Every Step: The Path of Mindfulness in Everyday Life*, New York: Bantam, 1992.

Nietzsche, F., *Human, All too Human: A Book for Free Spirits*, Cambridge: Cambridge University Press, 1986.

—, *On the Genealogy of Morals*, K. Ansell-Pearson, ed., Cambridge: Cambridge University Press, 1996.

Norval, A. J., 'Frontiers in Question', *Acta Philosophica*, 2: 51–76, 1997.

—, *Aversive Democracy: Inheritance and Originality in the Democratic Tradition*, Cambridge: Cambridge University Press, 2007.

—, '"No Reconciliation without Redress": Articulating Political Demands in Post-transitional South Africa', *Critical Discourse Studies* 6 (4): 311–21, 2009.

Nussbaum, M., 'Cosmopolitanism and Patriotism', in J. Cohen, ed., *For Love of Country: Debating the Limits of Patriotism*, Boston: Beacon, 1996.

—, *Frontiers of Justice: Disability, Nationality, Species Membership*, Cambridge, MA: Harvard University Press, 2007.

Nyers, P., 'Abject Cosmopolitanism: The Politics of Protection in the Anti-deportation Movement', *Third World Quarterly* 26 (6): 1069–93, 2003.

O'Grady, H., *Woman's Relationship with Herself: Gender, Foucault and Therapy*, London: Routledge, 2005.

O'Neill, O., *Towards Justice and Virtue: A Constructive Account of Practical Reasoning*, Cambridge: Cambridge University Press, 1996.

Owen, D., 'Political Philosophy in a Post-Imperial Voice: James Tully and the Politics of Cultural Recognition', *Economy and Society* 28 (4): 520–49, 1999.

Patterson, O., *Freedom in the Making of Western Culture*, New York: Basic, 1991.

Petit, P., 'A Republican Law of People', *European Journal of Political Theory* 9 (1): 48–69, 2010.

Pippin, R., *Hegel's Practical Philosophy: Rational Agency as Ethical Life*, Cambridge: Cambridge University Press, 2008.

Pitkin, H., *Wittgenstein and Justice: On the Significance of Ludwig Wittgenstein for Social and Political Thought*, Berkeley: University of California Press, 1973.

—, 'Are Freedom and Liberty Twins?' *Political Theory* 16 (4): 523–52, 1988.

Pitts, J., 'Political Theory and Empire', *Annual Review of Political Science* 13l: 211–35, 2010.

Pogge. T., 'On the Site of Distributive Justice: Reflections on Cohen and Murphy', *Philosophy and Public Affairs* 29 (2): 137–69, 2000.

—, *World Poverty and Human Rights: Cosmopolitan Responsibilities and Reforms*, Cambridge: Polity, 2002.

Polanyi, K., *The Great Transformation: The Political and Economic Origins of Our Time*, Boston: Beacon, 2004.

Prashad, V., *The Darker Nations: A People's History of the Third World*, New York: New Press, 2007.

Rawls, J., *A Theory of Justice*, Cambridge, MA: Harvard University Press, 1971.

—, *Political Liberalism*, New York: Columbia University Press, 1996.

—, 'The Idea of Public Reason Revisited', in S. Freeman, ed., *Collected Papers*, Cambridge, MA: Harvard University Press, 1999.

—, *Justice as Fairness*, Cambridge, MA: Harvard University Press, 2001.

Raz, J., *The Authority of Law*, Oxford: Clarendon, 1979.

Restakis, J., *Humanizing the Economy: Co-operatives in the Age of Capital*, Gabriola Island: New Society, 2010.

Richmond, A., *Global Apartheid: Refugees, Racism, and the New World Order*, Oxford: Oxford University Press, 1994.

Risse, M., 'How Does the Global Order Harm the Poor?', *Philosophy and Public Affairs* 33 (4): 349–76, 2005.

—, 'What to Say About the State', *Social Theory and Practice* 32 (4): 671–98, 2006.

Robeyns, I., 'Ideal Theory in Theory and Practice', *Social Theory and Practice* 34 (3): 341–62, 2008.

Rödel, U., Frankenberg, G. and Dubiel, H., *Die demokratische Frage*, Frankfurt am Main: Suhrkamp, 1989.

Rousseau, J., 'The Social Contract', in V. Gourevitch, ed., *Rousseau: The Social Contract and Other Later Political Writings*, Cambridge: Cambridge University Press, 1997.

—, *The Social Contract: Or Principles of Political Right*, London: Wordsworth Editions, 1998.

Sabl, A., 'Looking Forward to Justice. Rawlsian Civil Disobedience and its Non-Rawlsian Lessons', *The Journal of Political Philosophy* 9 (3): 307–30, 2001.

Sandercock, L., *Cosmopolis II: Mongrel Cities in the Twenty-First Century*, London: Continuum, 2003.

Sangiovanni, A., 'Global Justice, Reciprocity, and the State', *Philosophy and Public Affairs* 35 (1): 3–39, 2007.

Schell, J., *The Unconquerable World: Power, Nonviolence and the Will of the People*, New York: Henry Holt and Company, 2003.

Scheppele, K. L., 'The International State of Emergency: Challenges to Constitutionalism after September 11', Unpublished Manuscript: Princeton University, 2007.

Schor, M., 'Mapping Comparative Judicial Review', *Comparative Research in Law and Political Economy Research Paper Series* 3 (4): 545–67, 2007.

Schumacher, E. F., *Small is Beautiful: A Study of Economics as if People Mattered*, Tiptree Essex: Anchor, 1973.

Scott, D., *Conscripts of Modernity: The Tragedy of Colonial Enlightenment*, Chapel Hill: Duke University Press, 2004.

Scott, J., *Domination and the Arts of Resistance: Hidden Transcripts*, Yale: Yale University Press, 1990.

Seabrook, J., *The No-Nonsense Guide to World Poverty*, Toronto: New Internationalist, 2003.

Searle, J., *The Construction of Social Reality*, New York: Free Press, 1995.

Sen, A., 'What Do We Want from a Theory of Justice?' *Journal of Philosophy* 103 (5): 215–38, 2006.

—, *The Idea of Justice*, London: Penguin, 2009.

Shapiro, I., *The Flight From Reality in the Social Sciences*, Princeton: Princeton University Press, 2007.

Sharp, G., *The Politics of Nonviolent Action*, Boston: Porter Sargent, 1973.

—, *Waging Nonviolent Struggle*, Boston: Porter Sargent, 2005.

—, *From Dictatorship to Democracy*, 4th edn, Boston: Albert Einstein Institute, 2010.

Shelby, T., 'Justice, Deviance, and the Dark Ghetto', *Philosophy and Public Affairs* 35 (2): 126–60, 2007.

Shiva, V., 'The Greening of Global Reach', in S. Daly and P. Routledge, eds, *The Geopolitics Reader*, London: Routledge, 1998.

—, *Earth Democracy: Justice, Sustainability and Peace*, Cambridge: South End, 2005.

Simmons, A. J., 'Ideal and Nonideal Theory', *Philosophy and Public Affairs* 38 (1): 5–36, 2010.

Singer, P., *Democracy and Disobedience*, Oxford: Clarendon, 1973.

Singh, J., 'Beyond Free and Equal: Subalternity and the Limits of Liberal Democracy', PhD Dissertation, Department of Political Science, University of Toronto, 2012.

Sitton, J. F., 'Hannah Arendt's Argument for Council Democracy', in L. P. Hinchman and S. K. Hinchman, eds, *Hannah Arendt: Critical Essays*, Albany: SUNY Press, 1994.

Skidelsky, R., *The Prince of the Marshes and other Occupational Hazards of a Year in Iraq*, London: Harcourt, 2006.

Skinner, Q., *Visions of Politics, Volume II: Renaissance Virtues*, Cambridge: Cambridge University Press, 2002.

—, *Visions of Politics, Volume III: Hobbes and Civil Society*, Cambridge: Cambridge University Press, 2002.

Skinner, Q. and Stråth, B., eds, *States and Citizens: History, Theory, Prospects*, Cambridge: Cambridge University Press, 2003.

Smith, T., *A Pact with the Devil: Washington's Bid for World Supremacy and the Betrayal of the American Promise*, London: Routledge, 2007.

Solnit, R., *A Paradise Built in Hell: The Extraordinary Communities that Arise in Disasters*, New York: Penguin, 2009.

Stears, M., *Demanding Democracy: American Radicals in Search of a New Politics*, Princeton: Princeton University Press, 2010.

Stears, M. and Humphrey, M., 'Public Reason and Political Action: Justifying Citizen Behavior in Actually Existing Democracies', *The Review of Politics* 74 (2): 285–306, 2012.

Stephan, M. J., ed., *Civilian Jihad: Nonviolent Struggle, Democratization and Governance in the Middle East*, New York: Palgrave Macmillan, 2005.

Stiglitz, J., *Globalization and its Discontents*, London: Allen Lane, 2002.

Stout, J., *Democracy and Tradition*, Princeton: Princeton University Press, 2004.

Temelini, M., 'Dialogical Approaches to Political Struggles over Recognition and Distribution', *Critical Review of Social and Political Philosophy*, published online early 15th April 2013.

Thompson, E., *Mind in Life: Biology, Phenomenology and the Sciences of Mind*, Cambridge, MA: Harvard University Press, 2007.

Tilly, C., *Democracy*, Cambridge: Cambridge University Press, 2007.

Todorov, T., *Life in Common: An Essay in General Anthropology*, K. Golsan and L. Golsan, trans., London: University of Nebraska Press, 2000.

Tomasi, J., *Liberalism Beyond Justice: Citizens, Society, and the Boundaries of Political Theory*, Princeton: Princeton University Press, 2001.

Toulmin, S. E., *The Uses of Argument*, Cambridge: Cambridge University Press, 1958.

Tuck, S., *We Ain't What We Ought to Be: The Black Freedom Struggle from Emancipation to Obama*, Cambridge, MA: Harvard University Press, 2010.

Tully, J., *An Approach to Political Philosophy: Locke in Contexts*, Cambridge: Cambridge University Press, 1993.

—, *Strange Multiplicity: Constitutionalism in an Age of Diversity*, Cambridge: Cambridge University Press, 1995.

—, 'Reconsidering the BC Treaty Process', *Speaking Truth to Power: A Treaty Forum*, Ottawa: Law Commission of Canada and BC Treaty Commission, 2001.

—, 'Diverse Enlightenments', *Economy and Society* 32 (3): 485–505, 2003a.

—, 'La liberté civique en contexte de globalisation', *Les Cahiers du Juin 27* 1 (2): 1–10, 2003b.

—, *Public Philosophy in a New Key, Two Volumes*, Cambridge: Cambridge University Press, 2008a.

—, 'Thinking along with Feminism and the Abyss of Freedom', unpublished presentation at the American Political Science Association Annual Meeting, 30 August, 2008b.

—, 'The Crisis of Global Citizenship', *Radical Politics Today*, July 2009a.

—, 'Lineages of Contemporary Imperialism', in D. Kelly, ed., *Lineages of Empire: The Historical Roots of British Imperial Thought*, Oxford: Oxford University Press, 2009b, pp. 11–12.

—, 'The Crisis of Global Citizenship', Seminar in Political Thought and Intellectual History, University of Cambridge, 8 February, 2010a.

—, 'Consent, Hegemony, and Dissent in Treaty Negotiations', in J. Webber and C. M. Macleod, eds, *Between Consenting Peoples*, Vancouver: University of British Columbia Press, 2010b.

—, 'A Dilemma of Democratic Citizenship'. Paper delivered at the University of Victoria, 8 May 2010c.

—, 'Testing Freedom Clarified: Reply to Daniel Weinstock', *Literary Review of Canada*, February, 2010d.

—, 'Dialogue', *Political Theory* 39 (1): 145–60, 2011a.

—, 'Hannah Arendt on Violence and Nonviolence', President's lecture Series, University of Oklahoma, 25 April, 2011b.

—, 'Deparochializing Political Theory: The Dialogue and Interbeing Approach', *The Conference on Deparochializing Political Theory*, University of Victoria, 2–4 August, 2012a.

—, 'Human Rights and Enlightenment: A View from the Twenty-first Century', in K. E. Tunstall, ed., *Self-Evident Truths? Human Rights and the Enlightenment: The Oxford Amnesty Lectures*, New York: Bloomsbury, 2012b.

—, 'Middle East Legal and Governmental Pluralism: A View of the Field from the Demos', *Middle East Law and Governance* 4: 1–39, 2012c.

—, 'On the Multiplicity of Global Public Spheres', in C. Emden and D. Midgley, eds, *Beyond Habermas: Democracy, Knowledge and the Public Sphere*, New York: Berghahn, 2012d.

—, 'Two Ways of Realizing Justice and Democracy: Linking Amartya Sen and Elinor Ostrom', *Critical Review of Social and Political Philosophy* 16 (2): 220–32, 2012e.

Tully, J., ed., *On the Duty of Man and Citizen According to Natural Law*, Cambridge: Cambridge University Press, 1991.

Tyson, T., 'Robert F. Williams, "Black Power", and the Roots of the Black Freedom Struggle', *Journal of American History* 85 (2): 540–70, 1998.

Valentini, L., 'On the Apparent Paradox of Ideal Theory', *Journal of Political Philosophy* 17 (3): 332–55, 2009.

Vanier, J., *Finding Peace*, Toronto: Anansi, 2003.

Vitalis, R., *America's Kingdom: Mythmaking on the Saudi Oil Frontier*, San Francisco: Stanford University Press, 2007.

Waldron, J., 'Minority Cultures and the Cosmopolitan Alternative', *University of Michigan Journal of Law Reform* 25: 751–93, 1992.

Weber, T., *Gandhi as Disciple and Mentor*, Cambridge: Cambridge University Press, 2004.

Wiener, A., 'Constructivist Approaches in International Relations Theory: Puzzles and Promises', *Con.WEB* 5, 2006.

—, *The Invisible Constitution of Politics: Contested Norms of International Encounters*, Cambridge: Cambridge University Press, 2008.

Williams, A., 'Incentives, Inequality, and Publicity', *Philosophy and Public Affairs* 27 (3): 225–47, 1998.

Williams, R. A., *Linking Arms Together: American Indian Treaty Visions of Law and Peace 1600–1800*, Oxford: Oxford University Press, 1997.

Wittgenstein, L., *On Certainty*, Oxford: Wiley-Blackwell, 1969.

—, *Philosophical Investigations*, Oxford: Blackwell, 1997.

Wood, E., *Democracy against Capitalism: Renewing Historical Materialism*, Cambridge: Cambridge University Press, 1995.

Young, I. M., *Global Challenges: War, Self-Determination and Responsibility for Justice*, Cambridge: Polity, 2007.

Young, R. J., *Postcolonialism: A Very Short Introduction*, Oxford: Oxford University Press, 2003.

Zerilli, L., *Feminism and the Abyss of Freedom*, Chicago: University of Chicago Press, 2005.

Zinn, H., *Disobedience and Democracy. Nine Fallacies on Law and Order*, Cambridge, MA: South End, 2002.

Zinn, H., ed., *The Power of Nonviolence*, Boston: Beacon, 2002.

Index